How to Make Dances in an Epidemic

How to Make Dances in an Epidemic

Tracking Choreography in the Age of AIDS

David Gere

THE UNIVERSITY OF WISCONSIN PRESS

The University of Wisconsin Press
1930 Monroe Street
Madison, Wisconsin 53711

www.wisc.edu/wisconsinpress/

3 Henrietta Street
London WC2E 8LU, England

Printed in the United States of America

Library of Congress Cataloging-in-Publication Data
Gere, David.
How to make dances in an epidemic: tracking choreography in
    the age of AIDS / David Gere.
    p.   cm.
    Includes bibliographical references and index.
    ISBN 0-299-20080-9 (cloth: alk. paper)
    ISBN 0-299-20084-1 (pbk.: alk. paper)
    1. Homosexuality in dance.   2. Homosexuality and dance—United States.
    3. Dance—Social aspects—United States.   4. Dance criticism—United States.
    I. Title.
    GV1588.6.G47   2004
    306.4´84—dc22   2004005184

For
Peter Carley

and for my ghosts:
Joah Lowe (1953–1988)
Stephen Cobbett Steinberg (1949–1991)
Bill Huck (1947–1992)

Contents

Illustrations

Acknowledgments

Given that my work on this book has spanned nearly my entire adult life—a scary realization—it is no wonder that I have so many people to thank. I'd like to start with the San Francisco Bay Area choreographers and activists whose theatrical dances, site-specific works, films, movement meditations, and political protests first inspired me to think about the relationship between choreography and AIDS. I am grateful to have spent almost a decade participating as a dance critic in such a lively, iconoclastic, activist arts community. Though I moved to Los Angeles ten years ago and have kept loose ties to New York, the Bay Area remains my first dance home.

I also want to thank my dear friends and colleagues there, who helped me begin thinking about what it means to be a gay man making (or watching) dances in a time of great emotional, physical, and political turmoil, particularly my friend Daniel Goldstein, who was my willing sidekick during the years 1985–93 at both performances and protests, as well as Ellen Webb, Stephen Cobbett Steinberg, Bill Huck, Joah Lowe, Diana Vest Goodman, Danny Sauro, Janice Ross, Elizabeth Zimmer, Gay Morris, Tom O'Connor, Joe Goode, Djola Branner, Rachel Kaplan, and a hundred others whose love and support have meant so much to me. You know who you are. In addition, I must thank the editors of the publications that I wrote for during that time—especially Rob Hurwitt at the *East Bay Express* and a long string of supportive editors at the *Oakland Tribune*—for sending me out to see many of the works that are now the focus of this book. I also thank them for teaching me to write at the intersection of sophisticated ideas and straightforward communication, a value I remind myself of every time I sit down at the computer.

This book began as a dissertation at the University of California, Riverside, where I had the good fortune to work with Susan Leigh Foster, a gracious and indomitable force in the field of dance studies and a warm and dedicated mentor to me. I can't thank her enough. At Riverside, in what seems in retrospect to have been a golden age, I also had the opportunity to learn from an extraordinary array of scholars in allied fields, including Philip Brett, Sue-Ellen Case, George Haggerty, Marta Savigliano, Linda Tomko, and, when he was a visiting professor at nearby UCLA, Douglas Crimp. I am particularly indebted to David Román, of the University of Southern California, for initiating me into the study of AIDS cultural analysis. My fellow graduate students at Riverside continue to exert a huge influence on my work, and for that and for the levity and friendship they have brought into my life as a scholar, I blow kisses to ringleader Maura Keefe and to John Beynon, Jens Giersdorf, John Jordan, Janet O'Shea, Rebecca Rugg, and Karen Schaffman. I am also grateful to many far-flung friends and colleagues who sustained me through these years and, in some cases, collaborated in organizing conference presentations and lectures, or in commissioning essays for publication, especially Ann Cooper Albright, Bill Bissell, Suzanne Carbonneau, Ananya Chatterjea, Thomas F. DeFrantz, Deborah Jowitt, Alan M. Kriegsman, Sali Ann Kriegsman, Susan Manning, Allen F. Roberts, Mary (Polly) Nooter Roberts, Robert Sember, Marcia B. Siegel, Radhika Subramaniam, Lan-Lan Wang, and Tricia Henry Young.

I began teaching as a visiting professor at UCLA at the invitation of Judy Mitoma, the visionary founder of the new Department of World Arts and Cultures. Since that time a string of department chairs has supported me in this project, including Christopher Waterman (now dean of the UCLA School of the Arts and Architecture), Peter Nabokov, and David Roussève, not to mention my wonderful colleagues in WAC. The university itself has contributed substantially to my work through yearly research and travel grants offered through the Academic Senate's Congress on Research. Membership in the Interdisciplinary Queer Studies group of the University of California Humanities Research Institute, organized by Robyn Wiegman, gave me a big boost when I was just beginning the process of revising the dissertation into a book. Wiegman and colleagues Madelyn Detloff, Carla Freccero, George Haggerty, Eithne Luibheid, Lisa Rofel, Sandy Stone, and especially Nayan Shah, pressed me to think of my work in terms larger than dance studies. I am grateful for the challenges they put to me. I have also been enormously stimulated by the input of graduate students in my seminars on queer studies, particularly the spitfires who have aided me as research assistants: Peter Carpenter, Laurah Klepinger, Ann Mazzocca, Raquel Monroe, Jill Nunes Jensen, and Norah Zuñiga Shaw.

I must include words of praise for the librarians and archivists who have facilitated my work, including the staff at the Rivera Library of the University of California, Riverside; Margaret Norton and Kirsten Tanaka of the San Francisco Performing Arts Library and Museum; Ray Soto and Roberta Medford of UCLA's Young Research Library; Madeleine Nichols, Monica Mosely, Susan Kraft, and Lesley Farlow of the Dance Collection of the New York Public Library; Annette Fern and Beth Carroll-Horrocks of the Harvard Theatre Collection; Larry Billman and Saadia Billman of the Los Angeles Academy of Dance on Film; and Jeff Friedman of the Legacy Oral History Project. During the period that I was working on this book, I simultaneously conducted a survey of choreographers affected by AIDS in New York City, Los Angeles, and the San Francisco Bay Area for the Estate Project for Artists with AIDS. This work, conducted under the aegis of New York's Alliance for the Arts, extended the range of my research to such a significant degree that I now consider the finished on-line survey to be an informal companion to this volume. Thanks to the Alliance's Randall Bourscheidt, Patrick Moore, and Brennan Gerard for leading that project and to the literally hundreds of choreographers, and their friends and family, who dug into their personal archives to send me materials. I value these shards of life and work more than they can know.

When I was close to completing this book, I shared chapters in whole or in part with several artists and experts who possess direct knowledge of the material. Many thanks to Tommy DeFrantz, Joe Goode, Neil Greenberg, Keith Hennessy, David Román, Jim Self, Robert Sember, Don Shewey, Clyde Smith, Radhika Subramaniam, Joanne Sukaitis, David Weissman, and Bob Yesselman for sharing their opinions and for challenging me to think about the choreographies in this book from various points of view. Even when I decided to go in a different direction, their input was essential.

Working with Raphael Kadushin, Sheila Moermond, and Erin Holman of the University of Wisconsin Press has been a blessedly smooth and humane experience. This is my first single-author book, and I can only hope that every book in my future will be nurtured as warmly and carefully as has this one. I am especially indebted to the Press's manuscript readers, Sally Banes and an anonymous second reader, for their intelligent commentary and gentle prods. I also want to acknowledge Polly Kummel, my dream copyeditor, who not only has been an ace in matters of spelling and consistency but who has also grappled deeply with the ideas in the book. Our exchanges have been extremely fruitful and have rendered otherwise difficult chores a pleasure. My sincere thanks to you, Polly.

I have saved my Los Angeles friends and my family for last, because they will celebrate the completion of this book perhaps even more than I. Without a sprawling support system it would have been impossible for a hard-working dad to get any time for his book, and so I make this list to honor the people who have helped me stay sane: Barbara Allen, Ganga Amarasinghe, Mary Beck, Bonnie Brooks, Clark Brown, Victor Brown, Tom Burke, Mary Carley, Clay Crosby, Carol Endo, Dan Froot, Kelly Grief, Roberta Grossman, John Hamilton, Ellen Harrington, Berta Alicia Hernandez, Tom Keegan, Laurie Kilpatrick, Davidson Lloyd, Vic Marks, Christian Militello, Megan Morling, Sabrina Motley, Corine Motley, Laurie Newman, David Plante, Carra Robertson, Steve Rostine, Sophie Sartain, Robert Scheps, and Linda Timmons. Thank you for listening to me while tossing a salad or while pushing kids on the swing set at our neighborhood park. And thanks to my parents, my brother and sisters and their families, and my kids, Christopher and Isadora, for caring about me even more than about this book. As for Peter Carley, my partner of ten years, I can only think of one way to tell you how grateful I am. This book is for you.

How to Make Dances in an Epidemic

Introduction

In 1980 John Bernd and Tim Miller inaugurated a series of dance-based performances titled *Live Boys,* a multimedia chronicle of their evolving gay relationship. Bernd had arrived in New York just a few years before, a new graduate of Ohio's Antioch College, and was making a name for himself as a singer-dancer in the works of Meredith Monk. Miller, a native Californian who moved to New York to dance and found himself at the heart of a downtown avant-garde, had already cofounded P.S. 122, an alternative performance space in an abandoned public school. They met, quickly fell into a relationship, and almost immediately began to generate an autobiographical performance duet.

On its surface *Live Boys* celebrated being young, gay, and out of the closet. But the topography of the relationship that Bernd and Miller revealed to their audiences was most notable for its sheer mundanity. On a simple backdrop they projected slides by Kirk Winslow of the two of them lying in bed asleep amid tousled bedclothes. They took their audience on a fractured tour of their neighborhood. They ordered bialys, pumpernickel bagels, and cream cheese. Except for frequent repetitions of text and sharp intercutting of postmodern dance moves (that ranged from running to lying still, as if asleep), Bernd and Miller could have been any couple hanging out during a hot New York summer. They had rendered their gay relationship recognizable, normal even. In the *Village Voice* listings a critic wrote, "Highly recommended to anyone, nongays especially, who may enjoy seeing how generally interesting, in art, a particular same-sex relationship can be."[1]

At left: John Bernd (left) and Tim Miller in *Live Boys,* 1981. © 2003 Johan Elbers.

3

In retrospect *Live Boys* turns out to have been even more remarkable for the ways in which it presaged HIV/AIDS, just
months before the announcement of the first cases of the disease
in the U.S. Midway through the piece Bernd offers: "When I met
Tim, I had all these things wrong with my skin."[2] Kneeling at
center stage while shrugging his shirtsleeves up lanky forearms,
Bernd monotones: "About a week before I met him, I had a fungus on my skin, I had psoriasis where the fungus was, I had psoriasis on my scalp, I got poison ivy, and I was very depressed. . . .
I had to walk around with bandages on my wrists. And I looked
like I had tried to kill myself."

Miller asks Bernd, "How's your skin today?" to which Bernd
replies laconically, "Sort of a holding pattern. It's OK. It's not
bad." And then Miller, who has been shaking a can of spray paint
so that you can hear the sphere inside it rattling furiously, raises
his pajama shirt and sprays the letters *F, A,* and *G* on his chest.
Bernd raises his shirt now too and, after glancing at the audience
to ascertain that everyone is watching, offers his chest up for
Miller to spray *G-O-T.* Together they are a "FAGGOT" couple, the
unexplained aberrations on Bernd's skin blown up into a blatant
homophobic epithet, an angry scream rendered in black paint.

As we now know, a 1981 outbreak of Kaposi's sarcoma and
Pneumocystis carinii pneumonia provided the first indication that
something was amiss among groups of gay men in Los Angeles
and New York. A year later, in July 1982, the Centers for Disease
Control officially declared AIDS an epidemic. Six years later, at
the peak of the epidemic, John Bernd died of AIDS-related complications. He was thirty-five. Given the intertwined histories
leading from *Live Boys* to the announcement of the AIDS epidemic to the expansion in the number of AIDS deaths nation-
wide to Bernd's own death, the monologue in *Live Boys* takes on
a significance far beyond what Bernd and Miller could have
intended. This performance work is virtually fused with the arc
of the disease and cries out to be reconjured and seen anew.

I missed Bernd and Miller's *Live Boys* in 1981. I had just graduated from college myself and was teaching in India at the time,
completely missing the tremors that were then shaking up urban
gay communities in the United States. But when eventually I
moved to San Francisco and was confronted by my first AIDS
dance, it was not a theatrical presentation but rather a spectacular

pageant. I had come to San Francisco in 1985 to become a dance critic and, like all of us living there at the time, especially around 1987, became an unwitting witness to the effects of AIDS as they spread around us—from front-page stories in the gay papers to the growing contingents of AIDS volunteers in the annual Gay and Lesbian Pride Parade, from what we called "the look" of emaciated, lesion-blemished faces on Castro Street to the lurking subtext of long conversations that I shared with my friends concerning our sex fears. According to the U.S. Centers for Disease Control and Prevention, 1987 was the sixth year of the epidemic; twenty-seven thousand people had already died. But I didn't yet know personally anyone who was sick.

That summer a friend told me about a project that his roommate, Mike Smith, was beginning to work on with the gay activist Cleve Jones. The idea was to produce a warm fuzzy symbol of grieving, a kind of political graveyard for people who had died of AIDS, made out of three-by-six-foot pieces of cloth, slogans, and memorabilia. (The size of the panels was designed to approximate the dimensions of a grave.) By late summer I was walking down Market Street in the Castro District and was surprised to see a storefront with the first quilt panels hanging in the window and a sign that said "The NAMES Project." I went in and found Mike looking overwhelmed, awash in sewing machines, stacks of cloth, and reams of paperwork—the raw materials of this new grassroots organization. Danny Sauro, the project's first volunteer, greeted me with a handshake and a smile. I remember thinking that he was cute. I asked him what he was working on, and he told me that he was developing media contacts for the first display of the quilt in Washington, D.C., that October—he had only recently moved to San Francisco from New York and was volunteering while settling in with his lover, who had AIDS.

Mike told Danny that I was a writer for the *(East Bay) Express* and *Oakland Tribune* and that I knew a lot about newspapers. The next thing I knew, they had convinced me to join the NAMES Project media committee, where I would be in charge of finding celebrities, politicians, and AIDS volunteers to read the names from 1,920 quilt panels when the quilt was laid out for the first time on the National Mall. Garth Wall, Danny's blond and handsome boyfriend, bounded up the stairs a few moments later. Garth was on disability. He had been diagnosed with AIDS. But

with his boyish smile and radiant good looks, there was no way anyone could tell.

A central purpose of that first display of the quilt in Washington, in the fall of 1987, was to undo and reconstruct the meanings associated with AIDS, by sending word that it was nice boys, mother-loving boys like Garth, who were getting sick. The quilt itself was an overwhelming signification of the vast number of people who had died of AIDS-related causes and who were loved sufficiently that someone had cared to make a memorial. The American quilting tradition was evoked unabashedly: This was about mothers, fathers, sisters, brothers openly loving and caring for their family members. It was also an opportunity to influence the way that the media portrayed people with AIDS.

The quilt display was, at its root, a huge media event built around the perfect photo opportunity. Aerial photos dramatically revealed the enormity of the epidemic. Close-up shots of grieving family members—with the Capitol rotunda in the background—demonstrated the contrast between loving humane responses to AIDS and government indifference. Mini news conferences with the celebrity "readers" popularized the rhetoric of love and concern for people with AIDS through the nation's news organs. And interviews with handpicked AIDS volunteers reinforced the picture of heterosexuals jumping in to assist gay men who were dying of the disease. This was an appeal to the American spirit of volunteerism. And it was also, though perhaps not understood this way at the time, an attempt to reconfigure gay men not as objects of fear but as objects of pity.

We on the media committee recognized early that one of the most important things that we could do at the quilt display was to intervene directly with the reporters who were responsible for conveying this information to the general public. Wendell Ricketts put together a list of media do's and don'ts, based in part on his familiarity with the literature being published by the People With AIDS Coalition:

Do not refer to people with AIDS as "AIDS victims"; they are *living* with AIDS.
AIDS is a syndrome caused by a virus that affects the immune system; it is not a specific disease.
There is no such thing as an "AIDS virus"; AIDS may be caused by a virus known as HIV.

Do not assume that people with AIDS are all gay men
and that they were infected with the virus through
unprotected gay sex; the virus that causes AIDS can
also be communicated via unsterilized needle exchange, from mother to child in the womb, and via unprotected heterosexual sex.[3]

The list appeared in a packet distributed to all reporters when
they signed in at the Mall. Naively, we thought we would see a
significant change in the ways in which AIDS was depicted in
subsequent media coverage.

We did, in fact, see a huge rise in images of grieving and an up-
swell in discussion of governmental inattention to the epidemic,
with the inattention directly attributed to the fact that mostly gay
men were suffering. The sheer size of the epidemic seemed to
hit home, and newspapers couldn't get enough stories about
mothers stitching cloth memorials for their sons. The emotional,
sentiment-laden portions of our message got big play. But the
term *AIDS victim* appeared in nearly every news story.[4] HIV and
the subtleties of transmission and incubation were subsumed
under glossy verbiage about the "tragedy of AIDS." And the
press continued unabashedly to conflate AIDS and homosexuality. It was clear then that, as the medical theorist Paula Treichler
had articulated so trenchantly earlier that year, we were caught
in the clutches of two epidemics: an epidemic of HIV and an epidemic of signification, a proliferation of viral disease and a proliferation of unwanted meanings.[5] This was certainly evident in
the arena of AIDS activism. Soon I would discover that it was just
as true in the realm of theatrical dance. What, then, was the difference between the choreography of activism and the choreography of the theatrical dance?

Choreography and Corporeality

To make my point about the essential commonality of activism
and dance, I need to explain my understanding of choreography
and corporeality, two distinct but braided concepts that run
throughout this book. The initial impetus for this project was a
desire to study the theatrical dances—commonly called *choreographies*—associated with the AIDS era, in which I had become

interested as a longtime dance critic for various newspapers. But as an AIDS activist with my eye on the streets, it became clear that dances on the stage were part of a wider nexus of choreographies being enacted in settings that ranged from the National Mall to the sidewalk outside Macy's department store in San Francisco, from the steps of the Food and Drug Administration in Rockville, Maryland, to the streets surrounding Tompkins Square Park on Manhattan's Lower East Side. What difference was there, really, among choreographies enacted at these various sites, other than the physical fact of their being situated in or out of doors, or for paying or nonpaying audiences? It seemed that all these dances began with the gay male body in the age of AIDS, in fervent action. And each dance fulfilled even the most conservative notions of what choreography ought to be, from the astute arrangement of bodies in space to the intelligent ordering of form in physical movement.[6] It seemed clear, then, that I would not be able to get at the full meaning of the moving body on the stage unless I also investigated, for example, the AIDS funeral and its cultural surround, where the depth of AIDS mourning is instantiated in particularly unmediated form. Likewise, I would not understand the choreography of protests by ACT UP (AIDS Coalition to Unleash Power) unless I considered the abject, or outsider, masculinity embedded in the presentation of contemporary dance. As these individual instances of cultural production interfaced with each other, informing a mutual investigation, a deeper sense of what the gay AIDS body means in contemporary culture began to come to the fore. At the same time these productions shattered the boundary between the stage and real life.

Had these expanded notions of choreography not already moved into common parlance in dance by the 1960s, the concept of a funeral service as a choreography might be more radical. But ever since the experiments in unmatrixed performing that led to the creation of the Judson Dance Theater, beginning in the 1950s and continuing after the official disbanding of Robert Dunn's influential choreography classes in 1964, the boundaries of dance have been consistently stretched far beyond the confines of the enclosed theater.[7] Since that time dance has spilled out beyond the proscenium, into the theater itself, through the lobby, onto the sidewalk, ultimately even upon the sides of buildings, and finally—in the conservative 1980s and 1990s—back into the theater again. Meanwhile, the very criteria for what constitutes a dance have broadened to encompass the widest range of human movement possible. Beginning in the 1960s, dance critics such as Jill Johnston were writing about such movement phenomena as figure skating or strollers sauntering by. Pedestrian movement was valued and celebrated. In 1968 Johnston wrote: "The theatre must go. There is only one theatre. We are all actors and spectators simultaneously upon the stage of the world."⁸ Even the formalist dance critic Edwin Denby was caught up in the spirit of the times, titling his famous undelivered 1954 lecture to students at the Juilliard School in New York "Dancers, Buildings, and People in the Street."⁹

The idea of considering dance as a continuum, encompassing the theatrical performance of Bill T. Jones's *Untitled* as well as the outdoor quilt's unfurling, is not, then, without precedent; yet with the new conservatism that attached itself to postmodern dance performance and to related critical strategies in the 1980s and 1990s, such an approach appears no longer to be self-evident. The 1960s and their ethos are distant memories. Moreover, much contemporary criticism, by leading critics, seems to focus on defining what is acceptably dance and what is not.

But I would argue that studying an array of choreographies, such as those that I have chosen, deepens our understanding of the crucial ways in which one type of bodily performance informs another. For example, by attending to the corporeality of gay male bodies approaching death under the constraints of the symptoms associated with AIDS, one has already decoded a set of (indexical) bodily conditions or bodily signifiers that will turn up again in the (metonymic) depiction of corpses in an ACT UP die-in. These codes are modified when the death is not "real," yet they remain closely related. In fact, the ways in which they are *not* related—for example, the notable vitality of the ACT UP body as compared to the passivity of the corpse—indicate key points of resistance, in this case to death, to AIDS, and to government authority. The codes of dying are shifted yet again when the die-in is incorporated within a theatrical dance, where real death and activist death become mediated by abstract death: the simple act of falling. Yet another variation invites viewers to experience their own death by identifying with a protagonist who writhes in a casket. All these versions of dying, then—from bio-logical dying to activist dying to abstract dying to metaphysical dying—serve to illuminate one another, as the signs and codes of one are affirmed or contested by the other. As Philippe Ariès has argued so convincingly in *The Hour of Our Death,* every aspect of death is culturally constructed, from the apparatus and tech-niques of medical intervention to the funerary practices follow-ing upon biological cessation. And so it is that dances by gay men in the AIDS era can be seen as intricate concatenations of signs. An unbounded study of choreography by gay men in the AIDS era makes clear that these signs freely travel back and forth among the hospital, the street, and the theater, constructing, de-constructing, and reconstructing AIDS in a fury of meaning mak-ing. I hope that this analysis of a wide range of choreographies will lead to a new depth of understanding regarding cultural practices, particularly in dance.

Theorizing choreography in this expanded fashion has led in-exorably to my considering the bodies of the performers and the nature of bodiliness itself in the age of AIDS. In this way, my proj-ect joins the larger investigation of corporeality that is now tak-ing shape within the field of dance studies and is epitomized by the writings contained in *Corporealities: Dancing Knowledge, Cul-ture, and Power,* edited by Susan Leigh Foster. The introduction to that volume, which is playfully laid out in multiple typefaces to represent the overlapping voices and intelligences of the uniden-tified contributors, begins:

Corporealities seeks to vivify the study of bodies through a consideration of bodily reality, not as natural or absolute given but as a tangible and substantial category of cul-tural experience. The essays in this volume refuse to let bodies be used merely as vehicles or instruments for the expression of something else. They acknowledge that bod-ies always gesture towards other fields of meaning, but at the same time instantiate both physical mobility and ar-ticulability. Bodies do not only pass meaning along, or pass it along in their uniquely responsive way. They develop choreographies of signs through which they discourse: they run (or lurch, or bound, or feint, or meander . . .) from premise to conclusion; they turn (or pivot, or twist . . .) through the process of reasoning; they confer with (or rub up against, or bump into . . .) one another in narrating their own physical fate. In approaching physicality as a site of meaning-making, these essays lend greater precision to our understanding of the reality of embodiment. They also illuminate the corporeal play that is vital to cultural production and to theoretical formulations of cultural process.[10]

I could articulate my own goal for this book in similar terms: I am seeking here to investigate the bodies, the corporeal presences, of gay men in the time of AIDS as complex cultural constructions.[11] I recognize these bodies as their meat and bones, their "stuff," but also as the end result of a series of disciplinary actions, promulgated both from within gay culture (muscle building, piercing, a particularly frank come-hither stare) and without (the physical signs of oppression, skittishness, the walk of a man made to conceal the secrets of his sexuality, the tightly reined rebellion against that oppression). These bodies, and the bodies of those visibly ill with HIV, have much to tell us about living under the weight of homophobic and AIDS-phobic oppression. They gesture in the direction of the society and the syndrome that constrains them, begging for a closer reading of corporeality and choreography, of action and bodiliness, in a time of profound injustice and cruelty. But they also exist in a world of their own remarkable cognition, shaped by their own physical forms and communicative capabilities. They saunter. They storm. They camp. They march. They thrust their asses in the air. They form churches and steeples with wiggling fingers. They tap-dance in wheelchairs. They unfurl quilts. They lie inert in caskets. They flutter like ghosts. And they unabashedly reenact sexual rituals. Trying to figure out how and why is the driving force behind this book.

How Can a Dance Say "AIDS"?

As I began working on my dance and AIDS project at the University of California at Riverside, Susan Leigh Foster took me aside one day and asked what quickly became a central question: How can you tell that a dance is about AIDS? After vetting approximately fifty dances that I thought fell under the "AIDS dance" rubric—how? why?—I devised a three-part theorization of the features they held in common. At first, I thought of these three features as being of equal importance, but as I worked further on these ideas, I began to see that they were in a mutually dependent hierarchy, beginning with the prime factor: The dance must depict gayness. I call this the *abjection factor*, borrowing a term utilized to great effect by Judith Butler in her book *Bodies That Matter*. The gay man is abject, that is, marginalized, outside the mainstream, insofar as he cannot be a subject (that would be the heterosexual man) or an object (the heterosexual woman). To American society at large he is none of the above, simply because he is (or appears to be) gay.

The second necessary condition in this three-part formulation is the depiction—denotatively or connotatively—of male-male eros, of homosexual desire, which can manifest as eros fulfilled or, more likely, thwarted. The reason for this is that, without eros, the male-male bond could perhaps be mistaken for what Eve Kosofsky Sedgwick has termed homosociality, better known as male bonding, rather than gayness.[12] What I found was that intimations of eros buttressed the perception of abjection.

Last, in order for a dance to be perceived as having to do with AIDS, it must depict some form of mourning, ranging from the anticipation of loss to unabashed grieving. No loss, no conjuring of AIDS.

Recently, I had an opportunity to test my basic hypothesis, that all three factors must be present in order for a dance to conjure AIDS in a viewer's mind. My test consisted of screening Bill T. Jones's *Untitled* (a 1989 collaboration with the videographer John Sanborn) for a diverse group of fifty undergraduates at the University of California at Los Angeles, all of whom were newly enrolled in my course called Dance in the U.S.A.[13] Before showing the tape, I asked that any students who recognized the performer or the performance keep that information to themselves, but as I found out later, only a handful had ever seen Jones or heard of him before. Nor, on account of their youth, did they recognize any of his photographic references, such as the graffiti artist Keith Haring, the fashion designer Willi Smith, or the visual artist Louise Nevelson. Thus this was a near-perfect test group. During the screening I stopped the tape periodically to ask the students to describe what they were seeing and what, if anything, they thought it meant.

From the beginning the UCLA students described how Jones marches into the frame to assume a series of sharp, linear, martial postures, each emphasized by a sharp expectoration of breath. They interpreted these movements as conveying anger, frustration, and high emotion. They also noted, by way of contrast, the cool tone of the narrator's voice (the narrator is Jones's choreographic and life partner Arnie Zane, who, at this point in the showing, remained unidentified). With some prodding they articulated aloud what was almost certainly apparent from the first instant of the piece, that the performer is black, that he is muscular and sensual, and that, when he speaks—particularly in a sequence that repeats the phrase, "Do you remember"—he does so with what some students perceived as an accusatory tone, the sting of angry mourning. At this point several in the group theorized that the piece was about race in the United States and the legacy of slavery. No one mentioned gayness or AIDS.

But then a new episode of the piece began in which Zane's voice is heard at greater length. He is relating a dream about a piece of construction equipment that collapses on a workman. In the course of the narration Zane does two significant things: He slips into a languid, slightly sibilant, gay-identified delivery—a recognizable configuration of pacing, phrasing, and pitch—and he describes the construction worker, who has taken off his shirt, as "beautiful." Suddenly, hands shot up, their owners asking questions that clearly reflected a reevaluation of the earlier material. "Who was that other man?" asked one student, referring to a holographic image of a human that had appeared briefly in a pool of light earlier in the piece and that had attracted little attention at the time. "What is the dancer so angry about? Why is he feeling so strongly?" asked another. And then a male student raised his hand and asserted, quite definitively, that he was sure the piece was about AIDS. Why? I asked. Because he presumed the narrator and the performer to be gay—because of the reference to the "beautiful" construction worker, a description that a straight American man would never allow himself—and because the "Do you remember" sequence and the succession of black-and-white photographs that accompanies it made the student think about loss and death.[14]

As soon as all three triggers had been released—gayness, in the form of Zane's voice; eros or desire, in the sensuality of Jones's movement; and mourning, in the succession of black-and-white images—the wide field of meanings engaged by Jones's choreography zeroed in on AIDS. The formula was fulfilled, and AIDS appeared.

I am not pleased with myself for having arrived at this conclusion, for these three preconditions serve to reinforce precisely the meaning-making system that Paula Treichler and many other AIDS theorists and cultural analysts have worked so hard to disassemble: the conflation of gay male identity, gay erotics (especially anal sex), and death. The gay community and AIDS activists struggled for more than a decade to reconstruct AIDS as "not a gay disease" and succeeded to an extent only when heterosexual transmission was proved to be the cause of the spiraling HIV/AIDS epidemic in South Africa. But to my knowledge, not a single dance has been made in the U.S. in which an IV-drug user or a child or a hemophiliac or a straight woman is depicted as the person with AIDS.[15] As a result of popularly held conceptions that are reinforced in dance and choreography, it appears, then, that only gay men—or men who appear to be gay—signify as having HIV or AIDS in dance.

Singing the No-Sex Anthem

Interestingly, dance critics tend to respond to the moment when the three triggers are released—when the meaning of a dance coalesces around AIDS—with a strong tendency to de-eroticize the dance or to suppress the signs of their own gay viewership, in the case of those dance critics who are gay men. This strategy is effected with surprising consistency, as if the volatility of gay abjection, eros, and mourning were almost too dangerous to speak of in print. A case in point is the critical treatment of the central duet from Lar Lubovitch's *Concerto Six Twenty-Two*, which was featured in the Dancing for Life benefit at the New York State Theater in October 1987. Lubovitch had created the work, set to Mozart's Concerto for Clarinet and Orchestra, K. 622, during a December 1985 residency in France, and it premiered there late that year.[16] At its first performances in the U.S., at Carnegie Hall the following April, the *New York Times* critic Anna Kisselgoff effusively praised the entire three-movement piece: "There is something to cheer about when an already good choreographer comes gloriously into his own." Kisselgoff further underlined the "power" of the performers, the "inventiveness" of the choreography, the sense of "vibrantly alive human passion that emanates from the dancers at every moment. Why beat around the bush? The truth is that this is very exciting dancing and this is what dance is really about."[17]

When it came specifically to the central slow movement, however, Kisselgoff remarked that Lubovitch "surprises us and turns the middle adagio section into a tender duet for two men." Her next statement is emblematic: "Is the entire dance piece then a statement about the love two men can have for each other? It is possibly more about the way Mr. Lubovitch hears the music. And what he hears are musical themes that consistently suggest a cornucopia of movement themes." This is a fascinating passage because it turns toward a homoerotic reading of the dance and then away in an instant. Kisselgoff suggests, almost apologetically, that only Mozart's music inspires Lubovitch: Don't be afraid. But later in the same review she approaches her homoerotic reading again, in describing a particularly memorable motif in the duet. The dancers, she writes, "meet, place an arm around each other's shoulder and then form a linked pattern of two curved arms between them—as spiritual as the Gothic vault it suggests. . . . Chastely danced, it is also about caring."[18]

My theory is that dance critics in the U.S. are extremely reticent to speak openly about homosexuality in dance. And if I am right, it is notable that Kisselgoff gives so much space to these movements of complementarity and support. She does so, however, only in the context of the movement's "chaste" quality. This is not hard-core homosexuality on the stage—no hard cocks, no mimed anal coitus, she seems to reassure us—but rather benign homosociality, just a kind arm around the shoulders. In fact, what she tells her readers is that this is the safest sort of gay representation, the desexualized "noble neuter," to use the *Village Voice* writer Richard Goldstein's precise phrase.[19] This dance may be for two men who touch each other, but it is about caring, not about desire; about solace, not about eroticism.[20]

In the context of the fund-raiser *Dancing for Life*, where the Lubovitch piece was performed again in October 1987, other writers were, if anything, even more constrained in their reading of the piece's eroticism. Janice Berman in *New York Newsday* held her report of the duet for the final paragraph of her review, where she was saved from the problem of describing it fully even as she acknowledged its significance: "Yet perhaps the evening's most resonant moment came during the adagio from Lar Lubovitch's 'Concerto Six Twenty Two,' an extraordinarily moving duet for two men. . . . 'Dancing for Life' was originally Lubovitch's idea, and it seemed fitting that this piece was so warmly received."[21]

In a freelance article for the *Los Angeles Times*, Robert Greskovic, a critic for the gay weekly *New York Native*, called the duet "the sentimental favorite of the night."[22] Which sentiment he doesn't say. But Otis Stuart, who would himself die of AIDS in 1995, reported in *Dance Magazine* that, when the dancers began their slow walk toward one another at the start of the duet, "even the valiant tact pervading Dancing for Life cracked for just a moment. As the two men moved through their series of quiet encounters—unfettered by fears or fallacies, letting meanings fall where they might—the images of comfort and communion, of sustenance and support trumpeted a legacy of hope."[23] When Stuart speaks of the audience's "valiant tact" as having "cracked for just a moment," I can't help thinking that he is referencing a brand of repression, a controlled transaction between performers and audience, a transaction swollen with meaning but determined not to speak, certainly not about eros or sex.

Keith White, a writer for the gay weekly *Bay Area Reporter* who died of AIDS in 1990, came closest to identifying the eros at the heart of Lubovitch's dance when he wrote of a Berkeley performance in 1988:

The duet is tasteful, but unabashedly romantic, as the two men partner each other as daringly as they'd previously manipulated their female counterparts. But the most romantic thing they do—perhaps the most romantic thing people can do—is to look deeply into each other's eyes during their moments of repose. . . . The two men who performed the pas de deux . . . might not even be gay, though we recognize the dance's statement to be gay. This is what I imagine the heterosexual audience recognizes.[24]

Implicit in all these critical interpretations is the oddly thrilling sense that the Lubovitch duet is, in fact, highly erotic and that its eroticism tips its meanings in the direction of AIDS. But none of the critics quoted here actually writes the word *AIDS*, choosing instead to incorporate various—and decidedly indirect—turns of phrase to get their point across. They are by turns reticent, restrained, and obfuscatory. But even if these writers avoid explicit rhetoric as if it were its own kind of plague, they know what they are seeing on the stage. And they tell us this through a shared language of indirection.

The most remarkable aspect of Lubovitch's piece is, then, that it allows for two kinds of viewing: a secret, clouded, safe, "chaste" viewing of homosocial friendship; and a deeply erotic, highly sexualized homosexual reading, strongly inflected in the direction of AIDS. In creating a duet about two men who love, give solace to, and care for one another, Lubovitch managed to construct the AIDS era's most durable danced anthem, a performance positing gay male relationships as characterized by "chaste" love yet subject to an erotic viewing at the same time.

I make this assertion not as a critic—in which guise I too have been guilty of cloaking homosexual desire in the rhetoric of chaste friendship—but rather as a gay spectator with no investment in such cloaking. For me, Lubovitch's duet is highly and unabashedly erotic, even in the absence of any mimed intercourse or fellatio or other directly sexual activity.

The opening of the piece sets the tone. The music, which serves to provide an emotional palette, a structure, and a mood, partakes in a hundred variations of the arch, the cathedral arch, of the melody. But the fact of two men walking slowly toward one another and gazing directly at one another is, for me, frankly and deliciously homoerotic: two men, two *beautiful* men, facing each other at a distance, the separation between them eliciting a kind of electrical arc to match the arch of the music. If the clarinet melody is about tension and release of the breath, these opening moments in the dance are about desire: theirs for each other, mine for them, the audience's for some ideal of youth and love that they represent. This is the foundation of homoeroticism. Moreover, Lubovitch constructs the dancers as ready sites of identification for a certain gay audience, simply by costuming them in the polo shirts and khaki pants that are the uniform of the white gay man, and by casting two handsome men who physically fulfill a set of gay überideals.

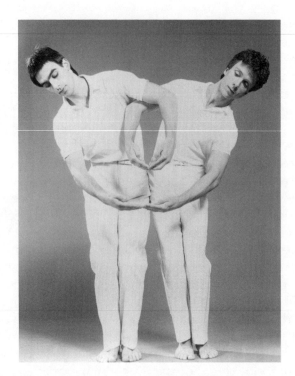

Sylvain Lafortune (left) and Rick Michalek in Lar
Lubovitch's *Concerto Six Twenty-Two*, 1987. Photo:
Martha Swope.

Then, as the dancers slowly approach one another, each raising an arm in a smooth arc until their two hands and arms are
pointed toward one another, their hands inevitably touch. I feel a
jolt at the moment when they do, continuing as they propel their
hands from the point of contact into an inverted *V* overhead. The
instant of touch is significant because the promise of two men on
stage walking toward one another has, contrary to expectation,
been fulfilled. Crucially, neither of the dancers turns out to be a
criminal, a sicko, a pervert, or any of the other stereotypes of homosexuality to which Hollywood films have accustomed us—
any one of which would have prevented that sweet instant of
touch. The moment is tender, but it is also, I would argue, blatantly sexual. I picture an entire audience focused on the beauty
of these two men with their arms around one another, walking in
sync to Mozart. The image fills me with pleasure.

When, finally, the dancers form two orbs with their overlapping arms, allowing the double circles to register on the eye, I am struck by the power of this image. Two people together creating a whole—lovers "completing" one another—is an image generally reserved for male-female pairings. For two men to express this image is a radical statement of same-sex possibility and an inherent critique of heteronormativity. Likewise, when the dancers begin to lean on and support one another, or when, ultimately, one of the dancers sits on one leg and extends the other on the floor as if he were a chaise lounge for his partner to rest upon, Lubovitch provides a model for homosexual relationships that is seldom seen in the popular media, one man providing solace, love, and support to another man.

Perhaps romantic love between two men is invisible where no terms to describe it exist. Perhaps the eroticism of the duet in an AIDS context makes it just too hot to handle. However, one thing is certain: Those of us who are dance critics or dance historians have to take responsibility for the way that we frame our interpretations, especially when it comes to AIDS. This is also a place where those of us who are gay and lesbian can play a significant role, for we may perceive things differently from our straight colleagues. I assert this to validate gay spectatorship, to request that those who read this text think hard about what it is that makes us see "AIDS" on the stage at all, and to encourage those who write about choreography and corporeality to declare openly and without embarrassment the homoeroticism inherent in so many dances of our time.

Silently Speaking AIDS

And now I must confess the irony of my reading Lar Lubovitch's duet from *Concerto Six Twenty-Two* in highly erotic terms, for Lubovitch himself has said that he intended the dance to be about friendship, not sex. In a 1986 interview about the dance, before it had been performed all over the world by the Lubovitch company and Mikhail Baryshnikov's White Oak Dance Project, Lubovitch said: "What I was intending was something nonhomoerotic, something on a very high spiritual level."[25] So where does the artist's intention stop and the viewer's perception begin?

This is an important question where AIDS is concerned, be-cause the terrain of signification related to AIDS is vast and, in many regards, volatile and uncontrollable. For example, even if a choreographer lets it be known that his piece is not about AIDS, it may still signify as such, even against his will. In short, the cre-ator of a dance may control the representation of eros and mourn-ing in his work, by shaping the choreographic imagery. But he cannot control his own status as a signifier and therefore cannot foreclose the spectator from associating the work with AIDS.

Bill T. Jones's choreography offers a particularly clear example of this phenomenon. While conducting the research for this book, I called Jones's office to request a set of videotapes. Two days later Jones called back, audibly wary, to ask my purpose. I ex-plained the nature of my study, that I was looking at a body of work by dance artists who in one way or another have reacted to AIDS, and that I was hoping to view the works that he made after his lover Arnie Zane died of AIDS. His reply: "I've never made work specifically about AIDS. I've made work about loss, about sex, about death but never specifically about AIDS. You may not believe it, but you can quote me on this."[26] I respect his intention. But even if Jones never intended to make work "specifically about AIDS," many critics and members of the public seem to find the subject unavoidably present in his choreographic frame.

For example, in *Still/Here*—a full-length, multimedia choreog-raphy with video projections and large-scale musical score that premiered in 1994 and has been both praised as a masterpiece and derided as "victim art"—Jones was extremely careful not to make any direct references to AIDS, even though the piece is based on a series of workshops across the country with people with life-threatening illnesses. The words *HIV* and *AIDS* are indeed never spoken.[27] None of the obvious physical markers of AIDS is present. The faces displayed in Gretchen Bender's videography display no visible Kaposi's sarcoma lesions, no rail-thin bodies suffering the effects of undiagnosed wasting syn-drome, no catheters, no tubes, no hospital garb, no medical appa-ratus whatsoever. Far more than half of the video images are of women or of older men; no obviously gay men are depicted. One clip showing an Asian American man engaged in high-velocity martial arts has been edited in a way that makes him appear invincible.

Likewise with the dancers themselves. Jones's company is made up of a diverse assortment of performers: black, white, Latina/o; tall, short; male, female; thin, stocky, even fat. But they are uniformly healthy, smooth-skinned, muscled, stretched, flexible, and sure-footed. As if to address any lingering doubt about their HIV status, Jones asserted in a preconcert talk in Los Angeles that none of the dancers was HIV-positive.[28] His publicist, Ellen Jacobs, responded to a *New Yorker* article by Arlene Croce with a letter to the editor designed to clarify misinformation. Among the items on the list: "The show's cast members are professional, international-class dancers, members of Mr. Jones's own modern-dance troupe—not 'sick people.'"[29] The dance was said to be about survival, and the inspiration for the choreography was a set of workshops held across the country in which Jones interacted with people facing life-threatening illnesses of all kinds.

But despite the intensity of his efforts not to signify AIDS in *Still/Here*, commentators on the work have talked of little else. Jones simply could not foreclose the representation of AIDS, and it washed over the piece, and him. From my perspective as a spectator of the work, this is not surprising, for AIDS seems manifest in every gesture of the choreography and every detail of the overarching conception, even when expressly unintended. For instance, consider Jones's text. The title itself, *Still/Here*, is an epigram (with strong intimations of defiance and denial) for "I am still here"—not dead.[30] A voiceover is laid over much of the piece, heard first in the voices of workshop participants and Jones himself, then transformed into scabrous song texts delivered by the folksinger Odetta. These texts are rife with associations that supersede their dictionary meanings. Take, for example, the scene where, under Jones's audible direction, a woman describes the moment of her diagnosis. She has been given a code number. (We intuit, therefore, that she is being tested anonymously.) She sits in a waiting room until she is called in to speak to a social worker. (Anyone who has been tested for AIDS at an anonymous testing site recognizes this scenario.) She is given the results: "positive." (For strep throat? Hardly.) The word *AIDS* is never articulated, but it is nonetheless conjured with undeniable force.

Much of the subsequent text concerns issues of women's health, with a recurring emphasis on cancer. The long section danced to the words *slash, poison,* and *burn* comprises the most

Arthur Aviles, Josie Coyoc, Rosalynde LeBlanc, Maya Saffrin, Gabri Christa, Odile Reine-Adelaide, Torrin Cummings, Gordon F. White, Lawrence Goldhuber, and Daniel Russell in "Still" of Bill T. Jones's *Still/Here*, Brooklyn Academy of Music, 1994. Photo: © Tom Brazil.

concentrated and focused choreography in the piece. The words *breast cancer* are not uttered here, but this medical locution is strongly implied, particularly in a gesture that sustains throughout this long passage: the dancer grasping her breast and her vagina, as if to protect her injured body parts. But when Lawrence Goldhuber performs a live monologue about his mother's cancer and her subsequent death, other silent words are conjured too. He relates a story about the moment when his aunt cannot bear to see her sister looking so ill and runs out of the room. "But not me," says Goldhuber, "'cause I've seen a lot of this kind of death lately, you know, the slow bit-by-bit kind. So I can just go right on pretending like it's normal, because it will become normal. And let's face it, it's always the same." For anyone caught up in the death and dying of the 1980s and 1990s, this is an unmistakable reference to AIDS. Moreover, many dancegoers who have watched the company over the years know that Goldhuber was at Arnie Zane's bedside when he died. In his memoir Jones relates how, at Zane's death, Goldhuber said Kaddish, the Jewish prayer for the dead.[31] A profile of Jones in the *New Yorker* before the *Still/Here* New York premiere includes a description of an informal lecture-demonstration in which Goldhuber spoke part of his monologue and ended with a variation on the version he ultimately performed: "Ever since I watched Arnie die, six years ago, it's been non-stop. And you know what? It's always the same."[32]

Virtually the same silent communication is enacted when the audience hears Jones's voice on audiotape; it evokes the information strewn throughout those countless preview articles, that he is HIV positive and that his lover died of AIDS. The correspondence between his identity and AIDS is further clinched when Jones's face and body appear on a small television screen at the conclusion of the piece. Disembodied there, he could already be dead, memorialized as a video apparition, conjured as a symbol by a series of quick-cut still images of internal and external body parts, corporeality and mortality evoked in a single instant. Jones may be a vision of health, but his silent lips nonetheless speak death.

This "silent speaking" is a phenomenon that runs throughout choreography made by gay men in the age of AIDS. The transactions of direction and indirection are constantly at play, as signs spew and viewers of the work sift through the meanings of the signs. The audience member's knowledge of the choreographer

or of the sponsoring group can speak AIDS. A whiff of effeminacy or obvious gayness can speak AIDS. A strain of elegiac
music, in the right (or wrong) context, can speak AIDS. Because
the word *AIDS* carries the stigmas both of transgressive sexuality
and of transgressive grief, we in American culture have already
learned to speak of it without words. We have practiced this silence and are expert at interpreting its meanings.

Scope of the Book

Among the thousands of corporeal events that might have become the focus of a book on AIDS and dance, I have chosen just
sixteen for close inspection, including two protests, two benefits, two memorial services, one processional funeral, three outdoor performances, one installation, and five theatrical dances,
including one that features an onstage erotic massage. My
choices are anything but capricious, though I lament that so
many performances—and please remember that I interpret that
term in its broadest sense—cannot be considered directly here.
(For documentation of other theatrical dances by choreographers associated with New York, Los Angeles, and San Francisco, please see the Estate Project's Internet site where my exten-
sive survey is posted: www.artistswithaids.org.) But rather than
treat only that list of well-known theatrical choreographies that
are best known as AIDS dances, I have sought to draw upon an
array of choreographies and corporeal events calibrated to assist
a reader in understanding the electric interchange between stage
and real life and to elicit the major themes of the AIDS era with
utmost vividness.[33]

It is important to note that I also made a decision midway
through the project to focus exclusively on gay male choreographers in the U.S., regardless of their HIV status, because I wanted
to understand the resonance of their choreographies in the context of the codes and conventions of gay male culture—not to
mention that I could not presume to understand all the intricacies
and variations of homosexual life, let alone the countless closely
allied cultures of straight women, lesbians, and even that rare
(and wonderful) coterie of supportive straight men. I fear, however, that this particular decision, with all its wider ramifications,

will be interpreted as a slight to some who have participated fully in the struggle to care for and protest on behalf of gay men with HIV/AIDS. When I shared one of these chapters in draft form with Janice Sukaitis, lyricist and playwright for the Angels of Light, a performance collective in San Francisco, she responded with encouragement and support but with a strong caveat: "Whenever a 'Gay' project comes along," she writes, "I'm always surprised to see that straight women, freaks, and persons who've fallen between the cracks, people that we so embraced in our group, are often excluded from this very history, in the way that gay men, people of color, and women have been excluded from mainstream history. It's ironic."[34] Sukaitis is right. The cultural production of gay men does not live in a vacuum, and the women, freaks, and marginalized others who are involved in the making of the work deserve attention too. I have thus done my best to revisit the text and to credit, insofar as possible, all those who have contributed to the choreographies that I am analyzing, whether they be gay men or not. In future work I will remember Sukaitis's words and seek to include a wider circle from an earlier stage.

In terms of geography, the choreography I write about here originates from locales all over the United States, with a strong concentration in New York and San Francisco, where the greatest number of AIDS-related works have been made. But this study makes no attempt to account for cultural production in other parts of the world where AIDS is just as prevalent as in the United States or even more so. This particular parameter is related to the degree to which my central thesis depends on the very specific conditions of gay life and cultural construction in the United States. Other studies need to be written of AIDS and the arts in other cultures, and my next project after the completion of this book will in fact be to look at cultural production in India, where public health officials are calling HIV/AIDS a "sleeping epidemic" that is about to skyrocket. We need other such studies, particularly in the nations of sub-Saharan Africa that suffer the highest incidence of HIV in the world. Someone with particular expertise in these cultures should write them. It would be impossible, however, to apply the same analysis to dances that grow out of U.S. gay culture and to dances from other gay cultures or, as in India and Africa, heterosexual populations.

If culture is a constructed category—a premise that is central to all my arguments in this book—then someone who is expert in those constructions must execute their analysis. Still, I do hope that this study may eventually offer an opportunity for scholars to survey the relation between AIDS and choreography across cultures. This must be a joint project, however, not a solitary one.

Methodology

Approaching the moving body semiotically, as a system of signs, I have viewed all the works included in this study repeatedly on videotape and at a very slow rate, as a result of which the video-taped choreography has come to exist in my mind in an integrated and comprehensive form.[35] As I worked on my analyses of each choreography, this mental image has lived alongside a textual interpretation of the dance—a kind of moment-by-moment verbal parsing—that I had earlier executed as a "tutor text." The discussion of each component of the dance therefore pertains not only to the verbal translation on the page but to my sensory memory of the piece as well. Lest this sound like a kind of apologia for a flawed process, let me also say that the repeated viewings of the piece necessitated by the verbal translation process have served to heighten my awareness of the choreography's details far beyond the bounds of my humanly limited kinesthetic consciousness.

I must acknowledge the intermediary quality of videotape or film, and its inherent problems. There is no exact substitute for the experience of live performance, certainly not where live performance is the intended format of the work. The camera sees monocularly and triangularly, whereas the human eye sees binocularly and peripherally. Video and film are two-dimensional, live performance three-dimensional. Moreover, most video and film cannot register images at low light levels, which means that the cinematographer must either artificially enhance the available light or make do. Undeniably, the camera sees something different than the live viewer can see; the limitations of video are well documented. However, it must be said that video and film are capable of expanding the perceptual range of the viewer to an astounding degree, and, as a researcher, I feel incredibly lucky to have had at my disposal videotaped documents of nearly every choreography or event in this study, save three (and one of the three, the beachside memorial of the choreographer Joah Lowe, was photographed extensively; the other two, the Dancing for Our Lives! and Dancing for Life benefits, have been reconstructed from written records and interviews). Without video this would have been a very different piece of scholarship and, in my view, a much poorer one.

The critic Marcia B. Siegel was one of the first to recognize the value of video and film to dance historical study. In light of dance's ephemerality, published dance criticism is often the only record of movement performance that lives beyond the memories of the performers and creators. But in many cases (and this is true of much choreography in the age of AIDS) such criticism is sketchy and impoverished, lacking in important details and clouded by homophobic niceties. Siegel's 1979 *The Shapes of Change: Images of American Dance* is based almost entirely on repeated viewing of dance documentation at the Dance Collection of the New York Public Library, and her reasons for taking this approach echo my own. "I've noticed that what I remember about a striking performance is impressionistic," she writes, "and that I seldom retain enough specific information to back up my impressions or to give me any new thoughts about the work."[36] And so, where it is available, she turns to video and film. These forms of documentation offer a perfect response to the epistemic ephemerality of dance: On tape we can watch a dance again and again, until it has impressed itself firmly upon our retinas and memories.

Regarding memory, I could not have known, when I moved to the Bay Area in 1985 and embarked on a career in dance journalism, that the dances that I was seeing then would become the basis and inspiration for this book. Luckily, I was continually writing reviews for weekly and daily papers, gay and straight, during those years when choreography seemed so often to be about AIDS. And even though many of these dances were insufficiently documented in the mainstream press at the time, I have saved all my working files, which contain innumerable press releases, programs, clippings, and, on many occasions, even my original notes upon viewing key choreographies in live performance. I have also maintained a complete catalog of my own journalistic writings from 1985 through 1994, as I reported on the Bay Area dance scene for papers ranging from the weekly gay press (the *Sentinel*) to weekly straight papers *([East Bay] Express, San Francisco Bay Guardian)* and the daily straight press as well *(Oakland Tribune, San Francisco Chronicle)*. These documents have formed the spine of the book, contributing to my view of the history of this era but also to a decidedly gay reception of choreography in the age of AIDS.

That a gay perspective on this work is needed accounts for my privileging queer theory and that subbranch of queer theory called AIDS cultural analysis. A guiding force in this area is Douglas Crimp, the art historian, critic, and theoretician whose work serves as a resource throughout this book. AIDS cultural analysis offers numerous tactics for seeing cultural production at more than face value, for getting under the skin of artistic and aesthetic projects in order to reveal the (often hidden) impetus for the work and for its reception. AIDS cultural analysis seeks to do this critical work from the perspective of an oppressed population, uncovering themes of homophobia and sex-based stigmatization from the point of view of gay men, lesbians, queers, and people with HIV/AIDS.

The Historical Frame

AIDS first entered public consciousness in the United States on 3 July 1981. On that day an obscure one-column article appeared on page A20 in the *New York Times*, reporting an explained cluster of cases of Kaposi's sarcoma, a rare cancer that until that time had almost exclusively affected older Italian men. The theater historian David Román—whose *Acts of Intervention* I summarize here as a springboard for my own study of dance in the AIDS era—begins his important book with a consideration of that *Times* article and the happenstance that placed it immediately adjacent to a large, if equally obscure, savings bank advertisement. The ad, configured as if it were a cut-out coupon, exhorted *Times* readers to sing "The Star-Spangled Banner" as a patriotic response to Independence Day, which was to be marked the very next day. (The sponsor of the ad was the eponymous Independence Savings

Bank.) In a Barthesian maneuver Román "reads" these neighboring newspaper items simultaneously, viewing the ad text as a communication to the "model citizen," an affirmation of fireworks, hot dogs, heterosexuality, and patriotism, in contradistinction to the proto-AIDS article, headlined "Rare Cancer Seen in 41 Homosexuals," which Román interprets as a perfect example of what Simon Watney calls "the contagion/seduction" model of homosexuality. The disease is contagious, invisible, and threatening, as well as a spectacle of erotic seduction. Román excavates the hidden messages: "Gay men are precariously implicated in the logic of page A20: either perform model citizenship or risk implosion with rare cancer. What's at stake is nothing less than the ideology of patriotic heterosexuality. . . . AIDS and performance, as A20 insists, are relational terms in the continuous negotiation of national identity and model citizenship."[37]

Román's tandem reading of those two items from the *Times*—which is characteristic of his scholarly approach in general—configures them as a kind of playscript, a window into American culture that reveals in verbal form the early themes of the epidemic. These themes will soon reveal themselves in theatrical contexts as well. Gay theater, which was already flourishing in New York in the early 1980s, would be irrevocably altered when the themes of page A20 collided with it and produced a new progeny: AIDS theater. As Román conceives of it, however, this new genre was more than a string of famous Broadway plays but rather a series of "acts of intervention," which left little or no trace because they took place at fund raisers, as part of education campaigns, in protest marches, or within memorial services. Any single performance, of trivial consequence on its own, became part of some larger ritual which "exceeded" it.

Performance, in this sense, was part of the more encompassing ritual that helped organize people's response to AIDS both in space and in time. The intervention had less to do with the representation or content imbedded in the performance proper—the song, the dance, the act—and more to do with performance's potential to bring people together into the space of performance. And once people are gathered in the space of performance, the possibility of intervention proliferates.[38]

Román's point is that the earliest AIDS theater consisted of performative acts whose primary purpose was to form a focal point
for gathering, not to put on a play. But even then these acts had a
larger social "ontology," which Román theorizes elegantly as ritualistic events functioning as acts of intervention: "The earliest
AIDS performances were located not in the theatre but in the collaborative, community-based production of social rituals. These
rituals set out to gather people into the space of performance in
order to raise money for research and care; instigate AIDS awareness; establish community-based service organizations; facilitate
discussion around such contested issues as sexual practices, be-
haviors, and identities; and honor the dead."[39]

In the early 1980s the primary purpose of these collective activities, Román writes (in what I take as a self-conscious echo of
his colleague Douglas Crimp), was intervention: "to stop the
epidemic."[40]

Román arranges and imbricates his archival research to create,
in part, a sense of the historical milieu in which gay theater
began to flourish but also as material for theoretical analysis. The
"gaying" and "degaying" of AIDS, the vicissitudes of homophobia, the nature of gay and lesbian political action—all these issues come into focus through his commentary. On the way, he
gives considerable space to the earliest responses to the epidemic, focusing on the earliest benefits, memorial services, political actions, and plays.

If John Bernd and Tim Miller's 1981 *Live Boys* was the first
theatrical choreography to make unwitting reference to HIV,
Bernd's solo piece later that same year was the first to all but
name it. *Surviving Love and Death* (1981) was an allusion to life
after the breakup of a relationship—it appears that the fishbowl
of Bernd and Miller's *Live Boys* had left their relationship shattered[41]—and it was also about the intensifying and increasingly
mysterious illnesses with which Bernd was having to cope that
year. Bernd describes the piece in his résumé as a "solo chamber
opera," and like other operas in the avant-garde multimedia tradition, including those of Meredith Monk, it includes singing,
dance, visual projections, and elaborate monologues.[42]

After performing *Live Boys* with Miller at New York's P.S. 122
and at Hallwalls in Buffalo, Bernd lands in the hospital. In a
monologue from *Surviving Love and Death* he says, "My guts

didn't stop bleeding."[43] His doctors at New York's Bellevue Hospital cannot figure out why. They wonder whether this is the "new gay cancer" but ultimately decide no, presumably because Bernd does not have Kaposi's sarcoma lesions or *Pneumocystis,* the two accepted markers for what at the time was being called GRID, or Gay-Related Immune Deficiency. The doctors rule out hemophilia and leukemia but eventually, says Bernd in a monologue, "they narrowed it down to a virus, which they know nothing about." He gestures conversationally while saying this, pacing back and forth. "And this virus creates its own antibodies within you, and the antibodies destroy the platelet cells in my blood, and the platelet cells are what makes your blood clot."[44]

Then, in a surprising flight of fancy and inventive stagecraft, Bernd announces, "I've decided to take control of this illness." He pulls out an old-fashioned blender, sets it on a rolling cart, and plugs it in. "Now, I decided to work on my diet, because that is maybe what I had the most control over." He proceeds to list all the things that he is taking, as food, in an effort to make himself feel better: the drug prednisone, 60 milligrams a day as prescribed by his doctor (he throws the pills into the blender); Mylanta to keep his stomach from becoming irritated (he pours in a big glug of the pink liquid); Brown Cow yogurt to replenish the bacteria in his system; 5,000 milligrams of vitamin C; watercress ("wonderful stuff"); potassium; banana; B vitamins in powder form.

"And never underestimate the power of the written word, for where I am today has a lot to do with it," he says, holding up a yellow pad upon which he writes a note to the virus: "SCRAM." In a quick stroke he tears off the page, rips it up, and places it in the blender. Last, he pours in a long chug of apple cider ("a great mixer") and, almost as an afterthought, throws in a gooey Entenmann's Danish, because "sometimes you gotta have it, you gotta follow your intuition, and if it says that's what you want, don't fight it."

Bernd starts the blender, shouting more text over the loud whirring sound (he is an irrepressible talker), then turns off the machine and guzzles directly from the blender glass.[45] In reaction he makes a disgusted face, then dries his mouth with his forearm. Becoming a medicalized body is a worthwhile degradation, he seems to say with this action, because he wants to live. And in fact he will for seven years more. But then, in 1988, the laconic,

John Bernd with blender in a scene from *Surviving Love and Death,* 1982. Photo:
© Sylvia Plachy.

handsome gay man from *Live Boys* and the stubborn mournful
shaman of *Surviving Love and Death* will meet his end.

Remarkably, this first formal choreographic performance of
the AIDS era not only fulfills the terms of the AIDS dance paradigm—depicting abjection, homoeroticism, and mourning—but
it also contains within its sixty minutes virtually every theme of
the AIDS choreographies to follow. I devote a chapter to each
theme: the stigmatization of gay sex (chapter 1); the linkage of
desire and deep mourning (chapter 2); the subversive and insurgent function of dance in the AIDS era (chapter 3); the theorization of the transformation of corpses to ghosts (chapter 4); and
the layering of gay male forms of sexual ecstasy within images of
heaven (chapter 5). Thus, from the very first choreographic activity conducted under the shadow of AIDS, gay men had already
activated a set of aesthetic issues relating to the political concerns
of homosexuals and people with AIDS. Not surprisingly, gay life
found its way into AIDS dance. And the politics of having AIDS
and signifying AIDS found its way into AIDS dance too.

I arrived at the terms attached to each of the five chapters in
this book through inductive rather than deductive processes.

After studying a substantial corpus of dances in the AIDS era, it became clear to me that certain themes and issues appear frequently and prominently throughout. The titles for each chapter grew out of those observations, with the pairings devised in such a way as to flesh out the rich territory of this time period. The relationships between the five pairs of terms are not analogous. They are not consistently oppositional, nor are they consistently similar to one another. Nor are the pairings exclusive to the dances discussed under each rubric. Rather, each pairing is designed to open a broad space for analysis and discussion. And, as in the case of Bernd's *Surviving Love and Death*, virtually any one of the choreographies featured in this study could be discussed in any of the five chapters. Placement under one pair of terms versus another is based only on subtle affinity.

Chapter 1, "Blood and Sweat," focuses on the forceful stigmatization of homosexuality and of AIDS that—especially in the early years of the epidemic—was manifested in inordinate fears of the gay man's bodily fluids. These fluids came to be seen as harbingers of doom, and dancing, by virtue of its association with homosexuality and its palpable activation of the fluid systems of the body, came to share, and in some cases amplify, that stigmatization. This chapter includes discussions of Keith Hennessy's *Saliva;* an ACT UP action on the steps of the Federal Drug Administration in Rockville, Maryland; and two early AIDS benefits—all by way of approaching a basic discussion of the body, particularly the gay male body, as inspiring fear and doom.

"Melancholia and Fetishes," chapter 2, offers a treatment of the inextricable connection between desire and mourning and the particular exigencies of mourning as demonstrated by the gay male community in the time of AIDS. Melancholia, as defined by Freud, is a special class of mourning that implies an inability for the grieving subject to return to normal. As Douglas Crimp suggests, gay men are melancholic in the AIDS era precisely because they cannot return to normal, for that which is normal—heterosexuality—is not an option (the feeble ex-gay movement notwithstanding). But if grieving is insufficient to heal the gay mourner, the literary critic Michael Moon suggests that our only hope of surcease will be the active embrace of fetishistic erotic mourning, a mourning that loves and clings and desires even as it elegizes. Tracy Rhoades's *Requiem*, with its profusion of clothing fetishes, is emblematic of this genre, as is the distinctly gay memorial service, discussed here as it relates to tributes to the choreographers Joah Lowe and Alvin Ailey. This chapter also features a close analysis of the work of Bill T. Jones, who takes fetishistic erotic mourning to a new level in *Untitled*, a vibrantly angry elegy that has been made into a (clothed) video and a (nude) theatrical dance. Jones's work is particularly volatile, I suggest, on account of his triple-marked abjection: that he is not only black and gay but HIV positive as well.

A discussion of the activist function of dance in the AIDS era is the main project of chapter 3, "Monuments and Insurgencies." Building on the theoretical writings of Bertolt Brecht, Douglas Crimp, and David Román, I argue that all dances have their politics as well as their aesthetics and that each category is best read through the other. Thus the politics of Rick Darnell's *Falling* can be divined in the specific aesthetic arrangement of its falling bodies and by the manner of their treatment once they hit the ground. The aesthetics of the AIDS activist Jon Greenberg's funeral can be seen as intertwined with the political beliefs that cause a group to raise a casket on its shoulders and march down a New York City street. And the unfurling of the NAMES Project AIDS Quilt—often described as "the world's biggest public art project"—can best be understood as a political act in light of the historical and theoretical significance of the National Mall, where its panels are billowed and laid to temporary rest. The quilt is a chillingly beautiful manifestation of mourning, but behind its beauty hides a political protest.

Chapter 4, "Corpses and Ghosts," reveals what are perhaps the key tactics used by gay male choreographers in the AIDS era; each tactic grows out of a long tradition of gay practices in the twentieth-century United States. Rodney Price reinvents the conventions of musical theater when he tap-dances in his wheelchair. Paul Timothy Diaz exhibits a powerful homo truculence when he performs as a corpse in a body bag on the streets of San Francisco. Joe Goode invents a new version of the gothic—AIDS gothic—when he writhes in a floating casket as part of a five-hour installation. And Goode also introduces viewers to the metaphysics of camp when he opens our eyes to a parallel world of ghosts and specters, with the help of a cheerful ghost concealed behind dark black glasses and blond bouffant hair.

The final chapter, "Transcendence and Eroticism," seeks to replace mainstream notions of heaven in the theatrical AIDS dance
with a highly eroticized, pungently gay view of transcendence.
Based on the importance of penetration in gay male sexual practices of the early 1980s, and on the heightened physical sensations facilitated by arousal of prostate, anus, and penis together,
this chapter makes the argument that gay choreographers have
remade heavenly transcendence in the image of sexual ecstasy.
The featured work here is Jim Self's *Sanctuary*, which includes an
onstage erotic massage as a key element.

Ultimately, *How to Make Dances in an Epidemic* does not tell
a reader "how to" make steps or what subjects to choreograph
about. But it does offer an analysis of gay male corporeality during the epidemic as well as an assessment of choreographic effects from 1981, when the epidemic was first recognized in the
United States, through the present day, with close attention to the
exigencies of gay culture and to best practices for bringing an
end of the epidemic. The approach is not chronological, although
the chapters move gradually from the most intense period of
AIDS-related choreographic activity in the late 1980s through the
end of the millennium. The book is not, strictly speaking, historical, either, even though the main figures appear and key events
are explored. I would like to think that it is, rather, anatomical. It
flays the body of the gay male choreographer and his choreography in an attempt to reveal skeletal structure, muscular activity,
and ultimately the gay male body's overriding intelligence.[46]

To close this introduction, I pause briefly to imagine a moment
of unexpected simultaneity, with each of the choreographies discussed in the book quivering on the verge of its enactment. This
is the moment when the performer takes a last breath before
stepping onto the stage or glances at his fellow protesters to
drink a draft of galvanizing solidarity or gazes from his preternaturally marginalized position as a ghost upon those who have
assembled for the enactment of his gay AIDS memorial. This is a
moment ripe with expectation, sensuality, and bodily possibility,
distinguishable from every other type of bodily activity that has
preceded or will follow it in the history of the United States.

This is the moment when abjection is fully embodied, when
the performer's gayness has been uncloseted and (regardless of
his HIV status) he comes to signify AIDS infection.

John Bernd publicity stills for *Surviving Love and Death,* 1983. Photo: © Dona Ann McAdams.

This is the moment when audacity, boldness, and insurgency ameliorate fear and even physical weakness, when the performer wheels himself to the head of the procession, rushes the steps of the building, or assumes a form so fleet and blithe that he will utterly escape detection.

This is the moment for belief in the efficacy of movement, when choreography is presented as its own reward, its own good, when motion equals action and action equals life.

This is the moment enacting the love of men for other men, made manifest in the fetishistic iteration of names, clothes, photographs, and movement, and in the delicious leer of cruising at the AIDS memorial service.

This is the moment when the body acquiesces to the virus, to bloating, neuropathy, visible lesions, shortness of breath, and profuse sweating, yet continues to enact its vivid corporeality.

This is the moment of high risk, when the performer allows himself to become, yet again, the object of hate, marginalization, and abjection, by taking his body where it is not wanted and absolutely refusing to budge.

And this is the moment when transcendence is imaged as a beautiful gay man lofting into space, the body blurred as if it had been transformed into spirit but still certain to return to earth . . . with a bang.

1

Blood and Sweat

[A] whole spate of crucial taboos turns upon superstitions about the nature, quantity, and powers of the bodily fluids. Perhaps it is not so much death as rather the leakage of the body that is the source of ontological anxiety.
Hayden White

In a July 1987 *MacNeil-Lehrer* news segment called "AIDS and the Arts," Bill T. Jones explained why he had counseled Arnie Zane, his lover and dance partner, against coming out on national television as a person with AIDS. "I am more than aware of the stigma attached to this illness," Jones said. "We had one person who was working with the company [who] said someone said to him, 'How are you working with this group of dancers? There are so many gay people there. Don't you sweat on each other?'"[1]

This remark highlights a plethora of issues that, in the late 1980s, were being projected upon the bodies of dancers in the United States. Three distinct presumptions are embedded in the statement reported by Jones: first, that some or all male dancers in Jones and Zane's company were gay; second (and this remained unspoken though emphatically implied), that a substantial number of these dancers would therefore be infected with HIV; and third, that coming into direct contact with the sweat of these dancers could be dangerous. In the late 1980s the standard

At left: Bill T. Jones (left) and Arnie Zane, 1987. Photo: Frank Ockenfels. Courtesy of Robert Longo.

dance-world response to these notions was to stonewall, by responding to a question with another question: What makes you
think there is a higher percentage of gay men in dance than, say,
in banking? The next line of defense would be to argue that AIDS
is not a gay disease and that, therefore, gay men should not be
presumed to be infected. On the third and final point, one could
invoke current medical research, pointing out that infection
by any means other than sexual contact, needle sharing, or from
mother to child in the womb was virtually impossible. What more
argument did anyone need?

Yet beyond the reflexive rhetoric, one must acknowledge that
the thoughtless speaker whose remark was reported by Jones
was actually correct about two of three assumptions. In 1987 all
six male dancers in Bill T. Jones/Arnie Zane and Company were
gay. Regarding the connection between gayness and AIDS,
within two years of the *MacNeil-Lehrer* segment, two men in the
Jones/Zane company would be dead and another would have
publicly announced his HIV-positive status.[2] Only the final pre-
sumption, regarding the danger of sweat, could definitively be
labeled erroneous. In 1988 Dr. Sharon Lewin reassured a group
of dance managers led by American Ballet Theatre's Gary
Dunning that it would take "buckets" of sweat to create even
the slightest possibility of transmission.[3] So what does this lone
anecdote reveal about the ways in which the public regarded
dance and dancers in the late 1980s? What exactly caused
dancers' bodies and their fluids to signify AIDS and death in that
period? Moreover, among choreographers, audience members,
and dance critics, what mechanisms of rumor, secrecy, silence,
and resistance—both misguided and enlightened—helped to
support these significations?

Simply put, for bodies and bodiliness in the age of AIDS, dancing is ground zero. This is the place where the meanings of
AIDS—the stigmas, the fears, the enduring assumptions, and,
contradictorily, the explosive power of life-giving metaphors—
are distilled to an elixir. From 1981, when the first cases of AIDS
(then called GRID, or Gay-Related Immune Deficiency) were
identified by the Centers for Disease Control, through the late
1980s and early 1990s, when AIDS deaths in the U.S. were approaching their grisly peak, the meanings surrounding AIDS
actively proliferated, attaching themselves to the dancing body

in a perversely symbiotic relationship. More specifically, these meanings attached themselves to the *male* dancing body.

The reasons for this are both simple and complex. By historical coincidence AIDS was, from the time of the first recorded cases in the United States, associated with gay men and their sexual practices, including anal sex. Meanwhile, as the dance scholar John Jordan has argued, the male dancer has been associated with effeminacy and homosexuality at least since the 1750s, when William Hogarth published his *Analysis of Beauty*.[4] It is almost too simple, then, for audiences in the U.S. to conflate AIDS, with its attendant gay markers, and dancing, with its own particular brand of gay markers. Hence, with nary a flip of the wrist, male dancer = gay = AIDS.

But even this undeniably potent, if irrational, chain of meanings may not explain the particular virulence with which dance more generally has become associated with AIDS since the mid-1980s. To understand the complexity of this larger move requires consideration of a set of fears attached to the body itself, as a container of bloody organs, fibrous tissues, and, most important, a panoply of body fluids. As the historian Hayden White has suggested in an essay on bodies and narrative in Western culture, "[A] whole spate of crucial taboos turns upon superstitions about the nature, quantity, and powers of the bodily fluids. Perhaps it is not so much death as rather the leakage of the body that is the source of ontological anxiety."[5] If I may then extrapolate from White's statement in ways that he might not even have imagined, it is not only the well-documented stigma associated with homosexuality in the contemporary United States that makes dance the ground zero of AIDS. It is also the fear-inducing notion of the body as leaky container, as permeable border, and as potential spreader of deadly contagion. Dance, then, is where AIDS and the body implode.

By the late 1980s the theatrical dance workplace was under daily siege, not by gay men or by a virus but rather by a set of invasive and unsupportable perceptions regarding bodies and bodily fluids. The rehearsal spaces and theaters where dancers studied and gathered to create new works in the late 1980s came to be perceived—by managers, choreographers, dancers, and, insofar as they noticed or cared, members of the general public—as sites of dangerous interchange, where a brand of virtually uncategorizable bodily intercourse was taking place. At the office the words "casual contact" might neatly circumscribe the extent of one's bodily encounters with other employees. Hands might touch. Doorknobs might bear the vague residue of a previous grasp. Toilet seats might host traces of sweat or urine or feces. The nation's more liberal doctors, including, oddly enough, the Christian fundamentalist C. Everett Koop, the surgeon general himself, took it as their responsibility to clearly and definitively allay such irrational fears.[6] But in the dance studio, where bodies were coming into decidedly noncasual contact with one another in the 1980s, concerns regarding contagion were not sufficiently addressed. In the course of a normal workday, dancers might in fact share bloodied shoes, tend one another's wounds and abrasions, and routinely participate in choreographed or improvised actions that could result in fingernail scratches or more serious blood-spilling collisions. In the dance workplace bodies touched, grasped, slid, lifted, rubbed, and, to a degree that had no parallel in office behavior, sweated profusely on one another. These dancing bodies were intimately connected, intertwined, soaked in each other's fluids. What is more, dancers were, at this galvanizing moment in the history of sexuality in the U.S., taking part in an uncomfortably intimate physical interchange, a blurring of the boundaries between one body and another, invoking fears of gender confusion and of sexuality more generally.

This highly charged moment is epitomized by a scene from the 1997 film *Alive and Kicking*, the screenplay of which was penned by the openly gay playwright Martin Sherman, the author of *Bent*.[7] The film offers a view of two dancers—a lesbian and a gay man—rehearsing strenuously in the studio. The man, Tonio, who is HIV positive, is sweating profusely. More to the point, he is sweating directly onto the body of the woman, Millie. All at once, and without warning, Millie loses control of her emotions and runs from the studio, screaming angrily. The issue is Tonio's sweat. She is furious at him for exposing her to his infectious fluid-producing body. This is a particularly surprising interchange, given that these two characters are the closest of friends and that they have, together, served as caregivers for numerous colleagues with AIDS. Surely, Millie knows that, medically speaking, sweat is not a danger. But when she makes up with Tonio, the next thing you know, the two friends are engaged

in a befuddled attempt at lovemaking, as if now that the un-
deserved fear of sweat has been overcome, a more intimate exchange of body fluids (albeit a "safe" exchange) becomes possible, even necessary.

What this scene demonstrates is the transformation of the
dance studio—a place for ritual action and rigorous, almost sacred, training—into a site where the signification of AIDS could
not be avoided, even in the thought processes of the most sympathetic and thoroughly informed colleagues. But the scene also
confirms, in dramatic terms, how one body fluid—sweat—can
come to signify another—semen or vaginal fluids—such that its
meanings begin to spill over the boundaries of its medical etiol-
ogy. I would suggest that, in the studio and at the place of performance, where anxiety about the signification of homosexuality prevails, any fluid exuded from a body is capable of becoming
conflated with AIDS infection. The body fluid becomes a sign of
the illness, a discomfiting aberration of the disciplinary distinction between the inside-ness and the outside-ness of the body.
Moreover, the source of those aberrant body fluids, the fluid
body itself, becomes a sign for contagious corporeality. Thus
sweat, though long understood by the scientific establishment
not to be a risk for transmitting HIV infection, is configured
within the public and private perception of the dance space as
extremely dangerous, as tantamount to death itself.

White calls attention to the possibility that existential anxiety
may not be the product of the human fear of death, as generally
assumed, but rather of "the leakage of the body," the anxiety-
provoking sense that the body is not capable of holding its boundaries, of serving as a durable container.[8] But to go a step further,
when leakiness becomes conflated with infection and disease, the
inability of the body to hold its fluids becomes even more fraught
with meaning. Now the HIV-infected body is not only in danger
of compromising its boundaries, but it may let loose a disease-
causing agent if it does so. This results in a double anxiety: the
fear of losing control coupled with the fear of death itself. This
two-headed anxiety—which White terms "ontological," insofar
as it pertains to the very condition of being—is fully volatilized
in the body and fluids of the male dancer in the age of AIDS. The
medical fact that sweat is benign with regard to contagion, or that
contact with other fluids that *are* contagion bearing, such as

blood, can be negotiated easily and safely with minimal training, does not prevent what White describes as "superstitions about the nature, quantity, and powers of the bodily fluids." In fact, the very nature of superstitions is that they are irrational and inexplicable. Thus the irrational treatment of the body's fluids becomes a conditioning aspect of the AIDS/dance interchange.

The anthropologist Mary Douglas addresses the closely allied concept of body fluid taboos in her 1966 *Purity and Danger*, suggesting that culturally promulgated ideas of pollution function to apply societal pressure on nonconformists, especially with regard to moral codes.

The laws of nature are dragged in to sanction the moral code: this kind of disease is caused by adultery, that by incest; this meteorological disaster is the effect of political disloyalty, that the effect of impiety. The whole universe is harnessed to men's attempts to force one another into good citizenship. Thus we find that certain moral values are upheld and certain social rules defined by beliefs in dangerous contagion, as when the glance or touch of an adulterer is held to bring illness to his neighbours or his children.[9]

Thus even though the male dancer's body may be invoked as a symbol of the ideal society—his perfect bodily proportion and muscular development viewed as a metaphor for order and virtue—that same body may simultaneously stand for homosexuality and disease and be sanctioned as such. As Douglas explains in her later book, *Natural Symbols*, originally published in 1970, the tension between the physical body and the social body, which regulates and controls the physical body, "allows the elaboration of meanings."[10] In the case of AIDS the meanings generated are frequently monstrous.

Just to complicate matters, even though sweat is medically benign, it may still serve as a symptom of HIV infection, thereby placing it in a special semiotic relationship to AIDS. For example, copious sweating is often a physical symptom of HIV; the virus can, at certain stages, cause what appears to be an extreme case of the flu. In the lexicon of AIDS in the mid-1980s through the early 1990s, especially before the advent of protease inhibitor treatments, night sweats were widely known to be a common condition. Such sweats were therefore widely interpreted as a marker of the disease—not just in the medical community but among gay men as well. Sweating, then, is a special case in which the connection between sign and signified is not arbitrary, as in virtually every other semiotic relationship, but rather indexical, to use the term as defined by the semiotician Charles Peirce.[11]

Daytime sweats are a complicating factor. When Jeff Wadlington, a dancer with the Paul Taylor Dance Company, was visibly sweating and had difficulty maintaining his balance in a 1993 performance on tour, my friends and I were concerned that he might be ill. When I asked, the publicist for the show told me that Wadlington had the flu. He died of AIDS a year later. Likewise, Mikhail Baryshnikov tells this story of his friend and fellow Soviet émigré Rudolf Nureyev: "We used to take class at Paris Opera together sometimes, and there he was with this Thermos of tea, totally sweating, wearing sweaters, and you could see that he was totally burning with fever. Yet he was taking class and dancing."[12] Based on his weakened and sweat-besotted appearance on stage, Nureyev had long been the subject of AIDS rumors. He never acknowledged that he had the disease, yet he died of AIDS in 1993.

Of course, sweating or other signs of illness cannot and could never be definitively linked to an AIDS diagnosis. The indexical relationship between sweating and HIV is not clear-cut, which accounts for the profusion of false rumors tying dancers to HIV when, in fact, these dancers may have been ill with other maladies or not ill at all.

Building on the convergence of these social and medical phenomena, by 1987 the conflation of gayness and AIDS—as analyzed so vividly in a volume edited by Douglas Crimp that was published that year—had managed to attach itself to dancers and choreographers, creating a new kind of seemingly incurable semiotic virus. The very bodiliness of dancers seemed to make them contagious. As demonstrated by the remark passed on to Bill T. Jones, the very functions that distinguish the work of dancing—sweating, strong blood flow, and the likelihood of bodily contact—now signified disease.

Semiotics and AIDS

Crimp's collection of essays, *AIDS: Cultural Analysis/Cultural Activism*, first published in 1987 as an issue of the journal *October*

and subsequently reprinted as an independent text, offers a revealing perspective on blood and sweat, not focused on the material concerns of the dancer in the studio but on the nonmaterial
meaning-making processes by which the body of a dancer could
become semiotically conflated with AIDS.[13] In their 1983 pamphlet titled *How to Have Sex in an Epidemic*, the AIDS activists Richard Berkowitz and Michael Callen had already argued for a sex-
positive response to AIDS, reasoning that gay sex and gay people
are not the culprits in this epidemic. "Sex doesn't make you
sick—diseases do," they wrote. "Gay sex doesn't make you
sick—gay men who are sick do."[14] This was perhaps the first attempt to resist the semiotic chain linking gay (especially anal) sex
to death, a chain that, in just the second year of the epidemic, was
already vigorously attaching itself to gay men. But it wasn't until
Crimp published his study in 1987 that this theoretical distinction was made with utter clarity, that we are in the midst of two
epidemics: an epidemic of HIV, and an epidemic of signification.
This theorization accounts for the particular semiosis of the
dancing body in the AIDS epidemic.

The writer in Crimp's collection who makes this point most
strongly and with the greatest sophistication is Paula Treichler,
who invokes the linguistic work of Ferdinand de Saussure to
suggest that AIDS consists of a plague of terminology, "an epidemic of meanings or signification," as well as a "real" disease:
"And until we understand AIDS as both a material and a linguistic reality—a duality inherent in all linguistic entities but extraordinarily exaggerated and potentially deadly in the case of
AIDS—we cannot begin to read the story of this illness accu-
rately or formulate intelligent interventions."[15] Treichler's project is an effort to lay out a Saussurian analysis of AIDS and its
significations by way of enabling such intelligent interventions.
She "narrativizes" the disease, exhaustively detailing its spread
as a linguistic signifier, observing closely as its meanings morph
over time. This observational work is crucial, she suggests, because the signification of AIDS is what controls the parameters of
action during the epidemic:

Whatever else it may be, AIDS is a story, or multiple stories, read to a surprising extent from a text that does not
exist: the body of the male homosexual. It is a text people
so want—need—to read that they have gone so far as to

write it themselves. AIDS is a nexus where multiple meanings, stories, and discourses intersect and overlap, reinforce, and subvert one another. Yet clearly this mysterious male homosexual text has figured centrally in generating what I call here an epidemic of signification.[16]

Treichler's research, inaugurated in 1985 with the news that Rock Hudson had been diagnosed with AIDS, offers a compelling theorization of the disappearance of the gay man's body and its reappearance as a kind of hypersignification, without a body beneath, as a figment of the imagination. Treichler mines the public record to dredge up some of the more idiosyncratic of these projections. U.S. Senator Jesse Helms, the North Carolina Republican, regards AIDS as a "creation of the media, which has sensationalized a minor health problem for its own profit and pleasure." John Langone, a science writer for *Discover* magazine, characterizes the popular view of AIDS in 1985 as an "Andromeda strain with the transmission efficiency of the common cold." A private citizen, Jonathan Gathorne-Hardy, suggests in a letter to the *New York Times Book Review* that AIDS is "the result of moral decay and a major force destroying the Boy Scouts."[17] This is exactly the sort of imaginative perseveration that comes into play in the reception of dances about AIDS. In fact, the epidemic of signification infects dance with particular virulence. As in the case of Bill T. Jones's informant, the male dancing body is presumed to be infected, or at the very least to stand as a surrogate for an infected body. From that moment the dancer is no longer himself, his own identifiable corporeality, but rather a scrim upon which countless semiotic images may be projected. General assumptions about men in dance rise to the surface, starting with those proffered by Bill T. Jones's informant:

1. All male dancers are gay.
2. Gay men are infected with AIDS; therefore male dancers have AIDS.
3. Dancers' body fluids are dangerous.

To these one might add a huge number of ancillary theorizations, many based on homophobic stereotypes or on notions of the AIDS-infected dancer as an object of pity. To list a few of the more benign:

1. The death of young dancers and choreographers is de-
   priving the nation of an artistic future.[18]
2. AIDS is a robber, stealing dance talent and morale.[19]
3. Almost all dances for men can be interpreted as alluding to AIDS.[20]

But then there are the baldly insidious projections:

1. Gay choreographers with AIDS use their victim status
   to manipulate viewers' emotions.[21]
2. Death saves dancers with AIDS from sullying the impression of their youthful gifts.[22]
3. Gay male choreographers receive accolades before they
   are deserved, because of the fear that they will die.[23]

Treichler's "mysterious male homosexual text" is ready and
waiting in dance, where he can be contemplated at length, made
to represent both that which he is and is not and spun into semiotic overload. He is his own disappearance and, in a bare instant,
his reappearance in a guise he himself would not recognize. His
blood. His sweat. Someone else's meanings.

Tumescence and Exudation

A central component of the experience of viewing dancing and
choreographic activities in general is the examination of the performers' bodies. Everything about the theatrical experience of
dance enhances and facilitates this operation of the gaze, especially with new developments in the aesthetics and strategies
of postmodern dance in the 1980s and 1990s. The costuming of
postmodern dances often reveals the body in degrees of partial,
complete, or simulated nudity. The feet, among the most sensuous of the human body parts, are stripped bare. Lighting enhances the audience's view of the shape, the curve, the three-
dimensionality of the dancer's physique. And those intimate
choreographies that encourage the audience to sit close to the
dancer—whether in theatrical or nontheatrical circumstances—
allow an unparalleled encounter with the dancer's corporeal
form, far closer than would normally be the case in ballet or traditional modern dance performance. This enhanced spectatorship allows the audience an unencumbered view of the dancing

body's basic characteristics, especially its qualities of tumescence and exudation.

Tumescence, literally, "swelling," is a physiological response to increased blood flow in dancers' bodies as they exert themselves and expend energy. The heart pounds faster. Circulation increases. White skin may display a rosy flush at the cheeks or shoulders or even on the hands. Indeed, in dancing the body's musculature as a whole begins to swell, to fill up with blood, to, as power weightlifters put it, "pump up." Like an erect penis engorged with blood, the dancing body becomes quite literally tumescent. Exudation, meanwhile, meaning "discharge" or "oozing," also accompanies the exertion of dancing, especially as the body seeks to cool itself through perspiration. Through its pores the body sweats a mixture of water and uric acid, especially at the armpits, the groin, the forehead, the midback. Exudation is evident in wet patches that seep into the dancer's clothing—dark patches revealed in bright light—or in a sheen on the face and body that is especially evident on dark skin. The boundary of the body becomes slick, wet, slippery. These qualities may be visible, but they are especially tactile. An audience member sitting in the first row may actually receive a spray of sweat when a dancer spins at high speed, throwing off a centrifugal shower.

This is where an inherent tension arises between body fluids as essential life substances and as fear-inspiring conveyers of contagion. Indeed, if male dancer = gay = AIDS, it now becomes clear that this sign chain operates in tandem with a diametrically opposed semiosis of tumescence and exudation: as signs of vigorous health. Hence, blood flush and sweat excite dual responses in viewers of dancing: desire in response to the presence of a powerful performing body and fear in response to the perceived presence of contagion.

The taut balance between two opposing sign chains heightens the viewer's awareness of the body as a kind of container, as fleshly, as mortal, requiring serious disciplinary action and training in order that its fluids are properly conserved. In this conception the body is raw, putrid even. Viewers are saved from its dank foulness only through the (tenuous) strength of the skin barrier and the (unreliable) rigidity of the skeletal and muscular systems. In this sense the dancing body is a kind of monsterish phenomenon, presented for view in order to remind us of our horrible mortality, of the unrelenting messiness of blood and guts, of brains and intestines, of sweat and mucous and earwax and feces.

At the same time, however, it is clear that there are important distinctions to be made between blood and sweat, tumescence and exhudation, as they pertain to the semiosis of dance, and these may be exploited by the savvy choreographer. Blood functions mostly as an internal hidden category, a metaphor for genealogy and class, that becomes dangerous and AIDS associated only when it is spilled (which is possible but uncommon in rehearsal or performance).[24] Sweat, meanwhile, is external, visible, legible in excess as a marker for illness or AIDS but otherwise signifying as a healthy sign of exertion and power—or of "worker" status. Capitalizing on these multiple significations of body fluids, some artists purposely complicate their viewers' perceptions. Some have specifically chosen to showcase the spilling of blood.

The best-known example of this in the contemporary United States is *Four Scenes in a Harsh Life* (1994), a work by the performance artist Ron Athey, presented at the Walker Art Center in Minneapolis, which featured onstage body scarification as one of its major effects. In a section of the piece titled "The Human Printing Press," medical paper towels were used to blot incision lines carved on the back of an HIV-negative African American man. The carefully blood-printed towels were then hung on a clothesline strung over the audience members' heads. This provoked an outcry from one Minneapolis spectator, which in turn resulted in fulminating rhetoric in the halls of Congress.[25] A related and lesser-known work, an untitled "community collaboration," was performed by Keith Hennessy in San Francisco the previous year. Hennessy's piece, choreographed by Hennessy and Stanya Kahn, featured six performers who inserted hooks in one another's backs. Strings were extended to members of the audience who, in Hennessy's words, "held them firmly enough to keep the tension, delicately enough to avoid unnecessary pain," and the intertwining of the strings became the work's major feature.[26] A third example of literal blood in performance was *The Test* (1995), a public HIV test conducted by the activist artists Elia Arce and Rubén Martínéz, in which the audience witnessed the performers having their blood drawn by genuine public health workers.[27] Predictably, performances that include elements of bloodletting raise inordinate fears for audiences and government officials: that potentially contagious blood is being allowed to gush beyond its bodily barriers and that it might seep into locales previously deemed protected and safe. Thus performance itself has, in these cases, been configured as a threat to public health.

Historically, body fluids become problematically foregrounded in dance only when coupled with fear of contagion. Otherwise they are embraced (the cult of the bloody toe shoe, the sweaty dance belt, the perspiration-stained costume). In such instances body fluids are not feared but rather fetishized. In the era of AIDS performance, however, such fetishized eroticization becomes perplexing because it is tangled up with the fear of death. No wonder, then, that body fluids—conceived as volatile, tainted substances—may be wielded by, or against, choreographers in such potent ways. Such is the case with the following choreographic events, made or performed in 1986–88, each of which signified AIDS for its audience. I discuss these choreographies—a theatrical dance, a political protest, and two AIDS benefits—by way of developing a clearer understanding of how late twentieth-century dances and danced events have come to interpret and shape the epidemic and our national responses to it. I will suggest that, while only the first two of these choreographies directly cite the fluids of the body, all four of these events are characterized by a key experience of bodiliness in the AIDS era: an awareness of the body's fluids as a circulatory support for lived experience as well as a set of dangerous contagion-carrying substances. Blood and sweat, tumescence and exudation—these are key categories for the production of meaning in AIDS-era dance. At the same time, virtually all choreographies in the age of AIDS reveal the effect of sexual stigma on the choreographic enterprise, for, as I hope to show, all dance in the AIDS era takes place in the shadow of proscribed gay sex.

The Gift of Spit

It is December 1988, and Keith Hennessy, a member of Contraband, the San Francisco performance collective, has put out word that he will be performing a new solo under a concrete highway overpass south of Market Street. The piece is called *Saliva*.[28] A group gathers under the imposing concrete dome, which vaguely muffles the sounds of cars zooming overhead. The audience is drawn to this offbeat location not by advertising or a listing in the daily newspaper but by word of mouth, signaling an affinity with the performer and his work. The Contraband associates Jules Beckman and Jeffree Mooney play drums, a kind of call in the urban jungle, while Hennessy makes his appearance in brown suit and skinny tie, a clean-cut 1950s professor offering a sacred ritual for his community. His audience is borrowed from Contraband's: a mix of gay and straight, manifestly countercultural, a slightly more down-to-earth manifestation of the 1960s hippie crowd combined with 1980s leather-jacket South-of–Market hipsters, virtually all of whom might describe themselves as "queer." There is a police presence tonight, two men in blue wandering among the crowd. Hennessy eyes them distrustfully while they maintain a low profile.[29]

Hennessy begins by singing what sounds like an invocation, a sweet, almost mournful lyric harmonized by Beckman—"Rain and wind, stir within, can't you hear me calling; spirits rise, dreams disguise, can't you feel me callin'?" As he sings these words, the crowd gathers around him, very still, standing in a semicircle, hands tucked deep in pockets to keep them warm on a cold San Francisco night. The singing, which is gentle and smooth, has a calming effect on the audience, which comes to receptive order. Hennessy can be a fidgety performer, dancing on the balls of his feet like a prizefighter. But tonight he seems calmer than usual, almost subdued. He still has an air of jauntiness about him—he was, after all, a street performer in Canada as a younger man, and a street performer has to ratchet up his energy to attract attention amid the relative chaos of street life— but tonight Hennessy is not quite himself. He is, instead, his professor self, a close approximation of William F. Buckley (licking his lips, affecting an upper-class accent). In this highway amphitheater words are scrawled on concrete buttresses, as if on a blackboard. One side—the good side—reads "breath, feeling, memory, self, anarchy, community love," and the other—the bad—reads "tension, numbness, forgetting, image, ideology, alienation, fear." A separate line connecting the two says, "i want lineage i want thanx fluids i want men." Hennessy has titled this section "Dad Speaking."

As the professor, Hennessy launches into a series of what he calls lectures, each a discrete chunk of text or movement. One is about boys and their attraction to father figures. Another is about his being an anarchist and why. (This particular lecture ends with a series of writhing paroxysms on the floor.) Yet another, more abstract and obscure, is about the disappearance of self in history, about the search for acknowledgment, for identity, about the desire for connectedness.[30]

The fourth lecture—"the shortest lecture, the biggest punch," Hennessy shouts out, eliciting a laugh—begins with a terse but quite remarkable movement solo. Essentially, it is a danced fist-fight. Hennessy's hands are clenched and ready to punch. His head recoils as if struck in the jaw. He kicks, turns in the air—not like a ballet dancer pirouetting but like a street tough evading an attacker—and falls down on all fours. Still in that position, he squiggles his head, then pushes himself to standing position, and, in an echo of the earlier movement, squiggles his hips. (He is passing the movement around to different parts of the body.)

After this quick phrase he bounces on the balls of his feet for a few seconds, skimming the ground as he locomotes: a boxing move. Then, all of a sudden, his body lurches as though he's been kicked in the chest. He kicks back, then appears to be struck again so that his body is thrown to the ground. Catching himself awkwardly, weight on two feet and one hand, he reverberates in place, almost like a comic strip character who responds to a hard slam with a visible "boiyoiyoing." As he does this, the fingers of one hand twiddle in the air. (Later this gesture will stand for ejaculating semen.) From this off-kilter position he scissors his feet into near splits, front and back, then spurts to standing, rolling his weight onto the sides and toes of his sneakers, swiveling in a circle as he does so. He repeats this last stylish maneuver—in contrast to the fighting moves, it seems saucy, smooth, dancerly, Twyla Tharpish—then claps his hands once and snaps his fingers. The end. He adjusts his pants.

After this mimed and slightly fractured battle scene, Hennessy embarks on a monologue that is explicit in its treatment of gay sex and AIDS, punctuated with dancing gestures (indicated here in parentheses). "Lecture number four is titled 'fluids,'" he says:

The Tao of circulation	(standing)
Sexual healing fluids	(leaning, yearning)
The sweat of hard touch	(hands in fists, holding an imaginary lover)
The saliva of mouth on tit	(fingers of both hands extended toward his mouth, lids of eyes lowered, mouth open, expression ecstatic, hands descending to his chest when he says "tit")
Flowing blood to warm heart	(hands at the heart)
Thickened phallus	(scooping downward to form a diamond at his crotch)
Exploding cum	(hands shooting forward together, the right hand sent outward like a projectile from the left, right fingers fluttering)
The distilled essence of ecstatic genetic history	(arms opening wider)
Just to name a few of my favorite	(slower tempo, slightly fey delivery—an effeminately gay moment)

This rush of text, this catalog of body fluids, this simulated sex act, from foreplay to tumescence to ejaculation, evokes such a raucous response in his audience that, riding the vociferous wave of their reaction, Hennessy repeats the entire phrase. It becomes now an iconographic act of memory, longing, an ode to a lost era of sex and gayness. In a self-conscious acknowledgment of his audience's affinity with him, of their queerness if not their gayness, he makes only one alteration of the text on the repeat. The last line is now "just to name a few of *our* favorites"—whereupon he plunges into a new text, his delivery stronger, more rhythmic, even more impassioned than before:

AIDS is a rip-off	(standing straight, tall)
Disease is a rip-off	(arms almost militarily at his sides, his gaze downcast)
I want your tongue up my ass	(staring directly at the audience)
Your juice in my mouth	(arms raised in an entreaty, forearms and hands traveling toward the mouth, volume rising, tempo quickening)

Why can't I taste your wounds,
   lick your life support system?

   (hovering on one foot, off-balance, vulnerable, his voice trailing off slightly)

Remember when our fluids
   could heal?

   (standing like a little boy)

It's important to remember this

   (bobbing awkwardly, arms akimbo and ungainly)

Close your eyes

   (he closes his; his head tips back slightly)

Remember how this could be true

   (the open fingers shadow his eyes)

How this could be you
Healing with your mouth
Your sex
Your blood

On these last lines, delivered as mournful punctuation, Hennessy opens his arms slowly until the gesture on *blood* is broad and floating. At the same time his head hangs almost wistfully. He seems to be remembering a time, perhaps just ten years before, when having gay sex meant finding surcease from loneliness, when the sharing of one's body fluids, of saliva and semen, was a kind of holy communion, a salve on old wounds perpetrated by a militantly heterosexist society. Indeed, gay writers frequently characterize the late 1970s as possessing a kind of sexual divinity, as having been akin to heaven on Earth, especially in such urban centers as San Francisco, New York, and Los Angeles, where large numbers of gay men congregated, formed visible communities, and shared sex. "AIDS is a rip-off" begins Hennessy's monologue, which is to say that he and other gay men had something then that has been stolen away now, something he would term *holy*. (In fact, Hennessy referred to his work in press and marketing materials in this period as "holy male performance ritual." Later he would add the word *trickery* to the list.) Holiness was ritualized in the sharing of what he calls "juice," a liquid locution that implies nourishment, not disease. Juice might be semen up the ass or down one's throat; or sweat shared between entwined bodies; or blood, conceived symbolically, as a sign for psychological and societal wounds assuaged by love; or the saliva of a kiss or a tongue up the ass or probing deep into what he sees not as a place of disease and contagion but as the "life-support system." This is a cry to a time before, when body fluids meant life, not death.

In the last section of the three-act piece, Hennessy takes his "holy male performance ritual" a step further by invoking the significatory power of saliva as a sign for all the body fluids and the healing power of gay sex. This finale is titled "Keith," or, in the earliest performances, "Keith, DANCING." It begins when he holds out a cut crystal bowl—the sort of bowl from which your grandmother might have offered chocolates—and instructs his audience to spit in it.

This is an extraordinary request and not only because spitting is such a highly regulated activity in U.S. society, indeed in most societies. (In the U.S. only certain types of people—blue-collar workers, street kids—spit in public. Those who do mark themselves as uncouth, polluted, or low.[31]) Hennessy asks not simply that you perform this bodily function in public but that you do it into a bowl already swimming with the spit of your anonymous seatmates. "[This] could be embarrassing, silly," Hennessy acknowledges to his audience. "You might just have a little bit, [or you] might have a huge amount. . . . Just work it up from now until you get [to the bowl]. I don't know of a good excuse, and I've heard many, not to spit in the bowl. So I expect you all to do it."

Following upon this firm injunction, a man whom Hennessy has designated his "acolyte" walks among the crowd, offering up the bowl and soliciting each person's expectorate like a Methodist usher requesting monetary offerings in a felt-lined brass plate. Some viewers back into the shadows until the bowl has passed. Others step forward and participate with apparent relish. Still others spit very quickly, perfunctorily. Remarkably, however, there is a growing sense of stillness and focus in the group as this process continues. Hennessy has moved deeper into the concrete catacombs now, and the audience has followed him there. The drummers are rendering a score of pitched, groaning drums, punctuated by cowbell. The music is languid and sexy. Multiple flashlights illuminate Hennessy as he crouches on his haunches on a piece of canvas, completely naked, back to the audience, squirming, snaking his spine. In the shadowy light the crack of his ample butt is visible, as is the curving shape of his undulating upper body as he opens and contracts his scapula. The light flickers on his skin, illuminating his musculature. In the

Keith Hennessy performing *Saliva* under a freeway overpass south of Market Street, San Francisco, 1988. Photo: Glenn Caley Bachmann. Courtesy of Hennessy and the photographer.

darkness the acolyte brings the bowl of spit and places it where Hennessy can reach it. Hennessy begins to speak over the sound of the drums while continuing to dance: "This is a play about my spine, about my double helix and electricity and information, my tree trunk of support, my dancing snake. About my system of nerves and bones that extends from head to butt, connecting skull to blades to ribs to pelvis, connecting sky to earth as my spine control. Connecting me to the connection in you to everything." This self-consciously New Age monologue—which likens Hennessy's body to a snake, perhaps the snake of kundalini yoga that is conceived as being coiled at the base of the spine as the fountain of life energy—configures Hennessy's body not as sick but as overwhelmingly sensuous. Moreover, he sees his body not as separate from his viewers' bodies but as contiguous with them. His words deny the existential separation of one human from another, whether man from man or homo from hetero. He is "connected."

Turning to the front now and straddling the bowl, Hennessy holds up a bottle and reads from the label as if he were Julia

Child displaying an essential cooking ingredient to her television audience. He declaims the text—"Pre-Pare Personal Lubricant with Nonoxynol Nine"—identifying the bottle as containing a common water-based lubricant for gay sex that contains a virus-killing spermicide.[32] Murmurs of recognition burble through the crowd. Hennessy squeezes the gooey clear substance liberally into the bowl. He announces a "secret ingredient," holding aloft a white envelope from which he pours what appears to be a powdered pigment into the glass receptacle. Then, ritually raising the serpent of his arm and hand, he stirs the spit with his fingers. The viscous fluid that has been exuded from the bodies of this audience-community—and which, under most circumstances, would be considered a filthy waste product—is now brought to center stage, as if it were wine in a sacred chalice.

Still sitting, Hennessy raises his left arm to the side like half an Egyptian hieroglyph, dips his right fingers into the bowl of spit, and spreads the inky mixture in a thick line along the angle of his forearm and bicep. He repeats the markings on the other arm, then connects the two across his nipples and chest, using both hands to draw a thicker center line down to the end of his penis. He stands and holds his arms aloft, displaying the "primitive" design. At this moment he brings to mind the graffiti artist Keith Haring—invoking a famous photograph of Haring's naked body decorated with thick black line drawings—and he is also Christ, for he has marked himself with the spit of his community. Our body fluids are smeared on his body. He bears the signs of our contagion, our "sin." He takes these signs upon his own body and attempts to transform them, to render them innocuous, harmless. This is the implied gift of his performance.

Of course, by the late 1980s we know that saliva bears only very slight traces of HIV infection, and Hennessy has made a point of protecting himself, and us (from our own fears, if not the contagion itself), by mixing an antiviral agent in this potion—albeit, in retrospect, an ineffective one. The physical danger of the ritual is ameliorated sufficiently that the audience does not feel compelled to intervene and stop him, to save him from himself—nor do the police. Yet this does not completely inoculate the audience from the associations between body fluids and death that flood the queer consciousness. Even in the 1970s, before widespread

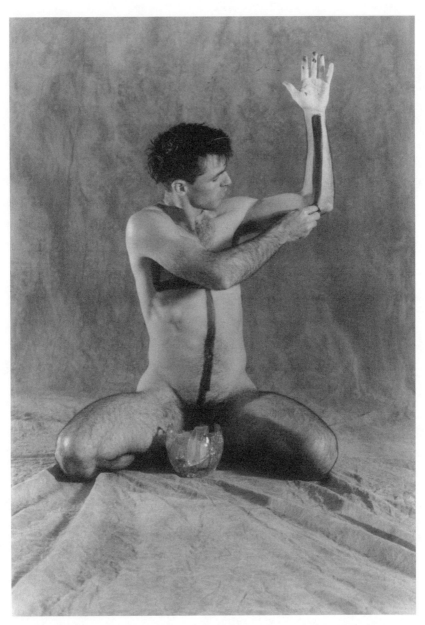

Keith Hennessy in *Saliva,* 1989. Photo: Steve Savage.

awareness of the HIV virus, this would have been interpreted as a proscribed ritual confronting fears of the body and its excretions, as well as homophobia. But in the late 1980s the collecting and smearing of body fluids in performance could be seen only as an act of gay priesthood: an attempt to desensitize the queer community to its sex terror. For Hennessy this requires a two-stage process: the symbolic ritual replacement of sexual fluids with saliva, and the rendering of saliva as safe, even healing, like a balm or salve. This ritual also requires that a designated actor carry out the action on the community's behalf.

Hennessy carefully designed *Saliva*—a ritual incorporating movement, text, and various symbolic actions—as a close analog to the gestural and textual maneuvers of the Roman Catholic priest preparing communion. (It is not that Hennessy's piece *is* communion, though it is surely a ritual, but that the choreography consciously configures the piece in such terms.) First, as I described earlier, the saliva is spread visibly on his own body, including the penis. Then Hennessy performs a series of movements that heighten his and our awareness of that penis: hiding it between his crossed legs—feminizing himself by placing his fingers and hands in a diamond-shaped gesture at his crotch, a symbolic vulva, then releasing the penis so that it swings freely, prominently. He is deconstructing and reconstructing his biological maleness, taking away his phallus, then restoring his phallus, in the process reframing it as bigger than life, as sacramental. These sacraments—connecting the body fluids to the sex organs—are calibrated to assuage profound existential anxiety focused on the body and its fluids. Thus they are meant to accomplish the work of transformation.

"This is a trance," Hennessy says in an epilogue, suggesting that we in the audience share in this trance by virtue of our breathing together, making us complicitous in the outcome of the ritual. He dons a black athletic supporter, black boots, and a black leather jacket emblazoned with the words *dead animal skin*. This is erotic foreplay, leather sex. The ensuing monologue is soaked in blood imagery: "Being hard is a way to feel my pulse. Alive, I am my cock. . . . I am no longer afraid of my own blood flow." He begins to sway, then whirls in a series of paroxysms that evoke the trance of disco dancing, with a strong flavor of anarchy and anomie. The rhythm changes, the tempo rises. Hennessy takes off the jacket, lights two torches, and spins them like batons. ("The New Man as flaming beacon," in the critic Rachel Kaplan's interpretation.[33]) Finally, Hennessy crouches on the ground and completes the promised sex act with a mythical partner, "Jake," not in movement but in a fury of words and accelerated breathing, outside and away from the body.[34] The text is replete with the liquid imagery of prolific body fluids, with Hennessy's voice rising finally to a passionate scream:

Taking weight, the cock, cum, slide, fuck, your body opened up, scream Jake scream; our fingers hearts tongue bathing where cocks locked up, scream Jake scream; how we flew, how we fly, fly, we can live it loving; our breath, kiss, those limbs shake off, can you shake me off, so good to know your cock in my face; loud, you need me; I hear the tremors crash against the walls of my skull; can you feel these verbs busting off my list every breath; I will hold you in my arms your writhing frame 'til the end of time because you pry me open, you pry me open, and I like it, I like it.

He is being fucked, and it is important to him that we know that he *wants* to be. Yet only moments later, in the postcoital stillness, Hennessy begins humming the tune of "Amazing Grace" in a grinding voice, painful, screeching, extending a hand beseechingly. It is as if he seeks redemption, but the request is a struggle. Homophobic Christianity won't let him have it. At his request the audience joins him, singing the words sweetly. One last time he has the audience hum "Amazing Grace"—now even Hennessy sings tunefully. Redemption received. And with that the piece, almost too abruptly, is over.

Kaplan's interpretation of *Saliva*, which deserves significant weight insofar as she was among the most insightful commentators on alternative dance and performance in San Francisco in the late 1980s, hinges on Hennessy's creation of a locus for his own identity and for his idiosyncratic spirituality that centers on his penis.[35] He is his penis. He is his ejaculate. He is his being fucked by another man's penis. He is his maleness and his gayness. While clearly enamored of Hennessy's performance, Kaplan critiques this notion of phallocentrism that, in its breathy reclamation, still obsesses upon the power of the male: Hennessy's penis presented as Lacan's phallus.

There is something reactionary about the attempt to *re-locate* power in the prick; the fetishism of the penis in Western culture is legion; the "penis" itself does not exist without its attendant symbolic representations. I can't help but think there's some over-compensation going on in the face of a feminist understanding of history profoundly affecting men of Hennessy's sensitivities. I understand the need to honor and love one's body, to perceive the self as a locus of power, but I do not believe we can afford to interpret our spirituality in such mechanical terms. God doesn't care about our equipment.[36]

The conception of maleness in Hennessy's *Saliva* deserves Kaplan's critique. His is an overpowering flood of maleness that can seem almost misogynistic, especially when the female is invoked only briefly in the second of the three acts when, in the guise of his mother, Hennessy dons a dress and enacts the nurturance of his "children," played by six volunteers from the audience. But Hennessy's effulgent masculinity could also be seen as an essential locus of phallic energy from which to speak back about AIDS abjection.

Hennessy's presentation of himself as a queer man is extremely complex in this regard. He is fully in control, fully possessed of his subjecthood, and patriarchally focused on the power of his penis even as he deconstructs his control, his subjecthood, his participation in patriarchy. But simultaneously, he presents himself as an object of desire, a beautiful man writhing for his audience and presenting himself for visual delectation. He makes himself abject too, feminizing himself as the bottom in a gay sexual tryst, the very definition of homosexual abjection. It seems, however, that, in part by virtue of his whiteness, and in part because of his access to the power of the phallus, he manages to embody a shifting array of subject-object-abject positionality. He is all these things, all these positions, at once. That he possesses such a high degree of control—he is not made abject but rather *makes himself* abject—is an indication of the phallic power he holds in reserve. No wonder, then, that Hennessy creates a locus for his identity that centers on his penis. Without his penis he is irredeemably abject. It is his penis that saves him.

This, I would suggest, points to the source of Hennessy's priestly powers in *Saliva*. Through the proliferation of maleness

Hennessy fulfills his urgent desire to recycle the bodily fluids of gay men as sacred liquids, to tear them from the grip of a signification that conflates gay sex with disease and death, and to restore them as life-giving substances. This is the remarkable project that is *Saliva*'s raison d'être. Our spit is smeared on Hennessy's body to make it fit to drink again.

Seize Control of the FDA

A procession of ten protesters advances on the front steps of the Food and Drug Administration (FDA) in Rockville, Maryland, surrounded by fellow ACT UP members, a huge and image-hungry media contingent, and a phalanx of riot police.[37] The protesters wear white lab coats whose front panels are smeared with what appears to be blood, their backs emblazoned with a slogan, "FDA HAS," accompanied by two very large handprints dripping red. Marching to the beat of a tenor drum, they hold their gloved hands aloft like prizefighters, prominently displaying them to the crowd. The gloves too are covered in blood. It is 11 October 1988, a crisp clear day in the fall of a year when one American is being diagnosed with AIDS every fourteen minutes.[38] The demonstration aims to symbolize the guilt that the U.S. medical community and government bureaucracy must bear for the deaths of tens of thousands of those new patients, many of them gay men. As protesters swarm around the building, the lab coat contingent is just one of more than a dozen separate groups from across the country, each focused on its own action. One cell surges at the front doors of the FDA and is repelled by the police guarding the entrance. Another enacts a die-in on the steps. Still another outlines "dead" bodies with chalk on the sidewalk, individual participants subsequently labeling the mute drawings with the names of deceased friends. But in the controlled bedlam of the overarching choreography, the demonstrators in the bloody coats are attracting inordinate police and media attention.

One protester, Patrick Moore, will recall later that the members of his "affinity group" from ACT UP/NY were nervous as they approached the front steps of the FDA building, unsure how the police would react to their parade in red-smeared doctor's

Protesters don lab coats bearing red handprints, which refer to the slogan: "The Food and Drug Administration has blood on its hands." Seize Control of the FDA, Food and Drug Administration headquarters, Rockville, Maryland, 11 October 1988. Photo: © Rick Reinhard/Impact Digitals.

garb. In fact, the members of his group would soon be among the 176 arrested—even though the police apparently were under orders to keep the number of arrests down.[39] Why was it that, among the legions of protesters burning effigies of then-president Ronald Reagan, hawking bargain-basement drugs on the FDA lawn, and staging noisy die-ins on the steps of the building, this particular group was targeted? "The police freaked out," Moore reports. "They weren't sure if it was real blood or not."[40]

By the late 1980s blood—especially the blood of AIDS protesters—signified strongly as a deadly substance. The safety of the blood supply in the U.S. had been at great issue since the early days of the epidemic. By December 1982 the scientific community had recognized blood transfusions as a potential means of transmitting HIV, along with the administration of blood products to hemophiliacs or the sharing of intravenous needles. Although the technology to test the safety of the blood supply became available in early 1983, in the form of a test for corollary hepatitis B antibodies, the blood industry had balked at instituting safety tests as a regular measure because of the expense.[41] After March 1983, when the Centers for Disease Control issued guidelines for blood-bank testing and mandatory exclusion of all people in high-risk groups, the blood of AIDS protesters came to radically symbolize "high risk."[42] The generally accepted notion was that if high-risk blood were to pass through a break in your skin, it would kill you, slowly. The genius of this particular ACT UP action, then, was in transforming the prevalent signification of AIDS. By smearing this supposedly tainted blood all over themselves, the protesters were able to transmute it into a sign not of gay contagion but of government guilt. This was no longer the HIV-tainted blood of gay men but rather the blood of hate, a red stain on the "hands" of the government. What was previously conceived as a matter of public safety was now configured as a matter of governmental honor.

Douglas Crimp, writing with Adam Rolston in *AIDS Demo-Graphics* (1990), details the context for the 1988 demonstration at the FDA and terms this protest "unquestionably the most significant demonstration of the AIDS activist movement's first two years."[43] The action was scheduled to mark the anniversary of the previous year's huge March on Washington for Lesbian and Gay Rights and to follow directly upon the second showing of the NAMES Project AIDS Memorial Quilt at the Ellipse in Washington, D.C. (The quilt provided a gathering place for AIDS protesters and proved to be a convenient way to bring together ACT UP members from all around the country.) Titled *Seize Control of the FDA* by its ACT UP organizers, the action began with a Columbus Day rally at the Department of Health and Human Services and continued the following day with the takeover of FDA headquarters in Rockville.

It was with a sense of dire urgency that ACT UP chose the FDA as its target, for the FDA was the sole gateway for new (and largely experimental) treatments for HIV infection. As of 1988 the antiviral drug AZT was the only new drug available. To put this in perspective, as of 1988 the life expectancy of people with AIDS was seven years from onset of infection. The best medical information at the time was that, following transmission of the virus, one could live symptom-free for some years, but the first direct symptoms of the disease—commonly Kaposi's sarcoma lesions or *Pneumocystis carinii* pneumonia; the symptomology would shift in later years—might occur just months before a serious final illness and death. The idea of waiting needlessly for promising new treatments to be tested was clearly ludicrous, yet that was the traditional and largely uncontested paradigm for testing drugs at the conservative FDA. A government agency whose top scientific administrators were appointed by the president, the FDA interpreted its role as protecting the population from dangerous drug therapies. This notion, along with a perception that President Reagan was openly hostile to gay people and people with AIDS, led activists to believe that the FDA was stonewalling access to a new generation of experimental drugs. Bolstering this analysis was Reagan's failure to substantively address AIDS in public until 31 May 1987, when he addressed the participants at the Third International Conference on AIDS and proposed mandatory HIV testing. (He was roundly booed.) In this atmosphere of distrust the FDA became more than just a symbolic target of ACT UP. (The AIDS Coalition to Unleash Power had, after all, been founded in 1987 in an effort primarily to speed new drug trials.) Rattling the policy makers at the FDA was literally the last bastion of hope for thousands of people with AIDS. Something had to be done to speed up the drug-testing process, and this was it.[44]

As Moore, who was a new ACT UP member at the time, remembers it, the idea for the FDA action came from the floor during the organization's weekly meeting, which was operated nonhierarchically, with all decisions requiring consensus. "At that point we weren't as paranoid about police surveillance as we were after that, so it was quite an open discussion," recalls Moore, who was then director of publicity at The Kitchen, a downtown New York performance space. From 1991 to 2001 he served as director of the Estate Project for Artists with AIDS. "Once we settled on the main point of the action—to go to the FDA and fling ourselves at the front door—once that was decided, we broke up into affinity groups. . . . We decided within each little group what our message was going to be and what, in addition to getting arrested, we wanted to do."

The members of ACT UP were, from the organization's inception, notably savvy concerning the use of graphic images to attract the attention of the media and to convey essential messages to the public. The SILENCE = DEATH slogan and its accompanying pink triangle—easily the most recognizable ACT UP image and among the most memorable graphic creations of the twentieth century—became the most famous and effective symbol of the AIDS activist movement in the 1980s.[45] In response to the stunning success and undeniable artistry of ACT UP's work, members of Gran Fury, a group of graphic designers associated with ACT UP, were invited to display their work at major museum spaces, starting with a 1987 show at New York's New Museum of Contemporary Art. Gran Fury exhibited boundless talent for attracting attention to its designs but also for conveying maximum meaning with minimal verbal information. This was partly a function of the expertise shared by ACT UP members, many of whom were "youngish gay men involved in publishing and media and graphic design," according to Moore.

Some members of the group would have been schooled in the science of semiotics and well versed in the theories of Roland Barthes. They might even have debated Barthes's theories during planning meetings. "I'm sure those sorts of discussions went on in Gran Fury," comments Moore. "In the discussions I was a part of, though, it was more heartfelt, just talking personally and intimately about people's feelings. Those discussions were more emotional than intellectual. But the ultimate effect appeared to be coming from a more considered viewpoint: This is how we feel, and, now, what image on the national news can portray this?"

For example, Moore's affinity group, which consisted of about fifteen gay men, met three or four times for two hours at a stretch in order to devise a choreographic concept to contribute to the action. "Ours was dramatic but very simplistic: blood," he reports, "the central theme of life and death, and bringing in the medical establishment as being the cause of our bloodletting. After three to four meetings we decided to do the bloody lab coats. Somebody bought the coats, somebody else the paint. And we painted [the coats] on the second floor of The Kitchen." Ultimately, the bloody handprints would become an overarching motif of the action.

Gran Fury had first used the bloody hands in July 1988 at a protest of New York City Health Commissioner Stephen Joseph's decision to downscale the city's official estimate of the size of the epidemic.[46] As part of that action, bloody handprints showed up in locations all over the city, printed there by roving ACT UP protesters who dipped their "latex-glove-covered hands" in red paint and pressed them to doorways, walls, sidewalks, newspaper kiosks.[47] Now, at the FDA, bloody-hand placards reappeared with the slogan THE GOVERNMENT HAS BLOOD ON ITS HANDS. ONE AIDS DEATH EVERY HALF HOUR, an image repeated on T-shirts and ubiquitous stickers that, like the bloody handprints, served as an enduring reminder of the demonstration. (Fifteen years later, these stickers can still be seen in various corners of New York City.) The particular responsibility in this crisis of the scientists and medical administrators of the FDA was brought home by a large subset of the protesters who wore white lab coats.

Seize Control of the FDA, which was organized by a national union of ACT UP groups called the AIDS Coalition to Network, Organize, and Win, evolved into a stunning daylong marathon choreography, extending from seven in the morning until five at night. In a video compilation of scenes from the day intercut with media footage and interviews with ACT UP protesters, Gregg Bordowitz and Jean Carlomusto depict the depth and range of those actions as background to and alongside a series of interviews with ACT UP participants.[48] One affinity group performs a die-in, bodies practically crisscrossing one another on the sidewalk. At their heads they hold cardboard tombstones

A die-in featuring tombstone placards critical of the FDA and AIDS drug man-ufacturers. Seize Control of the FDA, Rockville, Maryland, 11 October 1988. Photo: © Peter Ansin. Courtesy of Mikki Ansin.

with slogans such as I DIED FOR THE SINS OF THE FDA; AZT ISN'T ENOUGH; KILLED BY THE SYSTEM, or I GOT THE PLACEBO, accom-panied by the image of bloody red handprints. The protesters are surrounded by a platoon of police in riot helmets, shoulder to shoulder, balancing their riot sticks in black leather–gloved hands. Through a megaphone an officer demands that the pro-testers disperse, but he cannot be heard over the din of their rhythmic chanting: ACT UP. WE'LL NEVER BE SILENT AGAIN.

Another protester raises a ladder to the roof over the entryway to the building, and others quickly scramble up behind him, barely hoisting themselves to the top before an officer wrestles the ladder away from them, leaving the group happily stranded and taunting from above. Nearby, another protester lowers the Amer-ican flag and replaces it with a banner bearing the pink triangle and SILENCE EQUALS DEATH slogan that signify an ACT UP take-over of the building. Yet another hoists an effigy of Ronald Rea-gan and burns it. Protesters are pressing up against the windows of the building all around its perimeter, blowing kisses to the FDA workers inside, erecting banners and posters, and altering a

Rite-Aid drugstore sign to read "Fite-Aids." Multiple die-ins are taking place, some on the steps of the building, others in the street, with chalk outlining the bodies and the names of dead friends scrawled across the pavement. A circular march with placards protests the use of placebos in AIDS drug trials. One group sets up a corner store and hawks AZT at reduced prices, decrying the huge profits made by the drug company Burroughs Welcome at the expense of people with AIDS. Another group, prominently including a protester in a wheelchair, chants "No blood money," a further protest against profiteering drug companies—and another transmutation of the blood motif so that it signifies government, and now corporate, guilt.

The proliferation of overlapping actions is extraordinary—"uncontrolled yet controlled" is the way one protester describes it—especially in contrast to the monolithically stalwart response of the police. As is evident from the video, the police had been instructed to prevent protesters from entering the building, so it is there, in front of the lobby doors, that the police make their strongest stand. They form a human wall—dumb, mute, and monumental—and when groups of protesters surge toward them, they pick them off one by one, pushing them back until they lie in heaps on the steps. During this physical struggle the police reveal an arsenal of offensive and defensive weapons: riot sticks (menacingly deployed and occasionally used), plastic bands with which to tie the hands of the protesters, and latex gloves.

These gloves—sheaths, or condoms, to protect the police from even having to touch the skin or clothing of the protesters—show up in various guises throughout the day. Some police on the steps wear black leather gloves, part of their standard drag and psychological protection too. But at various points, and in response to particular actions, groups of police don latex surgical gloves before making arrests or directly encountering the bodies of the protesters. Some protesters wear gloves too, apparently to poke fun at the police.

The history of rubber gloves at protests—as a defensive response to bodies that threaten to seep beyond their boundaries—is an ignominious one. Even after fears about contracting AIDS through casual contact were debunked, the police continued to wear gloves at AIDS demonstrations. Most prominent of these

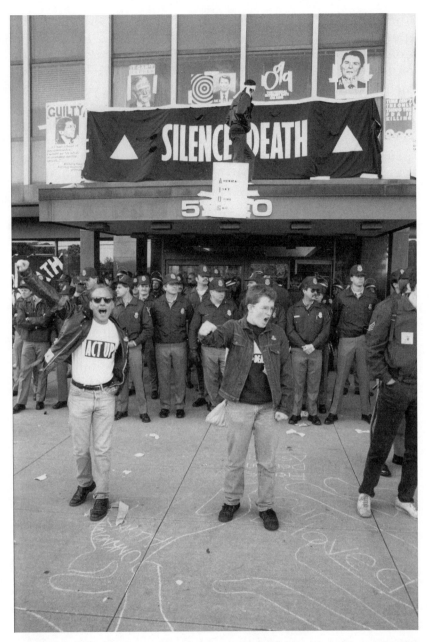

Protesters at the entrance to the FDA squeeze their bare hands into fists, while the hands of the police are sheathed in black leather or latex. Seize Control of the FDA, Rockville, Maryland, 11 October 1988. Photo: © Peter Ansin. Courtesy of Mikki Ansin.

cases was the demonstration that accompanied the first policy speech on AIDS by Ronald Reagan at the Third International Conference on AIDS. The following day, 1 June 1987, sixty-four protesters were arrested in front of the White House by Washington police, who protected themselves with bright yellow rubber gloves, the sort of heavy gloves used for industrial cleaning. As Crimp describes it, the demonstrators, many of whom were conservatively dressed in business suits and ties, "raised the very queer chant: YOUR GLOVES DON'T MATCH YOUR SHOES! YOU'LL SEE IT ON THE NEWS![49] This story played very well in the media and solidified the impression that the government was overreacting to the prospect of physical contact with people with AIDS. The police at the FDA demonstration more than a year later did not wear the bright yellow gloves. Nevertheless, understated milky latex gloves were part of their standard uniform.

The choreography of these gloved interactions is recorded for posterity because ACT UP considered video production to be an essential tactic.[50] Teams of videographers accompanied the protesters and moved in quickly whenever the police proved particularly menacing, to chronicle police abuses and to press home the point that they could not overreact with impunity. Indeed, the *Seize Control* video shows police reacting hotly in several instances, in particular when one police officer beats on the hands of a protester who is lifting himself onto the roof of the front walkway, or when a group of police begin to arrest protesters who are blocking traffic on the road and use more force than necessary. But, interestingly, much of the most vivid video at the FDA action was shot not by ACT UP crews but by members of the professional broadcast media, ranging from teams representing local news shows to national network news organizations, which had been tipped off to the action in advance. These television journalists had been so fully educated to ACT UP's concerns that they arrived with an inclination to represent the story in a way that was sympathetic to the protesters. Thus when Dan Rather on CBS or Dave Marash on ABC read the story to a national audience, they (uncharacteristically) positioned the protesters as reasonable and the FDA as irrationally stonewalling. "The action was a major success," says an ACT UP member in the *Seize Control* tape. "We did take over the running of the agency. For that day the eyes of the country and the world were on us, and not on what the FDA had to say. They were on our agenda."

Television cameras capture the choreographed action. Seize Control of the FDA, Rockville, Maryland, 11 October 1988. Photo: © Rick Reinhard/Impact Digitals.

The forwarding of ACT UP's agenda could be attributed in part to an experimental strategy described in the *Seize Control* videotape by Michaelangelo Signorile, who was in 1988 the co-ordinator of ACT UP's media committee and who is now a prominent author and cultural critic. His analysis of the organization's media savvy is revealing; let me quote him at length:

When you're working with the media, you're not dealing with feelings and that kind of thing. You cannot approach these people with compassion and say, please you must do something, people are dying. You cannot approach these people with anger, saying, please you must do this, you must be responsible. The media is there not to be responsible, not to be—as we were taught—the watchdog, or the watcher of our politicians, etc. The media is really there to make money. And what they want is something that will provide them with a story that they can really sort of . . . sell. . . .

So what we created here wasn't just a one-day media sensation. We created an issue. . . . We got incredible coverage for what actually happened. And a lot of that also has to do with the creativity of the demonstrations. I think once you get reporters there and camera crews there, they just run away with it. They love the graphics. They love the energy. They see the people. And there's a focus of the message. The message is focused and it's real, and it's honest, and it's people fighting for their lives.[51]

By 1988 ACT UP had already learned that, to be successfully distilled for the camera, choreographic messages had to be legible in a quick video bite of a few seconds or less and that they needed to be constructed in a way that invited a close-up view. With that knowledge ACT UP provided the media with a perfect set of movement images for video manipulation. In mere moments a viewer could register the meaning of a protester who was lying on the ground, holding a cardboard tombstone at his head: He is a corpse, and the government is killing him. Disciplined, defiant gatherings in the face of fully outfitted riot police conveyed a sense of enormous bravery on the part of the protesters: These people are placing their vulnerable bodies in support of a cause, even at the price of physical pain. And a march of demonstrators in lab coats smeared in blood, holding their guilty bloody hands in the air for public view, was an obvious satire of the FDA researchers who make the decisions and hold the power: If the government's doctors don't release new drugs now, the protesters' blood will be on their hands. By tipping off the press to its demands and its plans in advance, ACT UP configured the media as willing accomplices. Essentially, ACT UP taught the media how to "read" its choreographic protest. But even more important, through the theatricality of this non-theatrical event, the demonstrators refashioned their semiotically AIDS-infected bodies as exuberant, impassioned, audacious, even glamorous, just the way the camera wanted them.

In addition to the success of the FDA action as part of a concerted media campaign intended to influence national AIDS policy, it is worth noting the meanings and metaphors constructed for the participants themselves. One protester, a woman, remarks, "I knew that what good we were doing perhaps wasn't felt during the precise moment we were doing it. Looking back on it, it seems very surreal. The amount of physical action that was going on during that time, it boggles my mind now that I think about it, because all I was seeing was this little group of us, doing what we could do." The very "surreality" of the action highlights the degree to which *Seize Control* breaks the normal rules of engagement—gay and lesbian activists are not accustomed to feeling powerful or in control in a heterosexist society—but it also brings to the fore the possibilities for individual meaning making in a choreographic encounter. The very act of participation served to make some of the protesters feel as though they could conquer the world. For the length of the action, and in its aftermath, they felt swollen with power.

That the experience of participating in the action should render the protesters powerful (at least in the short term) says something crucial about the construction of the choreography itself. (I am speaking here of ACT UP's choreography in relation to the police and the building, not vice versa; I doubt that the wall of police felt empowered at the end of the day, after undergoing hours of physical and psychic siege.) The movement of bodies through space was not ponderous or stodgy, lugubrious or sentimental. Rather, it was darting and quick, light and sharp. The arrangement of participants in the space was not monolithic and undifferentiated. Rather, it was multivaried and unpredictable.

Also, the choreography was formed as a concatenation of indi-
vidually complete "cells," not as a smooth pageant, which meant
that the failure of any one action to have a choreographic effect
was of little consequence. The next action played out on a clean
slate. The loose joining of the parts made for a wildly energized
effect, with each action feeding off the one that preceded it or
overlapped it. Most important, this cellular organization—which,
significantly, resembles the actual configuration of small AIDS
organizations collectively seeking the end of the epidemic—
served to convey a central message, that this kind of relentless
choreographic assault was what the FDA could expect if it did
not accede to ACT UP's demands. And, in fact, in the months
after the protest, a shift in the government's position did occur.
"Government agencies dealing with AIDS, particularly the FDA
and NIH [National Institutes of Health], began to listen to us, to
include us in decision-making, even to ask for our input," reports
Crimp. Moreover, within a year ACT UP's proposal for "parallel
track" drug testing was instituted by the NIH and the FDA, leading to the wide availability of ddI (dideoxyinosine), "the first
antiviral AIDS drug to become available since AZT."[52]

Patrick Moore, the New York ACT UP member who marched
with his affinity group in bloody lab coats and gloves, knew that
if his particular action proved successful, it would help shift the
fear of AIDS contagion from his blood to the agency of the government. That had been the plan. "We wanted to have the bloody
hands be the things that people saw when we walked forward,"
he said, "and we also wanted to scare the police and have them
think that maybe it was real blood—because the idea of rubber
gloves was really abhorrent to a lot of people, and made them
feel like toxic waste." Moore was also inspired by another meaning for all that blood, "and that's rage. There's such rage and
such pain," he said of his feelings during the protest, "it's as if
the blood just poured out of us, so that we were just covered in it.
Like Sissy Spacek in *Carrie*, this blood dripping."

Dancing for (Our) Lives

Even when not visibly gushing, spurting, or dripping, body fluids
remain a key, if subcutaneous, component of every choreographic

action of the AIDS era. Although not always visible, the body's fluids remain in circulation, constantly sustaining and support- ing the body's basic corporeality, filling it, feeding it, cooling it— and signifying for viewers a range of meanings, some of which can be controlled by choreographers, others of which cannot. Keith Hennessy's *Saliva,* for example, accepts the signification of his fluid-filled body as gay but then blocks the expected chain of meanings extending from male dancer to homosexuality to body fluids just before it can render those fluids contagious and deadly. The ACT UP demonstration at the FDA begins by sub- mitting to the signification of its participants as gay and AIDS infected but, through vivid choreographic actions, successfully shifts the stigma of infected blood away from the participants and onto the government. These choreographies actively shape and permute the signification of bodily fluids in ways that re- sist the oppressive conflation of gayness with the fear of fluid gay corporealities. But what about AIDS performances in which body fluids are not directly evident—no glistening sweat, no spilled blood—but in which the operations of homophobic and AIDS-phobic oppression are still very much in force, very much fluid, pressing just beneath the surface of the skin?

The force of corporeal stigmatization in dance is made particu- larly evident in a comparison of two early AIDS benefits, both held in New York, one downtown, one uptown, that served as early sites of contestation regarding the homophobia and AIDS- phobia signified by the fluid male dancing body. A consideration of these benefits echoes the remark reported to Bill T. Jones with which this chapter began, a remark that defines an epidemic of signification leading inexorably from the preponderance of gay men in dance to the high incidence of AIDS in dance to the fear- inspiring contagion of the gay male dancing body. Though both benefits shared the worthy ambition of raising money for AIDS research and direct care, they went about managing the fluid sig- nification of AIDS in very different ways.

As will become evident in the discussion that follows, at the downtown benefit location, stigmatization is blocked at the cru- cial moment when the gay male dancing body is on the verge of being converted into an object of loathing, thus contesting the expected chain of meanings before it can conclude in stigma- tized death. This downtown event embraces the gayness of the

participants and admits to the wide reach of AIDS in the dance/
performance community but then utterly rejects the notion of
gay male bodies as contagious by drawing performers and audience together as one united group at the eye of the storm. At the
uptown event, however, stigmatization is not so much subverted
as denied, by disclaiming the connection between gay men and
the arts, arguing for the universal reach of AIDS (suggesting that
it far exceeds any losses in the arts) and forging a short-lived and
fundamentally fractured alliance between high-society heterosexuals and gay men in dance. The stigmatized fluids of the gay
male dancing body are thus in one instance embraced and reconfigured and in another blithely denied.

In the late 1980s ACT UP's combination of rage and choreographic action formed a crucial link between that activist organization, many of whose early members were artists, and the
downtown New York performance community, many of whose
members had been coming out in their work as gay men and as
people with AIDS.[53] By 1985 the choreographer Jason Childers
was very aware of Gay Men's Health Crisis (GMHC) and that
organization's urgent search for cure and care, not to mention
GMHC's Buddy Program, which paired volunteers with the first
people coming down with the symptoms of AIDS to offer emotional and physical support.[54] Childers signed up to be trained
by the Red Cross's AIDS program as a home attendant and saw
firsthand "how financially crippling the disease could be."[55] He
was shattered by the experience and saw that "there was a need
and a void of action." One night in late 1985 Childers was at
Bogart's, a New York bar, and met the lover of John Glines, a
prominent gay playwright and theater producer who in 1983
won the Tony and Drama Desk awards as producer of *Torch Song
Trilogy* and who, in 1985, won the Drama Desk Award and a Tony
nomination as producer of the AIDS play *As Is*. They discussed
the idea of a benefit organized by the dance community, and
someone suggested that Glines might help produce it. With the
confidence engendered by Glines's potential backing, Childers
approached Mark Russell, executive director of the downtown
New York performance space P.S. 122,

to see if P.S. 122 would provide the space (I had performed there a little and was working box office—I think

I had been promoted from janitor) and Mark was immediately into it. At some later point he recommended Tim Miller as adviser. Tim steered us in the right direction for the name of the benefit and found the beautiful picture of Ted Shawn's dancers for the flyer and program, among other things. And I just started asking around to see what choreographers would be interested. Lucy Sexton (of DanceNoise fame) was a great help—she knew everybody. I ran into Mark Morris (pre-Brussels) having a drink, who I knew from dance classes, and he accepted without hesitation. Mostly, it was the snowball effect; for once in my life no one said no to me. Everyone knew it was the right thing to do, a good thing to do, a necessary thing.[56]

And so it was that Russell, as executive director of P.S. 122, co-sponsored with Glines what was almost certainly the first official AIDS benefit in the dance community, a two-part evening held 13 January 1986, called *Dancing for Our Lives!* Childers conceived and coordinated the packed-to-capacity early-and-late-night programs, along with "special assistance and advice" from Tim Miller. (Among other things, Miller designed the benefit poster, which co-opted a famous John Lindquist photo of Ted Shawn and His Men Dancers, a gay world symbol of homoeroticism and secrecy.[57]) The *Advocate*'s Steven Greco and the *Stagebill* editor and dance critic Barry Laine served as hosts, in natty tuxedos. And the beneficiary was Gay Men's Health Crisis, specifically, the Buddy Program and the Financial Advocacy Program. The show raised more than $5,000. The *Village Voice*'s Deborah Jowitt, reviewing the first show, commented that, given the circumstances of the benefit, these dances by choreographers clearly identified as gay "acquire new poignancy or odd slants of meaning."

There's Steven Gross, trapped in a long black dress, his arms not through the armholes, bending and twisting while he meticulously describes the immediate aftermath of his mother's suicide. There's Jason Childers and Michael Levy fighting and embracing, using and helping each other, while Mimi Goese makes a short, potent appearance as a killer mom—now snarling, now all "honeybunch" sweetness. There's Doug Varone, whose beautifully performed theme and variations ends by petering out, as if there are no more alternatives. There's Thom

Dancing for Our Lives! poster, 1986. Design: Tim Miller. Courtesy of Tim Miller.

Fogarty, removing his female-entertainer costume, be-mused by phantoms—a blithe dancer (Kathryn Komatsu), a leggy boy who sits down to chat (Eric Barseness), and a vamp (Maria Lakis). He carries the vamp off, returns alone, and lies on a pair of trousers, fitting himself to their outline. Then he folds them like a flag and kneels, clutch-ing them. Head bowed. Shaking. There's Mark Morris and Teri Weksler, hilarious as decorous, middle-class, evangel-ical vampires. (Black humor overheard on exit: "Can't you see the headline?: VAMPIRISM LINKED TO AIDS.")[58]

It appears that none of these works was made specifically as a re-sponse to AIDS, but it is evident that each made a new kind of sense in this benefit context. Moreover, Jowitt's descriptions show that the audience for this nonmainstream dance and per-formance work was already attuned to gender critique and sharp commentary on death. A man dances in a dress and contemplates his mother's suicide. Two men alternately battle and embrace.

Movement invention runs its course and is configured as a kind of death, a loss. A cross-dresser is haunted by ghosts, then folds his pants as if they were the flag on a coffin, a fetish of lost love. Vampirism and bloodletting take on new meaning in a context where blood is considered tainted with AIDS. In a program in which politics and aesthetics can be read through one another, each work conveys its own potent meaning. Most of all, activism is on display.[59]

Also on display is gayness, presented by and for a community of dancers that actively embraces its gay and lesbian members. In addition to noting the vibrancy of the affair, Jowitt cannot help commenting that "hats passed for extra donations are stuffed with bills. . . . And the money will help, but more must be raised daily. It is not just his life, her life, your life, their lives that these people are dancing for, but the life of our community—*our* lives."[60] Here Jowitt echoes the very title of the event, *Dancing for Our Lives!* which neatly configures audience and performers together in a joint effort, alike and undifferentiated. That the downtown scene in the mid-1980s thought of gay artists as integral members, worthy of their dollars and their commitment, is significant, because the same could not necessarily be said of uptown larger-scale troupes. Writing in the gay magazine the *Advocate*, Charles Barber lauded the organizers of *Dancing for Our Lives!* for coming out of the dance-world closet and for placing their work in a sociopolitical context:

The *New York Times* described *Dancing for Our Lives* beforehand by somewhat breathlessly referring to those taking part as "self-described homosexuals." While this appellation may demonstrate a curiously antique point of view, it is nonetheless accurate, and raises an important point: visibility. It's as important today as it was before Stonewall. Amazingly, the dance-making community, like the theater community and others that are known to include a high percentage of gays, still includes some artists who cling to a vague understanding of the relationship between their lives and their work. Some say, a bit defensively, "My sexuality doesn't matter, so long as I produce good work." Qualities such as peace of mind and honesty of expression have been shown to matter tremendously, and nowadays, in the moral climate of 1986, fence-sitting is harder to justify than ever before. Happily,

Mark Morris and Teri Weksler in Morris's *One Charming Night,* in performance at *Dancing for Our Lives!* at P.S. 122, New York, 13 January 1986. Photo: © Tom Brazil.

the artists who took part in *Dancing for Our Lives* showed both with their participation and their art that they can flourish without the advantage of old excuses.[61]

The openness of the downtown scene to the depiction of gay sexualities, the independence of its artists, the intermixing of dancers and text-based performers—all these things lent an activist stance to downtown art making and venues that was missing from their upscale equivalents. ACT UP was so well regarded by the community of downtown artists that the organization was awarded a prestigious New York Dance and Performance Award, or "Bessie," in 1988 "for meeting the challenge of the AIDS epidemic and its crisis of conscience with vigilant acts of political and cultural provocation, thereby giving voice to the essential creative will of our humanity," according to a press release from Dance Theater Workshop, which sponsors the awards. Backstage after the Bessies ceremony, Bradley Ball, identified as the administrator of ACT UP, was asked whether he thought the arts community had rallied to fight AIDS in a successful fashion. "I think it's beginning," he said. "We've seen in the past few years very lovely benefits and very lovely memorials and very lovely mourning. Now it's time to get on . . . with focussing our rage and demanding some action."[62]

In the late 1980s ACT UP's call to action existed in stark contrast to the rampant homophobia of mainstream dance artists, for whom the stigma of gayness and AIDS loomed large, and who were, generally speaking, more conservative, more institutional, and felt they had more at stake than their downtown counterparts. By 1987 public denial concerning AIDS by members of the uptown mainstream dance world had grown from benign blindness to blatant lying. As Michael Bennett lay dying that year, he claimed that he was simply exhausted from overwork. The following year Robert Joffrey succumbed to what was euphemistically termed "kidney disease and asthma." And when Alvin Ailey died in 1989, the cause of death was given as a "rare liver ailment." In fact, among these choreographers' close associates it was well known that each suffered from complications of AIDS, and rumors to that effect circulated widely in the broader dance community. Yet these associates continued the not-AIDS ruse, sometimes long after the choreographer's death. It seemed that the public face of illness and death was simply incommensurable with the vitality, vigor, and youth that the dance establishment felt it needed to cultivate as its image, as its commodity for sale, especially during the dance boom of the 1980s.

These were the politics that the choreographer Lar Lubovitch confronted head-on when he first proposed the idea for a large-scale AIDS benefit organized by dancers, an idea that would take more than two years to come to fruition as *Dancing for Life* at Lincoln Center's New York State Theater. In August 1985 Lubovitch first made the personal commitment that "it was time dance did something for AIDS." But "it wasn't apparent for a long time that it would happen at all," Lubovitch told Thomas Connors in a 1987 *Village Voice* preview. "I knew I couldn't administer such a thing, but I was obsessed with the idea of interesting the major administrators and the artists they represent, so that they would accept the responsibility of putting this event together, so that they would agree with me—and decide as I had—that no matter what, we had to do this."[63] As it turns out, he had no difficulty in gaining the agreement of the managers, at least in principle.[64]

But given the politics of homophobia in U.S. dance and within the corporate funding structure, coming up with a workable format and nailing down the details proved far more daunting. The first proposal that the group entertained would in fact have involved all the nation's biggest dance companies, each contributing the proceeds from a single performance in their home theaters. As Lubovitch told Connors, however, a number of regional companies—which is to say companies outside New York—said no: "The boards wouldn't allow their companies to be associated with the idea of AIDS."[65] Years later Robert Yesselman, then executive director of the Paul Taylor Dance Company, who served as president of the benefit organization, would expound upon the reasons that dance board members were so squeamish: "The gay stereotype was already there, and it [the benefit] seemed to reinforce the connection between dance and gays."[66] To these unpaid, often corporately connected, often heterosexual board members, it was more crucial to protect their companies from the stigma of AIDS than it was to raise money to stem the disease. It quickly became clear that this broad-based national model had to be dropped. The next incarnation of the benefit idea involved consecutive Monday performances at three major New York venues, but the high costs of such an undertaking proved insurmountable, and the group feared that too large a percentage of the profits would be eaten up by expenses.[67]

In the end the committee settled on a relatively simple and elegant solution, with Jerome Robbins, the distinguished choreographer and co-ballet-master-in-chief of New York City Ballet, agreeing to serve as "artistic coordinator" for a single gala evening at Lincoln Center's New York State Theater. According to Yesselman, it took the group a full year of wrangling to reach that conclusion and then another year to plan and execute the event. In contrast to the quickly planned and executed benefit at P.S. 122, this one proved to be institutional and bureaucratic. But in contrast to P.S. 122's $5,000, it was also intended to raise $1.4 million.[68]

On 23 June 1987, four months before the benefit, the artistic directors of the participating companies held a press conference at the New York Marriott Marquis Hotel, which had joined AT&T and Philip Morris as corporate sponsors. The directors would officially announce the event, but they had also been prepped in advance by Ellen Jacobs, a prominent New York arts publicist, to field any difficult questions that might come up. Yesselman, who was there, recalls: "AT&T had given us their p.r. [public relations] firm, and we had them help us drafting questions that might come from the press, and the main one was about . . . the gays-in-dance issue. What we basically said was, if you're asked this question, here's what we feel, and if you want to say something else, say it. . . . We were saying, yes, there are gays in dance, as there are gays in movies, insurance, banks, every place else."[69] In fact, the question had already been posed in advance of the news conference by a *New York Times* reporter, who, upon direct request, received this joint written response from Robbins, Mikhail Baryshnikov, Twyla Tharp, Peter Martins, and Lubovitch, a statement that the reporter characterized in a front-page news story on 9 June 1987 as "taking strong exception to any suggestion that AIDS has had a special effect on the arts. 'AIDS is not a disease that discriminates,' the statement read. 'It strikes down people in the business community, the arts, government—every profession, every age group, every sexual persuasion.'"[70] Along those same lines a benefit preview article in the *New York Times* quoted Robbins as saying: "I'm tired of people thinking that AIDS equals only homosexuality and the arts, as if the disease could be contained within those communities. That's shortsightedness. AIDS is a world problem. It has hit certain sectors of the population simply by accident. AIDS is not the wages of sin. It's a disease that gets started anywhere."[71]

Meanwhile, at almost the same moment the *Village Voice*'s Connors was collecting comments on dance, homosexuality, and AIDS from among the organizers of and participants in *Dancing for Life.* This dogged reporter was unusually successful at ferret-ing out the issue hiding just below the surface, the very issue that had made the benefit so long in coming:

Despite growing public awareness, AIDS is still seen by some as a homosexual disease. Could the focus on dance—commonly perceived as a predominantly gay profession—reinforce this misperception? It's a question those active in "Dancing for Life" have considered. "That's a question I raised at one of our meetings," says board member Cora Cahan, who has been involved with the project since that first get-together. "There will always be people—no matter what we say, no matter what the statistics are—who are going to believe that the disease seeks out the homosexual. And that's a risk we're willing to take." While not anticipating a regression in public understanding, choreographer Mark Morris suggests, "Everyone in charge of this event has been very careful to act like there are no more gay people in dance. Of course, that's simply not true." Acknowledging the "stigma of homosexuality in dance," Eliot Feld states, "For those who want their prejudices reinforced, this event will cer-tainly do that. But for us not to take an active role, is to be immobilized by the fears and prejudices of others. We in New York are supposed to lead the way—that's why we're here. And hopefully, we are."[72]

The concatenation of issues and responses engendered by the benefit was fraught with complexity. On the one hand, Morris, who was still perceived as a downtown choreographer at that time, took offense at the suggestion that gay people were not heavily involved in the arts or, more specifically, in dance. He was correct on that score: Gay men led seven of the thirteen com-panies performing in the benefit. Yet many other choreographers and administrators involved with the benefit sought to suggest the opposite, that dance is *not* a gay haven. One thing can be said for sure: This was a situation that required a complex analysis to be fully understood, yet coverage by the mass media proved grossly inadequate.

The official press conference to announce the benefit was a case in point, a sterling example of the inadequacy of a media event to capture the subtle cultural and historical ramifications of an epidemic disease and its relationship to the arts. Yesselman was joined on the dais by Robbins, Baryshnikov, Laura Dean, Martins, Arthur Mitchell of the Dance Theatre of Harlem, and Taylor, as well as representatives of the funders (Zack Manna of AT&T, Peter Cantone of the Marriott Marquis Hotel) and the designated beneficiaries (Mathilde Krim of the American Foundation for AIDS Research, Nathan Kolodner of Gay Men's Health Crisis, and Richard Dunn of the National AIDS Network). A string of prepared statements dealt with the perceived link between dance and AIDS by ignoring it or by concentrating instead on the organizers' altruism. "Artists are humanists. The artist tends to see the human beings behind the numbers," said Yesselman in his introductory remarks. Peter Martins lauded the dance world's cooperative spirit, saying, "The dance community has risen in an incredible and inspiring way to make this a reality." Krim termed the benefit "an extremely moving initiative. It is very meaningful, for we see the whole world coming together to attack the AIDS problem."[73] Unmistakable here is the contrast between the downtown benefit, at which everyone pitched in together because this was about a community of dancers and creators, about "our" lives, and this uptown benefit at which the focus on a particular community was replaced by a generalized reverie on humanism. In fact, the subtle change in title from one benefit to the other is strong evidence for the shift. At P.S. 122 the benefit was called *Dancing for Our Lives!* but at the New York State Theater it was *Dancing for Life.* Semantically, the sense of participating in a joint venture had disappeared but so had the emphatic, activist exclamation point.

Having offered their various platitudes, members of the uptown group then were peppered by unfiltered questions from the press. Predictably, a reporter from the *New York Post* asked Martins and Baryshnikov to speak about whether any members of their companies were directly affected by AIDS.[74] Martins said no, that he was not aware of any members of the New York City Ballet who had become ill.[75] "Everyone who cares about human life is affected by this disease," he said. "We're doing it for everyone, not just for dancers. We're dancing for life."[76] Baryshnikov pleaded for restraint, saying that this was a family matter about which it would be inappropriate for him to speak.[77] No doubt, both artistic directors were in an awkward position, caught

The artistic directors (from left) Arthur Mitchell, Eliot Feld, Peter Martins, Jerome Robbins, Laura Dean, Paul Taylor, Lar Lubovitch, and Mark Morris share a curtain call with the performers at the conclusion of *Dancing for Life,* New York State Theater, New York, 5 October 1987. Photo: © 1987 Jonathan Atkin.

between board members who might have resisted any kind of participation in the benefit, dancers who feared being "outed" as having HIV, and their own homophobia. In the end their responses were more obfuscatory than revelatory, more concealing than revealing. These were the politics of secrecy and control surrounding AIDS in the late 1980s.

When, a few weeks later, the impressive benefit mailer was sent out—under the aegis of the New York City Ballet—big white block lettering spelled out the event's slogan:

> WHEN AIDS IS STOPPED
> WE WILL DANCE FOR JOY.
>
> ON OCTOBER 5TH,
> WE DANCE FOR LIFE.[78]

The logo for the mailer featured a silhouette of four ballet dancers (apparently female) performing joyous *temps levés,* a graphic rendition of a photo by Herbert Migdoll of Gerald Arpino's 1970 *Trinity.*[79] The honorary chair of the event was listed as none other than First Lady Nancy Reagan, whose husband had taken six years from the recognition of the epidemic to make his first substantive statement about the disease.[80] One of her cochairs would be Surgeon General C. Everett Koop, who, it was widely reported, had been trying for months to obtain even a brief meeting with his boss, President Reagan, to discuss national efforts to combat the spread of the disease. The other cochair was the actress Elizabeth Taylor, whose close friend Rock Hudson, a fiercely closeted gay man, had triggered national consciousness of AIDS when it was revealed that he was suffering with HIV-related illnesses in 1985.[81] The 8½-by-11-inch mailer delivered a confusing mélange of messages. Ticket buyers could expect a gala celebration, the theme of which would be a deadly disease; a dance performance at which gayness would—in the great American dance tradition—be closeted; and a society event whose honorary chairs would have little or nothing in common with regard to politics or commitment to fighting AIDS. This proliferation of competing discourses was, more than anything, indicative of the times. It expressed the essential ambivalence of homophobia layered upon AIDS-phobia, as manifested in an especially public form in the reception of a high-profile dance performance.

In a subtle sign of the organizers' inability to consistently control the signifiers extending from dancing to homosexuality to AIDS, the mailer's elegant paper stock was tinted a lovely shade of lavender, a color that in the late 1980s signified as gay. But when it came to the event itself, which was ultimately sold out and succeeded in raising $1.4 million for the beneficiaries, the word *AIDS* would never be spoken.[82]

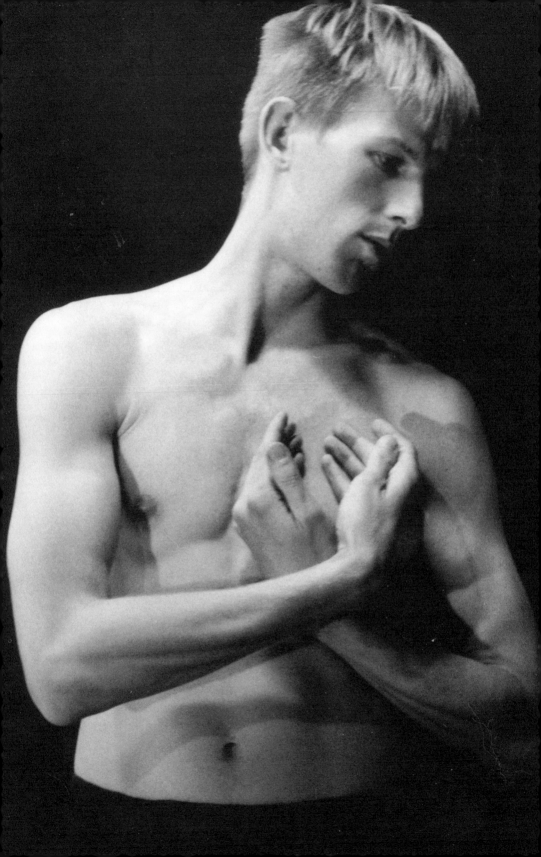

2

Melancholia and Fetishes

The complex of melancholia behaves like an open wound.
Sigmund Freud

Standing in a beam of light at center stage, and speaking in a voice as sweet as that of the choirboy he once was, the dancer-choreographer Tracy Rhoades lays out the premise of his 1989 *Requiem*.[1] "All of the clothes I'm wearing were either given to me by my friend Jim, or I inherited them after he died," Rhoades says, beginning methodically to peel off articles of clothing one by one. The socks, he explains anecdotally, conjure a battered chest of drawers in the apartment that Rhoades and Jim shared. A printed T-shirt, a souvenir of Jim's trip to Nogales, Mexico, elicits the story of Jim's effort to procure an experimental AIDS treatment. As he removes each piece of clothing, Rhoades lays it out on the floor in the shape of a body until, finally, the headless form is complete. Then he pulls on a pair of loose black trousers and begins anew, with what he calls "the Requiem that I give to Jim."[2]

Rhoades's dance is set to the "Pie Jesu" from Gabriel Fauré's *Requiem,* sung by a solo boy soprano in an impeccably pure tone. As the organ accompaniment begins, Rhoades rises to half-toe and treads in a long bourrée. He appears to float. His hands press together in a gesture of prayer, then open out to expose his vulnerable white forearms. (He holds each moment for the length of a long breath, sufficiently sustained to register fully in the viewer's

At left: Tracy Rhoades in *Requiem,* ca. 1988–89. Photo: G. Raven Traucht.

mind.) One hand folds up to touch the opposite clavicle, the bony triangle that supports the weight of the head, and is then echoed symmetrically by the other. The gestures are flat and formal, reminiscent of ecclesiastical images from a multicolored mosaic in a Byzantine cathedral. More gestures: The fingers intertwine overhead, tips of index fingers touching to form an upward-pointing arrow or the shape of a church steeple. Hands cup at the level of the throat like a chalice of wine, then transect behind the head, stick-straight fingers fanning out like the rays of a crown of light. One finger points up to the right, as if to touch, or perhaps to accuse, God. (The face betrays no affect either way.) Rounded arms and fingers cross on Rhoades's chest to suggest the sacred heart. Fleetingly, almost invisibly, a second finger joins it. The palms of the hands travel from Rhoades's mouth to the God place (an entreaty?) and then return unchanged (unheard?). Finally, the hands and forearms crisscross in a serpentine path in front of the body, drawing the shape of the caduceus, Hermes' staff, the symbol of the medical profession. This compact catalog of movement, which takes less than a minute, constitutes Rhoades's basic phrase.

Now, as the music moves into a turbulent central section, Rhoades repeats the phrase at increasing speed, still seeming to hover in place but now turning in a slow circle as he accelerates the gestures. The effect is as if a movie projector were running at double, now triple, now quadruple speed, rotating all the while. At moments this creates the effect of flying, arms beating the air as they elide from one gesture to another. At other instants the rapid gestures seem to be an expression of urgency, the repetitions signifying a need to ritualize and ultimately to purge this death ceremony of its sting. The phrase is on fire. The gestures now are snapshots, and we are flipping through them, over and over, until their edges begin to smolder and burn.

At the last repetition two gestures change slightly but deliberately. Rather than pointing one finger up toward God, Rhoades extends his entire hand, then quickly folds the fourth and fifth fingers back (to create a sign of benediction), the two remaining fingers popping apart to form a distinct *V*. The "sentence" of the basic phrase has come to a punctuation point. Then, at the tail end of the phrase, when the gestured "words" are sent up to the

God place, they come back not in an exact echo but as flowing water, hands rippling the air, a cool balm.

By the time the music returns to its original, soaring material, Rhoades has completed his single revolution and is facing downstage, arms extended to the sides, head hanging slightly, an unmistakable image of Christ on the cross. (As before, his facial expression remains neutral.) The liquid bourrée has ended, and now he is standing on his own turned-out feet, solid, rooted. He looks up slowly. The "opera" of the music is over. Facing the audience directly, he exhales audibly. A long pause ensues, after which he kneels down, rolls up Jim's clothes, and carries the wad of fabric offstage.

Rhoades created *Requiem* as an elegy to his lover, Jim Poche, who had died of AIDS in 1988. Rhoades performed the piece often and in various versions throughout the Bay Area—sometimes with its verbal preamble, sometimes without; sometimes in his underwear, sometimes in pants, or in a long elegant silk shirt.[3] In all its permutations *Requiem* received major ovations. Writing in *Ballet Review,* the critic Paul Parish praised the piece for its simplicity and "spirit of grace":

Dances that deal with AIDS have been part of every season since 1985. All have been heartfelt, although none has achieved a formal economy that could make it monumental, inevitable, simple. But this year [1990] a dance has emerged that evokes everything that needs to be invoked and nothing that doesn't, that affects everyone who sees it no matter what his or her background, and transforms the suffering of the dancer (who is wearing the clothes of his lover who died of AIDS) into a spirit of grace that has a great power to console onlookers.[4]

At first the catalog of disjunct gestures, repeated numerous times and with increasing energy, could be seen as a commentary on ritual practice: the reciting of mass, the fingering of beads, the chanting of the "Hail Mary" collectively evoked by the repetition of this single phrase of movement.[5] From this perspective the dance could be seen as a gently conservative palliative, the repetition serving to lessen the ache of grief.

But a focus on the subtly erotic aspects of this dance suggests another interpretive layer, a rich amalgam of homoeroticism and mourning, which lies at the heart of the piece and serves as its fuel. The "Pie Jesu" is taken from the Christian requiem mass, but how radical it is that in this case the priest and ritual celebrant reveals himself as a gay man, indeed, as the lover of the man who has died. His living body, dancing before us, is the body that once touched, gave solace to, caressed, and erotically desired his other, thus situating the living man as the sacred link in a continuous chain from life to death. Rhoades's body stands in for his lover's body, rendering the dancer and choreographer a corporeal fetish or replacement for that other body now dead and gone. Seen in this way, the effect is highly erotic, the piece initiated with what might best be described as an ecclesiastical striptease. (Only the simplicity and care with which Rhoades removes and places the clothing on the ground prevent it from being interpreted as a sexual come-on.) Thus Rhoades represents himself as both priest and lover, calmly carrying out a sacred ritual yet signifying intimate erotic knowledge, and knowledge of death too. One actually reinforces the other.

The clothing itself serves complex functions. Each item represents a distinct memory, which is to say that collectively the pieces of clothing trigger a flood of images from the period before Jim's death. They signify bodily presence, lived experience, everyday pleasures (the chest of drawers in a shared bedroom), as well as medical struggles (the aborted AIDS treatment in Mexico). But they also bear a sexual resonance, standing metonymically as they do for the shape and substance of the body. The socks are sensuous warm coverings slipped off to reveal vulnerable pink feet. The T-shirt is old and worn, so much so that the soft cotton hangs loosely on the torso, revealing the wearer's taut musculature, even his nipples. In one version of the dance Rhoades performs in his white underwear—simultaneously boyish and sexually knowing.

The dance also serves as a visceral embodiment of the tension between mourning and desire. A prominent gesture—two fingers pointing to the God place—echoes the pledge of love from the code of nineteenth-century ballet.[6] In *Requiem* we see the gesture repeatedly, from different angles, as the phrase turns on its

At right: the crown-of-light gesture from Tracy Rhoades's *Requiem*, ca. 1988–89. Photo: G. Raven Traucht.

center. The signification of devotion serves as a stinging reminder of erotic love, contained in a danced context of mourning and
set alongside an image of the lover's body made quite literally of
rags. The dance is flat and formal, evoking the gold-leaf angels of
Byzantium. And it is also about desire—skin, cloth, evocations of
nakedness. Rhoades and his late lover are etherealized by the
dance, and they are also configured as corporeal intimates, as
sharers of clothing and nakedness, as bodies entwined through
mutual love and loss. In the alchemy of mourning and desire, the
memory of a dead man is reconjured from the materiality—the
very fibers, the rags—of his possessions. He is not mourned and
gradually forgotten but rather reconstructed as a corporeal fetish
and kept close at hand.

For gay men living in major urban centers in the United States,
the year 1989 was dominated by the insistent and repetitive experience of death and dying and was thus a key moment in the
generation of the corporeal fetish as a signature tactic of erotic
remembrance. Not only were an extraordinary number of AIDS
deaths occurring during this period, but these were also mostly
deaths of young men at the peak of their physical and creative
powers. The numbers of deaths and of new infections that year
signaled the continuation of exponential, hyperbolic increases,
with deaths increased from 20,883 in 1988 to 27,639 in 1989—a
jump of 33 percent—and newly diagnosed HIV infection cases
rising from 35,481 in 1988 to 42,744 in 1989.[7] Although it had been
eight years since AIDS was officially declared an epidemic, the
range of available treatments—from potentially toxic chemical
compounds such as AZT and ddI to herbal remedies such as St.
John's Wort and Compound Q—remained largely untested, ques-
tionable in their effectiveness, and highly experimental.[8] And as
the breadth of the syndrome and its effects came slowly to be seen
and addressed, the catalog of AIDS-related opportunistic infections seemed only to get longer, from the purplish lesions of
Kaposi's sarcoma (the first marker of HIV/AIDS in 1981) to nervous disorders and severe stomach cramps associated with toxo-
plasmosis and cryptosporidiosis. As of 1989 the illnesses associated with women and HIV had not even been cataloged; hence
the numbers of women affected by HIV/AIDS were vastly underreported in the official calculations.[9] Even so, the numbers of reported cases for women and for other historically underreported
groups—black and Latino men—continued to climb steeply.[10]

Still, men having sex with men were estimated to comprise more than two-thirds of AIDS deaths in 1989.[11] And two factors intensified the grief of their gay survivors: the sense of premonition, that it could soon be happening to them (Rhoades would in fact die five years after Jim); and, as I discussed in chapter 1, the continuing and pervasive societal judgment that AIDS ought to be hidden, that it was cause for shame, as cancer was for a previous generation. Thus many gay men could not fully acknowledge AIDS and the grief associated with it, and it effectively blocked their integration into the shared epistemology of the community of survivors—with the degree of blocking related to such factors as social class and race, both of which I will discuss later in this chapter. These oppressive conditions favored a state of psychological limbo that Freud, in 1917, termed chronic melancholia, to distinguish it from successful and reintegrative mourning. "The complex of melancholia behaves like an open wound," he wrote.[12] More than seventy years later, in his 1989 essay "Mourning and Militancy," Crimp would describe melancholia as an unavoidable yet unnecessary side-effect of the stigma attached to the disease, as a sign of the depth and intensity of homosexual loathing in the United States.

During this period of the late 1980s many commentators began to offer up articles detailing the massive toll that AIDS was exacting on dancers and choreographers, as if to cry out, however meekly, for the nation's help. Lucia Dewey, in her 1989 year-end wrap-up in the *Los Angeles Drama-Logue*, listed a number of aesthetic breakthroughs that had occurred that year. But when she named the predominant theme of 1989, it was AIDS. "Although people in all fields are dying, losses are particularly damaging in dance," she wrote, not, as it turns out, to point out the high incidence of AIDS in this queer profession but rather to emphasize the "hands-on" oral transmission processes that characterize dance. But then, adopting a memorial practice that had been powerfully reinvented with the establishment of the NAMES Project AIDS Quilt in 1987, she listed the names of the sixty-nine most prominent dancers, choreographers, dance managers, teachers, and artistic directors who had died up to that point, starting her list with the words: "Now let the names speak for themselves."[13] Other publications, organizations, and dance companies demonstrated the effect of the rising number of deaths in similar ways. In *Dance Magazine,* the major popular journal for the dance field, for example, the number of male obituaries more than doubled from 1981 to 1988, in response to which the magazine ceased publishing obituaries altogether for five months in 1989.[14] The Dance Collection of the New York Public Library began collecting the names of dance figures who had died of AIDS for a lengthy public roll call held each December 1, World AIDS Day. Choreographers from Mark Dendy in New York to Joe Goode in San Francisco created works that featured the names of the dead.[15] As was the case with the NAMES Project AIDS Quilt (see chapter 3), these names began to function as memorial fetishes, as signifying devices of extraordinary power and resonance. Standing in for living bodies, now dead, these names served as corporeal fetishes too.

In this atmosphere of gloom and pervasive loss in the late 1980s, a signature set of memorial practices began to develop in the gay community and especially among gay male choreographers. These fetishistic practices—the metaphorization of the dead through shards of clothing, the calling out of names, elaborate memorials and direct choreographic address in the tradition of the literary elegy—were born of what could be described as a massive homocultural depression. Not surprisingly, this shared melancholic state grew intractable amid the rising tide of deaths and the inability to mourn these deaths fully or to be supported sufficiently in the practice of mourning, owing to the stigma associated with AIDS. The French theorist Julia Kristeva describes this state of darkness as analogous to living under the glare of a "black sun," an intense despair that she characterizes as following upon either a betrayal or a fatal illness, both of which have been indelible parts of the experience of AIDS in the United States.[16]

A particular conditioning factor in the response by the gay community to the omnipresent figure of death has been the recognition that the state of mourning is not beyond eroticism but rather incorporative of it. Just as Rhoades displays a movement language in *Requiem* that is both ecclesiastical and sexy, so have gay men in the age of AIDS learned mourning practices that express both the full depth of loss as well as erotic attachment to the lost object. Gay mourning is not chaste or churchly but ribald and sensuous. It is not pious, but it *is* devoted. Choreography in the age of AIDS, then, is necessarily imbued with both qualities, with the depths of mourning and despair as well as the heights of charged libidinal energy. Put bluntly, gay mourning bears the telltale traces of one last good fuck.

Desire and Melancholy

The relation between sexuality and mourning, between a constructed erotics and the existential state of grieving, is inextricable, for the simple reason that mourning presupposes desire and cannot proceed without it. Mourning is predicated on the loss of the desired object: no desire, no mourning. This classic formulation appears in writings from Homer to Lacan. And it is made manifest in the category of cultural production comprising choreography in the age of AIDS. This notion springs from a set of basic principles: The energy valence created between desire and mourning gives rise to various forms of cultural production, including choreography; it forms the basis of virtually all meaning-making activities engaged in by spectators of such forms of cultural production; and, during the age of AIDS in the U.S., it issues in a profusion of rhetorical choreographic forms linked to an evolving elegiac tradition. How, then, are desire and mourning connected? And how do they play out for gay men in the AIDS era?

In the context of AIDS, desire demands a particularly complex formulation for current gay male culture. For post-Stonewall gay men desire is a positive omnipresent force, suffused with energy and basic life drives in the service of sexual expression and human connectedness. These impulses are deeply woven into gay identity and gay culture. The control or forcible modulation of these impulses may therefore be regarded as restricting a primary cultural practice. Where desire is the organizing principle of a culture, attempts to curb, control, or channel that desire may be perceived as destructive of a core value. Death of the love object is a curb on desire but so are widespread controls on the practice of sex itself. Thus when major cultural practices related to desire are curbed or otherwise altered, mourning is a predictable result. (Public health advocates have been forced to grapple with this mourning as they encounter widespread resistance to using condoms in penetrative gay sex. Surely, the loss of pleasure is the major factor here but so is the mourning associated with a disciplinary shift in sexual practices.)

Mourning is generally conceived in more individual terms, however, a perspective that, with a bit of tweaking, serves to explicate the function of grief for gay men in the time of AIDS. Psychologists generally explain mourning this way: The subject cathects on an object and draws that object toward itself, but if the loved object either makes itself unavailable, is unavailable due to circumstances, or, in dramatic cases, disappears because it dies, mourning is the inevitable result. The broad arc of mourning, then, commences at essentially the same moment as desire. The two live as twins, with mourning resulting from the rupture of the expectation created by desire, and desire founded on the unpredictability of its finding its object. One might even go so far as to say that desire and mourning are two sides of the same coin, part of the same transaction, or a single tune rendered in transposed keys.[17] For a culture predicated on desire, then, mourning takes on a particularly powerful valence, magnified into melancholia.

Melancholia, meanwhile, is an especially intractable variety of mourning that, according to Freud, is akin to mourning but in an abnormal register.[18] Freud's basic conceptions have been quoted frequently:

Mourning is regularly the reaction to the loss of a loved person, or to the loss of some abstraction which has taken the place of one, such as fatherland, liberty, an ideal, and so on. As an effect of the same influences, melancholia instead of a state of grief develops in some people, whom we consequently suspect of a morbid pathological disposition. . . . Although grief involves grave departures from the normal attitude to life, it never occurs to us to regard it as a morbid condition and hand the mourner over to medical treatment. We rest assured that after a lapse of time it will be overcome, and we look upon any interference with it as inadvisable or even harmful. . . . When the work of mourning is completed the ego becomes free and uninhibited again.[19]

These observations posit mourning as a reaction to loss (of a person or an ideal) that recedes with time, leading inexorably to the mourner's rejoining the world of the living. But what if we were to apply Freud's ideas to desire and grief in the age of AIDS?

What if the subject—the gay male subject—is unable to recover from the loss of a loved one? Or what if he grieves not just a single person but the very "ideal" of an entire culture, with its own social and sexual practices? Or what if, by reason of his fear for his own life and his anger at political and cultural forces that failed to prevent the death of the loved object, he actually *chooses* not to complete his mourning? Or what if he cannot, will not, return to "normal"? Then he is subject to what Freud would call melancholia, an extreme state of mourning that he characterizes as a wound that will not heal.

Michael Moon, a Whitman scholar as well as a queer theorist, mines Freud's essay on mourning and melancholia in an extraordinarily fruitful way. In his essay "Memorial Rags" Moon identifies the central conundrum of Freud's concept of mourning for gay men—that healthy mourning requires eventual restoration to a "normal" state, but for a gay man, what's normal?[20] The "rags" of Moon's title may be read in at least two ways: as the bandages of Whitman's Civil War poem, "The Wound-Dresser" (bits of cloth torn from the American flag) and as scraps of elegy, the literary form within which mourning has traditionally been contained.[21] Moon seems to have chosen his title to draw a connection between the two major aspects of his own work: the historical construction of gayness in the writing of such poets as Whitman and the exploration of the role of AIDS in the continuing construction of gayness in the United States. But Moon's notion of "memorial rags" does more than draw a connection. It defines a new elegiac form soaked with the significations of homosexual mourning. These may appear prominently in poetics, as Moon discusses, but they may also, I would argue, display their essential characteristics in choreographic form.

Moon's "Memorial Rags" begins with a reading of Ralph Waldo Emerson's "Experience," an essay written two years after the death of the poet's five-year-old son. Moon hears in the essay's opening lines—which depict the experience of losing one's way—"an emblem of the collective mourning and grieving that have unexpectedly become central activities in the lives of gay men and our friends in the wake of AIDS."[22] Moon's purpose in enunciating Emerson's text is not, however, to empathize with Emerson's loss but to draw out the meanings of the rupture at the heart of "Experience." The rupture is this: Emerson's son is dead, but inexplicably the poet does not grieve for him. "This calamity . . . does not touch me: something which I fancied was part of me, which could not be torn away without tearing me . . . falls off from me, and leaves no scar. It was caducous. I grieve that grief can teach me nothing."[23] In Moon's analysis Emerson's lack of an emotional response to his son's death—interpreted by other literary critics as the "scandal" of Emerson's "indifference"—throws into relief the necessity of redefining mourning practices for each age, resisting another century's mourning customs (introspection, seclusion, the positing of transcendence) and replacing them with practices freshly adapted to reordered psychic and social conditions. If in his 1917 essay Freud had proposed a specific model for how grieving should look in the late nineteenth and early twentieth centuries, including the forms it should take and the emotions it should stir, then it stands to reason that the AIDS era ought to come with its own memorializing practices, suitably homoerotic ones. Thus Moon dismisses the outmoded Freudian process of grieving, healing, and reintegrating as consisting of "private psychological projects with teleological internal structures," as capitalist transactions that promise return to normalcy as the ultimate dividend.[24] For Freud grieving is a bounded process. The loss of the object is acknowledged and integrated. New objects are found. Grieving ceases. But for gay men and lesbians, the return to "normalcy"—a state of societal embrace—is not possible, for there is nothing akin to normal for a societal abject; all that remains for the queer mourner is, in fact, the return to abjection. Emerson's collision with Freud, then, provides the inertia for Moon's new theorization of erotic mourning and the re-envisioned memorial practices that he has in mind.

These new practices actively subvert Freud's definition of mourning, replacing visions of placidity and psychic healing with possibilities for fetishistic eroticism and psychic incorporation. According to Moon, it is common among critics and theorists "of elegy and the elegiac" to talk about the erotics of mourning only in the negative, as impotence or castration. But there is an alternative:

What if, instead of focusing on bodily deficiency in thinking about our own mourning practices, we focus on bodily

abundance and supplementarity? Resisting thinking of
the deaths of others as the making deficient of our own
bodies or body parts and resisting thinking of death as
absolutely rupturing the possible erotic relation of a living person to a dead one may make an important difference in our mourning practices.[25]

To paraphrase, Moon urges us to reject the notion of the infected,
stigmatized body as an unavoidable AIDS artifact and, instead,
to reenact and reverence our erotic connection with the AIDS
dead via the *fetish*—not the Freudian fetish, so predictably tied
to notions of feminine "castration" and "lack," but the Whit-
manesque fetish: rags—that is, the leavings or detritus of a life.
Moon goads us to refuse death as erotic rupture and instead to
defiantly animate the sexuality in mourning, to imaginatively
conserve corporeal fetishes as a means to maintain relationships
with the dead, especially by eroticizing the act and memory of
caregiving.

The Freudian conception of the fetish is so overburdened with
pathology and misogyny that it must be radically revised in
order to be embraced anew. For Freud the "perversion" or "ab-
normality" of the fetish stems from the male subject's failing to
recognize that females lack a penis,

a fact which is extremely undesirable to him since it is
a proof of the possibility of his being castrated himself.
He therefore disavows his own sense-perception which
showed him that the female genitals lack a penis and
holds fast to the contrary conviction. The disavowed perception does not, however, remain entirely without influence, for, in spite of everything, he has not the courage to
assert that he actually saw a penis. He takes hold of something else instead—a part of the body or some other
object—and assigns it the role of the penis which he cannot do without. It is usually something that he in fact saw
at the moment at which he saw the female genitals, or it is
something that can suitably serve as a symbolic substitute
for the penis. . . . The creation of the fetish was due to an
intention to destroy the evidence for the possibility of castration, so that fear of castration could be avoided.[26]

Moon's corrective avows that the fetish stands not for the lack of
a penis but for the corporeality of the male love object, for his

very bodiliness, and for the libidinal attachment to that bodiliness. These homofetishes might take the form of objects of clothing, possessions, photographs, locations, smells (Freud strongly invokes smell, and it functions in Moon's conception of the fetish too), or, I would argue, corporeal movement. In support of this notion Moon points to the imagery in Whitman's "Drum-Taps." These well-known late poems, incorporated in *Leaves of Grass* after the Civil War, "represent care-giving as erotically charged,"[27] a point demonstrated by a quote from the third stanza of "The Wound-Dresser" (from "Drum-Taps"):

> I am faithful, I do not give out,
> The fractur'd thigh, the knee, the wound in the abdomen,
> These and more I dress with impassive hand (yet deep in my
> breast a fire, a burning flame.)[28]

Noteworthy here is the eroticization of the poet's manner in tending to the wounded soldiers. The dressing of the wound serves to inflame Whitman's internal passions. As nurse, he is not only competent; he is "faithful." The very act of bandaging is fetishized erotically. The tending of the sick and the dead (do not decry it as necrophilia, Moon warns) is all but a metaphor for lovemaking. Writes Moon:

Recognizing and accepting the possible restorative effects of such processes can perhaps be helpful in reconstituting our relationship to the dead. Such recognition and acceptance can be part of a process that is not a displacement or a dismemberment—but not a castration—but *a re-memberment that has repositioned itself among the remnants, the remainders, and reminders that do not go away;* loss is not denied, but neither is it "worked through." Loss is not lost. (emphasis added) [29]

The power of Moon's essay emerges from his dynamic fusion of grieving and loving, integrating the concepts of what the philosopher Henry Staten has called "mortal" eroticism and what Moon terms as "a re-memberment that has repositioned itself among the remnants." This is not erotic connection to an idealized or transcendent version of the loved object; it is not an etherealization. It is, rather, libidinal connection to the corporeal form, the "bodiliness," the relics of that object. This leads not to the working through of loss (do we really want to be "done" with grieving, to abandon the loved object?); rather, it leads to the fetishistic renegotiation of it. The remnants of the erotic object—its "rags" or, in a reference to battle trauma, its "bandages"—are preserved not as transcendent ideals; they are held as fetishes, as emblems of love. In the production of gay culture in the time of AIDS, it is of such rags that meaning is made.

In "Melancholy Gender/Refused Identification," her 1995 essay based on Freud's notion of melancholia, the philosopher and feminist scholar Judith Butler offers a variant on Moon's fetishism, theorizing that the work of grieving results not in the smooth healing of loss and the dissolution of libidinal attachment but in the incorporation of that loved object in the melancholic subject's ego. This is, of course, the Freudian conception, subject to the contemporary critique of Freud's theoretical models as inherently misogynistic and homophobic. But by invoking the Freud of "Mourning and Melancholia" for her own purposes, Butler offers the possibility of a new understanding of fetishistic, erotic mourning as an essential element in the conservation of the mourned object. For it is in the fetishistic reconstruction of the loved object that it—he—is conserved within the mourning subject through a process that Freud terms *identification* but that Butler amplifies as an *incorporation*. Thus the fetish object ultimately becomes the fetish internalized—a fetish of supplementarity rather than of lack.

One might conclude that melancholic identification permits the loss of the object in the external world precisely because it provides a way to *preserve* the object as part of the ego itself and, hence, to avert the loss as a complete loss. Here we see that letting the object go means, paradoxically, that there is no full abandonment of the object, only a transferring of the status of the object from external to internal: giving up the object becomes possible only upon the condition of a melancholic internalization, or what might for our purposes turn out to be even more important, a melancholic *incorporation*.[30]

As a consequence of being incorporated or enfolded within the melancholic ego, the lost love remains vibrantly present, reconstituted and reconfigured as part of the grieving subject.[31] What Moon and Butler add to a discussion of choreography in the age of AIDS, then, is the possibility that the gay AIDS dead can be actively conserved, either in the form of fetishes and erotic memorial practices or through intrapsychic melancholy incorporations. The gay melancholy that they envision is rife with choreographic possibilities.

Melancholy Bodies

The gay AIDS memorial service is perhaps the most potent choreographic representation of the processes of desire, thwarted cathexis, and incorporation that has emerged during the two decades of the AIDS era. There is a tradition in the United States of giving the rituals of the dead over to designated ritual celebrants—priests or pastors or rabbis or imams—but gay men have taken this final ritual into their own hands, fashioning it as a highly charged and highly fetishistic reaffirmation of gayness and the loved object, including practices that serve to reconjure and revitalize the presence of the dead object in quasi-corporeal form. The AIDS funeral encompasses as many variations as does the art song or the pas de deux or the elegiac poem. From the lavish funeral featuring sprays of stunning flowers and high-powered eulogies to the modest outdoor ceremony at which mourners speak their own words of grief and strew the loved one's ashes, from elaborate rituals to stripped-down remembrances, gay men have turned the memorial service into a vibrant art form. Inherent in all these memorial variations is a belief in desire, in homosexual love and homosexual practices, and in the necessity of vividly conjuring the dead even while facing the irreversibility of death.

Daniel Harris, a notoriously acerbic commentator on gay culture, writing from within it, has investigated this phenomenon as it manifests in the obituary, the AIDS memorial in writerly format. In an essay originally published in 1990, he focuses his attention on obituaries printed in the late 1980s in the *Bay Area Reporter*, one of three gay San Francisco weeklies, which created a special two-page format for such notices in its pages. Significantly, these obituaries remained unmediated by editors and therefore grew to be almost obscenely sentimental and lugubrious. In a biting critique of gay mourning practices, Harris seems to find the whole thing just a bit too vulgar:

Few examples of this sepulchral new allegiance of activism and mourning are as genuine, poignant, and unguardedly grief-stricken as the fascinating amalgam of incomprehension, camp, sentimentality, and desolation in the obituaries in the San Francisco gay newspaper *Bay Area Reporter*. A weekly institution, this patchwork of bad photographs and amateurish copy written by the friends, families, and lovers of the dead men themselves is nestled like a portentous checkerboard of ashen faces among grisly advertisements for Ghia caskets, urns "at substantial savings," "plain wooden box" coffins, "dignified burials at sea," and funeral homes that promise to tell you "everything you wanted to know about funerals, but were afraid to ask." Amidst the black comedy of capitalism, the incomparable world of these stark over- and under-exposed images, which bleach the individuality out of many of the snapshots or darken them into anonymous black boxes, vacillates wildly from the chintziest mortuary sentiments ("he passed from here to the stars," one mourner laments) to comic, irreverent, and idiomatic elegies (like that written for a successful DJ, who could always be found on Sunday mornings "dishing up the best hip-shaking boot-bopping funk anyone could find"). With no well-paid professional intervening to mitigate or blunt the grief with apt banalities, a kind of anarchy of tastelessness, humour, and sheer ineloquent misery gives us direct access to the personal consequences of the epidemic through the quavering and uncertain voices of the "survivors."[32]

Harris's tone here is unabashedly cynical in the bitchy mode associated with gay camp—which makes his commentary notable for its double dose of camp, both his and his subject's. But beneath the bitchiness lurks a telling amazement at the sheer invention of this outpouring:

The mourners leap effortlessly from the intimate to the ceremonial, from the baroque to the laconic, from the dull rehashing of lives spent in the shadows of banks to hilarious instances of sacrilege in which the writers dump the corpses from their coffins and sling them around in their arms in an outrageous *danse macabre*.[33]

The result, Harris suggests—almost to his own amazement, it seems, given his judgment about the tastelessness of these memorial endeavors—is a powerful redefinition of grieving. New cultural forms for grieving are being created and are replacing those enacted by heterosexist society:

For a society that prefers to avoid death unless it has been dressed to the nines and laid in state in the parlour, we express grief in public only when we are armed to the teeth in the panoply of socially acceptable costumes and procedures. However genuine, mourning is one of the least spontaneous events in our lives, something that we censor and regulate with rigidly prescriptive rules whose reassuring formality prevents our corpses from unwinding their cerements, beating on their bone pots, and gibbering at us shrill reminders of a less cosmetic and aestheticized form of death. The *Bay Area Reporter*'s uncanny obituaries—to my knowledge the only regular forum in which friends and lovers can eulogize their dead compatriots— present mourning as we rarely see it in print: without our culture's presiding alter-ego, Emily Post, to give our grief that lustrous sheen of tactfulness and decorum. AIDS is represented here in appallingly personal terms, quite apart from politics, anonymous statistics, or the daily press's racy charnelese.[34]

Harris may critique these gay grieving practices, but he lauds them as well, perceiving in the sheer messiness of the undertaking a kind of grassroots resistance to the notion that grieving must be executed in a particular way. (He might have pointed out that gay people have accomplished the same for sex and relationships too.) Ultimately, he concludes that this particularly unvarnished, naive grieving carries enormous power. He calls it his "poison of choice."

How often does one hear the voice of real lamentation in the mass media? The elaborate editorial apparatus of the press is set up precisely to suppress voices that are too loud, angry, or emotional. In an effort to bring the reality of the epidemic home to us, the *Bay Area Reporter* has broken this rule, removed an unspoken gag order, and allowed real people to speak as they choose, sometimes with waxen formality, at others with shocking directness. In the piercing keens and ornate threnodies of disconsolate AIDS widows, the epidemic takes on an immediacy that no article, TV spot, or second-hand report, no matter how impassioned, can convey. After the obligatory reduction of the dead man's life to its handful of undistinguished milestones, his grieving lover will often address him in a chilling farewell, as if, like a mourner in Jerusalem, he were slipping his words into the chinks of this wailing wall of newsprint, this slag-heap of unremarkable faces.[35]

The "chilling farewell" planned upon the death of the San Francisco choreographer Joah Lowe in January 1988 demonstrates one version (a particularly *white*, New Age version) of these new aesthetics of mourning in a choreographic format.[36] After the thirty-four-year-old Lowe died, his friends, gay and straight together, began to plan a memorial that they hoped would prove sufficient to contain the size of their grief.[37] The first suggestion was to hold a dawn memorial on Mount Tamalpais, a beautiful mountain just north of San Francisco consecrated as a sacred site by the first Native American inhabitants of northern California. Lowe had loved this mountain, and several members of the group had hiked there with him. But when difficulties arose with securing permission to park cars and to strew ashes at that site, the memorial was quickly shifted to Baker's Beach in San Francisco, facing the ocean just outside the mouth of the bay and the Golden Gate Bridge. The group was intent on holding the memorial outdoors, with a feeling of raw nature surrounding the mourners. The liquid force of the ocean offered a setting for several key themes to be played out in choreographic terms: the powerful and unforgiving quality of the AIDS syndrome; the literal drowning that is the cause of death by pneumonia; and the wish that, although Lowe's corporeal body was gone, he would remain a melancholy presence in the constant image of the waves lapping at the shore. Unconsciously, the ocean also offered the possibility of a choreographic response to the recalcitrant stigma of AIDS—that it could be washed away.

At dawn—approximately 6:30 A.M.—on Sunday, 17 January 1988, a first group of mourners begins to assemble on the blustery

beach under a colossal cloth umbrella stitched with colorful Balinese designs.[38] Wrapped in bright slickers against the rain and
mist, and with scarves pulled around their necks to stave off the
January cold, the mourners trudge down the cold beach from the
parking lot, drawn to the site by the brightly colored umbrella.
They greet one another with wordless embraces. One of Lowe's
friends, a member of the Radical Faeries (a pagan spiritual group
that celebrates male sexuality and the exploration of androgyny),
begins to play rhythms on a deep-voiced African drum. The
mourners respond by creating a circle around an altar that is
being constructed spontaneously in the sand. At the center nes-
tles a delicately carved gourd bowl with a tight lid that had been
one of Lowe's prized possessions. Earlier, friends had poured
Lowe's ashes from the mortuary's plain brown cardboard box
into the decorative gourd, and now the gourd has become the
center of the choreography. Lowe—albeit just his ashes—lies at
the center of the circle. Around the decorative gourd are placed
small bunches of loose flowers—a pair of calla lilies, a handful
of pink roses, three red carnations, and several packets of white
jasmine blooms contained in small packages woven from palm
leaves. A few mourners have brought candles, some in brass
holders, which they thrust, burning, into the sand. The effort to
keep these candles lit keeps several people physically busy, as
they kneel to shield the flames or dig holes as bunkers to protect
the flickering votives. Others huddle together to keep warm,
reinforcing a desired feeling of closeness. By 8 A.M. the circle
has grown to about forty mourners.

The bodies of the mourners, as witnessed in photographs of
the event, appear frozen and numb, like statues of grief. The participants assemble side by side in the circular formation, their
feet solidly planted in the sand, hands stuffed in pockets, a few
grasping around each other's waists and shoulders with gloved
hands, which take on the appearance of outsized paws. Gay
men, straight men, gay women, straight women, and others of
undeclared sexual identity look much alike as they huddle together under a dark sky, concealed behind protective clothing
and their smattering of umbrellas. Their bodies are alert and still,
their postures formal, a sign of somber honor in the presence of
Lowe's ashes. Occasionally, the mourners stomp in the sand,
rendering the efforts to keep warm and to maintain emotional

control almost indistinguishable from one another. These are melancholy bodies: mute, frozen, grieving.

Immediately to the side of the gourd cask hovers a papier-mâché pod, the size of a giant turtle, supported by four stick legs stuck in the sand. The night before this ceremony, two of Lowe's friends constructed the pod in the kitchen of his house, painting it in bright colors: vertical stripes of hot pink and sky blue around the perimeter; interlocking triangles of purple, red, and hot yellow in imitation of Indonesian textiles; borders of yellow and indigo stripes, which make the pod shimmer like a brightly decorated sun. Now, hovering there next to the gourd with the ashes, the pod resembles a spaceship, prepared to take off at any moment. It also echoes the umbrellas, serving as yet another layer of protection from the drizzle descending from the atmosphere. In the tradition of the gay fetish, the homemade altar is garish, overdone, overflowing the boundaries of taste.

As the rays of morning light intensify, three of Lowe's women friends (Debra, Vicky, and Rucina), one of whom is a self-described witch, offer a ritual to the four directions. The origin of the ritual is unclear, but it serves to direct the mourners' attention to their physical environment, to the position of the rising sun on the eastern horizon and to the Pacific Ocean in the west. Then one of the ritualists leads the circle in singing a sweet, simple round, simultaneously performing an action she calls "sounding," which involves evoking the emotional and physical states of the participants in a kind of vocalized glossolalia. The melodies are smooth and wet, their own kind of drizzle. As the music continues, its tempo increases until the two friends who were with Lowe at his death are asked to hold aloft the gourd with the ashes and to pour it out so that all who want may sift the remains of his body in their hands or, if they choose, to take some of the ashes for private ceremonies and rituals of their own. The gourd is passed around, which rouses the circle of melancholy bodies into drowsy responsiveness. Confronted by the material remains of Lowe's body—his gray ashes—some reach in and touch the dusty chips, sifting them through their fingers. Others reserve small amounts of the ashes in their cupped hands or in handkerchiefs, lightly tucking these remnants back in their pockets for safekeeping. Others literally inhale his ashes, involuntarily, as gusts of wind stir the dry mixture from its languor in the green vessel. Thus

melancholy bodies become activist bodies, directly subverting any stigmatization of the corporeal traces of AIDS. Through intimate connection with the ashes, the participants deny any possible diminishment of the body of a dead friend.

At this point someone upends the pod, transforming it into a ritual bowl, into which the mourners pour the remainders of Lowe's body—the ashes—and the fetishes—the flowers, candles, paper messages. During this process two gay men, Charlie and Bill, the two close friends who had constructed the pod, pull off their rain gear and don wetsuits and fins. When the upended pod is full, they lift it between them and carry it to the water, the circle of mourners following them to the shoreline. At the water's edge the pod becomes not a spaceship but a boat, guided to sea by these two men who resemble slick seals in their black rubber suits and submit themselves to the harsh embrace of the ocean. At first, as Charlie and Bill plunge into the surf, the close-breaking waves strike hard at them, but the duo remains intent on keeping the pod-boat afloat and protected. Finally, they edge beyond the breaking waves and begin to swim out to open sea. The mourners on shore can see their heads bobbing in and out of the choppy waves, the pod-boat floating between them. In the January chill someone remarks that the ocean must be shockingly cold. Finally, when Charlie and Bill are about 150 yards from shore, they release the boat and let it float off on its own. Back on the beach, with the waves lapping at their feet, the mourners break up into smaller groups. Some stand alone, listening to the roar of the waves and watching the distant horizon. Others huddle together, tightly, protectively, wordlessly, their arms wrapped about one another so that their bodies touch along their full lengths. Some others begin to stroll back to their cars, contemplative as they traverse the length of the beach. Within a few minutes the boat, all but invisible now, has capsized and dissolved, spilling its form and contents into the gray-blue water. Sauntering back along the breaking waves, the mourners encounter a tangle of carnation stems and calla lilies eddying on the sand. Frozen melancholy bodies grasp one another for warmth and comfort against the sting of coldness and death.

Melancholy bodies. . . . I am a melancholy body. The very act of reconjuring Lowe's memorial, fifteen years later, is proof of that. (The wound of grief remains unhealed.) And yet, revisiting

Charles (Charlie) Halloran (left) and William (Bill) Samios transporting Joah Lowe's ashes to the sea, Baker's Beach, San Francisco, 17 January 1988. Photo: courtesy of Diana Vest Goodman.

Lowe's memorial at more than a decade's remove places the choreography of the event in a distanced light. I see it differently, and perhaps more clearly, now: the proliferation of fetishes and the psychic incorporation that are central to gay grief; the gush, the overflow of sentiment; the self-conscious tactility of the ceremony with the ashes. But I notice other things too, for example, the absence of anger. No stirring speeches mark this memorial event, nor do any protests. I also notice that, in contrast to my initial impression of the memorial, it is shrouded in the stigmatization of AIDS.[39] The location is chosen in part because, for the space of a few hours, it can be made private, safe, secluded—secret. As in so many other events in the AIDS era, the word *AIDS* is never spoken.

But the corporeal forms of the memorial and the attendant images are deftly configured to accomplish important work in the age of AIDS. Every possibility of fetishistic mourning is capitalized upon, and everything about the memorial is made to revolve around the image of water. The event is held at the ocean. The time of day—dawn—is chosen with full knowledge that a wet January mist will likely be hanging in the air. The props of the memorial signify the deflection of water, or holding wetness at bay. Slickers, ponchos, hats, gloves, umbrellas—symbolic and practical—and even the papier-mâché pod, all these things function to hold moisture off the participants' bodies. And off Lowe's ashen body too, for he is held dry and safe in a tight-lidded green gourd, under cover of the Balinese umbrella, with a wall of protective melancholy bodies ringing it. The environment is all liquid, all dank, but every effort of the choreography is aimed at keeping the participants dry, at staving off watery immersion.

But in the end the power of water to envelop and to cleanse is undammed. Umbrellas are discarded. The protective circle is broken. Casting off their slickers, Charlie and Bill suspend themselves on the waves to ferry Lowe's AIDS body amid a fetishistic profusion of love and care. Lowe's AIDS body is now submerged in the wet from above, below, all around. But far from an image to inspire dread—a reenactment of his drowning lungs at the moment of his death—it is transformed into an image of sweet peace, a liquid return to a realm of floating mystery. The act of taking Lowe to the water has rendered him omnipresent—dissolved in the ocean, awash in the waves, subject to a cyclical liquid passage from sea to land to air and back again. The melancholy bodies on shore can now imagine themselves floating in him, even (fetishistically) drinking him. His return to nature—conceived in protoromantic terms, in the best modern dance tradition—renders him immortal. And, perhaps even more important, it leaves him floating beyond the stigma of AIDS.

Race and Melancholy

In December 1989, two years after Lowe's funeral, more than four thousand mourners are filing into the Cathedral of St. John the Divine in New York, shuffling past an open casket in which lies the body of the choreographer Alvin Ailey.[40] One onlooker remarks at how soft his visage appears, especially when compared to the taut lined face that had seemed so strained at public appearances during the last months of his illness. Ailey has died of AIDS, a fact known to his close associates and to the members of his company, Alvin Ailey American Dance Theater. But publicly, the cause of death is given as "terminal blood dyscrasia, a disorder affecting the bone marrow and red blood cells."[41] The media simplify the medical terminology to "a rare blood disease," a statement that is true, if obfuscatory. In her biography of Ailey, Jennifer Dunning reports, "The disease, essentially a kind of umbrella term for any abnormal condition of the blood, had in fact been a partial cause of death. Alvin had asked the doctor not to disclose that he had had AIDS, which troubled many young company members and friends."[42]

The sole reason for obscuring Ailey's true cause of death was the stigma associated with the disease. According to Ailey's physician, Albert Knapp, Ailey was determined to spare his mother this final strain. But Ailey's death represented not just the stigma of HIV but the stigma of homosexuality and, in ways that must be theorized for dance in the AIDS era, blackness as well. This trio of stigmas—these *stigmata*—proved so motivating that the Ailey company would continue to deny that its founder had died of AIDS well after the death of Ailey's mother five years later.

Like most dance-world figures of the late 1980s—with the notable exception of Arnie Zane, who was white and of the post-Stonewall generation—Ailey was tortured about revealing his homosexuality and never openly discussed the nature of his illness. In his autobiography Ailey reports that his first quasi-sexual experience with a boy occurred when, at eight, he was pulled, half-drowned, from a water tank by a short muscular twelve-year-old named Chauncey, who thrust his body against Ailey's to pump the water out of his lungs. Thereafter Chauncey practiced his coital choreography on Ailey, who says he thus was introduced to "passivity, to being a kind of sexual object of an older guy."[43] By the time Ailey was eighteen, he had decided that he was gay, but he never revealed this to his mother—although she reportedly had some idea of Ailey's homosexual affinities by the time he was in his early twenties. Ailey was frequently described as embodying "manliness" in his dancing. Thomas DeFrantz refers to this as Ailey's "simmering hyper-masculine persona."[44] But when Ailey's mother came backstage to wish him luck before seeing him perform for the first time, at the premiere of his *Morning Mourning* for Lester Horton's company, seeing him in his stage makeup so startled her that she slapped him, hard.[45]

Significantly, Dunning reports only two extended homosexual love relationships in her Ailey biography—one with the white upper-middle-class "Christopher," his surname coyly omitted, and another with the Moroccan-Parisian "Abdul." Ailey's other loves are described as anonymous. To further buttress her depiction of Ailey's sexuality, Dunning quotes at least two psychologists who worked with Ailey on his inability to fully come to terms with his homosexual desire. One of these psychologists, Lawrence Hatterer, an admitting doctor at the Payne Whitney Clinic at New York Hospital, commented to her: "A lot of his complaints had to do with his guilt and conflict about his sexuality, though he didn't need or want treatment."[46]

If his being gay was problematic, it seemed he was of a mind there was nothing he could do about it. The same could be said of Ailey's feelings about being black. In his autobiography Ailey paints a harsh portrait of his Texas upbringing in the 1930s, in a town where the school for black children was rundown and sat at the bottom of the hill, while the school for whites was a "gleaming castle" perched up high, where racism and the lynchings inspired by it were all too common, and where Ku Klux Klansmen could be seen congregating menacingly in their white robes.[47] At the very end of the book, reflecting on the yearlong breakdown that landed him in a mental institution, Ailey writes:

I am an insecure man, a man who wonders who he is, a man from small-town Texas who never forgot walking through dirt with his mother as a child looking for a place to live. It's part of a great insecurity that I've always lived with. Zita Allen wrote an article in the *Village Voice* that said that "Alvin Ailey may be paying dues for fifty years of agony." My illness, I now understand, was the way that agony manifested itself. I never understood or faced that truth, not for many years. My way has always been to take things at face value, for what they are. The agony of being black, the agony of coming from small-town Texas and ending up dancing on the Champs Elysées in Paris, was a heavy load to carry. The contrast, the cultural distance between those two points, certainly had something to do with my illness.[48]

The cultural distance between black and white, poor and rich, gay and straight, marginalized and mainstream was not only evident in relation to provincial Texas, however. In New York Ailey railed against what he perceived as his company's second-class treatment among the pantheon of U.S. dance companies, especially when it came to funding. The net effect of racism, whether it be in Texas or New York City, is revealed in the extraordinary level of abjection under which Ailey labored in order to live his daily and creative lives. As a black man, a homosexual man, and, in the end, a man with AIDS, Ailey—like others similarly prominent who followed him—was abject in three ways, fighting against the tide to attain whatever power, access, and control he could.

In the opening chapter of his 1996 *Are We Not Men? Masculine Anxiety and the Problem of African-American Identity,* the cultural critic Phillip Brian Harper investigates the problematical nature of the experience of black men who strive to succeed in the white-dominated U.S., especially with regard to their perceived masculinity.[49] The main focus of Harper's attention is the African American newscaster Max Robinson, who from 1978 to 1983 was the Chicago anchor of ABC's *World News Tonight*. Robinson was, in fact, the first black news anchor on U.S. network television, and, to hear Robinson's obituarists tell it, he got there through a combination of good looks and white talk. Harper unpacks the themes at work here, from the taming of the threat of black male sexuality to the effeminacy that the black community associates with received standard English. But before Harper even gets started, the formulation takes on a stunning complexity, for along with Robinson's role as a model for African Americans striving to succeed in such visible occupations as newscasting, he is transformed into an (involuntary) object lesson for African Americans: that AIDS strikes not only white gay men but black people, irrespective of their sexual identification, too

Robinson died of AIDS in December 1988, and in the months previous he kept his diagnosis strictly to himself. In his last days, however, he told a friend that he "wanted his death to emphasize the need for AIDS awareness among black people."[50] If Robinson's wishes had been followed, then, his death would have inspired a direct and clear AIDS education campaign in the African American community, with straightforward information about the need to use condoms during sex and to clean needles before reusing or sharing them. But instead, the announcement was attended by a flurry of gossipy interest in how Robinson had contracted AIDS and a focus on whether he was homosexual.[51] In this context Harper repeats a joke from the early period of the

AIDS epidemic. It goes like this: "There's good news and bad news. The bad news is I have AIDS; the good news is that I'm an IV-drug user."[52]

Harper interprets this joke as emblematic of the exaggerated concern regarding masculinity that dominates in many African American communities and that is heightened by the anxiety surrounding AIDS. Worse than AIDS itself is the revelation of homosexuality, with IV-drug addiction viewed as a much-preferred mode of AIDS transmission. The revelation that Max Robinson had died of AIDS problematized his masculine identity, Harper suggests, in part because of Robinson's facility with white speech, for his very skill as a speaker in a white-dominated profession marked him as a compromised man, "as a white-identified Uncle Tom who must also, therefore, be weak, effeminate, and probably a 'fag.'" Harper continues: "Simply put, within some African-American communities the 'professional' or 'intellectual' black male inevitably endangers his status both as black and as male whenever he evidences a facility with Received Standard English—a facility upon which his very identity as a professional or an intellectual in the larger society is founded in the first place."[53] In Harper's view Robinson's silence about his AIDS diagnosis may be explained by this phenomenon, which also accounts for the inordinate public anxiety attending the announcement of his death, as well as the tragic absence of follow-up AIDS education. Thus AIDS mourning is complicated in the African American community by the instability of African American masculinity and its attendant codes of silence.

Even as Harper "explains" the anxious silence surrounding Robinson's death, he does not, however, condone it. Nor does he consider this silence intractable. Even in the anxious interstices of Robinson's story, modes of communication become evident that, in their own subversive ways, articulate a surprising amount of information, about AIDS, masculinity, and identity, within black communities. Harper provides as an example here an instance of "louding," or "loud-talking," for which Robinson was quite famous in the broadcast world. In 1981 Robinson had told a group of college students that network news agencies discriminate against black journalists and that the media, in general, serves as a "crooked mirror" in which mainstream white America considers its own reflection. For his candor Robinson was hauled before ABC News president Roone Arledge, to whom he defended himself by saying that "he had not meant to single out ABC for criticism," thus, in Harper's words, "performing a type of rhetorical backstep by which his criticism, though retracted, was effectively lodged and registered both by the public and by the network."[54] By using "louding," Robinson was able both to overstep and retreat behind an implied boundary, set in this case by the white establishment, in a single smooth maneuver. What might "louding" look like in choreographic terms? Or "softing"?

Harper's insights about the complexity of silence and speech in the African American community invite a self-consciously nuanced reading of the choreography of Ailey's funeral.[55] On the surface the conduct of the service appears to follow a safely white heterosexual pattern, with sufficient African American incursions to protect and stabilize the reading of Ailey's masculinity. But several instances of creative choreographic and rhetorical transgression shift the terms of the event in unexpected ways. To tie Harper's theorization of the instability of gender in African American communities to the notion of abjection that I posited in the introduction: The participants in choreographic events may enact the subtleties of abjection unpredictably and subversively. Blackness may be projected as a category of submission or as a sign of sexual dominance (a notion that Harper describes as the image of the black man as "walking phallus"[56]). It may be represented as a sign for the pitiable or as a site for the cultivation of anger. It can become the object of the white gaze, or it can stare right back.

This is to say that the representation of the black gay man with HIV offers up particularly volatile choreographic possibilities in relation to more stable subjects and objects in the contemporary United States. And the African American homosexual and his associates may, as choreographers of their experience, desire to shape and control the intensity of his abjection as part of the choreographic process.

Ailey's funeral is a case in point. Throughout the event, even with Ailey lying dead in a closed casket that had been transported to the chancel before the altar of the cathedral, a large cast of actors assists in shaping and controlling the conditions of his abjection. Ailey's blackness is represented by a string of African American speakers, from David Dinkins, the African American mayor of New York, to Maya Angelou, the poet. These speakers represent the power and success that can be attained by African Americans in the U.S., but, significantly, they frame that success within the context of white or Euro-American cultural constructs, much as Max Robinson did with respect to received standard English. Though the speakers are African American, their words are shaped and contained within a high Episcopalian service that features sweet and tightly controlled choral music sung by a predominantly white choir, by white forms of ritual and ritual speech, and by the building itself, a modern vestige of repressive medieval European aesthetics. In her words to the gathering, Carmen de Lavallade, Ailey's first dance partner, attempts to bring Ailey into a relationship with the imposing cathedral by suggesting that the building could serve as a metaphor for Ailey, its structural solidity juxtaposed with the delicacy of its stained-glass windows.[57] The European gothic monstrosity of the Cathedral of St. John the Divine destabilizes Ailey's black masculinity, requires that it be addressed. But at the same time the building confers upon Ailey the stature of a great man, of a black abject lifted up to commune with white heterosexual subjects. The cathedral itself is, then, part of the complex discourse of black-white relations activated at Ailey's death, and the participants at the service struggle to shape and mold its significance.

As Harper's analysis of the Max Robinson story demonstrates, unexpected incongruities "indicate the fundamental complexity of the relation between social structure and cultural practice at all events, and its especially intricate character in the African-American context."[58] I take this conceptualization of intracultural complexity as a challenge to search for deviations from the standard script at Ailey's funeral and to ferret out the secondary subversive activity.

For example, Angelou, who danced with Ailey in San Francisco very early in both their careers, delivers an eloquent speech that compares Ailey's passing to the falling of a great tree, an image that endows Ailey with a towering monumentality, albeit a vulnerable one. At the end of that speech, however, she breaches the barrier to Ailey's blackness by breaking into unmistakable black dialect.

> Lord help us, give a look at him.
> Don't make him dress up in no nightgowns, Lord.

Don't put no fuss and feathers on his shoulders, Lord.
Let him know it's truly heaven.
Let him keep his hat, his vest . . . and everything.
Let him have his spats and cane.
And Lord, give him all the pliés he needs into eternity.[59]

The exact meaning of this passage may have remained opaque to many in the congregation, but a listener with knowledge of Ailey's gay life could interpreted it only as a plea to allow Ailey his blackness in heaven, and his homosexuality too. The pregnant pause in the line, "Let him keep his hat, his vest . . . and everything," explodes with possible meanings. At the very least, it says, "Let the man be himself."

Another spillage over the barrier constraining Ailey's blackness and his gayness arrives in the force and fury of Donna Wood's performance of Ailey's *Cry*. In fact, several extracts from Ailey's *Revelations* have already been performed on a large stage erected before the cathedral's altar and directly behind Ailey's bier, with its banks of flowers and candles. But each of these performances has seemed awkward, weak, enervated, compared to their extraordinary resonance on proscenium stages around the world. It is as if the particularities of African American religious expression cannot speak within the gothic pomposity of the building and in the restrictive context of high Anglican worship. Wood's performance of *Cry*, however, crosses that divide, exploding like a bomb of sensuality and sexuality with unabashed joy and verve. Significantly, in these constrained circumstances the explosion could be contained only in the body of a woman.

Some of the most extraordinary choreography of the funeral, however, requires an attentive eye. A camera crew from WNET, the public television station in New York City, discovers a furtive gay male liaison as it zooms in on the congregation during Judith Jamison's oration, holding the camera there for a long five seconds. Sitting next to Arthur Mitchell—another black gay man whose abjection has been parlayed with great volatility—is Allan Gray, the African American mover-and-shaker with whom Ailey became very close in his later years (and to whom he left his private papers). Gray's hand is resting on the knee of an unidentified African American man. Gray and the unidentified man are intimately intertwined with one another through touch, intent and full of feeling. Mitchell, meanwhile, sits beside them ramrod straight, his jaw taut and constrained. Reading the whispers, the "softings," of the funeral, this emerges as a surprisingly homo moment, disapproved by Mitchell, in a service that otherwise erases both gayness and AIDS.[60]

The main homosexual choreography of the event arrives, however, in the form of a staged performance by Dudley Williams, the oldest member of the company and one of its most lustrous dancers, offering his interpretation of "A Song for You" from *Love Songs*. Wiry of build and androgynous in appearance, Williams joined Ailey's company in the 1960s and danced with him in the early years of Ailey's New York career.[61] Williams remains an anomaly in the company, his corporeality inviting the sort of anxiety about masculinity that Harper writes about. Williams is slender and fey, Sylvester in a unitard. He is unapologetically effeminate. And as he leaves the stage, he blows a kiss to Ailey's casket—a public though intimate gesture that could be read as a sign of their shared homosexuality.

Melancholy Incorporation

To make dances from a place of melancholy abjection is to wield power of immense proportion. As a black man creating avant-garde postmodern dances, Bill T. Jones has, from his very first work, activated himself as a site of fierce anger, actively resisting the forces that would cast him on the world stage in the role of the abject black man.[62] But he has also been known to use that abjection to his advantage. Deborah Jowitt, dance critic of the *Village Voice*, recalls a performance of his 1977 solo *With Durga* in which Jones publicly berated the audience for exoticizing and fetishizing his black male body. He did this while in fact presenting his body to be exoticized and fetishized: "'You want some?' he asked us, softly stroking his body, then cursed us out."[63]

It is important to note the multiple sources of Jones's abjection, including his being gay—although, historically, he and his partner, Arnie Zane, took pains to downplay their relationship. In June 1987 I interviewed Jones and Zane, and when I asked why people writing about their work regularly commented on the dimensional (tall/short) and racial (black/white) differences between them while making virtually no mention of their gay love relationship, both Jones and Zane were quick to explain:

Z A N E : No, we don't talk about it that much.
J O N E S : We were very careful about it.
Z A N E : We weren't making that an issue. . . . We were just
    who we were.[64]

Thus, both Jones and Zane actively resisted making their gay
relationship part of the frame through which the work would
be seen. Owing to the gay-erasing conventions of journalism in
the U.S., writers were more than happy to collude with them in
this project.

But then, in mid-1987, Zane became visibly ill and rumors
were circulating in the dance world that he was suffering from
AIDS. At a rehearsal in early June, Zane looked extremely thin
and was walking with a cane. He said he was having trouble
with his hip. When I asked Jones and Zane to discuss how AIDS
had affected their lives and art, Zane said, "Well, I think it affects
all our lives greatly. It's very touching. I mean, we're all affected
very deeply by it." Then there was a long pause, ten seconds perhaps, and he continued, "I don't want to get too involved in
that."[65]

Within a month Zane, with Jones, had made the decision to
go public with his AIDS diagnosis on a special edition of the
MacNeil-Lehrer Newshour, "AIDS and the Arts," which was aired
in July 1987.[66] This was a bold decision, for which he deserves
great honor. Until that moment, no other major dance maker had
come forward as having HIV or AIDS. (As I mentioned earlier,
Alvin Ailey, as well as Robert Joffrey and Rudolf Nureyev, to
name just three famous men in dance, would not reveal their di-
agnoses even in death.) During that PBS program Zane was particularly outspoken, in ways that would later irk critics on both
the right and the left. He spoke about the problem of losing control over the body. "There's not room for that in the marketplace
of the dance world," he said, refusing to ignore the hypocrisy of
a dance world that deals in commodities like physical beauty
and virtuosic skill as much as in art. He also tackled the question
of whether he thought that the arts had been particularly hard hit
by AIDS. "That's the controversial question this month, right?"
he said with a sardonic grin. "Of course I do. I'm in the center of
this world, the art world. My people, on a daily basis, I'm losing
my colleagues." How many colleagues? the reporter Joanna

Simon asked him. He paused for a long time, holding back tears. "Maybe twenty."[67]

The program ended with excerpts from 21 *Supported Positions,* a 1987 co-choreographed duet that emphasizes mutual male-male support. In the piece, Zane lifts the standing Jones, who is considerably larger than Zane, then lowers him carefully. Shifting the terms of their dependence, Zane then clasps his legs around Jones's waist, the two bodies slowly rotating in this pose, as objects of contemplation. As if to make a point about contagion, in the next phrase Jones and Zane roll over one another's bodies, purposefully blurring the boundaries between them. "It [the dance] related to the illness in showing the strength of my being able to handle this person's body, my lover, my friend, my colleague, and vice versa," Zane explained. "It was a sort of open letter to our friends and the world, saying, we're still working." The interview continued with a word from Jones:

> I think even now there's kind of *blinding pain* that comes down through my head and heart when I confront the possibility that I could lose this relationship. So we will hold each other. We'll build new works. We will deepen our relationship. We'll disagree. And we'll do what we do best, which is build and struggle.(emphasis added)[68]

The blinding pain that Jones acknowledges here can emanate only from the wound of anticipated loss, already open, already hurting. In the final image of their duet together, to a swell of operatic music Jones cradles Zane in a pose that summons up Michaelangelo's *Pièta.* Even before Zane's actual death, and in anticipation of it, Jones and Zane had searched for a choreographic metaphor that could encompass the size and intensity of their grief. For at least this moment, in the chaste, etherealized mourning of a mother for her dead son, they find it.

Ethereality, however, would be adamantly banished in 1989, the year after Zane's death, when Jones choreographed the highly erotic *Untitled,* a collaboration with the videographer John Sanborn, for the PBS program *Alive from Off Center.* This was among the first works that Jones created after the loss of his partner in life and dance, and not surprisingly it resonates with the full sensuous force of his melancholic longing. "I was just grieving," Jones explained to a student who asked him to comment on

Arnie Zane and Bill T. Jones in *21 Supported Positions,* a film by Robert Longo, 1987. Photo: Frank Ockenfels. Courtesy of Robert Longo.

the piece in 1998. "When you're grieving you're really trying to find a way to connect with the person you've lost."[69] And, as Moon has discussed so eloquently, one way for gay men to do this is through the corporeal fetish.

In fact, *Untitled* is built upon such a fetish, a phrase of movement created a dozen years earlier by Zane for his 1977 *Hand Dance,* a duet for Jones and Zane to Rhys Chatham's "Green Line Poem."[70] A shard of memory recreated, the movement phrase functions as a bodily and epistemic remembrance as well as a starting point for this memorial to Zane. Jones seems to have wanted to make this genealogy explicit when, two years later, for his company's 1991 appearances at the American Dance Festival in Durham, North Carolina, he programmed three pieces that alone and together served as memorials to Zane: *The Gift/No God Logic* (1987), Zane's last major work; the group version of *Continuous Replay* (1982), based on the phrase from *Hand Dance;* and his own performance of *Untitled.* Set directly next to one another, and with *Continuous Replay* featuring a near-literal repetition of the phrase throughout its fifteen-minute length, the derivation of the material in *Untitled* is rendered unmistakable. But even in the video version of *Untitled* (1989) Jones provides a telling clue to the danced material's having been created by Zane: a brief segment in which Zane appears in a holographic image, executing a short fragment of the phrase, immediately after which Jones steps into the dissolving holograph and takes over where Zane left off.[71] Jones steps into Zane's movement with his body, his corporeal "rags," wearing Zane's movement like a suit of clothes. The fetish of the movement is enacted in order to reconjure Zane from the only material that his death had left behind.

It is notable, then, that in the live version of *Untitled*, which is four minutes longer than the ten-minute television adaptation, Jones performs the dance completely in the nude.[72] (In the video version he wears black pants and a leotard top, which he rolls down to his waist halfway through.) The nudity reinforces the sense of the piece as simultaneously elegiac and erotic—the fulfillment of Moon's idea of erotic rememberment. It also invites the fetishization of Jones's body, with Jones actively eroticizing himself.[73]

As the live version of *Untitled* begins, we hear Zane's voice on tape—alternately languorous and focused—recounting a dream:

Last night, the third of March, first dream that I recall, I was involved with some type of almost, it was like a student protest. There was a huge mass of people, sort of scruffy with sleeping bags, knapsacks, tents, et cetera. There were the authorities, which in my mind, though I didn't physically see them at first, there were police in some form. And I sought refuge in a tent.[74]

As the spoken text begins, viewers see Jones's body in silhouette, standing in profile against a light blue-gray cyclorama. His penis and shoulder-length braids are completely visible, as

Bill T. Jones with a holographic representation of Arnie Zane in Jones's *Untitled,* from the video directed by John Sanborn and Mary Perillo, 1989. Video stills courtesy of Bill T. Jones, Bill T. Jones/ Arnie Zane Dance Company, Foundation for Dance Promotion; John Sanborn and Mary Perillo; and Twin Cities Public Television.

is his extraordinary physique, the powerful thighs and strongly curved buttocks, the flaring chest and shoulders. As he tilts his head forward slightly, his forearms sweep out in a circle as if to gather the air directly in front of his torso. Now the right shoulder rolls in a circle and the right arm levers forward, like the head of a mock dinosaur. This movement fragment is repeated almost mechanistically, three times. The staccato phrase conveys urgency. Then Jones lunges forward on one leg, arms scooping forward like the cup of a bulldozer. The elbows accent inward twice, as if squeezing something in their grip, before Jones twists sideways, chopping his elbows angularly. He configures his body as a machine.

Jones's performance is marked throughout by relentless physicality and continuous revision of the established formal structure. He offers the opening phrase now in a shortened version, again in a longer version, cutting from it, adding to it, always punching it up with a sense of enormous physical power, as if performing a martial art. Now, punctuating the phrase, he takes two marching steps, pauses, then takes two more. The arms scissor in opposite directions, until at their peak his hands fall and press against his head. He turns to the back, so that we can see the straight fingers of the hands now curling inward. He turns to begin the phrase again, just as Zane's text references his seeking refuge inside a tent. The movement and the text do not directly illuminate each other, but, then, perhaps they do. Zane's voice continues:

I was lying and sleeping by myself, with maybe three other individuals, two on one side of me, and one on the other side of me. And I peeked out of the bottom of the flap of the tent and suddenly in the distance I saw what looked like the inside of a fireplace moving toward me, but there were giant, giant logs completely burning, one stacked on top of the other, four or five high. They were being pushed by a bulldozer at tremendous speed, moving toward the tent.

In implied relation to the text, Jones's movement takes on a heightened urgency. The text speaks of danger, and the movement may be read as an evocation of that danger too, as well as a response to it. Jones continues to repeat the basic phrase, but on this repetition, when the hands press against the head, the arms immediately swing down with great force, forearms drumming

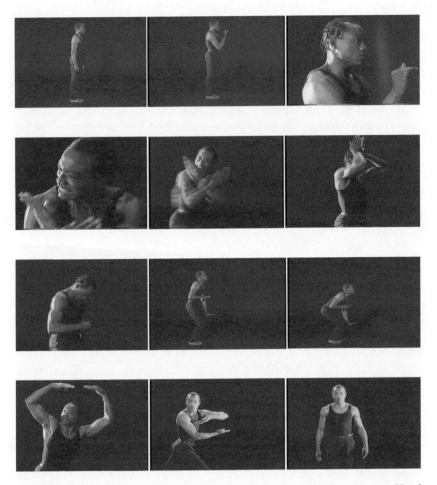

Bill T. Jones in *Untitled,* quoting movements from Arnie Zane's 1977 *Hand Dance*, 1989. Video stills courtesy of Bill T. Jones, Bill T. Jones/Arnie Zane Dance Company, Foundation for Dance Promotion; John Sanborn and Mary Perillo; and Twin Cities Public Television.

repeatedly in front of the body. At a key moment Jones collapses downward, one hand on one hip, head bent forward, almost as if he were crying. Zane's text continues: "The next thing I knew was that I, like a banshee, was whirling throughout this park, around flower beds, looking for coverage, so that the bulldozer with the burning logs would not get me. I woke up."

As the text and movement phrases come to an intermediate endpoint, Jones walks downstage into the light. And now, if one

gazes beyond the beauty of his body and the virility of his performance, he can be seen for who he is: a distraught lover, awash
in melancholy; a melancholy body. Jones's distress has been evident in the sharp mechanical quality of his movements, the audible expectorations of breath, even the formal segmentation of his
body, as if he were taking his limbs apart and putting them back
together, painfully. From this moment, however, the dance can be
seen as being about utter dissolution, about coming apart at the
seams, about the wound of abrogated desire and the inability to
heal, about memory, loss, and melancholy. Jones steps forward to
the microphone and gives that melancholy a strident voice:

You said, "A system in collapse is a system moving
forward."

As Jones intones this sentence, repeating it twice, it becomes an
accusation, as if he had been made a promise that was broken. As
he speaks, he begins counting the fingers of his right hand with
his right thumb. He does this mindlessly, as if he were counting
beads or rubbing a worry stone to quiet his turbulent mind.

At first, the content of the sentence, rather than its manner of
address, draws attention. The "collapse" can be interpreted as an
allusion to the collapse of the AIDS body, which is rendered here
not as dissolution but as evolution, as if death were not an ending but an opportunity to move forward. Presumably, Zane uttered these words before his death, and Jones, to judge by his impassioned tone of voice, has come to disbelieve him. "You said,
'A system in collapse is a system moving forward.'" Jones's implied response: Not true. This hurts. This system is not moving
forward. I am stuck.

But then, beyond the content, comes the realization that
Jones's words are aimed directly at his viewers. Jones's second-
person address—"You said"—has a curiously gradual effect, for
only in time does it become clear that, in gazing at us and speaking to us, he is configuring all the individuals in the audience as
corporealizations of his lost lover. Suddenly, it is we who are
dead, and the man we left behind is railing at us. We viewers are
thereby enfolded into the piece, forcibly transformed into stand-
ins for Zane, corporeal fetishes all. Jones speaks to us of shared
memories:

Do you remember Estella Jones?

Do you remember Gus Jones?

Do you remember Edith Zane?

Do you remember Charles Reinhart?

Do you remember Tye, the little half-wit who cleaned our room in Amsterdam?

Do you remember Lavonne Campbell, who said two young men shouldn't make such a commitment so early—they didn't know what they were doing?

Do you remember Keith? He loved those Puerto Rican boys.

Do you remember Juan? He loved those rich white artists.

Do you remember Stephanie, that time at ADF when I said I hate women, that time at ADF when I said I hate white people? And I tried to find their eyes later. I was invited back ten years later.

Do you remember Rhodessa, who cleaned your butt when you were so sick and dying you couldn't even raise your hand?

Do you remember . . . "a system in collapse"

Do you remember Willi Smith? . . . "a system in collapse"

Do you remember my mother? "Take care of my boy, he ain't got no education."

Do you remember . . . "A system in collapse is a system moving forward."

You said, "A system in collapse is a system moving forward."

You said, "A system in collapse is a system moving forward."

You said.

Jones's references encompass a panoply of people and events— both significant and mundane, with no distinction made between the two—from the life he and Zane shared together. He speaks of Jones's parents; Zane's mother; the director of the American Dance Festival (ADF); a boy who cleaned their room when, as young men, they traveled to Europe for a time. This is a glossary of life references, random fetishes of memory. Keith Haring, the white graffiti artist who had designed the sets for *Secret Pastures* (1984), is invoked as a man who desired other men, specifically, Puerto Rican men. (Haring died of AIDS in 1990.) Stephanie Reinhart, the codirector with her husband, Charles, of the venerable ADF, is conjured in relation to the recollection of a solo improvised by Jones at the dance festival in 1981 that offended some patrons and, evidently, the directors themselves.[75]

Tension builds as Jones further explores this world of memory, implied accusation, and personal revelation. He evokes unabashedly the intimate and vulnerable period when Zane was so very sick that Jones's sister Rhodessa had to wash him as if he were a baby. He revisits the degradation of the body—the system in collapse—in its horrifying details. Jones is configuring himself and Zane as objects of pity as he announces the factors in their abjection: Jones's blackness; his and Zane's homosexuality; Zane's—and perhaps his own—HIV infection. Yet now that there is no longer any secrecy about these root causes, Jones manages to transform his and Zane's abjection into sources of energy and power. Jones becomes a volatile aggressive subject. This is a radical subversive maneuver, and he uses it here to extreme effect.

At this point the ruminative quality of Zane's speaking is replaced by the dramatic delivery of the soprano Régine Crespin, whose voice matches the depth of Jones's grief. On tape she is singing the fourth of Berlioz's six *Les nuits d'été*, "Absence."[76] Crespin's delivery is particularly soaked with emotion, often rising to a catharsis, and the rich orchestrations support her in expressing unabated longing.

The music begins with the refrain "Reviens, reviens, ma bien-aimée!" (Come back, come back, my beloved), which Jones matches with a movement phrase that seems at first disconnected from the sharp point of loss expressed in the words: a side-to-side isolation of the hip sockets, more anatomical than sensual. But as before with Tracy Rhoades's *Requiem,* the disjunct or analytical quality of postmodern movement vocabulary serves Jones's choreography of melancholy in surprising ways, in this case by alluding subtly to the eroticism that smolders at gay melancholy's core. The grinding of Jones's hips causes him to fall to the side, metaphorically losing his balance. He allows his head to roll as he does so, repeating this movement fragment three times, in a choreographic sign for disorientation and anomie. The phrase is an echo of the ripe imagery of loss embedded in the text, which continues:

Comme une fleur loin du soleil,	Like a flower without the sun,
La fleur de ma vie est fermée	The flower of my life is closed,
Loin de ton sourire vermeil.	Separated from your rosy smile.

The flower, deprived of light, is dead. This is Kristeva's black sun. As the score continues, the verse of "Absence" is aswirl with pain and desire, painting musical pictures of the distance between the lovers, a distance so great that even strong horses would weary to cross it:

D'ici là-bas que de campagnes,	From here to where you are,
Que de villes et de hameaux,	So many fields, towns and villages,
Que de vallons et de montagnes,	So many valleys and mountains
A lasser le pied des chevaux!	To weary the feet of the horses!

To this text Jones dances a phrase replete with bodily dissections: more isolations of the hips; the head leading as the back tilts perpendicular to the floor; the spine shaken out like a rug. Pressing his body forward in a deep lunge, Jones now assumes what becomes an iconographic pose in the piece: right hand raised in front, left hand behind and akimbo, the fingers of both hands opening and closing like pincers. The arms scoop forward again, curving, pushing, as if clawing through deep loam. Quickly, Jones turns and stomps his feet on the ground three times, throws his head back, and beats the air overhead with his right arm. (In the video version of *Untitled*, this moment is shot from shoulder height with a handheld camera, which heightens the sense of madness and churning emotion.) Now Jones runs across the stage, legs scampering, arms wheeling overhead, before stopping at a fixed point, where he rises onto his toes and grinds his pelvis in an explosion of delicious sexuality. As his body falls forward, he throws his head and arms back, running in a wide circle as if he were ballet's Giselle, lost, lonely, and mad with grief. With his arms flung open Jones gazes directly at the audience until, at the end of the musical phrase, he drops his arms and head, spent.[77]

At the conclusion of Berlioz's music, Jones reapproaches the microphone and resumes his earlier monologue, which, as before, is directed to Zane and simultaneously to the audience. As Jones speaks, he pulls on a pair of black slacks, wipes sweat from his face, and dons a black shirt, black jacket, glasses, and hat—his clothes of mourning.

I think we're alone now.
There doesn't seem to be anyone around.
Do you remember Durham?
I think we're alone now.
The beating—
Do you remember Amsterdam, and the lights are playing, and all the places you can smoke all day long and have sex all night long?

> Do you remember Georgia?
> Do you remember Mespeth, Queens, when your daddy took the butcher knife and chased us through the streets and your mama hit me in the head with a rock? And I slapped her, and the natives said, the neighbors said, we know how to deal with people who hit women in this neighborhood, boy.
> Do you remember Rochester, New York, and my sister Jamie's house, and what the inner city meant in 1971, and what it meant in nineteen—?

Mundane, erotic, and dramatic events are intercut with lyrics from "I Think We're Alone Now," a 1967 hit tune by Tommy James and the Shondells, all soaked with the scent of homoeroticism, abjection, and mourning.[78] Jones invokes memories of his and Zane's dancing careers and of funding agencies and critics, right alongside images from gay life in New York, of famous gay bars in lower Manhattan and the chemical amyl nitrate (poppers), sniffed to enhance orgasm, of entire bathhouses devoted to gay erotic pleasures. He is mourning a lover, and he is mourning a culture of sex:

> Do you remember DTW and David White?
> Do you remember the NEA?
> Do you remember the New York State Council on the Arts?
> Do you remember The Cock Ring?
> Do you remember Man's Country?
> Do you remember St. Mark's Baths?
> Do you remember [sharp intake of breath] amyl nitrate on Friday night?
> Do you remember sex with strangers?
> Do you remember audiences?
> Do you remember the first time we heard the word "homoerotic"?
> Do you remember Bucharest, and the lady said, "Work not touched by the hand of God"?
> Do you remember the young man who said "too intellectual"?
> Do you remember Charlie?
> Do you remember Melissa?
> "A system in collapse."
> Do you remember Binghamton?
> Do you remember Johnson City in that little room?
> Do you remember the house in Valley Cottage?
> Do you remember the dogs, the dog who died of cancer, the man, the man who died of cancer?

Do you remember the art gallery, the place where we made repu-
tations, the place where we ruined reputations?
Do you remember the ADF?
Do you remember [he beats once on his chest]—?
"A system in collapse is a system moving forward."[79]

Now he shifts to events that immediately preceded and followed
Zane's death: a stay in the hospital when Zane was seriously ill,
his mother's rending her blouse in grief at the sight of her dead
son's body, the plot where he was buried. And then, inexplicably
and disjointedly, Jones points to their careers again, the line
between their shared experiences in life and in death, between
the mundane and the cataclysmic, all in a blur.

Do you remember Roosevelt Hospital?
Do you remember the cemetery?
Do you remember your mother ripping her blouse?
Do you remember the ambulance drivers who wouldn't touch
your body?
Do you remember ADF and the international choreographers?

Thus begins a steady dénouement as Jones, now fully wrapped in
the protection of his own clothing, as if he were reentering the
real world after floating in a universe of naked grief, begins to
address Zane for the last time, coupling that address with the
metaphoric pounding of his own angry, grieving, pained, suffering, melancholic heart. As he speaks, he steps farther away, gradually into the shadows and then complete darkness.

[He beats once on his chest, hard, with his fist] "A system in collapse is a system moving forward."
[beat-beat] I think we're alone now.
[beat-beat] I think we're alone now.
[beat-beat] I think we're . . . Do you remember?
[beat-beat] "A system in collapse—"
[beat-beat] Do you remember?
[beat-beat]
[beat-beat]
[beat-(slower) beat]
[beat (long pause) beat]

Arriving at the end of *Untitled*, Jones opens up the space between
the heartbeats as if to leave his audience suspended in time, floating in a space of inchoate desire and melancholy, where the two

categories are virtually indistinguishable. One can imagine Michael Moon clapping in the wings, celebrating a mourning that refuses to end and that is built so extraordinarily upon the fetishes of movement and memory. This is truly "a re-memberment that has repositioned itself among the remnants." At the strong beating of Jones's chest one can also imagine Douglas Crimp cheering what can additionally be seen as a vivid impulse toward a danced AIDS activism: defiant, erotic, and enraged.

At left: Bill T. Jones in *Untitled,* beating his chest at the conclusion of the piece, 1989. Video stills courtesy of Bill T. Jones, Bill T. Jones / Arnie Zane Dance Company, Foundation for Dance Promotion; John Sanborn and Mary Perillo; and Twin Cities Public Television.

3

Monuments and Insurgencies

We don't need a cultural renaissance; we need cultural practices
actively participating in the struggle against AIDS. We don't
need to transcend the epidemic; we need to end it.
Douglas Crimp

Choreography in the AIDS era lives in constant tension with the
stigmatization of the body, with gay male choreographers and
their audiences shifting back and forth between the acceptance
and rejection of AIDS as a core metaphor in dance. The chain of
signification from dance to AIDS serves both as a basic animating
substance, like blood, but also as a set of meanings to be resisted
and actively reconfigured. Dancing in this era also commonly
serves a mourning function, with fetishes of loss and longing literally embodied in the corporeality of the performers.

Significantly, the very visibility of gay mourning in dance constitutes a demand for caring and sympathy, coupled with the
self-assertion that is integral to public—as opposed to closeted—
grief. Thus the demand for public recognition proves to be a core
element of the AIDS dance, even when the reconfiguring of stigmatization or the working out of gay mourning practices remains its primary characteristic.

At left: the NAMES Project AIDS Quilt on the National Mall, Washington,
D.C., 11–13 October 1996. Photo: Paul Margolis, © 1996, 2001 The NAMES
Project Foundation.

Certain choreographies in the AIDS era, however, function directly as acts of resistance to civil authority, especially by offering an analysis of the power structures that animate the forces of homo- and AIDS-phobic oppression. The intent of such choreographies is to reveal the forces of oppression to the viewer, to render them blatantly visible, thereby destabilizing them. These dances, then, function in a realm defined primarily by what I term *insurgency,* or, to be more exact, by the tension between monumentality and insurgency, between the status quo and the attempt to subvert the status quo, between those who hold power and those who, through the use of subversive tactics, contrive to alter the configuration of power. Dances are commonly viewed as a concatenation of aesthetic effects—as beautiful, visually striking, structurally cogent, well crafted—or as vehicles for the evocation of sentiment, measured by the flush of heightened emotion that they are capable of exciting in their viewers. But with and through their aesthetic effects, dances also bear a politics, which is to say that audiences may view choreographic action in two ways at once: both as critique and as art, fused and inseparable.

This dual role for choreography—that it is simultaneously aesthetic and political—applies to virtually all choreographed action. The German playwright and theoretician Bertolt Brecht made this argument seventy years ago, using the word *sociological* to refer to the function of the work of art within the frame of society at large. As early as 1927 Brecht began to argue for the abolition of "aesthetics" in favor of a sociological view of theater.[1] The former, he wrote, concerns ineffable and insubstantial "eternal verities," while the latter is solidly "of the people." The problem with critics, he suggested at the time, is that they become mired in the aesthetic approach, even when their instincts would have them respond sociologically. That same year, in an essay on the new form of theater—"the epic theatre"—of which he was a champion, he wrote of the need to downplay emotional response in favor of reason, in order to facilitate the audience's ability to analyze the systems of power depicted in the play: "The essential point of the epic theatre is perhaps that it appeals less to the feelings than to the spectator's reason. Instead of sharing an experience the spectator must come to grips with things."[2]

Then, in 1930, Brecht penned an essay suggesting that, without an analysis of the system to which writers, critics, and musicians are contributing, "Their output then becomes a matter of delivering the goods," of providing support and sustenance for the system as it is already constituted:

Values evolve which are based on the fodder principle. And this leads to a general habit of judging works of art by their suitability for the apparatus without ever judging the apparatus by its suitability for the work. People say, this or that is a good work; and they mean (but do not say) good for the apparatus. Yet this apparatus is conditioned by the society of the day and only accepts what can keep it going in that society. We are free to discuss any innovation which doesn't threaten its social function—that of providing an evening's entertainment.[3]

In Brecht's entertainment model critical notions of what is good or what is bad in art come to be based solely on an evaluation of the art's efficacy in supporting the world as currently (and safely) constituted.[4] In this same essay Brecht goes on to critique the romantic vision of the artist, writing with determination: "No longer can [the individual] simply 'express himself.'"[5] Brecht critiques both the romantic and entertainment models, arguing instead for the utilitarian function of art and the need for the artist to take responsibility for analyzing and resisting the structures of power, of the "apparatus." Brecht's theater, then, emphasizes the active process, the pricking of the conscience, the heightening of reason. It is both political and aesthetic, with each term residing firmly within the other.

It is one thing, however, for viewers to be trained to uncover the systems of power embedded in the work of art—to clearly see the political in the aesthetic—and it is yet another for the artist him- or herself to assume an activist position in the artwork's creation, to literally make the work with the goal of goading the audience to action. The art critic and theorist Douglas Crimp has devised a model for artistic activism that is a direct response to the AIDS epidemic and that grows out of the analysis of stigmatization and of the mourning impulse that I discussed in the previous chapters. In two essays published two years apart Crimp theorized with concision the necessity of turning grief into public activism—and the efficacy of such activism in a time of urgent distress. Although I have referenced both essays in the earlier chapters, a reprise of the key themes remains necessary.

In the first essay, "AIDS: Cultural Analysis/Cultural Activism" (1987), Crimp puts forward an angry plea to artists in the AIDS era to do what is most important, when it is most needed. Is it enough for artists to produce lugubrious elegies? he prods. To hold benefits and raise money for AIDS research? To make art in the vague hope that the art itself will transcend our lives and our deaths? Or, conversely, is it the responsibility of artists to save lives, responding as activists would to the AIDS epidemic? "From the beginning my intention was to show, through discussion of these works, that there was a critical, theoretical, activist alternative to the personal, elegiac expressions that appeared to dominate the art-world response to AIDS. What seemed to me essential was a vastly expanded view of culture in relation to crisis."[6] Here, Crimp displays no patience for the aestheticists, for those artists and critics who rehearse clichés about the expressive necessity of art, specifically, "the traditional idealist conception of art, which entirely divorces art from engagement in lived social life." His views are best encapsulated in this unequivocal and oft-quoted passage: "We don't need a cultural renaissance; we need cultural practices actively participating in the struggle against AIDS. We don't need to transcend the epidemic; we need to end it."[7]

But then, in 1989, Crimp reveals a subtle shift in his position, a shift that will allow him to come to terms with the mourning-versus-activism battle within the gay community in the late 1980s. (This was a battle to which he had in fact contributed with his earlier essay.) As he lays out the issues in his "Mourning and Militancy," on one side are those for whom the candlelight march or the memorial service is a moving and profoundly cathartic experience, and on the other are the activists, such as Larry Kramer, who harness their anger to accomplish crucial societal goals and who therefore consider mourning to be profoundly suspect.[8] In attempting to articulate (and mediate) this conflict, Crimp searches for a way to understand the origins of mourning and militancy. Might these two categories, which appear on the surface to be so incompatible, actually be born of the same source?

Drawing upon the experience of his own painful grieving in response to the death of his father, Crimp ultimately locates his answer in a reading (across the grain) of Freud's concept of melancholia, a serious pathology that, according to Freud, shares all the symptomatology of mourning with the addition of drastically diminished self-esteem and the already discussed inability to return to "normal." (See chapter 2.) Moon, of course, had already pointed out how gay men were foreclosed from such promised healing.[9] But what is increasingly clear to Crimp is the degree to which the course of gay male mourning is systematically thwarted. The lover of the dead man sits in the back pew at the funeral, unrecognized by the family. The *New York Times* then refuses to list the lover's name.[10] The indignities mount up day after day. "Seldom has a society so savaged people during their hour of loss," Crimp complains, reminding us of Freud's warning: "We look upon any interference with [mourning] as inadvisable or even harmful." Crimp expands on that point:

The violence we encounter is relentless, the violence of silence and omission almost as impossible to endure as the violence of unleashed hatred and outright murder. Because this violence also desecrates the memories of our dead, we rise in anger to vindicate them. For many of us, mourning *becomes* militancy.[11]

This theorization of the connection between mourning and militant activism—that activism is, in fact, born from mourning—runs parallel to Brecht's conception of the integral connection between the aesthetic and the political. In both cases one term is inextricably connected to the other and cannot exist apart from it. Furthermore, it becomes impossible to conceive of one as coming before the other, because they are born simultaneously. This notion of interdependent simultaneity is crucial to any discussion of AIDS dances, because virtually every dance in this era participates polyvalently in the realms of elegy (mourning) and of activism (militancy), of aesthetics and politics. In fact, the application of Brecht's notion of the sociological to the specific circumstances of the AIDS era discussed by Crimp would suggest that the topography of gay mourning and gay elegy is a primary component in all the activist art making of these times. Or, rather, it is more than a component of activism: It is its twin, its double, its ghost, its shadow.

The cultural critic and theater historian David Román implements Brecht's and Crimp's ideas by expanding the definition of theater in the era of AIDS to encompass more than staged productions, as resonant as those theatrical productions might be. As I have already mentioned, Román includes the memorial service and the protest march in his analysis, in addition to the so-called AIDS play. This enables him to view the aesthetic content in the funeral rite alongside the political content of the Broadway show. In a similar vein, I am proposing that a consideration of dance in the AIDS era must encompass the entire range of "danced acts of intervention," from—as in this chapter, for example—the performance of the High Risk Group's *Falling* to the procession that culminated Jon Greenberg's political funeral at an East Village park to the unfurling of the NAMES Project AIDS Quilt on the National Mall. All these actions activate choreographic sensibilities, which inherently have their political effects. They also share a genesis in mourning. Significantly, mourning places these danced acts of intervention not in a soft, disempowered, or enervated condition but rather in a dynamic, insurgent relationship to oppressive monumentalities. These dances stand against the established order, against stone edifices as well as the invisible conditions of oppression.

The Strategic and the Tactical

To further focus the analysis of insurgent dances, and to buttress the theoretical triad of Brecht, Crimp, and Román, I will now examine key concepts of the strategy and the tactic proposed by the French theorist Michel de Certeau in *The Practice of Everyday Life* (1984). The overarching frame for de Certeau's text is his desire to investigate the involvement of the "user" or audience member in the dissemination of marketing and information in the capitalist system. He notes the existence of a great deal of scholarship on the material being disseminated but under the (incorrect) assumption that all "users" are receiving this material in a particular foreordained way. De Certeau argues that this is not the case and that the viewer—de Certeau's "consumer"—of commercial media responds in a nonlinear fashion, quite at odds with the response desired by the media's makers. The television viewer, for example, may channel surf through a commercial, noting its stylish effects without registering the name of the product being sold. Or the viewer may configure the advertisement as ironic or humorous, again disregarding the intentions of the image maker. De Certeau cautions that this analysis does not signal a "return to individuality" in our under-standing of reception, for there is no such thing as "social atom-ism." Rather, this rendering focuses attention on "modes of oper-ation or schemata of action":

> The purpose of this work is to make explicit the systems of operational combination *(les combinatoires d'opérations)* which also compose a "culture," and to bring to light the models of action characteristic of users whose status as the dominated element in society (a status that does not mean that they are either passive or docile) is concealed by the euphemistic term "consumers." Everyday life in-vents itself by poaching in countless ways on the prop-erty of others.[12]

This "poaching" reconfigures an uncomplicated schematization that sets the capitalist machine against the passive victims of that machine—in simple terms, the powerful exerting control over the marginalized—as a more complex configuration that allows for the possibility of both modest and substantive acts of resist-ance. De Certeau writes that such acts of resistance configure viewers: "As unrecognized producers, poets of their own acts, si-lent discoverers of their own paths in the jungle of functionalist rationality, consumers produce through their signifying prac-tices something that might be considered similar to the 'wander-ing lines' *(lignes d'erre)* drawn by the autistic children studied by F. Deligny (17): 'indirect' or 'errant' trajectories obeying their own logic." This leads de Certeau to theorize two categories cru-cial to capitalist society, both of which are defined in relation to their hold on power. A "strategy," he writes, is "the calculus of force-relationships which becomes possible when a subject of will and power (a proprietor, an enterprise, a city, a scientific in-stitution) can be isolated from an 'environment.'"[13] In other words, strategies are the means by which those in power scheme to remain in power. The realm of the strategic is associated with institutions, with business and government structures that seek to perpetuate themselves. A "tactic," meanwhile, is

> a calculus which cannot count on a "proper" (a spatial or institutional localization), nor thus on a border-line

distinguishing the other as a visible totality. The place of a
tactic belongs to the other. A tactic insinuates itself into
the other's place, fragmentarily, without taking it over in
its entirety, without being able to keep it at a distance. . . .
The weak must continually turn to their own ends forces
alien to them.[14]

By suggesting that the realm of the tactical is the realm of the
other, de Certeau draws the reader's attention to the efficacious
activities of the marginalized, the disempowered, the abject. The
tactic, he suggests, is not tied to durable institutions but to fragmentary or disjointed entities that "turn to their own ends forces
alien to them." Ironically, because the tactical requires the use of
means that are "alien" or unfamiliar to it, a quality of deviance,
grotesquerie, or disruption may be evidenced. By contrast, the
realm of the strategic is all too familiar with the means of power;
it exudes confidence.

The two sets of practices butting up against one another might
be metaphorized as the collision of stuffy stolidity with trickery
and wit, of conservative with radical, of strong with weak, of
giant with Jack. It is worth noting, however, that in the interaction
power may circulate and flow in unexpected ways. This is not just
a matter of who wins and holds the power. In fact, one may presume that the tactical will never replace the strategic. (If it does, it
is no longer tactical.) Rather, the tactical is calibrated to force the
strategic to shift on its moorings so that it can no longer function
monumentally. The tactical aims to destabilize the strategic,
while the strategic maintains and assimilates power relentlessly.

The importance of choreographic insurgencies (or tactics) in
the AIDS era becomes clear when considering the dearth of (strategic) response from the U.S. government to the AIDS epidemic.[15] Presidents Reagan, Bush, Clinton, and now Bush the
younger have turned a largely blind eye upon those who have
died of AIDS. As I discussed earlier, Reagan was so reticent to address the disease that he did not speak publicly about AIDS in
any substantive way until 1987, almost at the end of his second
term. The first George Bush was similarly quiescent, although he
deserves credit for increasing funding for AIDS research and care
through his support of the federal Ryan White Act. Clinton, as a
candidate, promised a response to AIDS that would rival the
Manhattan Project, the intensive research initiative that had led

fifty years earlier to the development of the atomic bomb. But throughout his two-term presidency, he failed to appoint the powerful "AIDS czar" who would guide such a project. As for George W. Bush, AIDS seems not to register on his meter at anywhere near the same level as international terrorism. He surprised the world in 2003 by proposing aid to African nations in the amount of $15 billion, specifically to fight AIDS, then posed for heart-wrenching photo opportunities with people with AIDS during a 2003 visit to sub-Saharan Africa. When it came time to propose his 2003–4 budget, however, President Bush included little more than $2 billion, just slightly more than he had allotted the previous year. No U.S. president has stepped forward to offer a commemorative speech or a transformative gesture that could be considered a sufficient response to AIDS. No president has capitalized on this opportunity to remake the United States as a nation that includes gay and lesbian subjects. No president has been inspired to transform a nation of AIDS corpses into a new vision of the Republic. If not a president, then who?

In the absence of an adequate response to AIDS on the part of the U.S. government, it has fallen to gay men, lesbians, and members of other affected groups to publicly pose the most urgent questions regarding health and homophobia in the AIDS era as well as to propose solutions, all from a marginalized position outside the center of power. In the process AIDS has been rendered public in an unabashedly tactical way. Our official addresses are not delivered by government leaders at major rallies—though the speeches of gay leaders at such occasions effectively mimic and sometimes parody such speeches, deriving power in the process—but rather by ordinary gay and straight citizens in their workplaces, by people with AIDS living from day to day, or by artists working in the street or on the stage. Given the heavy weight, the monumentality, of heterosexist, patriarchal, and homophobic U.S. society, such action is necessarily insurgent. That is, it signals a rising up, a revolution, a rebellion, against civil authority. And its means are those associated with de Certeau's tactic.

Choreography is especially capable of embodying such insurgency because of its essential characteristics: its ability to harness motion, its creative use of gravity, and its potential for darting and evasive quickness. The very solidity and rootedness of the monument can be seen as vulnerable weaknesses, in contrast to the dynamic mobility of choreographic insurgency. Static monumentality stands dumbly as bodily choreography parries around it. Monuments remain silent and static, insurgencies noisily active. Monuments rise from the earth, toweringly, imposingly, fixedly; insurgencies move closely along the earth, stealthily. Monuments conserve power; insurgencies disrupt power. Monuments are made of stone; insurgencies are made of energy and passion. Monuments in the age of AIDS stand cold and mute, as symbols of an uncaring nation, while choreographic insurgencies make the private public and struggle to overcome the stigmas of homo- and AIDS-phobia. The monuments of our time demonstrate indifference, while contemporary choreography activates public space, ritual action, and bold theatrical incursions as ways of teaching the nation what it means to live or die with AIDS.

High Risk Choreography

Choreographic insurgency is perhaps best exemplified in the work of the High Risk Group, a San Francisco–based dance company directed by Rick Darnell. Its very name declares its insurgent function: This is a company committed both to taking physical risks and to declaring openly the status of its members as gay and, physically or metaphorically, HIV positive.[16] (In the lingo of public health a "high-risk group" is one that is particularly vulnerable to a particular disease. For AIDS the high-risk groups have been designated as gay men, intravenous drug users, and, for a brief period in the mid-1980s, Haitians.) Most important, the title of the company poses a loud question to all who encounter it: Faced with the reality of AIDS, what are *you* going to do about it?

Darnell moved to the Bay Area in the mid-1980s and, before being directly affected by AIDS, began to create dances influenced by the aesthetics of the Judson Dance Theatre, the experimental dance movement that, from 1962 to 1964, had signaled the end of first-generation modern dance.[17] (With a bow to western kitsch, Darnell titled his first company Rickey Lynn and the Rangers.) Writing in the gay and lesbian press, the critic Rachel Kaplan praised Darnell for engaging in a dialogue with the historical art

Richard Board of the High Risk Group in Rick Darnell's *Brides of Frankenstein*, 1991. Photo: Robert Bryant.

movements that had preceded him. In particular, she suggested that Judson afforded the possibility of political commentary, which had been suppressed in an era dominated by slick postmodernism.[18] Kaplan aptly described the dialogue between Darnell and Judson as "eating the idiom and spitting it back":

It's exciting to see Darnell in his conscious relationship to dance history—as third generation post modern, he's directly descended from the Judson choreographers who challenged assumptions of dance theater in the '60s, expanding dance possibilities to include pedestrian movement, theatrical gesture, and political commentary.

It's clear Darnell knows his heritage and is aware of the variety of options this inheritance lends him, which is why I say having eaten the idiom, he spits it out at us in new ways. I think this kind of dance is the important dance because it stretches our ideas of what dance is; because it isn't attached to virtuosity but is attached to the formal challenge of exploring what works and what doesn't; because it's about relationships and gender and

communication and how we do and do not do it with one
another; and because it's made by someone under the age
of 30.[19]

In addition to citing Judson, Darnell made clear from his very
first performances at San Francisco's Centerspace, a small studio
tucked alongside Theater Artaud, that he was also interested in
adopting 1980s gay street culture and its insurgent critique of
capitalist society.[20] The dual aesthetic—part Judson, part street—
was dubbed "garage dance" by the critic Ann Powers, and Darnell immediately embraced the label for his own use, reveling
in its subversive associations.[21] In 1992 he told Kaplan, "Garage
is an aesthetic, not an imperative. It's a way of making theater
that's political, of recycling everyday elements into dance. We
take things we find on the streets and use them as props. We
dance on the streets we walk on. This dance is about living and
working in a common, diminishing space."[22] Thus even before
beginning to address AIDS issues in his work, Darnell had
adopted two choreographic tactics with insurgent associations.
Historically, Judson had positioned itself in an insurgent relationship to the monumental modern dance that had preceded it.
Where Martha Graham incorporated grand gestures and technical vocabulary in her dances, the Judsonites pointedly drew
upon mundane, everyday movements, like walking. Where Graham preferred a narrative structure, the Judson group reveled in
the nonlinear and non-narrative. But Darnell had also adopted a
contemporary "garage" aesthetic associated with the insurgent
San Francisco youth culture and the anarchist movement. Within
a year the two aesthetics, fortified in combination, would be put
to political use.

By 1987, the year after the group's San Francisco debut, the atmosphere of AIDS anxiety and fear that pervaded the San Francisco gay community began to have a direct effect on Darnell's
life, and with the death of Craig Marquette, a former teacher
from Bennington who had relocated to San Francisco, Darnell
made a bold and precipitous decision: to change the name of the
company from Rickey Lynn and the Rangers to the High Risk
Group.[23] In a self-published document that is one of many extraordinary histories and manifestoes that the company began to
produce in 1986, Darnell explains:

In 1987, about two years after being called "the Rangers,"
a grim reality began to set in on those closely involved
with the group and our community of punk rockers and
warehouse dwellers. AIDS was taking its toll. After nine
years of raging in the older community the epidemic had
begun to settle in the younger segment of the population,
a segment that until recently had been largely spared.

The death of a close friend and frequent collaborator with the group came as a hard blow. In the wake of
grief, anger, frustration and loss a heartfelt sense of reevaluation led to a complete overhaul of the group. What
had formerly been a laboratory for choreographic work
developed into a vehicle for cultural activism.

A commitment to political content quickly superseded the formal experiments of the company's first two years. Darnell's choreography was already capable of communicating clearly with
regard to issues of gender, sexuality, and class. During long
stretches of the company's history, its members were all men,
and they partnered each other both roughly and intimately,
which reflected a key interest in male-male love.[24] Other accou-
trements, such as visible nipple rings, brightly dyed hair, loose
sweatpants, and sneakers, evoked the aesthetics of the San Francisco youth culture. The signification of these elements as part of
a current, and fundamentally gay, counterculture was evident.
But with Darnell's shift in a self-consciously political direction,
the dancing proved insufficient to communicate the specific new
meanings that Darnell was aiming to explicate. For that, the
changed name of the company and textual incursions in the choreographic work began to play a role, to point the meanings of
the dances strongly in the direction of AIDS.

New Danger, for example, a work created in the late 1980s,
alternated between anger and gentle love as four dancers remained confined behind a chain-link fence, emerging from behind it only to spray-paint words on one another's bodies. Reviewing the performance at 1800 Square Feet, the garage space
that Darnell founded south of Market Street, Kaplan wrote:

The image of the High Risk Group is of young angry gay
men, and that's the image of this dance. Chained to the
fence and each other, leaning on each other for support,
leaping into each other's arms, their actions reminded me

of AIDS, of fear, anger and helplessness. The choreography spoke with a particular rage and tenderness; the dancers spat at the audience from behind the fence or moved into a dance where one blindfolded man relied on another to carry his weight.[25]

To an attuned viewer the gayness of the work was pointed, as was the commentary on life in the age of AIDS. In the final section of this piece, the dancers sprayed the letters *L, O, V,* and *E* on the front of their shirts, then *H, A, T,* and *E* on the backs. They randomly turned back and forth as they approached and retreated from the audience, speaking alternately, "I love you" and "I hate you," as if both love and hate were the same thing—at least where AIDS was concerned.[26] Then they took off their shirts and sprayed the letters *A, I, D,* and *S* in red on their bare chests, directly challenging the audience: "What are you gonna do about it?"

This was fundamentally a rhetorical question, insofar as the audience for High Risk's work was already highly attuned to AIDS issues and, presumably, was at the front lines in the struggle to increase funding for research and AIDS care and to counter the stigma associated with the disease. Audience members had bought tickets to a show by a company called the High Risk Group, after all. And yet the public goading, the presentation of the company as a group of mostly gay men ("a rough mix of gay and straight" was how the company described itself in the program), and the explicit assumption deriving from the company's title, let alone the "AIDS" finale of *New Danger*, that some if not all members were infected with HIV—all these actions served to notify the public that, at High Risk Group performances, the audience could not ignore HIV status. The direct and literal foregrounding of HIV was a radical act in theatrical dance performance, even several years into the official epidemic, especially in light of the company's equally radical performance of gayness and effeminacy, so long proscribed from the U.S. theatrical stage. Within a year Darnell would describe the company as a group of "teachers and performers engaged in cultural/artistic activism as labor . . . we dance about anger, alienation, oppression, injustice and our friends and selves that are dying."[27] The agenda was set, and Darnell was playing it out in unforgiving, relentless choreographic activity.

In 1991 High Risk took its agenda to a more "professional" level when it was invited to create a new piece for the sixth annual Edge Festival at San Francisco's Footwork Studio. High Risk's public goading around issues of AIDS and gayness reached a different type of audience in that work, which was evocatively titled *Falling*. After countless appearances at screenings of experimental video, at downscale AIDS benefits, and at new music clubs, the company had perfected the presentation of activist art outside the theaters where dance and performance are normally presented. By contrast, Footwork offered a relatively upscale atmosphere, although its location in the dusty, low-rent Mission District and its diminutive size (approximately seventy seats) still qualified it as an alternative space.[28] By 1991 High Risk was beginning to enter the mainstream in two other important ways: as a touring ensemble, with gigs in Santa Monica, Chicago, Cleveland, Buffalo, Philadelphia, and San Diego; and as the recipient of private grants.[29] In addition, Darnell brought in high-level—and, notably, female—collaborators for the creation of *Falling:* the filmmaker Greta Snider of the anarchist collective Shred of Dignity and the composer Khris T. Force, a member of Amber Asylum Electronic Chamber Trio.[30] The press release says that this new work was intended to metaphorically examine falling "as a reference from which to deconstruct the decline of the western white male heterocentric power structure." In the printed program Darnell waxes somewhat less ambitious:

FALLING is a metaphor for change that is occurring on a global, regional and personal level. Personally I see this change within the context of an international fight against AIDS both in a reference to current history and the outpouring of response that AIDS has generated. We all want to be free, healthy, live in a home and create unique nurturing relationships. This is an alternative to the american [sic] ideal and sense of family. Yet ironically in the myth of our country's creation there is room for this.[31]

The tone of the note is intimate and surprisingly conciliatory, as if Darnell were feeling a need to acknowledge the depth of response that the country had personally offered him and other people with HIV. But this was not to say that his art had turned less insurgent or less publicly offensive. In fact, quite the opposite. Perhaps the most dramatic demonstration of this was that the prologue

to *Falling* was staged on the cracked, dilapidated street outside Footwork, with five dancers performing a stylized die-in.
The die-in was a concept already perfected by ACT UP as a
highly visual performance capable of communicating, through
the media, the enormous toll and frequency of AIDS deaths in
the United States. Protesters at such venues as the Food and
Drug Administration in Rockville, Maryland, or New York's St.
Patrick's Cathedral would lie down on the street or sidewalk,
and their bodies would be outlined in chalk, leaving the visible
residue of their "deaths." At the premiere of Darnell's *Falling* the
mainstream media were not in attendance—there were no reviews in the daily papers and no coverage on the local nightly
news—but in addition to paid ticket holders and random passersby, Liz Weinberg, a videographer allied with the group, was
present and captured the performance on tape.[32] This was a formal dance that was, simultaneously, a public protest.

Prologue to *Falling*

To the vroom of a passing motorcycle, five men who look and
move like adolescent street kids gather on the sidewalk outside
Footwork and arrange themselves in a ragtag line. Darnell sports
a T-shirt and a black woolen cap. The others wear sweatshirts
with hoods; Clyde Smith's is distinctively striped. One man,
Myles Downes, has his long hair pulled up in a high ponytail.
Jesselito Cocjin Bie sports high-top sneakers. (All the men wear
sneakers of some sort.) Richard Board has cut his hair in a low
mohawk. Standing shoulder to shoulder, the men lean forward
and step off, each at his own pace, like members of a street gang
heading out to do some damage. They are crossing in front of
Footwork's front door.

Quickly, however, it becomes obvious that the five men are not
just walking on by. One man erupts in a brief skip and crumples
to the ground. Without histrionics another collapses beside him.
Two others spring into action, not to resuscitate the fallen but to
outline their bodies with white chalk on the sidewalk. They do

At right: High Risk Group in the prologue to *Falling,* performed on the sidewalk outside Footwork Studio, San Francisco, 1991. Video stills courtesy of
Rick Darnell.

so speedily, as if this fleeting moment cried out to be captured in quasi-durable form before dissolving away. The fifth man watches from Footwork's doorway, standing nonchalantly alongside the members of the audience. When the drawing is complete, the fallen men rise and join the others to cross the doorway yet again. For several minutes the choreography develops as a series of variations on this theme: the group of five traversing the entrance of the theater; one or two men falling to the ground; the remaining men dropping to their hands on the sidewalk to outline the bodies, or to watch from the sidelines, blending in with the audience; and, finally, all regrouping to start again.

At the end of nine passes Darnell speaks for the first time in a quiet drawl. As if to himself, he announces a set of grim statistics: "In about the time it took us to draw these silhouettes, about five more people have died of AIDS on the global level."[33] Without a moment's dramatic pause he then continues flatly, "Let's go back upstairs." As the thirty or so onlookers funnel in through the door, they are forced to step over the outlined and interlocking "bodies" that have been scrawled there, bodies that, not surprisingly, resemble the graffiti figures of the artist Keith Haring. When the door to the studio finally swings shut, it is as if the dead have been left behind, inconsolably, to be kept company only by the automobiles heading noisily down 22nd Street. In the last moments of the videotaped documentation, headlights become visible in the corner of the frame, shining directly and chillingly into the camera's eye. The chalk outlines now speak of a cold hard aloneness.

I describe this prologue to *Falling* in part to honor the meticulous choreography of these garage dancers and in part to attempt to register the powerful cumulative effect of the three-minute die-in. (The prologue serves as an introduction to the formal, forty-minute multimedia piece designed to unfold in the upstairs Footwork studio space.) The die-in is elegiac. The audience watches coolly as the figures fall, but it is impossible not to see in them the bodies of our own dead, our friends and lovers. The falling is executed by real people—five men whom we know or whom, through the dance, we are coming to know; with each collapse a viewer is required to suppress the impulse to offer a hand of assistance. (After all, no one should have to lie in the street.) And yet in each falling we also are confronted by a terse fact: another dead man, a man who once lived but who now is gone. We cannot forget this because of the chalk outline, the visible reminder of a body that once lay, in this exact configuration, inert and unmoving on the cold hard ground. The string of resurrections that accompany the falling are perhaps examples of facile transcendence. They give us false hope. But everything else about the dance—its incessant iterations in contrast to the quotidian walking steps—tells us that this is real. This is what death is like. And as the audience mourns these deaths, militancy becomes an inevitable response.

One thing that forces the audience to consider the reality of this dance of falling, of carefully measured death, is its presentation in a public space. The theater is the place for metaphors, where movement signifies beyond the bodies that produce it. The relative privacy of the performance place, even the small-scale studio, offers a protective intimacy. Once inside the four walls of such a space, we are safe with one another. We are separated from the street. And in the protection of this space—which in this case has been designated a site where gay performance signifying AIDS is welcome—we are free to construct private meanings, to grieve, take solace, be inspired, build community. But the street is the place where real life transpires. Not two blocks from Footwork Studio is the corner of the Mission District most regularly visited by the city's coroners, who regular haul up the bodies of the latest drug overdose or gang-violence victim or AIDS casualty. A mile to the northwest lies the Castro, Bay Area epicenter of the AIDS epidemic, where the bodies of the walking ill—young men turned old before their time—are a constant reminder of the very real corporeal effects of the disease. Scattered around the Mission District are many of the inexpensive apartments where dancers subsist, as well as the studios where they congregate to take class or rehearse. These are also the places where they sweat on each other and care for one another when they become ill. Thus the street in the Mission District where Footwork is located serves as a very different sort of stage from the relatively safe one that exists up just one flight of stairs. This is a place where questions about bodies and AIDS and death are inescapable, played out in full view of the public. And the public view will continue as long as the chalk lines on the sidewalk remain visible.

The crossings of the doorway offer repeated opportunities to contemplate the bodies, the dress, the carriage of the dancers. Freeze-framing the video on one return crossover reveals that each of the performers is displaying a slightly different attitude. This walking is not so much "neutral doing" in the 1960s mode, with deadpan faces and plain gait, as "characterological doing," redolent of high-attitude San Francisco street life of the 1990s. Darnell's eyes are cast downward, his head inclining slightly to his right, his feet dragging a bit. One might catch him lolling down the street just like this—part tough guy, part femme—on a nonperformance day. Smith strides more dynamically, shoulders aiming forward, head tipped back with a touch of defiance. Bie is the most determined-looking of the pack, his shoulders square, a red baseball cap pulled low and backward on his head. As a group, they send two distinct messages: that they are tough and strong, and that they are not constrained by standard "masculinist" notions of what toughness and strength should look like. They are defiantly effeminate.[34]

This challenge to standard notions of how gender should be embodied in movement is demonstrated in the precise contours of the choreography. The five men simply stride along the sidewalk, but then, to punctuate the pivot before the return crossing, or to alter the flow before falling to the ground, they break into skips, hops, low gliding steps, or, in one case, a surprising set of gliding skateboard maneuvers. (On one particular crossing Darnell pogos and shuffle-slides on the bottom of his sneakers.) These moves function as sturdy punctuation to each traveling phrase, but they also take on the appearance of parodic postmodern dancing, a blend of technical vocabulary and mundane everyday perambulation that characterized postmodern movement in the 1970s and early 1980s, before technique returned to postmodern dancing full force. This is to say that the men of the High Risk Group convey a compelling sense of everydayness, even as they perform each crossing of Footwork's door.

The same is true of each collapse to the sidewalk. There is no artifice in the choice of locale. The dirty sidewalk, with its patches of black asphalt and numerous stains of oil and bubble gum, is readily visible as the camera, tight and low, captures Darnell's cheek pressing into the concrete. This is urban reality. The sandaled feet of two audience members are caught in the frame, just inches away. At various points the dancers stand watching alongside the members of the audience, as though simply waiting for the bus. And yet the falls are notably abstract; they are not, after all, like real dying. There is no agony, no dramatization: just a descent to the earth. The impression of these falls, then, fuses the grittiness of photographic reportage with the distanced, illusory quality of such dance forms as ballet. Each fall is both toughly real and porously metaphoric.

These qualities are particularly evident in the outlining of the bodies where they come to rest. The white chalk is wielded very matter-of-factly. In one instance, for example, Downes reaches down with a piece of thick white chalk and begins to outline Darnell's body, starting from the crotch and continuing around a sneakered right foot. Downes is hurrying, pitching forward on one hand for support and executing the task as if he were fulfilling a timed assignment. But once the outline is completed, the body shape quickly enters the realm of the metaphoric, becoming a visible metonym for the statistical recitation that caps the prologue. The outline represents a death—or, more pungently, a murder. In the prologue to *Falling*, then, the epidemic is configured as a series of murders of gay men, on the street, by unknown and unidentified forces. The government is strongly implicated: Is it not the responsibility of the government to protect its citizens, especially in such places as a city street? Thus the enactment of this representation of AIDS deaths on the street is positioned insurgently in relation to the monumentality of government power and control. Why has the government abrogated its protective responsibilities? And if the casualties were not gay, would government response be of a different order?

The choreography of the prologue to *Falling* makes these points with particular clarity insofar as the bodies that are falling (that is, dying) are so palpably real, so physically close, and so like the bodies of the viewers standing just inches away that they cannot be dismissed as mere poetic abstractions. Even after the outlines have been drawn and have been left to the lonely street, they reverberate with the real corporeal presences that had defined these shapes. The vital physicality of the body is reduced to a thin, evanescent outline, to the slimmest evidence of its prior existence. It is no more than a trace. Yet it remains a pungent reminder of a human body, a life. This memorialization is not, however,

monumental. It is not made of stone or metal or any other durable material. It will not exist in a hundred years, maybe not even
in a hundred minutes. Moreover, it stands for no particular person. It does not have a name. It is just white dust, to be scuffed by
passing shoes, stepped over and around by passersby, and
eroded by rain and wind. Thus in its anonymity and in the anti-
materiality of its construction, it serves as a harsh critique of more
durable monuments. Therein lies this choreography's essential
insurgency: It is art with an analytical and critical function.

Aesthetic Activism

My analysis of the prologue to *Falling* has demonstrated how
choreography functions insurgently in the AIDS era. So too with
processions and rituals that mark the passage of the dead, especially when the death can be attributed to government neglect
and societal stigmatization. In fact, the choreographic treatment
of fallen bodies is a key element of insurgent critique, whether
those bodies are only metaphorically or actually biologically
dead. The cool fact of the dead body is perhaps the strongest rhetorical statement that a choreographer can make, and it virtually
always stands in an insurgent relationship to the monumentality
of stolid government power. The presentation of the mute, limp
body is not, however, in and of itself choreographically compelling. In fact, the very inertness of such a body renders it choreographically inept. The tactical efficacy of the dead body does not
derive from giving voice and action to the dead body itself—
which is, after all, beyond stating any claim of its own—but
rather from empowering those who bear the body in public, who
arrange for its display. The choreography of the public political
funeral is an opportunity, then, to transform grief to action,
mourning to militancy. Part shield, part ramrod, the dead body
itself becomes a catalyst to political action. That action then shim-
mers like ripples from a pebble thrown into water, motivating
family and friends, passersby (some of whom may be inconve-
nienced or affronted by the public nature of the funeral), and the
government, against whose monumentality the insurgency is ultimately configured.

On his deathbed the New York AIDS activist Jon Greenberg
stated a last ironic wish to his gathered friends. He did not want

a political funeral, he said: "I want you to burn me in the street and eat my flesh." Thus the stage was set for an activist's funeral of a particularly choreographic kind—reinforced by one of the participants in and planners of the funeral, Jon's younger brother, Neil, an openly HIV-positive choreographer with highly developed skills in the art of bodily action.[35] Neil reports that he was with Jon when he died:

He died July 12, 1993, and it was a huge experience for me to have to watch him die. To be there with someone who looks like me a little and who is dying of this disease. I have other siblings who I love as much as I loved Jon but I can't think of another death that could affect me the way this death has. It was like my own mortality rushing in on me.[36]

From his mourning for his brother, intensified by what Richard Staten has called "auto-mourning" and Peggy Phelan has termed "anticipatory mourning," Neil became a prominent participant in his activist brother's political funeral. Jon's coffin was taken in a procession from the First Avenue subway stop in the East Village, near where Jon lived, to Tompkins Square Park where the performance artist John Kelly sang and several speakers delivered eulogies.[37] In a videotape aired on New York City's AIDS Community Television, the most prominent of the eulogies is offered by Neil, who stands near his brother's open casket—a brother whose profile is, indeed, remarkably similar to Neil's—and speaks of the need to take responsibility for one's life:

He wanted to offer us the freedom found in acceptance and also the personal empowerment found in acceptance. He believed in being the sole person responsible for his own actions and deeds and not giving up that responsibility to anybody. This doesn't mean he refused help from people, but that he accepted the responsibility of asking for help. Jon found the joy in taking responsibility for himself. He said he did not want his life and death to be about George Bush or Bill Clinton or me or you. His life is. His death is. He took responsibility for his life.[38]

The view of the video camera captures the two faces, Neil's in vivid close-up, Jon's lying inert, eyes closed, in the casket that rests at Neil's elbow.[39] The scene is green and pleasant, the trees of the park in full leaf protectively shading the casket and a small gathering of friends. Although the emotion of the event is evident in the slight quiver of Neil's jaw as he speaks, the outward signs of the occasion are more picnic than funeral. Neil is wearing shorts. His haircut is clipped, young, and fresh. He sports a gold hoop in one ear. And yet the occasion also bears an unmistakable formality. Neil is speaking from a script into a microphone. His words are measured, the pacing rehearsed. The presence of the video camera so close to the speaker and to the casket marks this as an occasion designed for the media. At frequent intervals a still photographer darts into the frame, shooting directly at Jon's corpse. There is a stillness around the casket, a sense of reverence for Jon's life and a growing pall at the reality of his death. His friends and family are mourning. Yet ultimately, the occasion serves as a catalyst for both mourning and militancy. The funeral is a site where insurgency festers and where the tactical resistance of the marginalized other is brought into direct conflict with the strategic response of government power and societal status quo.

The tactical insurgency of this funeral is volatilized in part by its differentiation from the ceremonies of strategic monumentality epitomized by the funeral of President John F. Kennedy, perhaps the best-known example of ritual stolidity and symbolic strategy in the latter half of the twentieth century. As had the bodies of other presidents before him, Kennedy's lay in state in the Capitol Rotunda, at the symbolic center of the American polity. Mourners filed past the closed casket in silence, kept at a measured distance by an attentive military honor guard in crisp uniforms. Each and every symbol was calculated to produce the sense that Kennedy was resting at the font of government power. His body, for those few days, constituted the center of the strategic universe. Jon Greenberg's body, by contrast, can be seen in the videotape lying in state in Tompkins Square Park, at the symbolic center of the tactical gay and transgender universe. (The park, located in the East Village, is the site of the annual Wigstock Festival, a public drag show and rally. It is also associated with homeless encampments and illicit drug use. Hence, it is configured quite literally as the ultimate marginal space.) Although the occasion of Jon's funeral has a reverential stillness about it, the eulogists, photographers, and friends stand deviantly close to the dead body. They touch the wooden casket. They lean in close by Jon's face. They pass papers over his boxed torso. As she finishes reading each page of text, one speaker discards the sheets of paper by passing them to a friend on the other side of the coffin, touching the wood as she does so in a gesture one could read as familiarity or tenderness. Perhaps most significantly, no enclosure and no guards protect the body. It lies before the public as an unmediated object. The lid is open to make his dead face visible and directly accessible, and the camera is set up so as to capture the face in every shot. The tactical funeral, then, is choreographed as a public event, unguarded and informal, that spills over traditional boundaries, whereas the strategic funeral is shielded by enclosures (even as it is carefully disseminated to the public) and is bounded by guards and barricades. The tactical funeral is insurgent, whereas the strategic funeral is monumental.[40]

The final eulogy at Jon's funeral is read by a woman who, from beside Jon's bier, makes what is perhaps the most significant rhetorical maneuver of the Tompkins Square funeral. She reconfigures the notion of "status"—a designation generally associated with testing positive or negative for the HIV virus—as a category that separates gays and lesbians from heterosexual society: *status* as a term of identification based on sexuality.[41] Implicitly, she suggests that all gays and lesbians are infected, that all of us are "positive," that insofar as any in the gay and lesbian community are still suffering, or still seroconverting, we all are suffering and seroconverting. In this she indicts the media and the government for creating a false impression that the worst is over and that the need for activism is past. Don't listen, she says:

No matter what the media or government may want you to believe, AIDS is not receding in the gay community. Deaths are not declining. New infections are still occurring at an unacceptable rate. No matter what your HIV status is, if your status is gay or lesbian, it is our job to save our community from extinction, by whatever means is required of us. That's what Jon has been doing for the past five years.[42]

With this stirring call to action, marked by physical energy and gestural force from the speaker, the video of the funeral cuts to the procession.[43] The fanciful blue casket is now closed, a spray of flowers strewn across its lid. Six men raise it up on their

Mourners carrying Jon Greenberg's casket through the streets of the East Village, New York, 16 July 1993. Neil Greenberg is in a plaid shirt at right. Photo: © 1993 Donna Binder/Impact Visuals.

shoulders, using a metal rail that runs its length. At the front left corner stands Neil, who, like the others, expends visible effort to keep the casket aloft. The six pallbearers carry the casket out into the street, where a full-scale procession forms. On the right of the casket march two female drummers, one playing a Middle Eastern hourglass-shaped oud, the other beating on a larger frame drum. Just a few feet behind, a long-haired man holds aloft a photograph of Jon, a visual replica of him sitting relaxed and with a pleasant expression. The photo is decorated with flowers. The procession moves out into the middle of the street, in full view of passersby, shopkeepers, the public, the nation. At the intersections marchers join hands to stop traffic, the marchers in the rear peeling off to join the marchers at the front end of the line as the casket passes by. Their bodies serve as a wall of protection but a wall with manifold perforations through which to view the casket. The woman who earlier had delivered the eloquent eulogy now darts from front to back, monitoring points of interface with the crowd. She looks wary, concerned. Behind the casket march about two dozen participants, some walking alone,

Jon Greenberg's photo on display in the funeral procession. Photo: © 1993 Donna Binder/Impact Visuals.

trudging, eyes downcast, others with their arms twined about one another, caught in their own worlds of grief and solace. All are silent.

In many ways the procession of Jon's body now closely resembles the passage of Kennedy's caisson through the streets of Washington, D.C., and it thus demands societal validation. No one at Jon's funeral provides running commentary for millions of television viewers, no politicians march with bowed heads, no soldiers offer protection, no silent vigils are held by hundreds of thousands of onlookers. Yet the procession, announced by the simple noise of a drum, calls the public to solemn order. The participants gather protectively around and to the sides of the casket, guarding it now with the same alacrity with which they had earlier laid it open and accessible. The grief-stricken brother appears at the head of the procession, leading the pallbearers. He is cutting a swath down the street, daring anyone to stop him. Instructions pass up and down the line of march, lending a remarkable orderliness to the procession, even when blocking traffic at intersections. The participants are serving as their own police, their own uniformed soldiers.

But a kind of dare is implicit in this procession. The marchers are tactically co-opting strategic maneuvers associated with public pomp, in part as a means toward validating and empowering the procession—and of validating and empowering Jon's memory. The procession becomes a distinctly gay performance. The participants do not march in step. Rather, they loll at their own pace. They do not keep their distance from one another, like soldiers, but embrace like lovers—man with man, woman with woman. They also are not bound by particular partners but thread in and out of comforting liaisons. Their clothes are not black and formal but rather stylish, skimpy, colorful, sexy. While overridingly serious, some participants also smile and laugh, as if to subvert the expected parameters of mourning. The camera captures both soberness and rebellion, grief and spontaneity. Thus the procession is analogous to the monumental funeral procession but only in its broad outlines. The particulars of this procession are in every way deviant and insurgent.

The procession proceeds without a permit and without advance warning.[44] It is irregular, unwanted, even. These gay and lesbian bodies are determinedly invading spaces where they are not welcome, bearing an AIDS-infected body in a way that flouts laws pertaining to public health. Onlookers, who are busily tending their shops or going about their errands, are interrupted by the sight and—yes—the fear of the procession. Within touching distance of the corpse, fears of tainted body fluids and proscribed sexual practices come to the fore. The procession is, in that sense, a public health menace, transgressing the civil codes that separate the living from the dead, the healthy from the infected. The very danger that it poses calls for attentive response. Moreover, the funeral is an inconvenience, a problem, an aberration. It cannot be ignored. Ultimately, this is the power of death, and the power of a body—particularly an AIDS-infected body.

It is also the insurgent force of a political procession organized by the marginal as opposed to the empowered. Throughout the post-Stonewall era the silent candlelight march has afforded gays and lesbians the opportunity of public solidarity in a context of mourning. Such marches have served as collective responses to key homophobic events—such as the signing of anti-gay legislation—and have also catalyzed the enormous grief attendant upon AIDS deaths. These marches, whether in New

York, Washington, or San Francisco, follow a common arc. The participants gather at a rally site at dusk, tapping into a common sense of solidarity. As the sun goes down, a flame is passed from group to group and candles are lit. (Sometimes candles are provided; for more impromptu occasions participants bring their own candles as well as plastic cups to keep their flames from blowing out and to protect their hands from hot wax.) In Washington, D.C., such a memorial march might extend from the National Mall to the Lincoln Memorial, which requires prior permission from the National Park Service and city authorities. The process of gaining permission could be said to make such events less insurgent than they might otherwise be; to ask for the right to protest is to acquiesce in advance to government power and control. Yet the simple fact of gathering on the Mall, of taking over the streets of Washington, of completing the journey at such a resonant site as the steps of the Lincoln Memorial at twilight, with candlelight shining off the reflecting pool, is extraordinarily empowering for the marchers. This is true, in part, because of the sense that, as a group, the marchers are determinedly invading spaces where they are not supposed to be—or at least not as openly gay men and women. But also, as we stride down the street, our arms around our gay lovers and friends, kissing, laughing, and enjoying ourselves, we are subverting established protocols even as we mourn. When we mourn death by AIDS in public spaces, we are visible as homosexuals and as AIDS-infected bodies. Thus the marchers in the candlelight march, or the participants in Jon Greenberg's political funeral, are marked as AIDS infected, as physically weak and enervated, and yet, as a group, we know we are large, strong, even powerful. That an AIDS-infected dead body should possess any power at all seems a conundrum. Jon Greenberg, for example, is dead, which places him beyond efficacy, beyond power. Yet his survivors can fashion the very fear of him and of his disease as a tactic, to place demands upon a seemingly uncaring society and to unsettle the foundations of heterosexist monumentality.

The funeral procession serves a number of additional functions: For the participants, it constitutes a demand for their grief and loss to be taken seriously and to be respected. Few would dare taunt a marcher in a funeral procession. This is a sacred journey. If abjection is ever ennobled, it is at such moments as this. The procession also represents the (re)affirmation of emboldened activism: This grief will not be borne alone or in secret. It will be paraded down the street. For random onlookers the procession serves notice of the power of this grief and of the activist anger that attends it. Let this not be taken for granted. Mourning makes for powerful militancy. The procession is, then, a significant point of interface between those who mourn the effects of AIDS and those who, but for this public exchange, might never be touched by it. The dignity of the mourners becomes a resonant and lasting image for those who see it. The position of the mourners is elevated in the process.

The procession is also aesthetically beautiful. The sight of this large periwinkle box's being carried down the center of the boulevard is striking on its own terms. The shape of it, the color, the apparent weight, the gravity of it—all these things produce their aesthetic effects. And then there is the pulse of the drum, the rhythmic walking, the unhurried pace. These things alone offer a strange peace. And then there are the marchers themselves and the choreography of their passage through the street: the knot of men and women, some walking in unison, others stepping to their own internal rhythms; the band of black fabric tied around one arm; the color and design of the frame that decorates the photo of the handsome young man; and, finally, the paper cut-out shapes of the marchers who grasp hands at the traffic intersections, their bodies linked and aestheticized in the process. The funeral is an aesthetic act through which the political can be read. It is, above all, insurgent.[45]

Mall Dance

Actions conducted in public spaces by people who have been rendered marginal or abject are necessarily insurgent, which is why the unfurling of the NAMES Project AIDS Quilt ranks as one of the great choreographic insurgencies of our time. The abjection of the lives memorialized in the quilt is made explicit in a variety of ways, ranging from male-male declarations of love inscribed on the panels to the signifying appearance of the unfurlers themselves, many of them gay men and lesbians who, through their dress, body language, and reverence for the quilt panels, publicly perform their own abjection. Moreover, the quilt is a site for abject grief, for mourning lives that, by the terms of mainstream society, are not worth much. As Michael Moon might note, the quilt's fabric panels are elaborately and erotically embroidered with expressions of desire constructed from the "rags" or leavings of lives cut short; the survivors, by creating and displaying these fetishes, actively conserve and reexperience their erotic connection to their dead loved ones. As a ceremony intended to facilitate grieving on a mass scale, the unfurling reveals a portable graveyard attended by legions of "emotional support" volunteers; it is a site for public mourning. The unfurling ceremony that inaugurates most displays of the quilt is an AIDS dance, choreographically calculated to foment activism around AIDS.

It is Friday, 11 October 1996, 8 A.M. and large groups of white-clad performers are preparing to unfurl the Names Project AIDS Quilt on the National Mall. I am here to witness the event as part of my book project, as a participant-observer. But I am also here to pay homage to dead friends and to the late lover of my mate, Peter. Just as it was for the inaugural display in 1987, the Mall has been prepared in advance by paid and volunteer NAMES Project staff members, who have laid out wide runners of black plastic in a grid pattern to receive the large, twenty-four-square-foot sections of quilt. This bold template extends nearly a mile, from the base of the Washington Monument to the foot of the Capitol, transected at several points by busy roadways. Every few blocks on the north side of the Mall, a large gleaming white tent hovers at the perimeter, with signs identifying these as sites where "information" or "souvenirs" may be found. On the south side stand the volunteer tents, where readers, unfurlers, and captains check in, pour themselves free cups of coffee, eat a doughnut breakfast (Dunkin' Donuts is a sponsor), and stop to rest and chat. The air is very cold, about forty degrees. As the sun rises higher in the sky, it sends beams of light scattering across the open Mall and toward the Washington Monument. Now and then the sun moves behind a cloud, shrouding the scene in half-darkness.

The air seems charged with expectation. One organizer is calling directions into a megaphone, checking to make sure that every row of the quilt is matched with a team and a captain to guide that team. This is Youth Day, and most of the participants appear to be teenagers or their adult chaperones. Directly in front of me, a group of ten is forming: four adults and six teens. They are gathered at the sidelines, off to the side of the quilt, holding hands in a circle. Their heads are bowed, and it appears that they are praying. A white middle-aged woman, also wearing white, stands next to me and pleasantly initiates a conversation. "These are my kids," she says. "I'm so proud of them. They're only thirteen [years old]." I ask where they are from. "Drew Freeman Middle School in Prince George's County, Maryland," she replies. Subtly pointing, she draws my attention to an African American girl in the group who recently lost someone she knew to AIDS; her mother has joined the unfurling team with her.

I pursue the conversation with the woman from Freeman Middle School and learn that she is a teacher at the school, a health educator, as well as a member of the AIDS Education Board of the state of Maryland. She's been here on the Mall with her young charges since 6 A.M., preparing for this moment. As she watches the group directly in front of us, heads bowed, she says, "I told them they'd get me in trouble if they prayed, but they wanted to, so I said go ahead." The complexity of this communication is evident: These teenagers could be praying for the souls of the dead or for themselves that they not become infected. Whichever is the case, their spiritual communication creates an awkward tension on the quilt and on the Mall. Likewise with their interaction with NAMES Project staff. The captain for their team is someone they have just met: Juan, from Ft. Lauderdale, Florida, whose short haircut, mustache, and body language signify as gay. I ask whether the teacher has met any resistance to involving the kids in this project. No, she says. "But I've been doing this a long time, so I know better than to mention the word *homosexuality*. If you ask any of my kids, they're going to say, This is not a gay disease." Silently, I note the irony here: that the majority of the panels that these teenagers will be unfurling today are indeed those of gay men, and that Juan, their appointed leader, is a gay man too, and that here on the Mall gay men and lesbians are milling about on all sides. That her kids would deny the commonly held assumption that AIDS is a gay disease could be conceived as a positive breakthrough. (After all, this *is* what AIDS activists have been working for, isn't it?) Yet it is also a cruel travesty that the word *homosexuality* cannot be spoken in relation to the quilt, which was founded by gay men and memorializes so

The unfurling ceremony for the NAMES Project AIDS Quilt on the National Mall, Washington, D.C., October 1996. Photo: Paul Margolis, © 1996, 2001 The NAMES Project Foundation.

many gay men. Is gayness a secret that we must keep from their parents in order to invite children's participation?

A voice over the loudspeaker announces that the unfurling ceremony is about to commence. At this signal groups of eight begin forming circles around the folded sections of the quilt, each of which is situated in a space in the black plastic grid. Half the groups begin on the side where Peter and I are standing (the south side), with the other half beginning on the other (north) side. Far and near groups will cross and finish on sides opposite from where they began. The black plastic grid offers four rectangular openings from one side of the Mall to the other, each large enough to frame two quilt panels, each twenty-four square feet. Hence eight quilt sections are laid out like large folded flags for each group to unfurl as they progress across the quilt. The members of the group nearest me grasp hands, heads bowed, waiting for the first speaker to read the names of the dead.

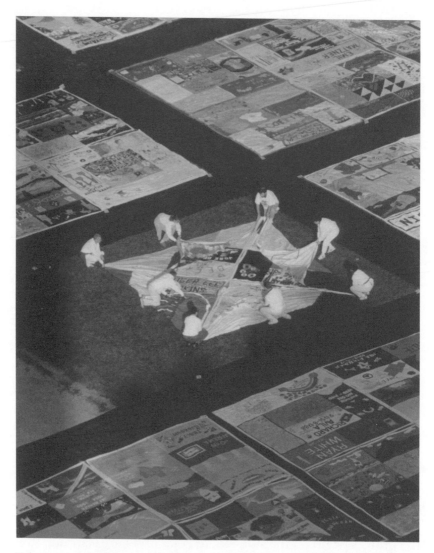

Volunteers unfolding a section of the NAMES Project AIDS Quilt on the National Mall, Washington, D.C., October 1996. Photo: Paul Margolis, © 1996, 2001 The NAMES Project Foundation.

The choreography involves alternate members of the group kneeling in to unfurl "petals" of the quilt—four layers of petals in all.[46] They reach down to pull back a corner of the fabric, then wait for the other group to do the same with the next layer. When the entire twenty-four-foot-square section is laid open, in a large diamond pattern, the unfurlers stand up and billow the fabric upward, over their heads. Simultaneously, they rotate the entire expanse a quarter turn so that the diamond shape fits the square in the grid pattern that is waiting to receive it.

The choreography is unabashedly pedestrian. As the group proceeds across the grid, opening panels in succession, some unfurlers remove their sneakers to avoid walking on the fabric, then put them back on again as they retreat. Onlookers run on to the grid to hold down the clear plastic that protects the quilt from the damp grass. Having laid down a section of the quilt, several unfurlers crouch and fuss with it a bit, tidying it into its location. Standing again, they walk to the next folded quilt section, grasping hands as they go, as if to participate in a form of communal protection. Their walk follows the pattern of a wide arc, the eight members of the team forming a standing circle around the next folded quilt section. The simple choreography consists of a combination of unfolding, billowing, and walking along curving pathways from one space in the grid to another. The pattern repeats eight times.

As the process continues across the breadth of the grid, the performers seem to slow down, to ease into their actions. My mate, Peter, standing by my side, observes, "They're kind of getting it now. It's working in synergy." Having completed the unfurling of all eight quilt sections in their row, the performers filter off the edges of the quilt to join hands at the perimeter. As they do this, they invite onlookers to join them. We grasp hands with the group on our side. Now the "circle" surrounds the entire expanse of fabric. This is a satisfying moment. Simple. Quiet. Contemplative. Communal. A long moment of silence offers the opportunity to gaze out on the mile-long sea of quilt and to absorb the symbolism of this danced action.

Framing a Dance

The physical location of the Mall, extending from the Capitol grounds to Fourteenth Street between Constitution and Independence avenues, forms a crucial context for the meaning-making activity of the quilt. Imagine, for example, that the unfurling were to take place in a Kansas wheat field. No doubt, that locale would strengthen the associations with the American quilting tradition and heartland Protestantism. At the same time an un-furling ceremony positioned on the docks at the terminus of Christopher Street at the Hudson River in New York City would reinforce the signification of the quilt as a gay art project, the docks being well-known sites of gay sexual assignation. But the National Mall, which extends as a formal boulevard between the Capitol and the Washington Monument, with the White House forming a narrow triangular relationship from its position slightly to the side, affords a more politicized rendering of the ceremony. The positioning of the unfurling at this site, along the base of a symbolic triangle, places the quilt in view of the nation's president, its legislators, and (rhetorically, at least) its founder and first president. The quilt display, while attracting crowds estimated to be as large as two million people, is acti-vated by its relationship to these symbolic viewers. The spectacle is heightened by its construction as a form of speech, the quilt panels fashioned as letters meant to be intercepted and read, as statements about love and compassion for people who are living with, or who have died of, AIDS. The codes and contexts by which these forms of symbolic speech will be interpreted are in-tegral to the history and location of the Mall.

In order to gather the full effect of the Mall as a site for the quilt display, it is essential to understand the location's gradual transformation from lush perspective on the winding Potomac River to symbolic gathering place. As the architectural historian Richard Wilson has written: "Out of what seemed an unkempt gardenesque park with little particular symbolic value, the Mall emerged to become the locus of American secular religion."[47] How did this happen? And what transformative process did the Mall undergo?

The city of Washington, D.C., was laid out in the late eigh-teenth century by the French engineer Maj. Pierre Charles L'Enfant, who drew upon the principles of French baroque de-sign to capitalize on the visibility of the site—it could be seen from miles around—and on the formalizing properties of a "grand avenue" that, like the one at Versailles, would reinforce the importance of this focal government building.[48] Until 1874, however, the area extending from the Capitol grounds to the

Potomac was not developed as L'Enfant had intended. Instead, it was divided into a series of modest gardens, each plot administered by a different congressional body—which, not surprisingly, resulted in a hodgepodge of landscaping styles. Complicating the jumble was a railroad crossing at Sixth Street, providing right-of-way to the Baltimore and Potomac Railroad.[49] In 1871 the Architect to the Capitol, Edward Clark—a presidential appointee—wrote in his annual report that the current development of the Mall was unacceptable and that an overarching plan for the gardens was desperately needed. In 1874 Frederick Law Olmsted Sr., the leading landscape architect of the day, was commissioned to propose a design, which he quickly accomplished.

   In line with his other large-scale civic projects, such as Central Park in New York City, Olmsted conceived of the grounds in "picturesque" fashion, configuring a series of gently curving oval pathways in a symmetrical formation to set off the grave importance of the Capitol—while cajoling it gently into a relationship with nature.[50] The aesthetic was essentially pastoral. Caught in a bureaucratic tangle, however, the plan languished, to be revitalized (in altered form) three decades later by Olmsted's son, Frederick Law Olmsted Jr., who delivered a rousing spseech on its urgency to the American Institute of Architects in 1900. In the younger Olmsted's view, not only was his father's landscape design ideally suited to the location, but it could be further strengthened by regulating the relationship among the buildings on the site as well. He was particularly convincing to his listeners on the subject of the treatment of the axis between the Capitol and the Washington Monument:

When I speak of the importance of treating the Mall in such a way as to relate strongly and visibly to the Capitol, I do not mean merely, or necessarily that a straight road should be slashed down the middle of it. . . . A different and more agreeable treatment would be a sort of compound "boulevard," marked by several parallel rows of trees with several pavements and turf strips. Such an avenue was that of the Champs Elysées. . . . The axis of the Capitol should neither be ignored by the use of a wiggling road and confused informal planning, nor

should it be marked by a mere commonplace boulevard,
but by an impressively broad and simple space of turf,
with strong flanking masses of foliage and architecture
and shaded driveways.[51]

Thus under the guise of establishing a plan that would conform to the informal, natural, accessible aesthetics of landscape
design promulgated by his father, Olmsted Sr.—a founder of the
City Beautiful movement[52]—Olmsted Jr. successfully convinced
his influential audience of the need for a measure of formality, a
wide boulevard, an unencumbered axis between the monument
to George Washington, symbolic fountainhead of the American
polity, and the seat of government where the work of the legisla-
ture proceeds. As the historian David Streatfield points out, the
irony here is that the models for this type of boulevard are pecu-
liarly royal—Louis XIV's great summer palace at Versailles and
"the avenues created during the late seventeenth century as
approaches to English countryhouses"—which is to say that
L'Enfant's plan had come full circle, ultimately winning the
day.[53] Olmsted Jr. and his partners in the successful McMillan
Plan—which would transform the Mall over the next five
decades—intended this portion of the Mall to serve as a great
populist open meadow, along the lines of Central Park. But in
fact they had duplicated the baroque formality of absolutist
France and England.[54]

One has to wonder what the designers of the Mall, from
L'Enfant to Olmsted, would think of this grand location's being
used as a gathering place for political protest, the use for which it
is now most famous. The historian Wilson finds a delicious irony
in the early landscapers' paper-and-pen renderings of the Mall,
"populated with well dressed, white citizens, properly subservi-
ent to the memorials and spaces. By visiting this place some ritual of patriotism ostensibly would be accomplished. Could those
responsible for the Mall have imagined demonstrations there by
the Ku Klux Klan, impoverished farmers, civil rights activists, or
gay rights groups?"[55] But regardless of their intended use, the
designs of absolutist Europe turned out to be especially conge-
nial as gathering places for protest, visible not only to the political elite but to the cameras of the Fourth Estate as well. This has

been true since the initial stirrings of political protest at this site. From the first mass march on Washington, D.C.—in 1894, courtesy of a ragtag group of grassroots monetary reformers known as Coxey's Army—through the famous civil rights movement's March on Washington of 1963 to the National March on Washington for Lesbian and Gay Rights of 1987 (at which the quilt made its debut), the grassy Mall has served as a place for citizens of the American Republic to gather to press their elected representatives to answer their concerns.[56]

The Creation of an AIDS Public Sphere

The notion that a city might transform itself into a site for the performance of grand-scale political theater—and, by extension, into a catalyst for the rise of a public sphere—is supported by the unfurling of the NAMES Project AIDS Quilt. A model for this analytical approach is offered by the literary theorist and historian Paula R. Backscheider in her book *Spectacular Politics: Theatrical Power and Mass Culture in Early Modern England* (1993). Backscheider's theory of state symbols, when applied to the performance of the quilt's unfurling, provides a compelling demonstration of the political efficacy of dancing, and it supports the notion that dance does not merely reflect history but rather *produces* it.

The salient portion of Backscheider's book focuses on the Restoration, that is, on Charles II's London—which would be irrelevant to my project were it not for the author's trenchant analysis of Charles's marshaling of political symbols. Charles was a master at orchestrating such symbols and at situating them in an effective array about the city of London, a preoccupation that Backscheider ascribes to Charles's early life experience: His father, Charles I, had made the mistake of paying insufficient attention to spectacle. The son, who had hidden in a tree as his father was carried off and killed, had no intention of repeating the error. Thus upon being invited back to take the throne, he devised a plan to discredit Cromwell's Commonwealth by staging—with gruesome theatricality—the desecration of Cromwell's body. Charles accomplished this by skewering its parts on poles around the city. The effects of such a desecration are theorized by Foucault, whose *Discipline and Punish* Backscheider quotes in brief: "The extreme point of penal justice . . . was the infinite segmentation of the body of the regicide: a manifestation of the strongest power over the body of the greatest criminal, whose total destruction made the crime explode into its truth."[57] A brilliant strategist, Charles II deployed the most potent symbol imaginable to demonstrate his mastery over the man who had killed his father: the dismemberment and display of the perpetrator's body. But this was only the first of Charles's symbolic acts. Backscheider highlights his staging of the reinstatement of the monarchy in solemn pageantry, as well as the production of theatrical satires—penned by Restoration playwrights under Charles's patronage—which subjected Cromwell and his regime to ridicule. Both strategies proved effective in reestablishing the monarchy. Political theater, then, whether presented on the streets of the city or on the stages of London-town, served as a key support for political power.

The October 1996 Washington weekend, which revolved around the unfurling of the AIDS quilt, offers a comparable nexus of symbols. I propose that these symbols be read, much as Backscheider has done, with an eye to their historical and cultural context. I have already discussed the potency of the Mall as a site signifying absolute power, with protest at such a site taking on a heightened valence. But many other symbols also come into play in the unfurling, most of them so obvious as to elude notice.

To begin with the most obvious of all, the unfurlers are charged with the laying out of a massive *quilt,* a symbol of mother love, a homespun creation signifying family, nurturance, and warmth. Significantly, the quilt places the person who has died of AIDS in a genealogy—he is born of a mother—which is to position him within a family tree (whether biological or chosen) in defiance of the message of the gay-hating society, which tells him he has been cast outside it. (One panel, for Dave Gass, actually outlines an entire family tree, dating to 1589 and ending in 1992, the year of his death. This is a resonant affirmation of his importance to the family unit.) The effect, from a theoretical as well as practical standpoint, is extremely powerful. Any person who is commemorated in a quilt panel is rendered not fully abject. He becomes a citizen, a constituent. He is not an absence but a presence. To quote Judith Butler's phrase, he is a body that matters.

A large nexus of ancillary symbols supports this transformation. The clothing of the unfurlers is white, a symbol of purity that collides with the societal signification of gayness as immoral, evil, degraded. Again, through the symbol of whiteness, abjection is rendered not fully abject. The ceremony being enacted at the unfurling is somber and funereal, in the great tradition of military or political ceremony. The panels of the quilt are stored in a manner that evokes the triangular folds of the American flag when it is lifted off a veteran's casket. The reading of the names of the dead, often by celebrities or highly respected people, lends gravity to the occasion. The very cooperativeness of the quilt, that it is made up of discrete units that, only when sewn together, create a stunning spectacle, speaks of support and complementarity. The slow walk, the carrying of the fabric, the deliberateness of the actions—all these signify respect for those who have died. Again, in the unfurling, abjection is rendered not fully abject.

The theoretical effect of the manipulation of these symbols turns out to be exactly the converse of the "silent speaking" that characterizes many AIDS dances. Here, abjection is announced, overtly signified, rendered public, flying in the face of prevailing societal norms that call for privacy. The theatrical AIDS dance often seeks to keep its meanings at least partially obscure. The nontheatrical AIDS dance strives for the reverse. The difference between these two treatments of abjection is significant, for the very act of *announcing* abjection serves to transform the abject person into a kind of subject, however unstable. Thus newspapers clamor to tell the stories of the dead. The unfurlers, panel makers, and readers—all the "actors" of the ceremony—are emboldened to face their government and demand action. Abjection is foregrounded by the performance of the quilt, but then it is quickly converted into a demand for the rights of subject citizens.

This demand, I want to suggest, signals the rise of a newly configured public, a public organized to stand before its government and demand accountability in relation to direct care, research funding, and basic civil rights. The riots that erupted after a police action at the Stonewall bar in New York City in 1969 have long been viewed as marking the advent of a modern gay and lesbian liberation movement. Stonewall made it possible for gays and lesbians to reveal their sexual orientations publicly, to "come out of the closet," to surmount shame with celebration. As a result of Stonewall, a gay and lesbian citizenry identified itself. I want to argue that yet another (overlapping) citizenry has now formed, in part through the symbolic valence of the AIDS quilt. Gay men, lesbians, parents, and family and friends of people with AIDS—all these citizens are standing together to demand equal rights and equal protection for people who are afflicted with HIV. Thus the AIDS quilt functions as a central symbol in a political movement not only to "regularize" homosexuality, to humanize gays and lesbians, to restore homosexuals from a position at the margins to a position at the center, but also, crucially, to bring government and public attention to bear on a health crisis of enormous proportions. I believe, then, that the quilt marks the advent of what could be called, after Jürgen Habermas, an "AIDS public sphere"—that is, a constituency marked by its overriding concern with the AIDS epidemic.

I must note that my framing of the notion of an AIDS public sphere is based upon, but decidedly different from, that proposed by the German sociologist. Habermas's theory—contained in his book the *Structural Transformation of the Public Sphere: An Inquiry into a Category of Bourgeois Society* (1991)—is laid out within the context of an analysis of bourgeois English, French, and German social classes in the late eighteenth century. In his configuration the central precondition for the rise of this sphere was a developing market economy, through which the emerging bourgeoisie was to take a mediating position between the absolutist bureaucracy and "the people." If the masses in the eighteenth century held little or no power and had not even the possibility of participating in government discourse, the new bourgeoisie—constituted as a public sphere—not only took part in that discourse but became a monitoring agent through which the government hierarchy was informed of the people's will. Habermas understands this political function not as an isolated entity but as intertwined with the rise of popular literature and political journalism—channels for public reaction, critique, and discourse. According to Habermas, these public spheres began to dissolve by the turn of the twentieth century with the rise of social welfare democracies, unrestricted public discourse having given way to public relations and other capitalist modes for channeling the business interests of popular consumer culture.

Habermas's concept of the public sphere is especially revelatory when applied to the performing AIDS project: Why perform AIDS? Why protest? Why mourn in a visible communal space as part of a public spectacle? Why make dances about AIDS that will be seen in national theaters? In other words, how do these activities embody the activity of a public that demands government response? The answers to these questions become clear in light of the vacuum created by government indifference in the AIDS era. At a time of crisis the performance of corporeality and the enactment of choreography become the most effective means available for a new public to assert itself and to state its demands for action and change. Thus the coming together of abjection, eros, and mourning, which are characteristic of virtually all dances about AIDS, serve to accomplish crucial cultural work, most centrally by creating a new public sphere.

Backscheider provides further support for the application of Habermas's theory to the performance of AIDS on the Mall, when she characterizes the openness with which the audience for late eighteenth-century gothic drama expressed its emotions and critiques, thereby personifying Habermas's notion of "public opinion": "As Habermas says, a public sphere had developed in which private people cast themselves as a 'forum' and came together to form a public ready to compel public authority to legitimate itself before 'public opinion.'"[58]

The stated purpose of the quilt is exactly that, to compel government authorities to support funding for AIDS research and AIDS care, in compliance with the weight of public opinion. Truly, then, the embodied activity of the unfurling of the quilt signifies a rise in public discourse, precisely the central condition of Habermas's public sphere.

Corporeal Fetishes and Mourning

What, then, is the power of the quilt's unfurling for those who take part? What does it mean for the people who perform it, for

those who see it, for those who write about it? On the second day
of the 1996 quilt event, I watched as a group of students from
Goucher College in Towson, Maryland, learned and performed
the choreography of the unfurling under the direction of Bob
Pine, quilt display coordinator for the Washington, D.C., chapter
of the NAMES Project. The preparations involved carrying the
folded quilt sections from storage out onto the Mall. Watching
people tug folded quilt sections into position is like watching
pallbearers heave limp bodies out to the cemetery. The quilt is
heavy, unwieldy, it resists their efforts. They do this in groups of
four. I notice that the groups are quite merry as they approach
the place where they are to pick up the quilt, but as they come
back with the fabric in their arms, they have turned serious.
Later I do this myself, with some of the Goucher students, and I
notice how difficult it is to hold on to the quilt. It resists our
grasp. In the sequence of actions there is a particularly graphic
moment when the handlers inside the storage tent heave the
quilt "bodies" up to be received. In the remarkable transubstan-
tiation of this ceremony, the fetishistic quilt panels are transformed into the flesh and bone of dead bodies, the bodies of
people we love. We carry the burden of their corpses out onto
the Mall, where we touch them, view them, give solace to them,
and grieve over them. Unlike the significations of the theatrical
dance, which tend to be indirect and mediated, these fetish bodies provide a direct, unmediated signification of the AIDS dead.
Nothing is abstract about the ceremony. After the quilt is un-
furled, people gather next to panels that memorialize their loved
ones, kneeling on the panels, offering flowers and notes. This
gathering is a wake.

While waiting for the cue to begin the unfurling, the Goucher
students assemble around the first section of folded quilt and
join hands with Bob, their leader, who uses these last moments to
explain the meaning of the quilt for him. He recounts the 1985
march to the Federal Building in San Francisco, at which the participants held pieces of paper inscribed with the names of loved
ones lost to AIDS. "It looked to Cleve [Jones, NAMES Project
founder] like a patchwork quilt of names. That's how the idea
came to him," Bob explains. He lists the statistics—thirty-eight
thousand panels, seventy thousand names, "and we'll read all

of them." And then he asks a question that surprises me: "Ever notice which years we've done this in Washington?" One student answers, "Election years." "Right," says Bob. "This is what we consider to be a protest, a nonviolent protest."

As the Goucher students walk back to pick up their coats and gear, I ask Erin Patterson, one of the young women with whom I had hoisted quilt sections earlier, what she thought about the experience. She cogitates for a moment and says, "You don't get a moment to look as you're unfolding, but there is one panel from my hometown, DeLand, Florida, and one with the same birthday as me. It's kind of scary. It hits home."[59] She pauses. "It's really difficult to process now." Later, in an article she has cowritten with Sarah Pinsker for her school newspaper, she will write: "Seeing the quilt in person makes you realize the magnitude of the AIDS epidemic. It also makes you realize how many people care. Most of all, it turns numbers into people. It drives home the fact that AIDS touches everyone: in ten years, you could be making panels for loved ones, or they could be making one for you."[60] For Patterson the quilt conveys its meaning in at least three ways: as a chastening symbol of the exponential growth of the epidemic; as a teaching tool for interpreting the human dimension of AIDS, beyond homosexual stereotypes; and as a cautionary tale—you could get AIDS too. But perhaps most significantly, the quilt's unfurling causes participants to engage in a kind of Brechtian choreographic analysis, revealing the political in the aesthetic and the aesthetic in the political.

When the quilt was first laid out on the Mall in 1987, it was situated in an insurgent relationship to the monumentality of the location and its symbolic representation of the American polity. That first display of the quilt took place against tremendous odds. The National Parks Service denied a permit until literally the last minute, for fear, parks officials said, of the quilt's damaging the lawn. (U.S. Rep. Nancy Pelosi, D-Calif., ultimately brokered a deal.[61]) The walkways were slightly curved that first year, highlighting the quilt's imperfection. The white dress of the volunteers seemed particularly ragtag. And the only official access for the media, via a hydraulic lift, quickly became overrun by gay and lesbian participants, who wanted personally to witness the visual spectacle of the quilt from an aerial perspective.

The first version of the quilt was truly a project of disempowered people, energizing the marchers who attended the 1987 March for Lesbian and Gay Rights and disturbing those who resided in Washington's halls of power. The media grabbed on to the quilt as a remarkable visual symbol, creeping toward the Capitol and the Washington Monument, threatening the foundations of government inaction. The quilt constituted an insurgent skirmish, to which elected officials—the purveyors of the monumental—were forced to respond.

Since 1987, however, the quilt has come under increasing attack from within the gay and lesbian community as a regularizing force. Increasingly, the quilt's organizers accepted corporate sponsorships, ranging from Dunkin' Donuts to Clos du Bois wine, which made it a witting tool of mercantile advertising. Government officials, rather than avoiding the quilt, began to volunteer to read names. (Thus in 1996 both President Bill Clinton and Vice President Al Gore visited the quilt with their wives, the first president and vice president to do so.) Discussions continued with the National Parks Service, but the issuing of permits became almost a cordial formality. Meanwhile, the essential gayness of the quilt began to be suppressed in favor of a predominantly heterosexual Midwestern image built upon the faces of the mothers and fathers of the dead, rather than the dead themselves. Eventually, the base of operations moved from San Francisco to Atlanta, Georgia. This is not to say that AIDS activism was no longer the quilt's agenda. Even at the 1996 unfurling, Cleve Jones could be heard on numerous television programs goading government officials to support programs of AIDS research and direct care. The timing of the event remained calibrated to precede elections by just a few weeks. But a percentage of the quilt's insurgency had been co-opted by the forces of monumentality, the very forces that it was meant to unsettle. And to that extent the quilt itself had become a kind of monument, albeit a fragile one.

De Certeau would suggest that, by assuming the strategic methods of the status quo, the purveyors of the quilt had jettisoned a portion of its tactical efficacy. And in fact they had. By building an institution with a budget and an office and a plan to build a museum to house the entirety of the quilt, they had turned some measure of their attention away from insurgent activity and toward the maintenance of their own profile, as well as the guarantee of their salaries. In that sense the quilt now serves as something of an object lesson about how to make dances in an epidemic: The choreography must remain light on its feet. It cannot be monumental. It must be quick and evasive. Above all, to be effective it must remain insurgent.

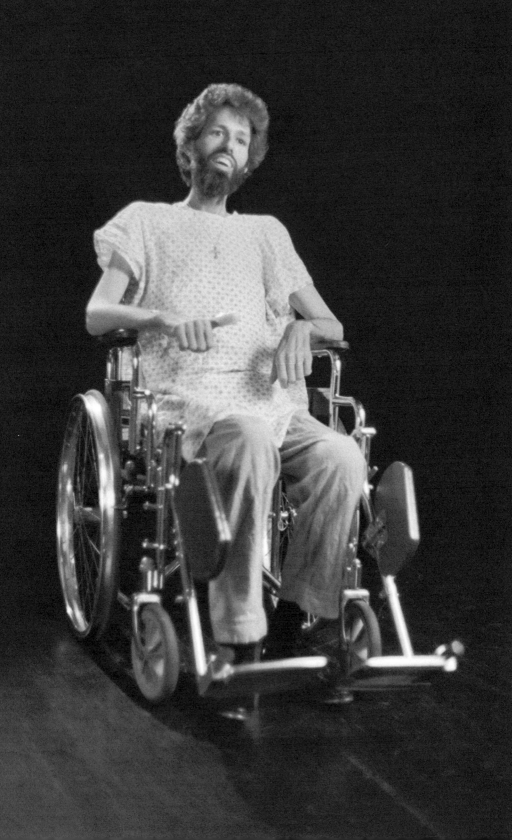

4

Corpses and Ghosts

A mortal can only start from here, from his mortality.
Jacques Derrida

Rodney Price is sinking into his wheelchair. With head and eyes drawn downward, his bony forearms balance precariously on the arms of the chair, his feet tucked behind the stirrups as if to save him from free-falling into oblivion. In the videographic frame he is positioned exactly in the middle, straight-on, matter-of-fact, his hair and beard gray, face gaunt, body sheathed in hospital pajamas. He is only thirty-eight years old, but he looks as if he were eighty. He will be dead in two weeks.[1]

Music by Kurt Weill begins: 1940s piano honky-tonk played in a dire minor key.[2] Price sits absolutely still, as if catatonic, during the ominous introduction. But then, exactly on cue, he lifts his head and commences to sing Janice Sukaitis's updated verse: "There's an element of doom and desperation / when I'm the subject of the conversation." The camera is in close-up now, which makes tiny details of his face visible: the sunkenness of his cheeks; the bones pressing beneath the skin; the teeth jutting, prominent, overlarge; and the crabbed geometric print of the pajamas at his wizened neckline. As he sings, his eyes grow large, frighteningly so. But his tenor voice is surprisingly light, smooth, lilting, marked by a stylish touch of vibrato. Continuing in the

At left: Rodney Price in David Weissman's film *Song from an Angel,* 1988. Photo: © 1988 Daniel Nicoletta.

same plucky spirit, Price gestures mimetically, musical comedy–style. "Locals agree I'll never see my washboard stomach or my derriere. / Or my youthful, abundant head of hair." Simultaneously, he draws his hands along his ribs, then motions to his buttocks, which are lost in the depths of his chair. In sync with the lyric about his hair, he runs his fingers through his surprisingly thick mane, immediately inspecting to see if the hair has fallen out in his hands.

The key of the music abruptly shifts to major and the patter turns more lighthearted. "And though I shouldn't boast of it / If I am aided by a cane I'll make the most of it. / If there's a blemish on my cheek / I'll learn to host with it." He touches the skin stretched over one cheekbone and then stares at his hand as if gazing into a mirror, shocked. "If I'm the one to roast, / then let me be the toast of it." He punches in the air and slows the tempo to punctuate the word *toast*. It's time for the chorus:

> I start the day every morning
> Inspiring angels like you.
> You say I'm thinner, take me to dinner,
> 'Cause I've got less time than you.

With a quick cut reminiscent of that famous moment in *The Wizard of Oz* when the film goes from black-and-white to color, Price then suddenly reappears in top hat and tails, grinning broadly. Still swallowed up in his wheelchair, he is nonetheless tap-dancing on the stirrups and the floor immediately before him. His routine consists of straightforward rhythm tap, closely conforming to the beat of the tune, but it is heightened by the use of the chair's metal stirrups, which produce a sharp ping rather than the customary click of metal taps on a wooden floor. When the camera shot shifts to a close-up of Price's feet, a viewer may even hear Price snapping his fingers, a sprightly touch. The rhythm is languid, slow-paced, but the tapping is bright, sparkling. This is Price's novelty act, a throwback to the days of the 1920s and 1930s vaudeville circuit, which he performs even as he faces death.[3] The film ends with Price's head supported on his folded hands, eyes downcast, as though a spell has been broken. A final mute close-up reveals him smiling benignly and looking straight into the camera, as if he were actually more than a little frightened and knew that we were too.[4]

Rodney Price, transformed, in David Weissman's film *Song from an Angel*, 1988.
Photo: © 1988 Daniel Nicoletta.

Song from an Angel, the five-minute film of Price's final performance, which was directed by David Weissman, invites a dual
analysis—first from the standpoint of gay culture, for this is a
quintessentially gay performance, and second from the standpoint of a man standing on the precipice, facing his mortality.
Unlike other choreographies that I have discussed thus far, *Song
from an Angel* is not primarily concerned with the stigma of AIDS.
In fact, Price seems calculatedly oblivious to that stigma—
though the contrast between his pitiable state and his humorous
response to it is surely calibrated to shock any AIDS-phobic
viewers. Price's performance is also not primarily about mourning, in the sense of mourning for a dead lover. Nor is it primarily
insurgent in its functions (although it has a calculated power to
tweak). Instead, Price's presentation of this little ditty draws attention to its very particular means—its twists of gay humor, the
use of irony and camp, as well as frequent citations from gay
Broadway style. At the same time it focuses on the strangely vulnerable position of the man who performs it, for, as he reminds
us in the chorus of the tune, he's got less time to live than do
most viewers of his performance. The resulting piece is frankly
macabre: undeniably funny but tragic too.

The performance theorist Peggy Phelan has remarked on the
huge effect that AIDS has had on the lesbian and gay community,
particularly with regard to the experience of living in the constant shadow of death and grief. She writes: "Exiled from the
Law of the Social upon which heterosexuality is based, many gay
men and lesbians may have introjected the passionate hatred of
mainstream homophobia and taken up an embattled, aggressive,
and complex relation to the death drive. The aggressiveness of
this relation may make it possible for us to survive our (first)
deaths. While we wait for the next, we perform queer acts."[5] Living outside the comfortable house of heteronormativity lends an
outsider perspective to gay and lesbian life and also allows for a
wide range of options regarding affiliative practices. In any case,
the gay or lesbian person is marginalized, kept outside the heterosexual encampment. But Phelan suggests that this "passionate hatred" of heteronormative homophobia results in a state beyond marginalization, marked by the kind of angry response
that makes it possible to face imminent death without psychological collapse. This is what she refers to as the first death, the

psychological realization of mortality, along with the concomi-
tant onset of anticipatory mourning—a state generally unavailable to the young or to those untouched by death. The space
between this first death encounter and real biological death—the
second death—she configures as a free zone, open territory beyond the reach of hetero-oppression and arrived at before the silence effected by biological death. This is the space for queer acts,
for acting out our marginalization, and for performing our grief.

I would suggest that this space is what is opened up and remarkably filled by such performances as Rodney Price's wheelchair tap routine. The look in Price's eyes tells us that he has
faced his first death and anticipates his second. He knows his
end is near. His body is failing. This is a man all too aware of his
coming demise, yet, unlike most humans approaching imminent
extinction, he fixes his eyes firmly on the fact of his mortality,
forcing his viewers to see it with him too. Thus even as he faces
mortality, he has become more queerly alive. He has checked
himself out of the hospital, walked into the film studio of his
own accord, and performed a defiant song and dance for the
camera—a quintessential queer act. As it happens, when Price
was admitted to the hospital to be treated for lymphoma, six days
before the scheduled film shoot, it appeared to the filmmaker
Weissman that Price might not live to record his performance. At
one point Weissman asked Price whether he would be disap-
pointed if the film didn't work out. "And he said, '*Yes*,' very
firmly," reported Weissman. "He said, 'This is my last hurrah. I
don't want to die sedately. I want to do everything I possibly can,
while I can still do it.'"[6] Thus Price's *Song from an Angel* begins by
facing death squarely and then turns death into a joke. It admits
the intractability of death yet plays games with it, teases it, con-
fuses it. Price draws attention to corporeal dysfunction—to loss
of weight, thinning hair, dissipating muscularity—and yet he
says, I'm still alive—hah! And he incorporates tap dancing, the
indomitable entertainment-at-all-costs genre of the American
music hall (borrowed from the culture of African and Irish Americans, two other oppressed groups) to accomplish his humorous
sleight of hand.

Perhaps only in such dire circumstances as those imposed by
AIDS can gay tactics for art making become absolutely essential—tactics ranging from the darkly macabre to the wildly

camp, from the terrors of gothicism to the chuckles of the music hall, and from the depths of the funereal to the heights of metaphysical transcendence. During the AIDS era the contrast between frightening and funny has taken on a compelling significance to gay male choreographers, defining the broad parameters of a new aesthetics of death. But just as important to the dances of this time period is a shared phenomenology of corpses and ghosts, upon which these aesthetic tactics have been liberally grafted. (The graft takes with surprising ease, for ghosts are almost by definition both fearsome and humorous—corpses too.) This phenomenology is based in part on the undeniable physical facts of the biological progress of the diseases encompassed by the AIDS syndrome. Kaposi's sarcoma lesions, wasting, and premature aging are the daily facts of AIDS, so it is not a surprise that these physical symptoms would emerge in dances as signs of the disease or that the AIDS corpse would bear its medical tattoos. But beyond these physical symptoms, and in accord with the harsh patina of stigmatization that accompanies both homosexuality and AIDS, a surprisingly consistent phenomenology of ghosts and haunting has also evolved during this twenty-year period dominated by AIDS. This phenomenology has not been written about before in any consistent way for the gay and lesbian community, although images of corpses, ghosts, specters, and hauntings proliferate in the cultural production of AIDS.

Given the importance of mourning to the gay psychological response to AIDS, it does not seem surprising that the dead would be configured in such imaginative ways. Perhaps more remarkable is that in the phenomenology of AIDS death and subsequent haunting, the very delicacy, tenderness, and—in large part—ineffectuality of the gay AIDS ghost serves as a cognate for the marginalized, tracery-like presences of gay men in U.S. society. Thus our corpses and our ghosts are anything but neutral entities or blank slates. Rather, they bear all the varied signs of the marginalized lives that we have been made to lead in the late twentieth century. My point, as will be demonstrated by the works I analyze in this chapter, is that all the tactics for survival that gay men devised in the last part of the twentieth century are displayed on our dead bodies and are integral to our ghosts. These characteristics define the culture of gay death and, with it, the choreography of AIDS.

Theorizing Gay Corpses, Gay Ghosts

Gay AIDS corpses bear the signs of at least three sustained sets of practices: one as gay men, as participants (or active nonpartici-pants) in a plethora of gay cultural modalities; another as sick people, as bearers of a concatenation of opportunistic infections that systematically destabilize, choke, and ultimately kill the body; and yet another as bodies striving to stave off death and disease. These three sets of practices are written on the gay AIDS corpse. Certainly, gayness is inscribed there but so are the infec-tions that prey on the body that has HIV, as well as the medical practices devised to defend it.

Such gay cultural practices as nipple piercing are an obvious example of cultural residues left upon the gay AIDS corpse. Tat-tooing and manicuring are others, as would be a never-ending array of gay hairstyles. But a highly developed bicep muscle that has wizened from disuse also has a distinctive shape and feel, as does a body shaped by the cultural performance of gender and sexuality in ways that could emphasize its length or its curves or its blocky stalwartness. None of these practices disappears at death. Corpses are gendered and sexualized as profoundly as are their living counterparts.

The other discourse written on the gay AIDS corpse is the his-tory of the disease itself. These histories are manifested in such signs as lack of pulchritude, skinniness, bony-ness; premature aging, hair loss, or wrinkled skin; the appearance of being "drawn," wasted, especially in the face; pallor, or the lack of blood flush; translucence; marks on the skin, especially lesions (as in Kaposi's sarcoma); or swelling of the abdomen. Each phys-ical symptom might be associated with illness in more general terms, rather than AIDS-related illness in particular, and some might not appear at all. But the appearance of several of these features together, especially with such identifying conditions as K.S. lesions, constitutes a direct indexical signification of AIDS.

Equally determinant of this signification are the signs of par-ticular medical interventions, such as the Hickman catheter in-serted in the chest for the easy administration of intravenous medications, or the mouth twisted from its normal shape and form as a result of the insertion of an intubation tube. Treatments and their histories fashion an embroidery upon the body. Thus these three discourses, one of gay bodily practices, the other of HIV disease, yet another of specific medical interventions, are all marked on the gay AIDS corpse.

Gay AIDS corpses are also marked upon the consciousness of the living in ways that parallel the reception of the living gay AIDS body. Corpses are, by their very nature, inert and still. They lack the will to resist gravity, and so, in most Western cultures, they lie supine, as if sleeping. (In southern India, where I lived in the early 1980s, corpses sit up, which requires the body to be tied to its supports and the jaw to be trussed shut with a wide band of fabric.) Historically, in the West this supine posture has been likened to rest, as if a sign of relief after the suffering inherent in death. Whether quick or prolonged, the death is followed by the corpse's ease. It has no work to accomplish, no medical travails to endure. The corpse exists in a state beyond effort.

And yet, at least in its early stages, the corpse is far from dead. The body is, after all, a machine, which has been burning fuel and pumping blood, right up to the moment when the heart stops beating and brain cells cease sending or receiving messages. The newly dead body is loose and warm, a condition that persists for some time—as long as an hour, perhaps—before the body's blood settles into cool stillness, pooled according to the dictates of gravity, and the musculature and bony substrata of the body stiffen into rigor mortis. In this state the gay AIDS corpse becomes a harbinger of fear and loathing, even for those professionally trained to deal with the technologies of death and embalming. Beyond its direct representation of that which we fear most, simple death, the AIDS corpse is viewed as a dangerous effulgence, inert yet still brimming with fluids over which consciousness can no longer exert control. The handlers of AIDS corpses don rubber gloves, goggles, and masks. The fluids of the body, which, regardless of the cause of death, may ooze beyond the skin barrier or beyond the boundaries of muscular control after death, are treated as dangerous contaminated substances. The body itself is zippered into a bag for transport.

A haunting example of the technologies of AIDS death is Bill T. Jones's report of the deal that was struck with the ambulance drivers who came to pick up his dead lover's body. "They refused to enter the house," writes Jones. So that Arnie Zane's mother would not have to see him placed in a zippered bag, his father carried his body down the stairs and met the ambulance service employees on the porch.

The procession wound its way through the chaos of the living room and out through the lower porch, where, contrary to the agreement, the ambulance drivers stood holding a bright red body bag. Lon, with all the grace of a professional quarterback, deftly slipped Arnie's body to them and rushed back to tackle his beloved wife so she would never see. Arnie was placed in the bag. . . .

I reached out—and at that very moment, the nervous driver spun the tires and peeled out of my driveway. . . . Arnie was gone. His ashes would be mailed back to me in a box a few weeks later.[7]

Fear of contagion may explain the unusually frequent choice of cremation as a method of bodily preparation and burial in the case of gay AIDS corpses. This procedure is generally conducted outside the view of family members and mourning survivors by undertakers who are specialists in this work. The body is subjected to kiln heat, the temperature of the "firing" so high in fact that all that remains at the end of a period of time regulated by the state is a mixture of indistinct bone chips and gray ash. This mixture is scooped and swept into a receptacle—generally, a plastic bag sealed in a cardboard box, sometimes a pottery urn—and is turned over by the crematory specialist to the undertaker, who in turn delivers or mails the remains to the designated relative, mate, or friend.

The gay funeral generally proceeds in the attendance of these ashes, to which the face of the dead person is appended with a prominently displayed photograph, generally portrayed in a posture—smiling, alone, or with beloved friends—that signifies life. Thus begins the theater of the funeral, a vivid cultural conflation featuring such distinctly gay icons as diva singers, remembrances of special gay events and occasions, acknowledgment of homosexual friends and lovers. On occasion, as in political funerals, the ashes are catalyzed as weaponry, strewn over the bars protecting the White House as a protest against government inattention or inaction. In some dramatic cases corpses are in fact transported to the White House gates as the focus of ACT UP protests and media actions. (Officers donning rubber gloves regularly escort the funeral procession and the casket away.[8]) More often the ashes and their cognate photograph are presented to friends and gay family as fetishes of grief, as foci for mourning.

Death does not end here, however, and at this juncture the French theorist Jacques Derrida's notion of "hauntology"—a play on *ontology*—becomes useful.[9] An inescapable spectralization often occurs at this point. In fact, at any of several points in this process, survivors may begin to experience a haunting that runs parallel to the existence of the ashes or corpse. Especially in cases of massive medical intervention, the ghost of the gay AIDS corpse may appear even before the corpse is declared dead. In such instances the ghost serves as an overlapping replacement for the corporeal presence of the soon-to-be-dead gay man.

The notion of ghosts as posited by gay men has a remarkable consistency, one that is revealed in conversations about "visitation" experiences among those who have lost friends and lovers to AIDS. In my experience almost every gay man has such a story and will share it if gently prodded. Such accounts are, in fact, nearly as common as the ubiquitous coming-out tale, the most frequent subject of conversation in gay culture. Surely, there are a myriad of differences among individual hauntings, yet the manifestations of gay ghosts possess a kind of genetic similarity, akin to the way family members share the same jaw line. It is not so much that such stories resemble each other but that the hauntings they describe mirror the marginalized outlines of gay life. To the degree that gay men in the United States share a common culture, history, and oppression, so do our ghosts.

This phenomenon of resemblance is in contrast to the diversity of religious backgrounds and beliefs of gay men. In fact, the notion of gay ghosts seems largely disconnected from the theological apparatus of any particular religion—although it bears closest connection to mystical traditions of evanescent transcendent spirituality contained within Judaism and Christianity. Such notions could be described as New Age, yet it is worth noting that even men who would not ascribe to New Age theology commonly speak of ghosts.[10] Certainly, those who hold to firm religious beliefs within codified systems are most likely to frame and shape their ghosts to fit within those systems. Having been labeled sinful or deviant by their familial religious systems, many gay men have wrested free of those systems and, having practiced and perhaps even *perfected* nonconformity, they may not be inclined to shape their transcendent religious experiences to any particular teachings. This is exactly why the concept of the AIDS ghost is operative in gay culture. Such ghosts are deviant and nonconforming (like gay men). They are tender and erotically connected to other men (like gay men). And they are frustratingly incapable of changing the construction of the heterosexist world (like gay men). Within the received knowledge that comes from participating in gay culture and the culture of AIDS death, a number of normative characteristics emerge with regard to the hauntings of gay ghosts. I offer these as an activist ethnographic informant; I have gathered reports, rather than verifiable phenomena, from inside gay culture.[11]

The gay AIDS ghost manifests as a better version of the dead man, beyond carnal forces, beyond sexual desire. Thus the dead man becomes a more perfectly altruistic version of himself. The ghost is subtly active and can be perceived best in moments of stillness and quiet. It is recognizable as corresponding to a particular dead person insofar as it constitutes a distillation of that person's qualities, especially as perceived in moments of love and vulnerability, in sex, friendship, relationship, political work, grief. The understanding person becomes a particularly sympathetic listener in ghostly form. The sensitive person becomes a preternaturally intuitive ghost. This distillation process also requires that less-pronounced characteristics, or negative ones—such as bad habits, cynicism, crabbiness—dissolve away. What remains is a new, improved incarnation, idealized, spiritualized. This is not to say that carnality and sexual desire may not surround the aura of the ghost, but in the absence of solid, bodily corporeality, fleshly desires are transmuted into other forms of intense connection—spiritual connection, for one.

Another key characteristic of the gay ghost is that it does not haunt indiscriminately. It does not, for example, haunt a house after its inhabitants have moved away. Nor does it attach itself to a person with whom it enjoyed no direct relationship in life. Gay ghosts are closely connected to the people whom they loved in life. They are not transferable. In addition, the efficacy of these ghosts is limited. They do not lift cups of tea or manipulate Ouija boards. Rather, they communicate through more subtle means—smell, sound, fleeting sense memory—and their subjects are cosmological or theological. The gay ghost does not, for example, tell fortunes or foresee the future, at least not in individualistic terms. Instead, its messages pertain to the nature of reality, providing glimpses of worlds that transcend our own.

A major mission of gay ghosts is reassurance. The messages delivered by these ghosts predominantly concern the safety of the dead, especially signs that the dead person is "OK." Often this message is carried by the dead person himself, the mere fleeting encounter with whom serves as its own kind of reassurance. A calm ghost, whose presence induces feelings of peacefulness, proves his own well-being. It is not uncommon, however, for ghosts to bring along messages of other dead friends, lovers, and associates—celestial gossip. The ghost's primary function, however, is to open, however briefly, a window between the temporal and post-temporal worlds. There is a place where our dead friends go. Death is not the last word.

Gay ghosts may not lift cups of tea, but they do manifest in ways that are perceptible through the senses. Joah Lowe's ghost wafted through my living room, trailing a scent that was immediately recognizable as the smoky perfume of his San Francisco bungalow. Ghosts often manifest through smells. They may also appear as visual apparitions, as bodily tracery rather than firm corporeality. These appearances may take place in dreams, liminal states between waking and sleeping, or in meditations, the ghost characteristically failing to conform to the physical rules imposed by gravity and materiality. Sound is a key means of communication for ghosts, which may take the form of music or words. Yet, interestingly, words are not generally heard directly from the lips of the ghost but rather are perceived internally by the living human. Gross sound waves are eschewed in favor of direct brain reception. Those who receive such messages describe them in verbal terms even though no sound is audible.

Although gay ghosts do not generally perform actions in the world on the scale of the horror-movie poltergeist—no hovering dinnerware, no crashing through walls—certain subtle actions do seem to fall within the ghost's purview. A clock that stops, especially to mark a significant time of day, is one such action. Another is the switching on and off of lights. Both occurrences are quite benign—unexplainable, perhaps, but nonetheless harmless. Annoyance would be the strongest possible reaction to these hauntings, but gay ghosts do not, by and large, perform harmful actions. They are light, not dark, providing assistance rather than inflicting harm. The deep sadness surrounding ghosts is not so much a function of their having died as of the shared sense that they are incapable of manifesting on the earthly plane forever. In fact, the "life span" for ghosts—or for contact with ghosts—is limited, following an arc of greatest intensity immediately before, during, and after the death and then gradually dissipating over a period from one week to perhaps one year.

The gay ghost is, then, marked by many of the same tactics associated with choreographic insurgency. It does not hold power, but it unsettles power. It is incapable of large-scale action, but it is remarkably effective in small-scale incursions. It lacks muscle, but it boasts ethereal form. The gay ghost's inability to register as fully corporeal causes it to lack durable monumentality. But what it lacks in monumentality it makes up for in capricious unpredictability. It does not haunt the nation as does George Washington, from his phallic perch on the Mall. But it will never burden the nation, either, for it will leave and make way for other blithe spirits to follow. It may linger for some time, reassuring, playing, even mocking, as does Rodney Price in his wheelchair dance. And then it will go away, leaving just a trace of memory, like the chalk outlines around the bodies of Rick Darnell's dancers in the prologue to *Falling*. Perhaps the most important function of the gay AIDS ghost is in demonstrating to gay men that, for all our travails and hardships, we are not saddled with oppressive earthly responsibilities and commitments. We are here and we are gone.

In the bodily syntax of AIDS, the transformation from healthy, sexy body to sick, emaciated body to inert corpse to meat in cold storage to ashes and, finally, to ghost is repeated every day. Each stage of the bodily process subsumes the one that came before, obliterating its predecessor and taking its place. At the end of the cycle this series of replacements allows for a double formation at its terminus: when ashes and ghost coexist. On the table lies a man's body, his ashes, in a box. His ghost, meanwhile, might "speak" through the inexplicable on-and-off of a light switch. Neither ashes nor ghost is equivalent to the person's body as it had been in life. The ashes represent his corporeal presence in a "purified" postcontagion state, burned down to a concentrated form of carbon, all other elements virtually expunged. These ashes remain inert, stable, lifeless, functioning solely as fetishes of memory and devotion. The ghost, however, appears in numerous guises, transmuting easily from one slippery form to another. It might, for example, manifest as invisible and mute, just efficacious enough in worldly terms to be capable of nudging open a musical greeting card. Thereafter, the ghost could appear in one's dreams, waft a trail of familiar scent through one's living room one late evening or return at significant moments over the years to proffer a sort of ethereal hug. And yet, for all its initial activity, this ghostly form gradually fades away.

This double existence—durable "remains" on the one hand and ephemeral "specter" on the other—is what is so vividly depicted in the choreography of AIDS. What is the relationship of corpse to ghost for gay male choreographers in the AIDS era? How do corpses and ghosts manifest? What work can they do? How does dance make corpses and ghosts especially visible? What is the usefulness of corpses and ghosts to the gay community? And how do their choreographic representations embody the tactics of stubbornness, camp humor, and transcendent spirituality that are key characteristics of the gay culture of death?

Homo Truculence

The San Francisco choreographer Paul Timothy Diaz raises money for AIDS organizations by performing on the streets, especially in a piece popularly known as the *Body Bag Dance*. The actual title of the piece is *One AIDS Death . . .* , the ellipses acknowledging that when Diaz first made the dance in 1990, one AIDS death occurred in the United States every ten minutes. By 1991 the figure was every eight minutes. Diaz has developed a particular fondness for performing this dance in and near Union Square, the busiest shopping district in the city. This is a good place to collect donations. But it is also a prime location for a streetside corpse to make a statement.[12]

Diaz performs the solo dance wearing a tube of Pepto-Bismol pink Lycra. He remains completely concealed within the stretchy fabric, his actual visage or bare forearms never revealed to passing viewers. This tactic configures Diaz as a gay masked man. (He has suggested that he decided to work under cover because

Paul Timothy Diaz in *One AIDS Death . . .* , 1993. Photo: Eric Luse. Courtesy of the *San Francisco Chronicle*.

"I didn't want anyone to know about my status."[13]) The recorded music is by the appropriately titled Dead Can Dance, the world music band, and the chosen track is "Persephone," a reference to the Greek goddess of spring who restores life after the austerities of winter. Whether performed at the corner of Geary and Stockton streets, at Rick Darnell's 1800 Square Feet studio, or (illegally) in the rotunda of San Francisco's City Hall, *One AIDS Death . . .* always proceeds along the same lines, with minor allowances for improvisation. The first two minutes of the music accompany the laying out of the gay AIDS corpse in its hot-pink body bag. The dirgelike score plays from a small boom box, while Diaz lies on the sidewalk stiff as a board, his arms crossed over his chest. Then, at a cue in the music, he folds at the waist and stretches his arms behind him, forming the recognizable shape of a pink triangle as the fabric stretches between his head and elongated fingers. Thus he shifts in a single instant from signifying death to signifying the gay movement through its most prominent post-Stonewall symbol (which, of course, derives from the pink patch worn by homosexuals in the German concentration camps). From there the dance develops as a series of similar triangular-shaped poses—arms stretched down; arms stretched up—interspersed with silent gape-mouthed screams and evocations of homoerotic sculptures by Michelangelo. Stretching against the fabric of his body bag, Diaz appears at times as though he were trapped by or emerging from pink marble.[14] Nearby, three pink signs with black lettering provide information for passersby: MOVEMENT TO RECOGNIZE ONE AIDS DEATH EVERY 10 MINUTES; ALL DONATIONS TO BENEFIT AIDS; and PLEASE DO NOT BLOCK THE SIDEWALK. Diaz often collects money for the Maitri AIDS hospice operated by a group of Zen Buddhist monks in San Francisco's Castro District, or for the Parachute Fund, a San Francisco–based organization that supports dancers who are facing life-threatening illness. On any given day in the mid-1990s Diaz might perform this eight-minute dance as few as three or as many as a dozen times, and many of these iterations have been captured on video. He is dogged in his resolve to perform this corpselike dance.

One particular video document of *One AIDS Death . . .* reveals Diaz performing outside Macy's department store on a December day in 1990.[15] In the background a Salvation Army Santa

Claus rings his bell. The plate glass window beside Diaz's body features a brightly decorated Christmas tree. Shoppers stream by, and many pause for a moment, with their shopping bags in tow, to drop a donation in his pink bucket. On this particular day, however, a San Francisco police officer and a Macy's security guard have determined that Diaz's show must not go on. The soundtrack of the video document reveals the police officer, during Diaz's third run-through, questioning Diaz's videographer, Peter Nolan.

OFFICER: Excuse me. Are you with this man?
NOLAN: Yes.
OFFICER: Macy's doesn't want this on their property. So you are going to have to leave.
NOLAN: OK. alright.
OFFICER: [Emphatically.] So you have to stop now.
NOLAN: He does have a permit.
OFFICER: He can do it anywhere but not on their property.
NOLAN: OK. Is it because of the subject? Is it because of AIDS?
OFFICER: No, it is because it is on their property.
NOLAN: There was a guy who was performing here earlier though.
OFFICER: Right. When it's their property, they, they . . . The opera guy is okay. But he [Diaz] does not have permission.
NOLAN: So he [the opera singer] got permission from Macy's?
OFFICER: This is private property.
NOLAN: He got permission from Macy's?
OFFICER: Yup. OK.
NOLAN: OK.
OFFICER: OK, so why don't you go and stop the performance now, OK?
NOLAN: OK. Alright.[16]

Throughout this exchange Nolan maintains a stubbornly indefatigable tone, even when he appears to be acquiescing to the officer's requests. His delivery is completely nonthreatening, quiet, even bland. Meanwhile, Diaz continues to perform the dance, with the pink triangles and the catalog of Michelangelo poses. He too is unflappable, even when, without any warning, the police officer walks over and turns off the music at the boom box. In response, Diaz immediately and reflexively interrupts the movement section of the dance and resumes his original position as a corpse: flat on the ground, arms across his chest, unmoving. He has gone dead. One could call this response homo truculence.

"I staged a die-in," Diaz writes in a catalog to the collection of his videotaped work, which is housed at the Dance Collection of the New York Public Library. "The bag was very warm, I did not mind. I could have easily fallen asleep." In hindsight Diaz feels that he should have continued to dance in silence. Having already undergone frightening medical interventions—and, by implication, having faced death—he ought not to have allowed the officer to intimidate him. "I had nothing to lose," Diaz says.[17] In Phelan's terms, Diaz was living between his two deaths and was primed to perform queer acts.

But rather than view his response as cowardly, it could just as easily be argued that transforming himself into a dead body constitutes the quintessential act of gay choreographic disobedience. Immediately, passersby begin to question and taunt the police officer for stopping Diaz's music: "Why did you turn it off?" "What is he doing wrong?" "Glad to see our tax dollars going to such a good cause." By going dead rather than going ballistic, Diaz has placed himself beyond reproach. He is not hurting anyone. And other citizens, gay and straight alike, respect his disobedience.

Soon a Macy's security officer is involved and approaches Nolan, saying, "Excuse me, can you tell me why he doesn't want to move on?" To which Nolan replies: "I think because he wants people to see this." Diaz continues his pink die-in. He does not budge. A minute or so later the guard is beginning to sweat: "He is going to put us in a very embarrassing position, and I really don't want to be embarrassed. You think you [Nolan] might be able to talk to him? I really would appreciate it." The guard sounds plaintive. Nolan responds, "Maybe you should talk to him." Nolan refuses to be the middleman, forcing the guard to face the pink dead man himself. The guard asks Diaz's name. Nolan gives it. And with that, the guard moves into the camera frame and crouches beside Diaz's supine body, talking to this pink corpse that doesn't move. As a result of this interaction, the attention of all passersby is drawn directly toward the sidewalk

Paul Timothy Diaz performing *One AIDS Death . . .* outside Macy's, San Francisco, 1990. Video still courtesy of Paul Timothy Diaz.

and to the explanatory pink signs propped against the building. The camera reveals two gay shoppers hovering close by, like protective sentinels. The pace of donations continues. One shopper declares loudly to a friend, "It's a protest." Diaz still does not budge. Another shopper says somewhat derisively, as if to reassure a child who is afraid of the sight of a dead body on the sidewalk, "He's alive. Give him a hundred dollars, and I bet he'll get up and dance."

But, of course, Diaz is already dancing his immovable corpse opus, marked by a surprisingly effective antivirtuosity. The place where he lies on the sidewalk begins to implode. All eyes are on Diaz, and on his signs, and on his bucket requesting donations. The security guard, uncomfortable as he is to be in this position, is now configured as a supplicant, a mourner, kneeling at graveside, saying prayers, begging forgiveness, talking to the AIDS dead. This is a stunning choreography, replete with its inaction, bellowing with its muteness.[18]

Of course, this is only one example of this vividly tactical phenomenon. The ACT UP die-ins are a close cousin, made more

truculent by their frequency and unpredictability. The authorities never know when to expect the next one. Any AIDS choreography performed continually fits the bill. But one of the best
examples of homo truculence is the refusal of so many gay choreographers to stop their mourning and get on with their lives.
At the 1998 meeting of the Dance Critics Association, a board
member leaned over to me conspiratorially to offer a description
of the San Francisco choreographer Joe Goode's latest work. She
liked parts of it, she said, but did Goode really need to make yet
another piece about grief and AIDS? "Enough of the mourning,
Joe," she said.[19] The refusal to suspend his fixation on mourning
makes Goode a prominent purveyor of homo truculence too.

AIDS Gothic

You climb a coil of twisty stairs in the dark, feeling your way as
you go. Stepping out on the landing, you look down over the rail
and see our protagonist—let's call him Joe—lying on his back in
an open casket floating five feet in the air. You see him from
above, arms crossed over his chest, legs stretched down below his
writhing torso, eyes unfocused, glazed, as if transfixed on a distant scene invisible to all but himself. Candles burn from below,
creating a shimmering halo around the black hole that is the coffin. Joe squirms there in the murk, stretching and fumbling like a
corpse not quite dead. A chill runs up and down your spine.
    You rush down the stairs and are forced directly into a neigh-
boring chamber, lit, again, only by flickering candlelight. Two
spectral figures appear, swathed in white rags, their skin the un-
earthly pallor of chalk, hair scraggly and unkempt, eyes dark as
black saucers. You cower in the shadows, peering cautiously as
they move slowly toward one another. They begin to nuzzle, two
ghosts slow-dancing. They pull apart from one another, then
grapple in cool slow motion, as if engaged in the ritual reenactment of some long-remembered mortal struggle. One ghostly
figure, wrapping its arms around the other's torso, cantilevers its
legs into the air like a pair of fishhooks. The other ghost turns the
tables, grasping its opponent tightly around the solar plexus,
forcing the air out of its lungs in noisy expectorations, squeezing
the life out of it.

Joe Goode Performance Group in *The Reconditioning Room*, Capp Street Project, San Francisco, 1990. Photo: Ben Blackwell. Courtesy of Joe Goode Performance Group.

You run trembling from this room, only to find yourself in yet another chamber, cold and dank, floor covered in mounds of musty earth, where huge and fearsome images appear before you: a succession of faces in attitudes of horror and revulsion, their distorted visages looming closer and closer. You search madly for the door but cannot find the handle.[20]

The choreographer Joe Goode's *The Reconditioning Room* cries out to be interpreted through the language known as the gothic, that set of durable aesthetics both macabre and strange that has made frequent, often end-of-century, incursions into the forefront of Western culture.[21] First performed in February 1990 at San Francisco's Capp Street Project, this installation piece unfolds over five hours with the six members of the Joe Goode Performance Group taking turns hanging in a floating casket, perching themselves on diagonal suspension wires attached to the walls, and appearing (spectrally) on the video screen in evocations of Edvard Munch's famous lithograph *The Scream*. Video footage of the piece, from one of the sixteen performances spread over February and March 1990, reveals Goode himself in the casket, which was suspended by heavy metal chains from the ceiling. The audience is allowed to gaze upon Goode's writhing body from various positions in the room, including from a balcony directly above. Candles burn in a mound of earth directly below the casket, so that those who watch from the balcony see the candlelight as a mysterious haze. At certain points in the performance, only a single activity is enacted. At other times multiple activities occur simultaneously, requiring audience members to decide where to direct their attention. Always, the mood is of disease, a sense of premonition or impending doom. In sharp contrast to the shimmery vision of heaven and angels that is commonplace in Western popular culture, this AIDS gothic version of afterlife resembles purgatory: a dark waiting room with no exit.

A key feature of this installation piece is a duet between two androgynous figures (danced originally by Wayne Hazzard and Liz Carpenter) lit only by flickering candlelight. These "spectral" incarnations appear in a small black room, musky and dank, which conveys a distinctly subterranean aura. Standing just feet or even inches away, a spectator is able to witness their evolving relationship in suitably claustrophobic circumstances. They appear to be engaged in a relationship duet. But it would be inaccurate to describe this as a love duet or as a pas de deux. By virtue of their ragged costuming and chalky body makeup, the dancers resemble nothing so much as performers in the post–World War II Japanese form known as butoh, in which the body is served up raw and unmediated. Moreover, their genders are rendered indistinct, no obvious differentiation having been made between the movements and embodiment of one dancer versus that of the other. Throughout the dance their interactions veer between harsh struggle and the evocation of languid private suffering. The choreography represents anxiety made physically manifest.

Goode's installation exhibits virtually every convention associated with the gothic, as defined by the literature of the late eighteenth and early nineteenth centuries, from the mysterious to the supernatural, from the eerie to the subterranean, from the erotic to the terrifying, forming a nearly complete catalog of the genre. Following upon the romance novel, the new genre of gothic fiction arose in Europe during the period of the Enlightenment, particularly in England and France. Manifested in more than three hundred works between the 1764 publication of Horace

Walpole's *The Castle of Otranto* and the 1818 debut of Mary Shelley's *Frankenstein*, gothicism is immediately identifiable by certain key characteristics. It is generally set in a place of murky historical (hence, "gothic") provenance, in a dark, cramped, or subterranean setting that encourages feelings of paranoia and claustrophobia. Sexual oppression, lurid libidos, a sense of looming sexual threat predominate. Mysterious doubles, twins, and doppelgängers make frequent appearances. And the world of the supernatural is liberally invoked, offering opportunities for visits by ghosts, specters, and other "spiritual" phenomena.[22] Thus a rich aesthetic canon from the late eighteenth and early nineteenth centuries offers means for treating subjects ranging from sexual desire to sexual oppression, especially as these relate to women.

As many scholars of the period, including Eve Kosofsky Sedgwick and George Haggerty, have noted, however, this canon is also particularly adept at providing a framework for the expression of rampant anxieties concerning homosexuality. In *Between Men*, her study of homosexuality and homosociality in English literature, Sedgwick writes that, in the late eighteenth century, when the category of homosexuality was first being invented and reified, "The Gothic novel crystallized for English audiences the terms of a dialectic between male homosexuality and homophobia, in which homophobia appeared thematically in paranoid plots."[23] The aesthetics of the gothic, then, served in part as a fictional construct for the fear and loathing attached to male-male affectional bonds, whether homosexual or, more loosely, *homosocial*. Haggerty takes this idea even further, suggesting that "gothic fiction is at last partly about 'homosexual panic,' the fear of acknowledging those forms of desire that threaten society's regulation and control of sexuality. But it is also . . . about the debilitating quality of that control. The force of cultural subordination is itself a Gothic nightmare, and these novelists are as ready as anyone to acknowledge that force and perhaps to defy it."[24] Haggerty proposes that the oppressive atmosphere of the gothic—in which the male protagonist is as likely to be locked in a dungeon from which he will never escape as he is to be lost to uncontrollable and unacceptable sexual desires, thereby inviting his banishment from society—is a fictional manifestation of sexual regulation. As cultural production, then, the gothic novel serves an important societal function in proposing appropriately lurid punishments for sexual excess. Norms are thus fervently and fervidly protected. But, says Haggerty, the oppressive force of sexual regulation is the gothic's equally potent shadow subject. Those who engage in the aesthetics of the gothic canon are as likely to be acting *against* the forces of sexual oppression as they are to be acting *for* it, titillating and exciting even while striking fear in the hearts of those deviants who indulge in proscribed sexual practices. (Homosexual pulp novels of the 1940s and 1950s served a similar duality: offering prurient material for the delectation of gay readers while being packaged with dire warnings of the consequences of homosexual desire.) If eighteenth-century novelists could "defy" these forces of sexual regulation through the perverse application of the gothic sensibility, as Haggerty suggests, then why not twentieth-century choreographers as well?

In *The Reconditioning Room* the oppression of AIDS death and homophobia is everywhere manifest. It is, first of all, visible in the extended duration and unstoppability of the choreographic imagery itself. A body hangs in a casket for what seems an interminable period, longer than most viewers would be physically and emotionally able to endure. The nightmare of this scene is compounded because the body in the casket is not dead but rather appears to be very much alive, squirming on its floating bier. Likewise, the silent screams are repeated over and over on film, one face replacing another until they are transformed into a cascade of mourning, anxious worriers offering no hope of surcease. The bodies floating on diagonal wires are caught in limbo, their fate sealed. Overall, the force and impact of the choreography is to embody the inescapable horror of AIDS. We cannot get away from it. And lingering in the background is the unavoidable sense that the cause of it all is homosexual sex. Sex has led us to this version of Dante-esque purgatory. It draws us into the dark heart of the installation, but it also makes us want to run for the door.

But there are other, perhaps subtler, ways in which the choreography of *The Reconditioning Room* offers resistance to the inescapability of Dante's inferno. By virtue of inviting viewers to cohabit this space for any duration of their choosing, one minute or five hours, Goode challenges us to face our fears directly and to render them benign, or bearable at the very least. After watching

Goode writhing in his casket for ten minutes, the scene appears less frightening, perhaps even formally intriguing. Moreover, there are beauties to be experienced in this dark place. The candles glowing below the casket are warm and beautiful. The floating movements on the diagonal wires appear weightless, free. The smell of the loamy earth is rich and fecund. *The Reconditioning Room* is a sensory feast.

Even more significantly, Goode's squirming in the casket can be seen as the primary sign of his resistance, that he will not simply lie down and die (a variation on homo truculence). In fact, Goode stated this idea quite explicitly when explaining his reason for lying in the casket. At a public event timed to coincide with the opening of the installation, he said he was working toward an out-of-body experience. His goal was not to give in to the floating casket, to succumb to it, but rather to float out of it and his body altogether.[25] And wouldn't that be the ultimate resistance: leaving the ailing body to lie in its wooden box while floating effortlessly out of reach of disease and death? To conceive of the body as buried yet alive, tied yet floating, screaming yet serene, is to imagine it in the grip of a horrifying oppression yet also capable of transcending that oppression. In that sense, *The Reconditioning Room* is not a hall of AIDS horrors so much as a site for disciplinary practices. If strictly adhered to, these practices might serve to release a participant (or viewer) from the tight grip of mortality in the age of AIDS.

One additional element is even more crucial to a reading of the piece as resistant to the oppression that it depicts, and that is the presence of ghosts, the two white-smeared specters grappling with each other in the near dark. On the surface they too are signs of sexual control. They seem disembodied, devoid of warmth, unable to escape the endless loop of their struggle-filled encounter. But in fact their very ghostliness can be interpreted as a victory over oppression. They are dead but not dead. They are not of this world—they are not flesh and blood—but they have not been obliterated or extinguished. Moreover, they remain in contact with those of us who remain on the mortal plane. We can see them, almost touch them, even talk to them if we wish (though they are unlikely to answer). The mere fact that we have access to them, however, even in this ghostly form, is strangely reassuring. Death is not the end.

Literary and performance scholars are quick to interpret the ramifications of this gothic view of death. Mandy Merck, in a 1996 essay on Andy Warhol—a gay ghost in his own right—traces a dominant line of inquiry in contemporary queer theory regarding "a representational strategy that renders homosexuality as a haunting invisibility."[26] Patricia White, for example, reads the 1963 horror film *The Haunting* as an example of lesbian desire "deferred to manifestations of supernatural phenomena."[27] Homosexuality cannot be depicted straightforwardly but only through the oblique lines made available through the supernatural horror genre. Diana Fuss notes a frequent tendency in contemporary queer theorizing to configure the homosexual "as specter and phantom, as spirit and revenant, as abject and undead."[28] (Sue-Ellen Case's "Tracking the Vampire" is a prime example.) The very marginality and liminality of the homosexual is metaphorized in ghostly form, a category of exclusion that also denotes a degree of menace. Merck goes on to cite Terry Castle's argument in *The Apparitional Lesbian* that, in Merck's gloss, "the homosexual phantom gains entry to representation by virtue of its deniability: its ghostly appearance allows the culture both to register and to refuse its existence."[29] Thus the trope of the ghost is, as Haggerty's analysis of the gothic would suggest, a sign of gay oppression—an invisible presence, to be affirmed or denied at will by heterosexual society. And yet its mischievousness, its call on our attention, defines a notable agency.

I have already reported on this agency in the earlier ethnography of gay ghosts, and the depiction of the ghosts in *The Reconditioning Room* is consistent with it. These are ghosts who are recognizable as real people. They have bodies and faces that, even concealed behind white paste and costume rags, may be identified as the dancers in Joe Goode's troupe. They have weight and shape. They also are remarkably accessible. They do not exist on some distant plane but are within arm's reach. And they communicate directly, even if not through words. Their dancing itself conveys a simultaneous sense of direction and indirection, a quality of immediate presence modified by the marvelously porous qualities of movement metaphor. This is true of Goode's ghosts. (In *The Reconditioning Room* and *Remembering the Pool*, the ghosts also emit an occasional sigh. This might cause a viewer to start, involuntarily, and to respond: "Who's there?") In short, then, the gothic elements in Goode's installation piece accomplish what the gothic has always accomplished: on the one hand, they metaphorize punishment, purgatory, a prison from which there is no escape; but on the other, they offer a position from which that punishment may be critiqued and from which the punished may "speak" back. Perhaps the ultimate rejoinder is that, after their five-hour subterranean ordeal, the dancers will come back out into the light, as will the viewers of the installation.

Another prominent citation of gothic practices, also by Joe Goode, further capitalizes on the gothic's ability to create and theorize the efficacy of ghosts. *Remembering the Pool at the Best Western* is the choreographer's transformation into a theatrical format of *The Reconditioning Room*. (The first version of *Pool*, titled *New Work*, was made the same month as *The Reconditioning Room*, and Goode has acknowledged their self-conscious interconnection.) And yet the three-act, full-length theatrical work accomplishes a different sort of work, primarily because it is a metaphysical comedy.

The Metaphysics of Camp

Remembering the Pool at the Best Western begins in the kitchen, the most domestic of spaces, in the early morning.[30] A laconic disembodied voice in the dark, Goode begins his monologue:

GOODE / DISHEVELED MAN: Nine twenty-two a.m. I wake to the sounds of Frankie Valle on the clock radio: "Walk Like a Man." Huh. I disentomb myself from the death of sleep and drag my weary legs to the kitchen. The left knee is uncustomarily creaky today, even louder than the right. So much for joy in the morning.[31]

Light comes up to reveal Goode's lanky figure, wrapped in a bathrobe, seated at a small stylized kitchen table. One elbow is on the table, his head in his hand. His expression is drowsy.

DISHEVELED MAN: I transport myself to the kitchen table, in the only corner of the room with even average light. I sit for a while, stooped and dazed, reprising my dreams. But only the haziest and most fragmentary images come.

From left, Liz Carpenter, Wayne Hazzard, Joe Goode, and Liz Burritt in a publicity still from Goode's *Remembering the Pool at the Best Western*, 1991. Photo: Bill Pack. Courtesy of Joe Goode Performance Group.

Likening sleep to death, the Disheveled Man seeks to recall his dreams—which, in a small leap, might be considered an allusion to life after death. From the start Goode transports us to a world that is dark and murky, the boundaries of reality failing to hold firm.

While Goode delivers his last sentence, his arms begin to float off the table, his head juts forward, and his eyes take on an expression of surprise. He is dumbfounded. The audience erupts in laughter as an unexpected companion appears onstage from behind Goode's head. She is a tall bespectacled woman in a blond bouffant wig, white polyester pants suit, and feather boa. She stands just inches behind Goode and mirrors his floating gestures. He resumes his monologue:

DISHEVELED MAN: I see a woman, a tall striking
    personage.

At this, Goode and the Apparition strike parallel poses, heads in profile, arms held high to either side, mock heroically. In fact,

Liz Burritt, the Apparition, shadowing Joe Goode, the Disheveled Man, in Goode's *Remembering the Pool at the Best Western,* 1990. Photo: Robert Bryant.

Goode cannot physically see her because of her physical position. But owing to the unison of their gestures, clearly he can sense her or she him. He continues:

DISHEVELED MAN: It's someone I don't know, gaunt
    and ethereal, with this enormous hair.

On each phrase of the line this unlikely duo mimes a different gesture. The word *gaunt* brings their palms into a narrow, worried configuration, both faces pinched. *Ethereal* registers as a radiant lift of the head, fingers placed on the chin, while the "enormous hair," timed to coincide with an effulgent upward curve of Goode's speech line, is indicated with a huge rounding of the arms overhead, punctuated by a pat at the ears, just where a 1950s hairdo might curl up.

DISHEVELED MAN: Her gestures are soft and vague,
    like she's not quite sure if she's part of this world. She
    beckons to me.

In tandem they incline forward with their right arms extended, cupping their fingers back rhythmically as the Apparition speaks:

APPARITION: Come here. Come here. Hey, you, come
     here.
DISHEVELED MAN: I hesitate. After all, I don't know
     her. And something about her sense of style puts me off.

The audience laughs, in part because of Goode's wide-eyed, ter-
rified expression, in part because his body recoils exaggeratedly.
He delivers his line about the Apparition's sense of style with
two fingers coyly pressed against his chin, his head tipped back,
his eyes confused and suspicious, which draws an even bigger
laugh. A particularly humorous component of this gesture is that
the Apparition performs the move at the same time but with relish in place of suspicion.

APPARITION: No, really, come here. I have something
     to tell you. It's very important.
DISHEVELED MAN: I allow myself to be sucked in to
     the velvet tone of her voice and the soft caressive qual-
     ity of her movements.

The gestures are now sensual and tactile, the forearms rubbing
along their length, two fingers of one hand lifting to the chin and
inscribing two circles in the air, like puffs of smoke.

APPARITION: I know you've been wondering about
     certain things, like what it's like to be dead, and where
     it is exactly that your dead friends go.

All at once the gestural choreography turns staccato: The two
hands are tilted up to shield the eyes, expressing shock. Both
Goode and the Apparition freeze in this position, then pop the
gesture outward, pressing hands into fists that then punch into
the stomach, thereby contracting the upper body. This chain of
gestures reads as fear, angst.

DISHEVELED MAN: I think, What is she talking about?
APPARITION: You know what I'm talking about. I'm
     talking about your dead friend. I'm talking about how
     much you miss him and how you wonder where he is.
     I'm talking about the knowledge that you have that
     you don't know you have. I'm talking about the . . .
     the possibility that you could live beyond, the miracle
     of . . . of . . .

The bodies retract, but the gestural phrase repeats, beginning with the two fingers, chin level, nonchalant, drawing a circle in the air. Then, as the Apparition stutters, the gestures take on a frantic tone, reaching up and to the side, first right, then left, in a mixture of fright and anticipation. Finally, both bodies appear deflated, heads hanging, hands clinging to chests, energy drained away.

At this moment the center of the stage is vaguely illuminated to reveal two dancing figures. As the dialogue between Goode and the Apparition continues, a duet of these figures is beginning to unfold in half light.[32] They cannot literally be "seen"— that is, our protagonist senses the dance but cannot directly perceive it with his sense of sight. (The choreography here is a direct quote from the spectral duet in *The Reconditioning Room.*) Rubbed with white makeup and costumed sparingly in what could be white rags, or white leaves—not unlike Vaslav Nijinsky's costume for *Le Spectre de la Rose*—the two dancers begin by standing close to one another, practically embracing, then shift their focus upward, forming balletic port de bras as if toward heaven. But heaven, in this case, is not of the balletic sort, and it is not populated with angels. One dancer hangs on the other, lifelessly, as if she/he were Spanish moss draped on an oak tree. This is not so much dancing as hovering—balancing, reaching, in a timeless void. Meanwhile, Goode continues to sit at the table, eyes fixed into the distance, as if he were watching this duet of decaying cadavers in the privacy of his imagination. The Apparition continues to echo his gestures and he hers.

Moments later, when she slips off into the darkness, Goode continues his monologue alone, hunched forward in his chair, eyes staring, arms folded into his chest in a gesture of shock and self-protection.[33] He seems to be resisting the state of unbounded consciousness that made the ghost duet visible, and in fact the duet has disappeared into near-total darkness. He speaks of shaking himself "back to some semblance of reality." Instead he finds himself overtaken by an "overwhelming sadness," a melancholic state.

"Hey, compadre. Why so sad?" The Apparition reappears and sits across from Goode at the table, more accessible than before, like a friend commiserating over tea. She continues to mirror his postures and gestures, which are calibrated to particular comic effect as she describes his dour expression: "Why the long face, the furrowed brow, the creased, careworn, dark expression, the pitiful, haggard, bloated—" Goode interrupts her:

DISHEVELED MAN: Wait, I'm not sad. I'm enclosed in a world without dreams, in a narrow, airless, stagnant, straight-ahead world, with no sideways movement.

APPARITION: But there are dreams there. You just need to open yourself up to them. There are connections to the dead. Life beyond body. You just need to let yourself expand into it. Think: What do you dream of?

DISHEVELED MAN: I dream of Lumina, Lexus. I dream of Acura Legend. I dream of Maxima, Integra, Infiniti.

APPARITION: No, no, no, no, no, no, no. Please, what else do you dream of?

DISHEVELED MAN: I dream of my dead friend. I think I see him talking to me or talking to someone. Only he looks different, spooky.

APPARITION: You just need to look more closely, see him as he really is.

DISHEVELED MAN: I can't seem to understand anything he's saying. I want to communicate with him.

APPARITION: He's not scary.

DISHEVELED MAN: I want to understand how he's feeling.

APPARITION: He's still the same.

DISHEVELED MAN: I want to know if he's lonely, if he misses me.

APPARITION: He still needs a friend.

At this, soft music (by Erik Ian Walker) begins to seep in as accompaniment to the duet of ghost-cadavers, mysterious and Satie-like. The two dancers—one of whom I will call the "dead friend," the other "Joe," for reasons soon to be made clear—are locked in an embrace, rocking slowly side to side, except that Joe's arms are hanging down and the dead friend is performing the work of consolation. They break apart and crouch on the floor. Then, without more than a moment's hesitation, Joe springs up, turns in the air, and—arms upstretched, mouth gaping—is caught from behind by the dead friend. Three times the dead friend jostles Joe there, until Joe crumples, his head slumped back, arms sinking, torso ultimately hanging over at the waist

Wayne Hazzard ("dead friend") and Liz Carpenter ("Joe") in Joe Goode's *Remembering the Pool at the Best Western*, 1990. Photo: Robert Bryant.

where the dead friend grasps him. As he is lowered to the ground, Joe becomes robotlike, his arms hitched up at right angles, mouth hanging open, leaning forward on one leg. (These movements seem to signify shock, stupor, living life as if one were going through machine motions.) The dead friend brushes

Joe's neck with his mouth, grasps Joe's forehead in his hands and swivels him to embrace him from behind, as if he were a romantic ballerina, before lifting and rushing forward with him in an ungainly torrent. Then, in a sudden paroxysm, the dead friend lowers Joe to the floor, falls to the floor himself, and makes himself into a support upon which Joe cantilevers his legs into the air—a movement image read earlier as appearing like two fishhooks stabbing into the dead friend's back. As they both recover to their feet, Joe takes a ride on the dead friend's back, floating, legs pedaling in the air, arms thrown back. And then the light shifts to the kitchen table, where the Apparition explains to the "real" Joe how to read the dream he has just recalled.

APPARITION: Do you remember the dream of your dead friend? You were in it, only it didn't look like you. You were unhappy, and he was consoling you.

At this, the dead friend falls down noisily on all fours and begins pumping his ass in the air, as if being fucked from behind.[34]

APPARITION: He was telling you not to worry about whether or not he was with you, because he *was* with you. He was telling you everything was normal. He could still see colors, feel touch and sensation, only it didn't matter what he looked like in the morning. He was telling you, it certainly is a ride he never intended to take. It certainly is a ride he never intended to take.

At the last moment of the dance and of the Apparition's monologue, the music swells and the ghost duet too, climaxing in a series of turns in the air and passages of circular running. The Apparition exits, as does the ghost dancer representing Joe. The real Joe remains at the table, hunched forward as before, head jutting forward, seemingly overwhelmed by emotion.

Then the dead friend from the ghost duet emerges into the light at the kitchen table, a hand first, then his whole body. Joe sees him and, in an extended pause, seems to recognize him, at which point the dead friend assumes the place of the echo, the double, just inches behind Joe's head, the dead friend's hand resting lightly on Joe's shoulder. Silently, in parallel, they reach forward, precisely beckoning "come here," heads tilting, two fingers inscribing a circle in the air, arms floating.

D I S H E V E L E D   M A N : It certainly is a ride we never intended to take. It certainly is a ride.

This is only the first section of the three-part piece, but already
it is clear that Goode has substantively transformed the material
of *The Reconditioning Room* into something at once more narrative and more directly focused on metaphysical conjecture. His
purpose seems to be to address a very specific set of questions
concerning what happens when our friends die of AIDS and
whether we may remain in contact with them.

The urgency of these questions is perhaps obvious. The year is
1990, and the AIDS epidemic has already been raging in San
Francisco for nearly a decade. Young people, particularly young
gay men such as Goode, are being called to serve as caretakers
for their dying friends, to face their own mortality, and to ponder
metaphysical questions that are insufficiently addressed by a
secular culture predicated on the primacy of science—of things
that can be proved—and, not inconsequentially, on the irration-
ality of ghosts. In newspaper interviews Goode has explained
that *Remembering the Pool at the Best Western* was made during a
period when his close friend Vernon Fuquay, the artistic director
of Dancers' Group Footwork in San Francisco, was dying of
AIDS.[35] The piece is dedicated to Fuquay. Goode helped care for
Fuquay during his final illness—he was one of Fuquay's
"wound-dressers." And it was Fuquay's death that prompted
Goode to address the proverbial big questions: What is the nature of life? Is there an afterlife? If so, what is the connection
between the two? Significantly, Goode places these questions in
the mouth of a mysterious half-visible creature who attends the
protagonist closely, shadowing him, doubling him, beckoning to
him. She is gothic, but she is more than that too.

The Apparition serves a very different function from that of
the two gothic dancers in the ghost duet. To start, the Apparition
is not so much a foggily defined ghost as a mysterious erotic
sylph. The conventions of the character seem to be an update of
Filippo Taglioni's 1832 *La Sylphide*, where, in an early scene, the
winged sylph appears beside the Scotsman James as he sleeps
in the comfort of a wingback chair, fading in and out of view—
capriciously, as though in a waking dream. In Goode's version
of this encounter the Apparition similarly appears and reappears

at whim, and she is described as being "gaunt and ethereal," an apparent reference to the nineteenth-century sylph. Moreover, in her blond wig and feathered white costume, she is oddly alluring. (The feathers might be seen as a dance in-joke about sylphs and swans.)

But Goode has recontextualized the Apparition in a world that is overridingly gay. Whereas the sylph's function in the nineteenth century was to embody heterosexual desire, here she is conceived as Goode's buddy, or "girlfriend." She may be erotic—with big breasts, exotic feathers, gargantuan hair—but in a comic form, certainly not as the object of Goode's affection. Also, rather than being presented as a figure who might trick a young man into falling out of love with his betrothed, this sylph emerges as a deeply knowing, deeply wise fairy godmother, whose advice bears heeding. Most significantly, this sylph is not a source of erotic terror but of erotic humor. She is the embodiment of the gay notion of camp—a combination of exaggeration and loving homage whose oversized coif puts an audience member in mind of Marie Antoinette or of the country singer Dolly Parton. Her job is simple: to talk about what happens when we die.

That Goode should use such a strong dose of camp in this scene of utter seriousness highlights the efficacy of this tactic, especially in concert with the gothic doom and gloom epitomized by the material drawn from *The Reconditioning Room*. "What *is* Camp?; *is* Camp gay?; . . . *is* Camp political?" the literary historian Gregory W. Bredbeck asks. "My own Camp response would be: *only her hairdresser knows for sure*."[36] And so it is that camp both invites and evades definitions; the very process of defining camp renders it lifelessly tame, like a domesticated tiger. But there are ways to approach camp that, by a process akin to gay cruising, might bring it into perspective and reveal some of its important uses in Goode's work. Thus a quick review, beginning with "Notes on 'Camp,'" Susan Sontag's foundational essay on the subject, may help to contextualize current perspectives.

Throughout her 1966 essay Sontag identifies exaggeration as a key element of camp. "Camp is a vision of the world in terms of style—but a particular kind of style," she writes. "It is the love of the exaggerated, the 'off,' of things-being-what-they-are-not."[37] But what exactly is being exaggerated, what is it that is "off"? Sontag precisely identifies the point of distortion as localized at the site of the rigid conventions legislating gender roles. The displacement of these roles results in the creation of what Sontag calls the image of the "androgyne," a smooth blend of male and female choreographed in the gestures and postures of the body.

> Camp taste draws on a mostly unacknowledged truth of taste: the most refined form of sexual attractiveness (as well as the most refined form of sexual pleasure) consists in going against the grain of one's own sex. What is most beautiful in virile men is something feminine; what is most beautiful in feminine women is something masculine. . . . Allied to the Camp taste for the androgynous is something that seems quite different but isn't: a relish for the exaggeration of sexual characteristics and personality mannerisms.[38]

In Sontag's conception, then, the attraction of camp lies in its ability to subvert standard notions of gender and amplify elements of the individual personality, as opposed to facilitating quiet acquiescence to gender roles, rigid roles that inhibit personal expression. Beauty lies in "going against the grain," a concept that can easily be translated into choreographic terms when so-called feminine gestures are performed on a male body. (Indeed, the dynamic embodiment of gender, the set of physicalizations that we perform every day of our lives, is a constant, ongoing choreography: the dance through which we define ourselves and society defines us.)

At its most provocative, then, Sontag's essay clarifies the degree to which gender is a performance, a concept that Goode would almost certainly embrace. Sontag writes: "Camp sees everything in quotation marks. It's not a lamp, but a 'lamp'; not a woman, but a 'woman.' To perceive Camp in objects and persons is to understand Being-as-Playing-a-Role. It is the farthest extension, in sensibility, of the metaphor of life as theater."[39] Perhaps unwittingly, then, Sontag provides support for the central notion of modern feminism: that gender is a cultural performance, that it is not natural but that it is constructed.

But almost in the same instant Sontag denies a central tenet of feminism: that consciousness of gender construction is fundamentally political. Sontag suggests repeatedly in her essay that camp is only about style, with the result that she unconscionably downplays content—especially *political* content. For Sontag, "It goes without saying that the Camp sensibility is disengaged, depoliticized—or at least apolitical."[40] But what could be more political than a man, dressed like a man, gesturing like a woman? With such an action a man says: I am fully aware of the arbitrary nature of these codes, and I resist their hold on my body. This is not about "style" but about challenging societal restrictions. It is about transgression, which Michel Foucault, in a stunning metaphor, likens to a flash of lightning illuminating the limits of darkness—"its role is to measure the excessive distance that it opens at the heart of the limit and to trace the flashing line that causes the limit to arise."[41]

Countless writers have roundly criticized Sontag over the past four decades for having removed camp from its necessary, integral relationship to the political subversiveness that is part of the gay sensibility. The literary critic D. A. Miller, in a 1989 essay titled "Sontag's Urbanity," thoroughly disses her "Notes on 'Camp.'" According to Miller's analysis, Sontag establishes camp as "a primordially gay phenomenon, emerging within the formation of a specifically gay subculture, at the interface of that subculture with the homophobic culture at large."[42] So far so good. "But when once Sontag has evoked the gay lineage of Camp, she proceeds to deny it any necessity." Miller quotes Sontag: " 'Camp taste is much more than homosexual taste. . . . One feels that if homosexuals hadn't more or less invented Camp, someone else would.'" Miller again: "That unblinking embrace of counterfactuality can only be understood as not just expressing, but also fulfilling, a wish for a Camp theoretically detachable—and therefore already detached—from gay men.[43] In other words, when Sontag argues against the gayness of gay camp, she is not only dishonoring but attempting to disempower gay men.

More recently, the cultural critic Moe Meyer has echoed Miller's criticisms. In the introduction to his 1994 collection of essays, *The Politics and Poetics of Camp*, Meyer suggests that Sontag's version of camp, "with its homosexual connotations downplayed, sanitized, and made safe for public consumption," serves to remove discussions of camp (as sign, in the semiotic sense) from homosexuality (as referent). The result: "The discourse began to unravel as Camp became confused and conflated with rhetorical and performative strategies such as irony, satire, burlesque, and travesty; and with cultural movements such as Pop."[44] And to unravel the discourse is to drain away its power, to neutralize it.

Like Miller, Meyer takes the view that Sontag's discussion of camp as "style" or "sensibility" has served to depoliticize what is inherently political. Seeking to undo Sontag's move, to roll it back, Meyer highlights the use of camp as a "political and critical" strategy in the work of ACT UP and Queer Nation, two political groups that remind us of the "oppositional critique embodied in the signifying practices that processually constitute queer identities." Through their work—primarily to provide access to AIDS funding and care but also to unmask homophobia in the culture at large—these organizations seek to demonstrate that being queer is, by its very nature, a critique of heteronormativity. Which leads Meyer, at the outset, to constitute a new camp manifesto:

Camp is political; Camp is solely a queer (and/or sometimes gay and lesbian) discourse; and Camp embodies a specifically queer cultural critique.[45]

The implications for Sontag's definition of camp are devastating: "un-queer" uses of camp such as those proposed by Sontag are now reconceived as mere appropriations and "no longer qualify as Camp."[46] In Meyer's view, which I support, Sontag's camp is no camp at all.

Placing key metaphysical musings in the mouth and gestures of a camp creation such as the Apparition, therefore, is intended to make clear that the knowledge she speaks is *queer* knowledge. It cannot be separated from gay culture. Integral to this knowledge is the idea that through laughter, exaggeration, and gender critique, our minds may become large enough to take in the mind-expanding possibilities offered by ghosts. There is more to life than Luminas and Lexuses. There is meaning beyond the material world.

In fact, the Apparition's detailed and lucid interpretation of the danced ghost duet emerges as a remarkable opportunity to define the nature of ghosts and of life after death in a way that conforms to the ethnography of ghosts developed by gay culture, as opposed to the oppressive theology offered up by established and homophobic religious institutions. The Disheveled Man sees his dead friend but finds him spooky. The Apparition instructs him not to fear but to "see him as he really is." The Disheveled Man fears the loss of his friend's essential characteristics and of his ability to communicate emotionally. The Apparition reassures him that his dead friend is the same as before. The Disheveled Man wonders whether his friend still needs him, whether their intimacy is durable. The Apparition explains that, even in the place where he has gone, the dead friend still needs contact, even friendship.

The dance of the two ghost figures reinforces the metaphysical training. When the two figures hold each other, it is the dead friend who is depicted as consoling. When the figure representing Goode ("Joe") threatens to spin up and away from gravity, as though losing control, the dead friend grabs him, grounds him. Their relationship plays out in a way that is more than vaguely erotic. The dead friend submits his ass for fucking and careens across the stage with the Goode character in a rush of romantic feeling. But the connection is not idealized. It is replete with physical struggle: the tight grip, the ungainly lift, the sense of being "hooked" or stabbed in the back. Their frolic together is further marked by a strong sense of what Freud calls the uncanny.

At the climax of *Remembering the Pool*, this sense of the uncanny is multiplied kaleidoscopically when the line separating imagination from reality breaks down utterly. As the camp sylph recedes, uttering her last reassurances about everything's being "normal"—a remarkable assertion in a gay culture awash in AIDS—she is replaced by the dead friend himself. Goode finally finds himself staring his dead friend full in the face. The cadaverous figure has yanked off his wig and is standing directly in front of Goode, breathing hard from the dance, his bare muscled skin and bald head glistening with sweat. The intensity of the long silent moment is shattering. Questions about spirit and the body— does the soul have a physical form? where are our dead friends?—explode in the mind. Then, with the Apparition fully receded into the darkness, the dancing specter takes the Apparition's place behind Goode. He gestures and beckons, just as the sylph had done before, in the role of the otherworldly double. Attending Goode closely, he remains felt but only half-seen. (Perhaps the soul *does* have a physical form, and perhaps our dead friends *are* with us.) Most audience members could not know this, but the dancer in the role of the dead friend is in fact the surviving lover of Vernon Fuquay, who was the inspiration for *Remembering the Pool*. As the lover, Wayne Hazzard, hovers behind Goode, beckoning in unison with him, it is as if Fuquay's haunting has become palpable and complete. Hazzard is the medium. This is Goode's direct encounter with his dead friend's ghost.

5

Transcendence and Eroticism

Eroticism opens the way to death.
Georges Bataille

Recently I viewed the 1990 film *Longtime Companion* for the ump-
teenth time, watching with the kind of obsessive fascination one
usually reserves for a slow-motion train wreck or for the video-
loop collapse of two gigantic buildings in lower Manhattan: You
know what's going to happen, you're horrified, yet you simply
cannot turn your eyes away. Written by the gay playwright Craig
Lucas, *Longtime Companion* was the first Hollywood film to deal
with the AIDS epidemic in the United States, and, predictably, it
concerns itself almost exclusively with gay men of the sort who
spend part of each summer at Fire Island and part of every day at
the gym. It is mediated for middle America through the point of
view of a straight woman—homosexual culture for the masses.
But for all its shortcomings, *Longtime Companion* remains, at least
for me, as riveting as it was when it was first released, moving
inexorably as it does from 1981, when the first cases of a rare cancer were identified in gay men and reported in the *New York
Times*, to 1989, when those gym boys with their Fire Island tans
have reluctantly, through loss and anger, been converted into political activists.

At left: Anastasis on Fire Island, the final scene of the film *Longtime Companion*,
1990. Film still courtesy of MGM Home Entertainment.

Especially remarkable is the final scene, a kind of apotheosis of wishful yearning, in which our trio of central characters, Will (played by the divine Campbell Scott); his boyfriend, Fuzzy (Stephen Caffrey), butchly attired in an ACT UP T-shirt; and Fuzzy's sister, Lisa (Mary-Louise Parker), amble down the beach at Fire Island, musing upon all they've lost while simultaneously conjuring a wish to be there at the moment when the cure for AIDS is found. Suddenly, as if the peaceful inhabitants of the island had just been sprinkled with fairy dust, the beach is rent by a surge of sweaty, muscled, mostly male bodies, many in fresh summer whites, whooping and shouting at their release from what must surely have been purgatory. For these are not just any pulchritudinous men but rather the dead men of Fire Island, all revived, embracing one another, joking, camping, catching up on old times. The cure for AIDS has been found, and it is not only for those sick and still living but also for those dead and long gone. This is a resurrection of a distinctly gay disco variety, set to the composer Zane Campbell's aptly titled "Post-Mortem Bar." And until the fantasy bursts in a final plummet to the reality of three dreamers alone on the beach, a gay male viewer, especially one who lived through the 1980s in the U.S., is suspended in pure bliss. Not only have the hot bodies of Fire Island been restored to all their shapely allure, but the perfume of sex is in the air again, sex in the dunes, sex in the morning and in the afternoon, sex as reason for being.

In his 1993 essay "Dante on Fire Island: Reinventing Heaven in the AIDS Elegy," the literary critic James Miller terms this final scene a paradigmatic example of the "anastatic moment," the word *anastasis* taken from the Greek for resurrection.[1] In Miller's reinvigorated usage of the term, however, this is a resurrection from graves dug by failures of government agencies, by rampant apathy, and by homophobia, as well as by a virus. "In AIDS elegies anastasis comes as a blessed moment of recovery," Miller writes, "when the dead rise from the mass graves dug for them by the fatalistic discourse of public health and join forces with the living against the World, the Flesh, and the Virus."[2] Thus the anastatic elegy is both a consolation and a form of action, a vision of transcendence as release, yes, but—I would argue—an earthbound transcendence soaked in gay male eroticism and founded on the sensations of sex. This may be heaven but it is not just any heaven. This is *gay* heaven.

In my research on AIDS and dance, which has now consumed almost two decades of my life—starting from the time when I was working as a newspaper critic in the Bay Area and first watching the collision of AIDS with dance and dance with AIDS—I have seen dozens, maybe hundreds, of theatrical dances that seek to paint a picture of heaven. Most are so benign as to be immediately forgettable, bearing not a wisp of the particularity of these times and not a wisp of gay culture, gesturing instead toward neoromantic heterosexual otherworldliness.[3] A smaller set of truly anastatic choreographies, however, not only envisions a time when AIDS will be cured but when those who have died of AIDS will be erotically restored to us. In my view that distinctive tinge of eroticism is essential to AIDS dances about heaven, because without it heaven would be just another opiate of the gay people, an empty attempt to mollify survivors by creating images of an afterlife where all is made right again, where old grievances are redressed, and dead bodies are not just made whole but are sexlessly beatified. Those of us who have managed to survive AIDS thus far need some consolation, but the wrong kind of consolation would tell us to pitch our sexual practices overboard, to murmur quiet remembrances in private, and to refrain from upsetting the heteronormative status quo.

But what if we could have our mourning and our militancy, our consoling and our street marches, our dreams of dead friends made whole again alongside our angry tirades against a system that ignores the deaths of those deemed immoral, unworthy, or just plain expendable? And then have back our gay erotic pleasures as well? What would such choreography look like?

In David Rousstève's 1995 *Whispers of Angels* sharp social commentary mixes with the unabashedly sentimental narrative to create a new kind of scabrous poetry for the AIDS era, one that is both melancholic and militant and that comes to an orgasmic climax.[4] The piece begins with a monologue in which Rousstève details, perhaps autobiographically, perhaps fictionally—he never lets on for certain—his early quest to make it in show business.[5] Standing at a microphone in the guise of the stand-up comedian, he regales us with tales of his first part in a soap opera, in which he ends up playing not a well-heeled party guest, as promised and expected, but a down-and-out black dude flipping burgers at a barbecue for those self-same guests. Thus from the very outset Roussève forces his viewers to confront the racial inequities that endure, even for an honored Princeton graduate, in the world of television image making. A second monologue turns dreamy, spooky even, as Roussève recounts another soap opera episode, with scenes set in sub-Saharan Africa, in which he is typecast as the victim in a ritual sacrifice. Race, AIDS, fear of death—these are the themes of the first half of Roussève's piece, which premiered at the Brooklyn Academy of Music and was performed at a string of major U.S. venues by Roussève and his Reality company.

The intensity of the piece ramps up incrementally, unstoppably, until act 1 ends with a scene of Roussève dying in a movement vocabulary that draws upon the grizzled, expressionistic body language of butoh. (The music, by contrast, is a whiskied version of "The Twelfth of Never" by the African American chanteuse Nina Simone.) As he slowly descends toward the floor, his nude body not so much falling as crumbling, Roussève exhales sharply in an urgent pattern that defines a verbal drumbeat, insistent and punctuated, but with text that remains unintelligible until the final iteration when he clearly articulates the words, "Hold my hand, I'm dying." Meanwhile, a string of five nude dancers has remained facedown on the floor, each dancer's hands touching another's feet, like a chain of paper cutouts. At the last, the nearest body in the string arches upward, a hand reaching out as if to grasp Roussève's spirit into its constellation.

At the conclusion of the piece this death is echoed and won back in a perfect example of the gay anastasis that Miller identifies in *Longtime Companion,* except that Roussève's heaven turns out not only to be gay in its sensibility but distinctly African American and vocally erotic as well. Roussève begins this final scene by repeating the verbal component of the dying scene in act 1, this time while sitting in a chair. "Hold my hand, I'm dying," he intones, strongly punctuating each syllable. After the final death rattle he stages a literal crossing-over to a promised land that is decorated with the stuff of backyard altars and Fantasy Land gardens and peopled with the long-dead members of his family, his grandmother in the rocking chair, his mother by her side.

David Roussève in *Colored Children Flyin' By*, P.S. 122, New York, 1990. This scene was later incorporated in Roussève's 1995 *Whispers of Angels*. Photo: © Dona Ann McAdams.

B. J. Crosby, a fabulous gospel singer with a powerful set of lungs, fills in for the angel Gabriel, welcoming this new saint to Technicolor heaven. "Glory, Glory, Hallelujah"—she belts out this well-known gospel hymn while leading Roussève's character across the waters, represented by the dancers now lying side by side on the floor. But when I suggest that she *belts* the tune, I really mean that she erotically *excites* us with its melodic contours. Her shimmering high notes, which she sustains into eternity, have the effect of clawed fingers on soft skin, and the quality of her voice is at once piercing, insistent, overstimulating, and penetrative. At the song's climax the entire cast and audience celebrate by breaking into a lusty version of "For All the Saints," finding sustained ecstasy in a scene that had begun with a painful death. A gay man with AIDS is risen from the dead, and a gospel diva is there to render this resurrection akin to sex, in the form of musical ecstasy. This is anastasis redefined for the AIDS era.

Similarly consoling, activist, and erotic at once is Terry Creach's 1997 *Study for a Resurrection*.[6] Made specifically for the serene atmosphere of St. Mark's performance space in downtown New York, the piece is heightened by the live performance of simple polyphony by the choral group Lionheart. The consolation of this particular anastasis is contained in the smooth, soothing tones of these beautiful male voices, echoing and resonant under the high-pitched roof of this active church, but it is also embodied in the dancers' liquid movements and in their soft touch.[7]

Creach has taken visual and aural images associated with a brotherhood of monks and adapted them to a context that is now about dead men, dead *gay* men, depicted in a frame of shimmering spirituality that configures them as saints. When I described this piece to my mate, Peter, detailing the succession of scenes in which as many as six men tenderly hold one another, swirling from the arms of one partner into the arms of another, I wistfully offered a rhetorical question: "Doesn't that sound like heaven?" Peter's response: "Sounds like a back room to me," by which he was referring, of course, to the darkened enclosure behind some gay bars where men meet for furtive, and anonymous, sexual assignations. Thus *Study for a Resurrection* is about spirituality, yes, but it also about sex—and about falling into the abyss of death, only to be lifted out of it again, literally, per Creach's title, resurrected.

Paul Matteson (in handstand) with Lionel Popkin and Keith Johnson (at rear), accompanied by the singers of Lionheart, in Terry Creach's *Study for a Resurrection*, 1997. Photo: Sue Rees.

One of the most enigmatic titles for a dance in the AIDS era is Arnie Zane's 1987 *The Gift/No God Logic*.[8] Reviewing the work that year, the *New York Times* critic Jennifer Dunning mused aloud, "Whatever could that title mean?"[9] In fact, by 1987 it was an open secret that Zane was ill with AIDS, but perhaps Dunning felt some need to protect him. With the benefit of hindsight—Zane died 30 March 1988, nine months after the New York premiere of *The Gift*—the meaning of the title seems self-evident: The piece was a final gift of himself, and he created it at a fraught moment when he could not fathom the possibility of a just or loving God.[10]

The choreography of *The Gift* is an abstract study, a series of variations, each of which begins with four dancers who assume the shape of a pinwheel, shoulder to shoulder, then fall back into a neat row.[11] In this sense it is situated in the center of Zane's compositional practice, his astringent postmodernism. But layered upon the sharply drawn choreography is a set of semiotic qualifiers that reconfigure abstraction in raw emotional terms. The music is by Verdi, two arias from *La Forza del Destino*

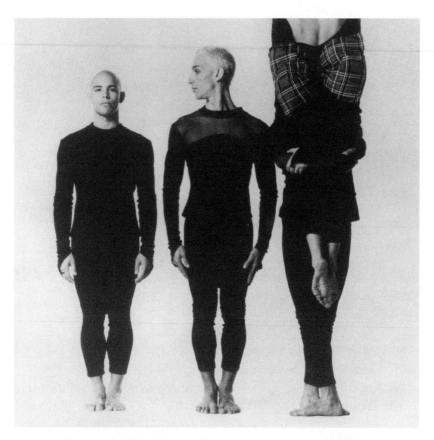

Arthur Aviles, Demian Acquavella, Sean Curran (partly obscured), and Heidi
Latsky (with bow) in Arnie Zane's *The Gift/No God Logic*, 1987. Photo: Lois
Greenfield. Courtesy of the Bill T. Jones/Arnie Zane Dance Company.

(The Power of Destiny), sung by Zane's favorite soprano, Mont-
serrat Caballe. The lighting by Robert Wierzel, with its harshly
angled rays and fog effects, suggests one world being gazed
upon by another. And then there is the bow on Heidi Latsky's
back (costumes designed by Jones/Zane company member
Demian Acquavella), the bow that renders her and the piece itself as a gift to the people Zane loved and to posterity. Indeed, of
the twenty-two works identified by Elizabeth Zimmer and Susan
Quasha as having been created by Zane alone (as opposed to in
collaboration with Jones), this is the piece most frequently performed by the Jones/Zane company in the thirteen years since

Zane's death.[12] It remains firmly in the current repertory. The piece itself is therefore a kind of anastasis—Zane is dead but his choreography lives on. Those of us who see the piece may even feel soothed by this sense of continuation. Less obvious on first view, however, is that *The Gift/No God Logic* is a very erotic piece, made so by the stiff erectness of the dancers, the way they firmly tug and grasp one another, the way the dancers' bodies resist any hint of subsiding, in steadily consistent response to Caballe's wrenchingly orgasmic vocalizations.

Anal Divinity

What these three works have in common is a set of images that point toward heaven but are distinguished by doing so in a kinesthetic, dramatic, or musical language that is redolent with the sensations of gay sex. Especially anal sex. The particularities of gay male sexual practices of the 1970s and 1980s are brought into clear relief in a self-published primer written by Peter Larkin and released just before HIV was identified in the U.S. Though long out of print, Larkin's *The Divine Androgyne According to Purusha: Adventures in Cosmic Erotic Ecstasy and Androgyne Bodyconsciousness* (1981) is so popular that used copies cannot now be gotten for less than $200.[13] I initially intended to study the book from a photocopy, as a means toward theorizing the ways in which anal penetration has permeated images of gay transcendence in the time of AIDS. But a friend advised me that it was essential to hold the original text in my hands, to view its pictures in color, and to experience a sensuous engagement with it as a work of art as much as a primer for sex. And so I consider the book here first as a material object: a large-format book with a thick cardboard cover, quite lavishly illustrated and printed, four-color, with elegant black endpapers. Facing the first chapter is a full-page photograph of Larkin himself, in a white pouch loincloth, nipples pierced, staring frankly into the camera, standing out of doors amid tall grasses. Larkin cuts an attractive figure, with his short beard and fringed hair, his body relaxed and toned though not overly muscled. The image and its placement seem calibrated to inform the reader that the book will be about gay pleasures.

Other images tell us that the book will have its ponderous (or humorous, depending on your point of view) elements too—as in its cartoon-style cover, which depicts thirteen hunky men engaged in a daisy chain orgy, encircling the sun and floating in an egg-shaped sky. Another loaded illustration is a photo of freshly washed dishes and a spanking clean dildo sitting side by side in the dish drainer. Indeed, if the sexual philosophy of the book were to be boiled down to a few words, the tag line could be William Blake's from an aphorism quoted in the text: "You never know what is enough unless you know what is more than enough."[14] Remove all constraints, Larkin seems to cajole his readers, and prepare to explore.

For all its density as an erotic art object, the book is also surprisingly print- and theory-heavy, comprising two hundred pages organized into seven chapters with titles like "Lifting the Repressions" and "Advanced Androgyne Relationships," and subtitles like "Erotic Pain and Piercing" and "Yoga of Cosmic Erotic Ecstasy." The text for the initial chapter, "The Awakening," begins thus:

Call me Purusha—Purusha the Androgyne. That is the name I have given to my *unrepressed self,* who emerges from within me each day like a mysterious new dimension of my identity, or like a different person. By now I feel that the unconscious components have merged and recombined with my conscious self to become the whole me—the original, natural, primitive, erotic and mythological version of what I have been trying to be and would have been from the beginning of my life, had I not gotten so mixed up in repressing and self-invalidating. The experience has been like falling in love again with all those mysterious strangers I've been falling in love with all my life, only now this intense experience is happening primarily within myself and only secondarily with others.[15]

Relying heavily on the rhetoric of pop psychology, Larkin, aka Purusha, tells us that he has developed an erotic philosophy that presents a sharp contrast to the sexual repression exhibited by society at large and reinforced by a societal bent toward materialistic gain. Larkin's vision, as explicated in subsequent passages, is proto-Marxist in its analysis of humans as pawns of social systems and the people who run them, but his solution is distinctly gay (though, initially, he doesn't use this word) in its focus on erotic experience. He liberally lards the text with quotes laid out in large typeface, from an eclectic bunch that includes Blake, Native American ritual texts, Christian liturgy, Herbert Marcuse, Betty Dodson, Jesus of Nazareth, Norman O. Brown, and Freud, all conveniently converging at the point of gay eroticism. Larkin's erotic primer is thus positioned as a work of philosophy, as an argument for a distinct brand of pleasure and autoeroticism aimed at spiritual realization. Its tone is deadly earnest.

It is notable that Larkin frames his text in this way after having spent ten years in training to be a Christian priest and five as a lay practitioner.[16] In his view he has merely uncovered "sublimated forms of erotic ecstasy" inherent in Roman Catholic religious life and has lifted them out of their repressed state: "I now achieve my greatest happiness in reintegrating and balancing out my body, as unrepressedly erotic as possible, with my consciousness, as fully aware and unified as possible: re-discovering myself 'a bodyconsciousness' and dancing out my own personal myth within the great flow of Nature and Universe."[17]

Any reader familiar with Roman Catholic theology will recognize that the language that Larkin chooses to describe his new path is not so much Catholic as New Age.[18] He speaks of "Universe" rather than of "God," and of "cosmic oneness" rather than "sin." He explicitly praises as key influences the Human Potential/New Age Consciousness movements, which were flourishing in California in the 1970s. But ultimately what he advocates is a mix of New Age ideas and urban gay male sexual practices, a mix that will mark a "new tribe" consisting of people who traverse the two worlds "to go beyond the greatest taboo of our civilization: the fusion of sexual ecstasy and religious spirituality."[19] At this key point in the text Larkin tellingly appends an illustration of a man's head thrown back dramatically, which could be interpreted either as Christ on the cross or a gay man lost in intense sexual pleasure.

The notion that pain can be pleasure, and that sex can be a religious practice, is not new with Larkin and he is certainly aware of this—hence the dizzying array of quotations ranging from Tantric Hinduism to Christian hagiography. His erotic theology is therefore posed as a return to prior knowledge, as a restoration rather than as a break with the past. At the same time Larkin is

quick to discount heterosexual models of spiritual realization
in Tantric Hinduism, or erotic pleasures available to women
through anal stimulation, suggesting that male autoerotic or homosexual models are superior—especially on account of the
erotic possibilities inherent in the stimulation of the prostate
gland, that organ that lies close by the anus in the bodies of men
but is absent in women. For accumulated wisdom on the erotic,
and transcendent, possibilities of stimulating the penis, the anus,
and the prostate gland simultaneously during sex, Larkin looks
to gay men. "Nowhere else," he suggests, "do I experience the
raw, naked energy and power of unrepressed eroticism as I do
among this group, in the uninhibited discotheques, bathhouses
and private sex clubs of their well-developed subculture."[20] The
reference to "their" subculture can only be read ironically. Larkin
toys with the role of the disengaged scholar but is clearly the en-
thusiastic gay practitioner.

The reason for gay male sexual superiority, Larkin posits, is
that in general gay men are interested in exploring a wide range
of masculinities and femininities, thereby blending the reductive
aggression/submission paradigm associated with insertive male
and submissive female sex roles. Beyond these broader experiments in androgyny by gay men as a class, however, he particularly cites the sexual explorations of "erotically advanced males"
in New York, San Francisco, and Los Angeles, where certain gay
men have developed

> erotic sensations in their anal zones to the point where
> they utilize and enjoy them as females do their vaginas;
> by stimulating and developing their chests and nipples
> until they experience them as erotically and sensitively as
> females do their breasts; and then combining these *yin*
> sensations with the *yang* sensations they already experi-
> ence in their cocks, until they experience themselves sex-
> ually and psychologically as "androgyne"—as "man-
> woman." Personally I consider the term "gay" to be a
> euphemism and trivialization for what these people
> really are: Androgynes—whether beginning, advanced,
> or Divine.[21]

Twenty years after the publication of Larkin's book, the notion
that the gay male—especially the gay white male—possesses unrestricted access to this form of erotic divinity is highly suspect.

Jack Morin's classic manual on anal stimulation for men *and* women, *Anal Pleasure and Health,* for example, lists any number of gender-neutral possibilities, and some that are available only to women.[22] But the self-assurance with which Larkin narrates this information reveals exactly how he views the sweeping topography of his particular formulation of eroticism—a formulation arguably adhered to not only by Larkin but by other gay men as well, as demonstrated at least a little by the continuing popularity of his book. This is a view that, along with its proud trumpeting of gay men as spiritual seers, positions gay male erotic submission as key to witnessing the divine.

Tellingly, deeper into the text, in a discussion of the three stages of the Androgyne and the practices associated with these stages, Larkin begins to write about the submissive posture and the gay man's anus in the same joking way that a mother talks about her son's love of food:

Of all the body's orifices, whether male or female, the ass-hole—including the anus, rectum and lower (descending) colon—holds the greatest potential for erotic experiences of being penetrated/fucked, primarily because of the great amount of extremely sensitive interior tissue area involved and because, when fully relaxed, the anal canal allows for the deepest, most intimate penetration of the human body by means of large cocks, large dildoes or the human hand and arm. The way to an advanced male Androgyne's heart is through his asshole.[23]

Gay men who become curious about submissive anal eroticism might—on the advice of a friend or by means of a standard Internet search engine—find their way to bodyelectric.org, a website offering videos, books, and workshops under the auspices of Body Electric, a business based in the Bay Area that was founded by Joseph Kramer in 1984 and that, since 1992, has been owned and operated by Kramer's associate Collin Brown. After checking out the website myself, I call the Body Electric phone line and ask so many questions about the materials available that I am referred to the direct "customer service" line, where I am delighted to find myself talking with a surprisingly knowledgeable representative. After conversing for a few minutes, the man on the line suddenly and unexpectedly identifies himself as Kramer, whereupon I am treated to a guided phone tour of Body

Electric's stock on anal eroticism, including two how-to videos by Chester Mainard, one audiotape, and a more professionally produced video on anal massage titled *Uranus: Self Anal Massage for Men*. None of this material is produced as pornography but rather as self-help information for men seeking to learn more about how to develop the anus as an erogenous zone. Though this is serious business, in the multiple meanings of that word, Kramer does have a sense of humor about this material. He tells me how Mainard, widely regarded as the guru of anal eroticism—the "Avatar of Assholes"—had supported himself by teaching medical students to conduct prostate exams at the University of Wisconsin, Madison. As an appreciator of the male asshole, Kramer says he thought "that sounded like a pretty good job," which led Kramer to seek similar work at Stanford University.

Kramer was born and grew up in St. Louis, the son of devout Roman Catholics. After a thorough Catholic schooling he joined the Jesuits and began preparing for the priesthood. In 1972, seven years into his training, he was taking classes at Berkeley's Graduate Theological Union when he got caught up in the spirit of the day and was compelled to celebrate his being gay. Four years later he moved to New York, "from a monastic tradition in seminary to a sex monastery," he told Don Shewey in an interview for the *Village Voice*. "Everybody was having sex everywhere. And when I went into sex, I wanted to drink life to the lees."[24] By the early 1980s Kramer had packaged his blend of theology and sex into a workshop called Celebrating the Body Erotic, an homage to the homoerotic poetry of Walt Whitman that often features, among other organized activities, an anal massage ritual.

After introducing me to the literature on the anus, Kramer kindly puts me in touch with Bert Herrman, author of *TRUST/ The Handbook* (1991), a compilation of information on ways to engage in what he prefers to call "handballing"—because it has more loving connotations than "fisting," that is, inserting the hand or forearm into the colon via the anus.[25] Herrman's foreword presents a mini history of the practice, suggesting evidence from erotic pottery in Southeast Asia, South America, and Rome, with a modern efflorescence dating from the gay sexual revolution of the 1960s and '70s, variations on sexual tastes notwithstanding. "By the heyday of gay liberation in the late 1970s," writes Herrman, "handballing was a standard part of the gay male sexual repertoire, especially in San Francisco, Los Angeles and New York. A joke popular on the East Coast went: 'What's the difference between a San Francisco gay and a bowling ball?' The answer: 'You can only get three fingers into a bowling ball.'"[26]

Herrman specifically references Larkin's *Divine Androgyne* and laments that immediately after the book came out, in 1981, "AIDS struck the gay community with a vengeance. Handballers, weakened by heavy drug abuse, unprotected sex and a history of combining handball with traditional anal sex (a lethal combination), died in inordinate numbers."[27] Indeed, Larkin himself died of AIDS in the late 1980s. The practice of penetrative sexuality as a means toward glimpsing the divine did not, however, die out with Larkin and his generation, even if gay male sex in general veered in the 1980s in the direction of practices thought to be "safe" or "safer," such as mutual masturbation, oral sex before orgasm, and body frottage. Kramer, for example, continues to sell his videos and books dealing with anal massage, and a recent Body Electric workshop was titled "Butt Camp: The Pleasure of Anal Massage."[28] But the focus here is on healing.

Undoubtedly, one reason that Kramer's philosophy centers on healing has to do with AIDS. Shewey, an astute writer on both theater and on sex, offers this assessment:

Much of Kramer's work emphasizes massage as a way of restoring a healthy attitude toward sex and intimacy among gay men threatened by or afflicted with HIV disease. It's no accident that he named his school after Walt Whitman. A major part of Whitman's legacy comes from the years he spent during the Civil War nursing the wounded and dying—an all-too-common experience in San Francisco over the last decade. Kramer formed the first AIDS hospice massage team in the United States, and both his teaching and his private practice revolved around touching people with life-threatening illness. "From very early in the epidemic, the major thing I saw was men terrorized," he says. "Not just in fear, not just in depression—those were states that all kinds of human beings had. I never saw so many people in terror in all my life. Terror just shuts down everything. Psychotherapy takes a long time to deal with terror. But breath work and massage and touching and caressing is like spring thawing out the ice."[29]

Those who are attracted to Kramer's philosophy and methods yearn for that thawing, and in at least one case, the warmth of spring morphed into a theatrical dance.

Performing Gay Eroticism

A public performance of a work by the choreographer Jim Self at St. Mark's Church in Manhattan is not, perhaps, the place one would expect to witness Kramer's philosophy in action, but for a weekend in January 1993 the erotic and the divine coincide for the price of a performance ticket. Self's *Sanctuary: Ramona and the Wolfgang Work for a Cure* is advertised alongside performances by the New York City Ballet and Alvin Ailey American Dance Theater in the *New York Times,* the *Village Voice,* and other key New York journals. In fact, the *Times,* the *Voice,* and *Dance Magazine* all review the piece in their pages, as a production of the well-known and well-respected Danspace Project.[30]

A former dancer with the Merce Cunningham Dance Company and an often witty experimental choreographer in his own right, Self is known for having said yes to many of the same things to which the 1960s experimental choreographer Yvonne Rainer said no: theatricality, costume, virtuosity, work on a large scale, and the guilty pleasure of popular music. In 1990 for the Serious Fun festival at Lincoln Center, for example, Self premiered *Jim Self and Julio Torres in Getting Married—A Wedding for the '90s.* According to the dance historians Sally Banes and Noël Carroll:

This was a literal enactment of a marriage ceremony between Self and his real-life male lover Julio Torres, accompanied by comic metamorphoses such as the newlyweds jumping into a basket that becomes a car, while the song "I'm putting all my eggs in one basket" fills the auditorium. The geniality and humor here is vintage Self, while the affirmation of gay rights represents Self's effort to give voice to social content that until recently has been suppressed.[31]

Self has a reputation for making work that is political and wryly humorous at the same time, and he brings that reputation with him to this performance at St. Mark's Church.

Self presages the nearly two-hour performance of *Sanctuary* with a quiet, serene solo in the church nave, which has been cleared of its pews.[32] Barefoot and dressed in comfortable loose clothing, he walks a serpentine path through the space, occasionally holding his hands high in the air and shaking them, almost in the style of a gospel church parishioner. (A program note explains that "Uncle Jimbo, a showman, shaman, and sometime pervert, and the community of dancers, musicians, performers, and healers are preparing the space for the evening's ritual."[33]) At times in this relaxed, almost languid, solo Self touches his head, as if to massage or stimulate specific points, and at other times he seems to be metaphorically brushing cobwebs away from his body, cleansing and clarifying his body and the space around him. He does this in a very casual way, as if for himself (even though he is being watched), and the effect is soothingly beautiful. As I watch I note the gradual calming of my own breathing and pulse. After standing still in the space for what seems a very long time, Self then begins to crawl on his knees, gradually snaking and slithering his way down the center of the floor, literally licking the floorboards, as if to arouse them. Arriving downstage, he crouches on his haunches and looks forward, very simply scanning the audience, taking the people in, right to left, very slowly and steadily. He stands, presses his hands overhead in a gesture of prayer, and lingers with his arms extended to the side with his back slightly arched in a posture of yielding—or a presage of ecstasy.

Breaking out of performance mode, Self then saunters downstage to greet the audience directly. "Good evening. Welcome." Now his hands gesture unconsciously. He seems shy and a little fey. "Thank you for coming." He tilts his head forward just slightly in a diffident acknowledgment of the audience, his body again just slightly curvilinear, slightly effeminate.[34] "I meant to give you a little idea of what to expect tonight," he says, explaining that the first part of the event is essentially a "concert," with audience and performers in their expected positions. The second half, however, is to be "an actual healing ritual." And for that he requests that the audience participate more actively, by witnessing—in apparent distinction from watching, by engaging in "intentional breathing," and by changing seats from time to time, to "spread the energy out so it doesn't get all focused down here"—that is, at the center of the church nave, which is functioning like a proscenium stage. Then he explains how this performance came to be: "Many of the collaborators in this event have done the erotic massage work of Joseph Kramer, and we began to ask the question what could we do now as artists, performers, and healers, to actually bring together the community that worked on healing at this point in time. What could we do? So with that question in mind we started stirring up ideas." Don Shewey reports that, in 1992, the composers Dan Martin and Michael Biello organized a special Celebrating the Body Erotic workshop for New York City artists and that Self was one of the attendees.[35] Presumably, this event was the inspiration for *Sanctuary*. In his preamble to the performance Self does not explain the Body Electric context nor does he say the word *AIDS* aloud, but it is clear what he means: "What could we do" . . . in this time of AIDS. He then signals the performance to begin. "Just be present and enjoy yourselves," he suggests before disappearing into the makeshift wings.

With this simple preamble behind us, the first half of the event unfolds fairly conventionally, like a standard dance concert, except that the mythic narrative shaping this first hour seems at odds with the simultaneously plain and humorous work for which Self is known. To start this part Self leads a trio of muscled men, dressed only in dance belts, who possess none of his plain, loose, unaffected movement quality. They follow the outline of his steps, but their approach—all pulchritude, little finesse—bears no resemblance to his. The music too is a strangely treacly assemblage of musical theater tunes by collaborators Martin and Biello, bearing titles like "The Dance," "Let Me Love You Now," and "When I'm Hard I Remember"—and, yes, the hardness in this case refers to penile tumescence.[36] Later in this first half Self reappears, covered in black-painted tattoos and donning a long black wig. He's a man-woman now, Larkin's "Androgyne," and he lifts his butt in the air to be symbolically penetrated by a black male partner. Minutes later he gives "birth" to a young girl. This mythic melodrama fills out the "Ramona" half of the performance, and, according to a program note, it involves Self's possession by the "She-Wolf Goddess of the universe who calls on all her relations to focus energy on establishing cellular and universal communication for healing purposes." Audience members simply could not discern this from the dance, nor could they guess that the "Wolfgang" of the title refers to all the beings—a metaphoric pack of wolves—gathered together in the goddess's sphere. Clearly, some important intentions are not made clear in the performance itself.

Self saves clarity for the "Ritual for Exchange of Knowledge," which constitutes the second half of the piece. Here Self provocatively invokes the notion of sanctuary—which coincidentally was the name Larkin chose for his publishing company as well as for the plan he hatched but never realized to build a spiritual commune—as a place of safe spiritual refuge. This second chunk of the performance begins with Self, still done up as Ramona, wig, tattoos, and all, intoning this text into a microphone:

In the Northwest Native American tribes they tell stories about young children who are turned away from their tribes and sent out into the wilderness to die. In this case, the young man is sent away from his tribe and he goes out into the forest and instead of dying he asks Great Spirit what he should do. Great Spirit says, pretend to be asleep. So the young man pretends to be asleep. And eventually wolves come to him and carry him off to their cave of healing. And in the cave of healing the wolves teach the young man the power of life and power of death. And they ask that when he goes back to his tribe he share that knowledge with them. So what we're going to do now is re-create what might have happened in that cave of healing.[37]

If the earlier Wolf Goddess narrative was confounding, this reference to Native American mythology appears to be calculatedly outrageous, for in addition to representing the New Age co-optation of a Native American myth, it suggests the possibility that the danced enactment of this narrative is meant to find a way of healing HIV/AIDS.[38] Equally remarkable is that, in the retelling of the myth, the esoteric healing knowledge given by the wolves to the outcast man is filled in by a central gay trope from Self's and his collaborators' fervid imagining: erotic ecstasy as agent of healing, as source of divinity, as transcendent antidote to the debilitating effects of HIV/AIDS. This fleshing out (or adaptation) of the myth addresses the specific sexual cosmology of gay men dealing with HIV/AIDS, offering up the ritual stimulation of the body as a site of pleasure *and* as wisdom, as medicine, as agent of health and healing. Sexual ecstasy is thereby posited not as homosexual taboo but as healing elixir.

This second section of Self's piece begins with two sacred masseurs, monklike figures swathed in red, carrying in a massage table and setting it on a large round rug laid out in the middle of the church floor. A tall, lithe man walks directly to the table, disrobes, and mounts the table flat on his back, feet pointing toward the audience. The table is covered in a bright white sheet, so that his thin, white, toned body stands out in stark relief upon it. The man is fully naked, and it is worth remarking that his nakedness takes on a special valence in the nave of an active Christian church. A religious air permeates these doings but an air of transgression as well. Two more monk figures enter with a drummer, leading the man on the table—and presumably those audience members who wish to participate as well—in a series of twenty fast breaths, followed by five counted inhales and exhales. Before the final exhale the man clenches his body into a contortion that appears not unlike a Martha Graham contraction, his solar plexus pressed down into the table, so that his feet and head rise in rigid counterbalance. When the fifth breath is released, the man's body relaxes deeply into the table and the masseurs prepare to begin.

Speaking into a microphone, Self explains during this preparatory phase that the final breath is called "a big draw" and that what we are about to witness—again, what Self and his cocreators imagine might have happened in the Native American cave of healing—"is taoist erotic massage, and the person on the table is going to receive his massage from people who are trained to do this. It's designed to awaken the spirit, awaken the sexuality, awaken the whole body, and move the erotic energies around the body. . . . This is designed to be a pleasurable experience. It is pleasurable for the person on the table. For all of you, please enjoy it. If you feel like breathing or moving around, please do that. Don't be shy."

Shyness is not really an option. Having removed their red cloth wraps, the masseurs, in loincloths now, rub their hands together, presumably to warm them. Approaching each other, they press their hands as if to form a bridge over the man's supine body stretched out on the table. Slowly, they lower their hands, echoed in movement by the monk-priests around them, until they land their touch directly on the man's prone body. Drumming begins in a languid four-beat pattern rife with exotic signifiers—a buzzing percussion instrument, a rattle, a pitched drum. Some rhythms are flavored with tinges of the Middle East, as if this were the sultry accompaniment to a belly dance. Self circles the room and presides over a group of eight male and female acolyte figures, each swathed in the red fabric, who are sensuously and erotically stimulating themselves, writhing on their swaths of fabric. Situated in a wide circle of crimson cloths that limn the edges of the church nave, these acolytes face in toward the massage table, wiggling and gyrating loosely.[39] Some perform idiosyncratic mudras with their hands.

Within a few minutes the languid drumming is rent by the shouts of the man on the table, who now has one masseur rubbing his chest and the other encircling his genitals. He is writhing on the table and shouting as his attendants rub and rub, fondling his genitals as clearly and firmly as if they were kneading a knotted shoulder. One masseur encircles the penis and scrotum, rubbing at a furious rate, while the other reaches onto the man's abdomen and down his legs in long strokes. Meanwhile, the musicians wander around the periphery of the table, play their instruments, and sing while continuing to incite and encourage.

The man on the table seems to subside for a minute or two when the masseurs retreat, allowing him to calm down. They are pacing the action. But before long the masseurs reapproach and recommence their erotic work. At this point the man on the table is rendered absolutely frog-legged, his legs turned out, knees bending and flexing, in urgent response to what appears to be an overload of erotic stimulation.

About five minutes into the massage the percussion music gives way to a piano trill, and the acolytes on the outside circle respond by clapping their own rhythms. The effect is serene, and indeed the man on the table appears relatively calm now. Loud rhythmic breathing can be heard over the sound system, and a drum joins, signaling a break, but before we know it the masseurs are back at the man full force, eliciting ever more shouting and wailing from his prone figure. The acolytes are now swirling their red fabric sheaths. The man on the table is, if anything, more decontrolled, more uncentered, than before. He seems lost.

I wonder: How must it feel to achieve this state of erotic loss of control in a public place? Or does his presence in a public place actually intensify his reaction?

One masseur is still focused directly on the man's penis, while another rubs his chest and sends energy out his arms in long strokes. The acolytes are yelping and wailing, swirling their fabric, creating an atmosphere of bacchanal while circulating the nave counterclockwise. The man on the table, the acolytes, the sound/music—all the participants and ancillary features of the event are beginning to take on a borderless quality. The man's body is now so overstimulated that it seems his skin cannot contain the immensity of his sensation, and the body boundaries of the people in the space seem to have been rendered fuzzy, indistinct, by the tumult of touch, sound, and swirling fabric.

Just more than ten minutes into the massage, a steady beat sounds on a tenor drum and a male voice begins to shout out directions for breathing. "Inhale one, exhale, inhale two, exhale, inhale three, exhale, inhale four, exhale." This is a repeat of Kramer's "big draw." The masseurs now back off from the man on the table, and all the ancillary figures hold still as pillars while the man rises up in a repeat of that earlier Graham contraction, now a trembling orgasm. His muscles are clenched so tight that his body seems like one big nerve. As the lights fade, the man lets out a loud shout, "Ahhhhhhhh," a softer echo, and then just loud breathing, in the decelerating rhythms that indicate recovery.

Now all is dark and the room falls silent, except for the labored breathing of the man on the table and, occasionally, the sound of his high groaning. Two or three minutes go by and the space remains dark. A high light flute—an ocarina, perhaps—floats a barely distinguishable tune in extremely long tones. Some awkward coughs from the audience are audible as the space remains nearly pitch black for another minute. Gradually, we hear light arrhythmic music in the upper register of the piano, rolling, with a surfeit of sustained pedal. Darkness prevails.

Quietly, almost imperceptibly in the shadows, the participants begin to gather around the massage table. A high male voice sings another sugary song by Martin and Biello, "You Are Gift," with lyrics like "You are kissed. . . . You are joy. . . . You are grace." The music is again in musical theater style, lyrical and tremulous. "You are fear." The music crescendos and the singing coalesces in a gradually clarifying rhythm. During this time the masseurs

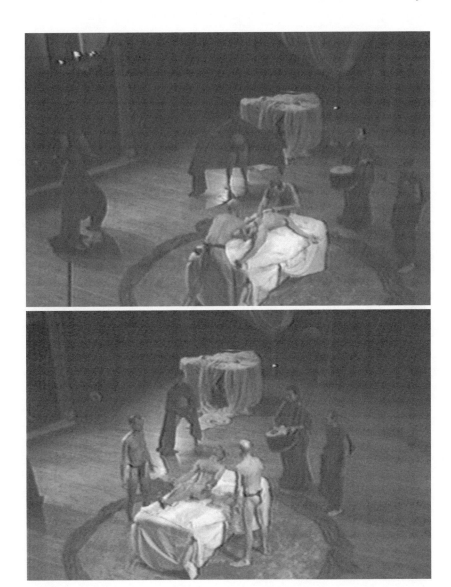

The culmination of the erotic massage in Jim Self's *Sanctuary: Ramona and the Wolfgang Work for a Cure*, 1993. Video still courtesy of Jim Self.

offer the man on the table a covering of red cloth, and the ancillary performers gather around him in a circle, holding hands. A voice over the loudspeaker suggests that members of the audience may want to join another circle around the table. Thirty or forty people respond to this invitation.

One monk figure begins to speak, acknowledging the assembled group for its courage. "Take a moment and see who is around you." He encourages the onlookers to touch hands or to hug. On the videotape we can now hear the sound of a woman crying softly. "Let's all breathe in together." The crying continues. "The space we've created is a sacred space." And then the woman, presumably the same woman heard crying, shouts out at the top of her lungs, "You're all sick," followed by the sound of feet scurrying from the space. This sends a shock wave through the room but without any notable physical response. Muscles tense, vibrations are felt, but bodies do not move. The audible breathing continues now for a time, as the members of the group seem to recoup themselves from this surprising interruption. During this time one monk figure breaks the circle and exits, moving through the outer circle. Meanwhile, the man remains on the table, and the onlookers continue to stand silently in their two circles.

After a time the monk figure takes the microphone again to explain that raw emotions are not unexpected, "because we are in the presence of power and sacredness. What to do except to love and to be with what's there?" He then, rather abruptly, declares the performance at an end and explains that the man on the table, who now has a name, Stephen, "has asked that people visit him and be with him and touch him and talk to him. If you feel moved to do that, please do that." The members of the circle then drop arms and clap, at first hesitantly, then long, loud, and full.

For the next quarter hour many audience members continue to stand where they are in the outer circle. Some hug one another or just continue standing. Soft music plays in the background. Some few people approach the table and seem to kiss Stephen through the fabric, to bow to him. Audience members continue to mill and linger, their attention centered on the man on the table. For a period the documentary camera zooms in on one of the masseurs, who is greeting a succession of men with deep embraces, gentle strokes, and warm extended hugs. After another ten minutes Stephen sits up and locks in an embrace with one of the masseurs. Many people remain in the space, milling, talking, hugging, until the documentary tape goes blank.

Self's *Sanctuary*, beyond the expected debates about its aesthetic value, may be the clearest example imaginable of a performance that seeks transcendence, and healing, through the excitation of erotic energy. It is certainly unique as a dance event that includes images of unmediated male eroticism. There is literally nothing separating Stephen's presence on the table, with his hard cock and his complete immersion in the physical experience of what Kramer calls "full-body orgasm," from the viewers who have bought tickets to the event. Everything is visible, literally everything—Stephen's body, his tumescent cock, his frog-legged response to being rubbed about the genitals, and his final quivering orgasm in what looks so much like a modified Graham contraction. This is a rare perspective to offer in concert modern dance, and it stems, in Self's own words (shared in an explanatory e-mail), from a desire "to use ritual performance as a way to loosen the response around AIDS" and as part of "a research project related to studies of ritual as a healing tool," not to mention Self's expressed intention "to create a forum for various perspectives to interact."[40] A program note further frames the performance of the erotic massage as research, as an opportunity for the exchange of knowledge among:

> *healers/teachers/performers/critics/anthropologists/virologists/*
> *therapists/observers/spiritualists/sex*
> *workers/faeries/queens/homos/family/friends/former*
> *lovers/etc.*
> *The purpose of this simple ritual is to formally provide, in a*
> *movement context, a forum for the exchange of information for*
> *those who are working in the areas of healing, movement*
> *research, ritual studies and practices, performance, etc.*

Presumably, one might watch this event or participate in it—by breathing rhythmically or moving about the space as directed—and learn from it how to engage in personal healing or how to approach death or how to envision healing unto death, the kind of healing that is not necessarily evidenced in physical remission and glowing health but rather in the attainment of a kind of grace in the face of impending death. The proposition that Self offers us is that eroticism bears intrinsic healing powers, perhaps by opening up a window to another realm, a realm of transcendence, the beyond. It is notable that "critics" are invoked among the group of people who might exchange knowledge through this event and that three critics did indeed seek to address the piece in their published writings. Yet it is also significant that, in each of the three published reviews, the exigencies of public writing and public mores seem to have prevented these critics from addressing what happened in and through the erotic massage, other than to refer to it coyly. In fact, my description of the work begins where theirs, of apparent necessity, drops off.[41]

By focusing on the details of the choreography of the erotic massage, I am hoping to participate in exactly the exchange that Self is requesting, to concentrate on what can be learned through this experimental public ritual. And with that as my goal, it appears to me that the piece represents an extremely brave attempt to make available the vital energy of sex, to bottle it, if you will, for medicinal consumption. Setting aside an evaluation of the piece in an art context, which is invited, perhaps even required, by its presentation in a dance series—for paying customers, no less—the second half of *Sanctuary* does manage, however uncomfortably, to spotlight the pure sensation of erotic excitation and to reposition it as not just a solitary or coupled activity but as a community event. This is extraordinary, unprecedented even, and it opens the way to a particular gay male understanding of heaven as a distillation of eroticism.

Encountering Bataille

In the 1950s, when Georges Bataille wrote the line "Eroticism opens the way to death,"[42] he could have been referring either to the little death of orgasm or to the existential death that ends in extinguishment or—who knows?—a kind of heaven. He might even have been summoning a notion of transcendence constructed upon the distinctive experience of one's body's being penetrated. As a pious Roman Catholic who turned to eroticism as a replacement for, or extension of, theological passion, Bataille bears a more-than-passing similarity to the key figures of this chapter: Peter Larkin, aka Purusha, and Body Electric's Joe Kramer.[43] If this trio can be taken as in any way exemplary, it seems that religious fervor and sexual ecstasy are closely intertwined, or at least that they can be.

Bataille was born in France in 1897 and grew up in Rheims, the son of a syphilitic public servant whose symptoms intensified from blindness to near-complete paralysis and madness during the course of Bataille's childhood and youth.[44] These biographical details would not be worth mentioning, were it not that Bataille's pornographically philosophical writings bear undeniable traces of his fascination with the public bodily functions that were so much a part of his early life. Furthermore, Bataille's conversion to Roman Catholicism at seventeen, his year studying in a seminary, his aspirations to the priesthood, and his ultimate rebellion against the church notably follow the pattern of his fellow eroticists.[45]

Bataille's first novel, *W.C.* (1926), was reportedly so scurrilous that he later burned it. All that survives is the first chapter, republished as the opening of *Blue of Noon*, in which Dirty, the female heroine, is depicted as a foul-mouthed drunken aristocrat who throws lines at her red-faced maid like, "And as for you— you, the nice girl . . . you masturbate."[46] In a lost passage of *W.C.*, we are told by Allan Stoekl, editor and translator of Bataille's *Blue of Noon*, Dirty and the narrator engage in an orgy among fishmongers' stalls.[47] A contemporaneous poetic essay titled "The Solar Anus" (1927) celebrates the notion of planetary rotation and sex as twin animators of the universe, interestingly conceived not as the sun and the penis and/or vagina but rather as the sun and the anus.

> The two primary motions are rotational and sexual movement, whose combination is expressed by the locomotive's wheels and pistons. . . . Thus one notes that the earth, by turning, makes animals and men have coitus, and (because the result is as much the cause as that which provokes it) that animals and men make the earth turn by having coitus.[48]

For Stoekl these lines foreshadow Bataille's theory of "heterogeneous matter," that is, "matter so repulsive that it resisted not only the idealism of Christians, Hegelians, and surrealists, but even the conceptual edifice-building of traditional materialists. It was indeed an all-out assault on dignity."[49] Rather than an assault on dignity, one might consider Bataille's writings an attack on Cartesianism in favor of a celebration of the body, the physical, the erotic, in their most excretory forms. In the 1930s the surrealist André Breton would fling the epithet "excremental philosopher" at Bataille, arguing that heterogeneous matter and reason are at odds with one another and that Bataille was ill advised to claim the possibility of their union.[50] As a dance scholar, I cannot resist making the counterargument that thought cannot exist apart from the materiality of the body and that Bataille's assertion of the flesh and its excrements is fundamental, especially to a philosophy that argues for a radical reprivileging of the body and its pleasures. The starting point here is not theological reflection but rather the permeable threshold that is crossed whenever desire imbues flesh.

In 1957, three decades after *W.C.* and "The Solar Anus," Bataille brought these ideas to fruition in *Erotism: Death and Sensuality (L'Erotisme)*, in which he clinches the link between erotic feeling and death. "I do not seek to identify them with each other but I endeavour to find the point where they may converge beyond their mutual exclusiveness."[51] In its fundamental aspects *Erotism* thereby foreshadows Larkin's, Kramer's, and Self's projects by entwining spiritual longing with eroticism and by refusing to view these twin categories as antithetical.

In a further parallel with our more contemporary gay erotic trio, *Erotism* puts emphasis on the notion that sexual taboos have prevented humans from fully exploring their erotic potential. Bataille writes that long before his book was published, it became socially acceptable to discuss, write about, and philosophize upon the realm of the erotic. But it is not difficult to read between the lines that these discussions began to transpire in public not so very long before the publication of *Erotism* and that taboo's shadow remained long. Furthermore, the sexual studies of Bataille's day were largely couched as science, which was problematic for Bataille insofar as he believed that "eroticism has a significance for mankind that the scientific attitude cannot reach. Eroticism cannot be discussed unless man too is discussed in the process."[52] So again we might recognize a common thread in Purusha, Kramer, and Self, who assert that eroticism is akin to divinity or that the search for erotic pleasure is a religious or spiritual quest.

Bataille recognizes that this is not the same message as that expressed by Roman Catholicism. "This is certainly not a return to the faith of my youth," he writes. "But human passion has only one object in this forlorn world of ours. The paths we take towards it may vary. The object itself has a great variety of aspects, but we can only make out their significance by seeing how closely they are knit at the deepest level."[53] Thus even if his theories are scatological by Christian theological standards, Bataille still refuses to allow them to be pried apart from a central religious impulse. He continues: "Let me stress that in this work flights of Christian religious experience and bursts of erotic impulses are seen to be part and parcel of the same movement."[54]

At this point in the text Bataille dispenses with the preliminaries and lays out his central premise, that eroticism opens up the possibility of a continuous, dissolved state of being in the same way that death does—which is to say that eroticism is a kind of death, or a practice for death, and that its appeal is therefore intrinsically human. Only in pleasure and in death, he suggests, can our radical discontinuity as beings be broached, bridged, defied.[55]

Bataille writes this point in two different ways, within a few lines: "Eroticism, it may be said, is assenting to life up to the point of death," and then, "eroticism is assenting to life even in death."[56] This conundrum may be difficult for some readers to fathom, but Bataille is placing eroticism as a bridge *between life and death,* extending on either side of its span. And he is also placing eroticism as a bridge *between individual lives,* as an extension of what he terms "the passions." In a discussion of physical eroticism, he explains, "The whole business of eroticism is to destroy the self-contained character of the participators as they are in their normal lives."[57] Thus the boundaries between human beings are broken, in a process that bears the traces of an inherent violence.

Bataille further explores this quality of violence or cataclysm in language that emphasizes the sense of violation accompanying it and that ultimately positions eroticism as a portal to death. Hence, "What does physical eroticism signify if not a violation of the very being of its practitioners?—a violation bordering on death, bordering on murder?"[58] Bataille is not asserting here that the erotic action itself need be violent but rather that its *effects* are intrinsically violent, that it shakes a person to his or her core. This is yet another way in which eroticism is akin to death. Not only does eroticism mimic death in creating a continuity between one being and another, but it foreshadows death in its inherent tremulousness. Eroticism is thus a primary means by which to metaphorize continuity, as an echo of the dematerialization and subsequent continuity only imagined in death. "We achieve the power to look death in the face and to perceive in death the pathway into unknowable and incomprehensible continuity—that path is the secret of eroticism and eroticism alone can reveal it," he writes in a key passage. Or more succinctly: "Eroticism opens the way to death."[59]

The Writer's Body (After Bataille)

I feel near death. How can this be? So many men and women I have known have been diagnosed with the virus but not me. When Joah came home with the results of his antibody test, the ironically "positive" but oh-so-negative results, we held each other for a very long time. And then, holding my breath, I went for my test too. When I shared with my mother the "negative" outcome, she reflexively belched out huge sobs of relief. Now that I am a parent I can imagine how she must have felt while waiting for the test results—so trepidatious and yet so hopeful.

Like many gay men in the United States and the gay, lesbian, and straight caregivers among us, I have since learned to compartmentalize in locked sections of my brain the memory of those first illnesses, those night sweats so intensely enervating that they left the sheets literally soaked and the bodies on them lying limp. The muscled, toned, firm, and shapely bodies that seemed to shrink to bone and sinew before our eyes. The thick curls that unexpectedly came out by handfuls, until the few remaining wisps lay damp and lifeless on gray foreheads. Gray. Gray. Bodies seeming to lose their color, their pinkish blush, their deep bronzes, turning gray. Gray.

These are the bodies I have not wanted to see and the body I have not wanted to be. But tonight I feel near death, sicker than I have been in the ten years that Peter has known me, he says. Here I am, curled up on the floor of my office wrapped in a leather coat, though the thermostat registers 74 degrees on this unseasonably warm winter evening in Los Angeles. I am hot and then I am cold. I ache all over, especially deep in my joints. I feel like an old man. I am not an old man, but the feeling is palpable. This is what old age must be like, I think. This is definitely what sickness is like. This is what my now-dead friends must have suffered, or something like this, in the grizzly days of their protracted illnesses.

I am being histrionic, a drama queen. But this is how my mind goes. The Pandora's box in my brain, the little compartment in which is contained all the fearsome memories of those bodies, those gray bodies, opens up and the memories come flooding out. I am sick. They were sicker. Sicker than I. And for much longer. And then I realize what has happened to trigger this flood of memory.

Last night we had sex, in a different way than we have in a very long time. It was more like we used to in the early 1980s, when the pleasure of doing what we wanted, when we wanted, how we wanted, ran so deep and rich and was so suffused in us that everything felt better than it does most times now. Even things that hurt. Teeth on cocks, butts, assholes, lips, shoulders, nipples, balls, toes, fingers. All of it. All the body. All that pleasure. We went there again last night. Too often we hold back—on account of the way sex scares us now and forces us to confront the locked box, the compartment in our brains, which is where we hold the memory of what we have lived through. Irrationally, many of our fears have become attached to sex, and to the vulnerable parts of our bodies—especially the parts that have come to symbolize both pleasure and death.

Some of us have always been afraid of our assholes, now even more so, given what this part of our bodies has come to mean. Leo Bersani wrote an essay whose title articulates that fear in the form of a question: "Is the Rectum a Grave?"[60] Is the asshole death? And yet the rectum, the anus, the asshole, is there in the back of our minds, so powerfully, so close to consciousness, as the place of pleasure that we remember, the place that our first lovers taught us to know, and in respect of which they whisperingly guided us to expand in order to accept their love, their penetrative love, their fucking love. It is this place in the body that has become like death itself, this place that we had learned so painstakingly and so productively to view as a site of pleasure.

Why should anyone care about this? What difference do gay assholes make? I cannot even begin to say. Our bodies, our gay bodies, our American male bodies, our 1980s and '90s homosexual bodies, were made in their current forms, mapped by their

current desires, through a set of practices we learned and then unlearned and then perhaps relearned. But even those of us whose ability to compartmentalize may in some ways be all too good still falter when it comes to controlling the meaning of the anus, this body part that in the early 1980s seemed to turn deadly on us. We went there last night. Can it be only coincidental that today I feel near death?

The asshole and the act of penetration have been the hall-marks of gay male sexuality through my entire life as a gay man in the U.S., starting in the late 1970s and continuing into the twenty-first century. Certainly, other body parts and other acts are larded with feeling and desire for gay men, but the asshole is singular in puckering so privately at the crossroads of fear, pleasure, and stigma. This effulgent trio predates AIDS yet is unmistakably volatilized by it. Homosexuality and its practices aside, the asshole is in its ordinary function the orifice of the body from which wastes are expelled. It is the body's garbage chute. At the symbolic level, however, it marks what Mary Douglas would call a "margin" of the body, that is, a boundary between what matters—the living flesh—and what doesn't—that which is ex-creted.[61] Unlike that other margin, the skin, however, which serves as an outline of the body, as its functional and physically stimulating container, the anus is more freighted with meaning, although it remains almost always a bodily secret concealed from view. Even as a site of pleasure it leads a double life, as the secret valve through which flatulence and feces exit the body. It exists under constant pressure—always holding back the con-tents of the intestines, feeling the load that accumulates behind it and that must be evacuated. Depending on where and how we are raised, we will have spent a considerable length of time working out the proper ways to control the anal valve, when to open it, when to hold it closed, how to clean it, and the impor-tance of that cleanliness in relation to health and disease. Thus the anus is, as a matter of degree, unlike any other bodily orifice in existing as a key portal over which the individual learns to exert a seriously consequential control. This control is closely linked to fears not only of "body dirt"—to use another phrase of Douglas's—but of contagion and disease as well.

Erotic actuation of the anus, then, requires an adult relearning of information inculcated within the first impressionable years of life. Most of us are taught to think of the anus as dirty (like the character in Bataille's *W.C.*)—best kept out of sight and under tight stricture. To suggest, alternatively, the anus as a site of pleasure, and generative pleasure at that, inviting touch, stimulation, and penetration, would seem ludicrous. One could hardly expect mental agreement with this new premise to be translated into immediate physical receptivity. As anyone who has ventured into the territory of anal eroticism knows well, rigorously disciplined muscles do not automatically allow venturesome fingers, dildos, or cocks to enter. Early attempts to allow penetration are often, though not always, painful. But once the initial pain has been endured, enormous pleasure, suffusing pleasure, awaits. And so I assert that this part of the body that has come to symbolize death is present in everything we make, every cultural artifact we produce, every dance we construct, and every choreographic activity in which we participate. It is our axis mundi, imbricated with meaning as a touchstone of our bodies and as the key to our very corporeality. The rectum may be a grave, but it is also life itself. Thus no transcendence for gay men can be posited without accounting first for the enduring experience of anal eroticism.

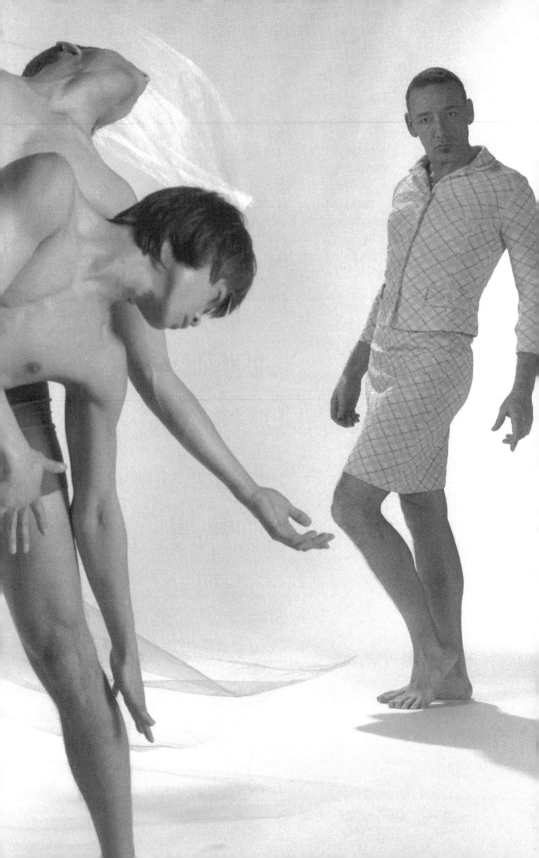

Epilogue

A live performance of Mark Dendy's *Dream Analysis* at Dance Theater Workshop in New York City has catapulted to its conclusion, and the audience is in a decidedly giddy mood. This dance-theater show is a comedy, after all, a thinking person's comedy peopled with multiple Martha Grahams and Vaslav Nijinskys, and it leaves one feeling lighthearted, buoyant, free. But then, even before the applause has died down, Dendy saunters to the edge of the stage in his skimpy "faun" costume and makes this plaintive appeal: Dancers with HIV and AIDS are in need of support during this time of continuing crisis. Won't you please give a donation to Dancers Responding to AIDS?

Depending on your point of view, this postperformance oration is either annoying (must he spoil a lovely evening?) or gracious (somebody ought to thank this guy for caring). And therein lies the split that has grown in the arts—and particularly in contemporary dance—as we speed toward the official twenty-fifth year of the AIDS epidemic in the United States. Nobody would argue with the proposition that AIDS has been with us too long already. A feeling of exhaustion seems inevitable. Denial too. But at the same time "it ain't over," as the choreographer Bill T. Jones intoned repeatedly from the stage of the Brooklyn Academy as part of a recent pitch for Dancers Responding to AIDS. The AIDS epidemic can't be over when you hear anecdotal reports of those who don't respond to the new drugs or can't afford them. Or

At left: Felipe Barrueto Cabello and Vong Phrommala (left) with Joe Goode in Goode's *Deeply There,* 1998. Photo: © Terrence McCarthy.

when you contemplate the estimated 750,000 to one million Americans living with the knowledge that the virus is still active, perhaps replicating, in their bodies. Or when you read that new cases, especially among young people and women, continue unabated. Or when you learn that middle-aged white men, the same white men who in the 1980s had heeded calls for safer sex and survived, are now seroconverting in rising numbers. Indeed, if the activism and efforts to raise money stop now, history will surely berate us for quitting too soon.

What's more, even if the epidemic *were* over, its crucial artistic effects would remain. For even while HIV knows no particular target, it has had an undeniably devastating effect on the performing arts in general and dance in particular, contributing, for example, to ancillary debates regarding the question of whether most male dancers are gay, and casting a pall of mourning over much of the creative work of the last two decades. Whatever happens with the new advances in medical science, AIDS is a defining event—perhaps the defining event—of late-twentieth-century theatrical dance.

One striking bit of evidence for the omnipresent effect of AIDS is the degree to which the postperformance financial pitch and the benefit performance have evolved into vibrant art forms in their own right. One of the most distinctive AIDS events of the New York season, the *Remember Project* of Dancers Responding to AIDS (DRA), takes place each year on or near December 1, World AIDS Day, under the auspices of the Danspace Project at St. Mark's Church. This annual dance marathon, from noon to midnight, supports DRA and its umbrella organization, Broadway Cares/Equity Fights AIDS, in distributing $250,000 annually to subsidize rent and health care for dancers with HIV. About eighty companies and individuals commonly take part, and honors are given to the organization's major fund-raisers.

But whether or not more money is raised, or a cure found, it seems clear that AIDS will endure in choreography as an indelible cultural artifact, preserved in the politics and aesthetic practices of this era's diverse dance artists. In her infamous screed in the *New Yorker* a decade ago, the dance critic Arlene Croce decried the rise of this sort of work, calling it "victim art."[1] I would not use that scurrilous phrase, if only because people living with AIDS make it a practice not to think of themselves as victims.

Nor would I want to denigrate art that speaks directly to the issues of our time. In my view, that is exactly what art does best.

But even if, owing to the cumulative effects of exhaustion, denial, and homophobia, a segment of the public actually wanted artists to stop making financial appeals from the stage, or creating work about loss, or finding ways to speak about AIDS in their choreography, such efforts would have negligible effect. Death and grief, mourning and AIDS activism have, in fact, become so integral to the culture of the arts at the start of the millennium that the stamp of AIDS will surely remain on us long after the epidemic actually comes to an end—assuming it does. Moreover, the moment when the dancer becomes a spokesman in the fight against AIDS, verbally or choreographically, is highly charged. This is the moment when the dancer looks his (sometimes her) audience in the eye and says, AIDS is not over, the needs of my colleagues are overwhelming, and until a day arrives that I cannot now imagine even in my wildest dreams, I must continue to mourn, publicly and militantly. This is my Holocaust, and I must always remember.

In choreography the form and content of AIDS remembering endure even as they undergo subtle shifts. Though hundreds of explicit "AIDS dances" have been created since the early 1980s, only a very few dances in the late 1990s and early 2000s make direct reference to AIDS. But these days choreography need not specifically refer to AIDS for an audience member to sense its reverberations. David Roussève, for example, whose *Love Songs* (1998) toured widely, did not set out to make a work about AIDS, though he has in the past. Still, he says, "I have been so altered, changed by the AIDS crisis—particularly emotionally—that AIDS is very much reflected in this piece."[2]

Resonances of AIDS can therefore turn up quite unexpectedly. In building a work around the narrative of two African American slaves who fall in love and are brutally separated from each other, Roussève asked his dancers to contribute material that was as intimate as possible without being directly sexual. Julie Tolentino, one of Roussève's dancers, devised a scene in which she enters to find another dancer, Ilaan Egeland, lying perfectly still on the floor. Tolentino then changes Egeland's clothes. As Roussève explains: "In real life, Julie had once actually gone over to a friend's house who had died of AIDS, and she had changed him into his

Julie Tolentino and Ilaan Egeland in David Roussève's *Love Songs,* 1998. Photo: Lois Greenfield. Courtesy of David Roussève.

burial clothes. And it was the most intimate and disturbing thing she had done in her entire life."[3] Roussève believes that some viewers divine the literal reference in that scene. But others will see it as "an abstract image of trying to get something that you'll never be able to get from a person, from a lover." Regardless, he adds, "The emotional core that's feeding that scene is certainly the AIDS crisis."

But even as artists like Roussève find the resonance of AIDS at a deep, almost unconscious, level, others continue to create works that directly address recognizable aspects of the syndrome, often to disturbing effect. Joe Goode's works since the early 1990s have all, directly or indirectly, addressed the omnipresence of AIDS, and his 1998 *Deeply There (Stories of a Neighborhood)* is a musical centered on the character of Ben, an unseen figure—the prototypical gay man dying of AIDS—symbolized by tousled bedclothes on a movable bed. In a review of the New York premiere the *New York Times* critic Jennifer Dunning likened the effect of the work to the ache at the heart of James Agee's novel *A Death in the Family*. But after the San Francisco premiere of *Deeply There,* Goode received a letter from a longtime supporter who was distressed by the theme. The letter described in moving terms the truthfulness of Goode's portrayal of the caregivers who surround Ben as he becomes sicker and sicker and ultimately dies. But then, the writer, a gay man, continued, "Why are you making a piece about AIDS now?" Goode was taken aback, interpreting the query as a fervent argument for denial: "We are in this respite from having to go to memorial services, so why am I making him think about this?"[4]

For Goode and other gay male choreographers, making dances about AIDS or asking for money from the stage or dedicating time to other volunteer efforts (Goode is head of the fund-raising committee of the Parachute Fund, the San Francisco equivalent of Dancers Responding to AIDS) is not so much a matter of choice as an unavoidable imperative, a compulsion to overcome melancholic ennui. The energized alternative, as Douglas Crimp has argued, is a rigorous and committed melancholic activism.

Indeed, in the resolution to *Deeply There,* Goode sings a soliloquy to Ben that seems to suggest that his grief will one day come to graceful closure. "Don't worry, I will be fine," he croons in a

Notes

Introduction

1. Weinstein, "Acts: Live Boys."

2. I transcribed this text from the videotape of *Live Boys,* performed in April 1981 at Hallwalls performance space in Buffalo, New York. I want to thank Tim Miller for providing me with a copy of the tape. Glen Johnson, professor of media studies at Catholic University in Washington, D.C., is preparing a transcript of the videotaped performance of *Live Boys;* he plans to include the transcript in his book of texts by Tim Miller, *A Tim Miller Reader,* forthcoming from the University of Michigan Press.

3. A portfolio of related material published in the *PWA Coalition Newsline* from June 1985 to November 1987, and from *Surviving and Thriving with AIDS: Hints for the Newly Diagnosed,* both texts edited by Michael Callen, is reprinted as "PWA Coalition Portfolio," in Crimp, *AIDS,* 147–68.

4. The "victim" appellation was also commonly applied to those with diseases such as cancer, which at one time had been stigmatized nearly as strongly as AIDS. See Sontag, *Illness and Metaphor; and AIDS and Its Metaphors.*

5. Treichler, "AIDS, Homophobia, and Biomedical Discourse," in Crimp, *AIDS,* 31–70. This essay is reprinted in Treichler, *How to Have Theory in an Epidemic,* 11–41.

6. For a standard notion of choreography see Lincoln Kirstein, who writes: "Choreography is a map of movement—patterns for action" (*Movement and Metaphor,* 4).

7. For a history of this period see Banes, *Democracy's Body.*

8. Johnston, *Marmalade Me,* 189.

9. Denby, *Dance Writings,* 548–56.

10. Foster, *Corporealities*, xi.

11. The notion of bodies as being "constructed" is not meant to deny their biological formation but rather to reveal the ways in which knowledge shapes their discursive formation. This formation may take physical shape, for example, in bodily practices such as body building that literally transform the body's physiology, its physical facts. But it may also take the shape of beliefs about the body and its meanings.

The concept of the discursive formation of the body, building upon feminist readings of the construction of gender, has been explored to great effect by a group of scholars working on the historical construction of the body in the West. One fine example is the collection edited by Catherine Gallagher and Thomas Laqueur, *The Making of the Modern Body: Sexuality and Society in the Nineteenth Century.* In its introduction Gallagher summarizes the impetus for her project in a way that could easily apply to gay male bodies in the time of AIDS:

Scholars have only recently discovered that the human body itself has a history. Not only has it been perceived, interpreted, and represented differently in different epochs, but it has also been lived differently, brought into being within widely dissimilar material cultures, subjected to various technologies and means of control, and incorporated into different rhythms of production and consumption, pleasure and pain. (vii)

These are the phenomena that I explore in this book.

12. Sedgwick, *Between Men.*

13. Jones, *Untitled.*

14. Another student in the class thought that *Untitled* was about AIDS for a different reason: because the penultimate section of the piece is accompanied by an aria that she associated with Tom Hanks's operatic scene in the AIDS film *Philadelphia* (1993).

15. A possible exception is Anna Halprin's *Positive Motion: Dancing with Life on the Line,* which features a mixed cast of men and women, gay and straight, infected and uninfected. Still, since it was impossible to distinguish HIV-negative and -positive women from one another in performance, all tended to signify as HIV negative. The same was true of the men, but they all tended to signify as HIV positive, at least for this viewer.

16. Parks, "Passion's Progress," 55–56.

17. Kisselgoff, "Dance: Lubovitch Troupe."

18. Ibid.

19. Goldstein speaks of the "noble neuter" in Hollywood films of the 1990s that allow homosexual characters to take starring roles but only on the condition that they have no sex lives ("No Sex, Please, We're Gay," 51).

20. Kisselgoff's interpretations are echoed in a review of the company's November 1986 season by an openly gay man, the *Village Voice* writer Burt Supree. He too writes of the adagio's unintimidating quality, describing it as "chaste and tender, with that open-hearted spirit" ("Bright Spirits," *Village Voice* [9 December 1986]).

21. Berman, "An Evening of Commitment to 'Life.'"

22. Greskovic, "13 Troupes Join 'Dancing for Life' War on AIDS."

23. Stuart, "Dancing for Life at the New York State Theater," p. 38.

24. Keith White, "Passionate Communions."

25. Parks, "Passion's Progress," 56. Parks reports that at this point Lubovitch's smile wavers and, his mouth set, he continues:

There were other things motivating it, though. The dance was also motivated by AIDS, because so many dancers have been stricken with AIDS, something the dance world doesn't own up to, much to my regret. I felt that I wanted to show a version of male love on a platonic and high-minded level, to show the dignity of men who love each other as friends, that all men do have another man in their lives that they love so dearly, not in a homosexual relationship, but just all men, homosexual or heterosexual, have men that they love in their lives. But it's such a delicate subject, and such an embarrassing subject for so many men that it's very hard for them to deal with it, [and therefore] it's so rarely dealt with.

26. Bill T. Jones, interview by author, telephone, 1 April 1998.

27. I base my discussion of *Still/Here* on three live performances that I saw in Los Angeles and Pittsburgh in April and June 1995, as well as repeated viewings of a videotaped performance document from the Brooklyn Academy of Music (2 December 1994).

28. My handwritten notes, Wiltern Theater, Los Angeles, 28–29 April 1995.

29. Jacobs, "In the Mail: Who's the Victim?"

30. In the public talk preceding the Los Angeles performances of *Still/Here,* Jones explained the title thus: He had just returned from touring a colossal full-evening work, *Last Supper at Uncle Tom's Cabin/The Promised Land,* when he received a call at his office from a donor who wanted to know the title of his next work. "Tell them I'm *still here,*" Jones shouted in frustration at the person who answered the phone in his office. The name stuck.

31. Jones, *Last Night on Earth,* 183.

32. Gates, "The Body Politic," p. 123.

33. This accounts for the lack of discussion of classical ballets in this text, for in almost every instance the AIDS ballet obfuscates its meanings to such a degree that an AIDS interpretation can appear farfetched.

Often this results from casting a heterosexual couple as the central figures. Or it may be a result of skewed point of view, for example, focusing on the bond between mother and son rather than between son and lover. I hope to write about these twinned phenomena in a separate essay.

34. Janice Sukaitis, personal communication, 10 December 2002.

35. Felicitously, my very first act in relation to the book was to attempt a frame-by-frame analysis of Lar Lubovitch's duet from *Concerto Six Twenty-Two* in the style of Barthes's *S/Z*. This process proved revelatory for me and subsequently came to inform all my research for this project. (I have spared readers the complete analytical sketches, but these lengthy—one might even say laborious—discursive texts have formed the basis of the more reader-friendly description and analysis here.) What aspect of Barthes's semiotic approach have I adopted? In *S/Z* Barthes appropriates Balzac's novella *Sarrasine* and "manhandles" it. That is, he cuts the written "tutor text" (description) into 561 fragments and categorizes each within a scheme of five codes: hermeneutic, semantic, proairetic, cultural, or symbolic. Having shattered the story into bits, irrevocably interrupting its narrative linearity, he specifically chooses not to put them back together. In place of a traditional "reading" or interpretation of the narrative, Barthes then undertakes—like certain ascetic Buddhists he has heard of—"to see a whole landscape in a bean."

This procedure of minute parsing and detailed inspection can be adapted quite easily to the reading of dances, which leads to a study of dance in the AIDS era that is based on approaches drawn from semiotics as well as contemporary critical theory. The application of Barthes's procedure to dance, however, requires a preliminary step that Barthes's did not: the text of the dance—its language of bodies and movements— must first be transformed into a verbal text. It must be set in words, as what Barthes calls a "tutor text." This translation process (and, indeed, it is a form of translation as radical as shifting from Mandarin Chinese to English) puts a certain problematic distance between the dance and its analysis. Such a wealth of information is contained in a body, let alone a moving body, that attempts to verbalize its corporeality might easily lead to a verbal avalanche: a single moment could become two hundred printed pages and even then not satisfactorily capture the body's semiotic capabilities. This is so because the body is continually spewing "signs," which are subject to meaning-filled interpretation. And so a decision must be made in moving from dance text to verbal text: what to include and what to leave out?

For the purposes of this study I have chosen what I consider to be a middle ground, which I have further mediated by modulating the level of specificity of the written descriptions. Neither have I glossed the chosen dances the way I would if I were writing a piece of journalism, nor have I sought to mine each choreography's every subtlety.

36. Siegel, *Shapes of Change*, xviii.

37. Román, *Acts of Intervention*, 5.

38. Ibid., 8.

39. Ibid., 10.

40. Ibid., 9. The first AIDS fund raiser was at the activist playwright Larry Kramer's apartment on 11 August 1981, five weeks after the *Times* article about gay cancer. The ensuing early years of the epidemic brought a proliferation of fund raisers, notably a 1983 circus benefit that directly addressed the dialogue between homosexuality and patriotism begun on page A20 of the *Times*. The identity markers "homosexual" and "American" were finally brought together at New York's Madison Square Garden in 1983 when Leonard Bernstein conducted the orchestra of the Ringling Brothers and Barnum and Bailey Circus in "The Star-Spangled Banner."

> Less than two years before, when the *New York Times* first reported AIDS alongside the perforated sheet music to "The Star Spangled Banner," gay men had no counter-effective tactic to unsettle the ideology of heteronormative patriotism. On April 30, 1983, the lesbian and gay community, along with the ever-expanding AIDS community, joined forces to stage an unprecedented response to AIDS. (Román, *Acts of Intervention*, 20)

Not surprisingly, "The *New York Times* failed to report the occasion" (20).

41. In snatches from the apparently autobiographical monologues in the piece, Bernd says, "A lot of the problem was competition, two artists, it's hard, a lot of jealousy," and later, "The only way it could end was for one of us to go away."

42. The résumé is one of hundreds of documents in the John Bernd Papers housed at the Harvard Theatre Collection, Houghton Library. I am grateful to the library, and especially to the head librarian, Annette Fern, for allowing me access to these materials.

43. *Surviving Love and Death* was performed at P.S. 122 in New York 25-28 December 1981 and 22-25 January 1982. A video document is housed at the Harvard Theatre Collection.

44. Earlier in the piece Bernd had intoned: "You have something within you . . . something within you . . . we don't know," in what appears to be a loop of phrases he heard from his doctors. "I'm always tired," he responds, "I am tired."

45. Loose pages in the Bernd papers at Harvard appear to constitute the script for this section. The complete text to be "spoken during blending" is given as follows:

what to do what to do what to do
oh what to do
I do not wish to die until I have been
of service to my gifts
and is to my destiny to love and seek look [*sic*]
and where is the meeting of heaven and earth
it is the line on the horizon which we shall never reach
and things don't end they change
and I am man
I am woman
I am Christ
I am Lucifer
I am the queen
I am the prince
I am a shamin [*sic*]

Please note that the John Bernd Collection at Harvard was thoroughly catalogued after my August 2001 visit. All paper documents related to *Surviving Love and Death* have been gathered in the box designated "Series: 1. Choreographic Works, file folders 35–42. For an on-line guide to the collection, see http://oasis.harvard.edu/html/hou00151.html (15 September 2003).

46. The "how to" reference in the title positions my project in a lineage of AIDS texts dating from near the beginning of the official epidemic in the United States, generally established as mid-1981. Three key essays since 1981 have chosen this construction as a frame for the presentation of critical analyses. The first, "How to Have Sex in an Epidemic: One Approach"—a primer written and self-published by the AIDS activists Richard Berkowitz and Michael Callen, using money from Callen's income tax refund—set out to instruct gay men in methods for engaging in sex without exchanging body fluids. (The radical nature of this proposal becomes clear if one realizes that Berkowitz and Callen were writing even as sexphobic public health advocates were advising gay men, essentially, to stay indoors and keep their hands and dicks to themselves.) The second text in the lineage, "How to Have Promiscuity in an Epidemic" (in *AIDS*, 237–71), was penned by Crimp within months of the publication of Randy Shilts's *And the Band Played On*. Printed with unusual speed, Crimp's essay in the academic journal *October* encompassed a fervent critique of Shilts's widely read account of the epidemic, which, in line with mainstream U.S. thinking and values, had blamed gay sexual promiscuity—personified by a sexually voracious flight attendant whom Shilts dubbed "Patient Zero"—for the spread of AIDS. (Shilts's motives were made clear during an encounter

I had with him at a book-signing party in 1987, when I directly challenged him on the politics of his "Patient Zero" scenario. His response,
accompanied by an unforgettable grimace: "Yeah, but it sure sold a lot
of books.") The third essay, Treichler's "How to Have Theory in an Epidemic," doubles as the title of her 1999 collection of essays written during nearly twenty years of the AIDS epidemic in the U.S. Virtually all
her essays seek to analyze—to theorize—the accompanying epidemic
of fraught meanings. Taken together, the three "how to" essays rank as
exemplary achievements of AIDS cultural analysis because they focus
attention on the most volatile issue attaching itself to the epidemic in
the United States, and that is gay sex. Homosexual intercourse, I argue
in this study, also becomes the central issue in the production and reception of choreography about AIDS. Precisely because Americans
equate dance and homosexuality—specifically, to the practice of man-
on-man sex—choreography has attained ground-zero status in the
cultural and antihomosexual wars characterizing American public discourse since the early 1980s. Dance equals homosexuality. Homosexuality equals AIDS. Dance equals death. This fevered knot of criss-
crossed meanings, with festered origins long predating the AIDS era,
has, in a deadly irony, been activated by the very visibility of gay choreographers and dancers as they become ill, die, mourn, or make
dances in full view of the public. Thus the issues that were central to the
earlier writers of the "how to" manuals for gay men are the very same
issues that are central to a study of choreography in the age of AIDS:
how to perform (choreographic or sexual, take your pick) activity in the
face of sexual stigma and the fear of death?

1. Blood and Sweat

1. "AIDS and the Arts," videocassette.
2. The dancers included Jones and Zane as well as Demian Acquavella, Arthur Aviles, Sean Curran, and Lawrence Goldhuber. Goldhuber was, in fact, closeted in 1987 when he joined the company, but he
came out later (Goldhuber interview). Zane died in 1988, Acquavella in
1990. Jones revealed his HIV-positive status in an interview with the
Advocate after Zane's death (Jones, *Last Night on Earth*, 250); as of this
writing he remains asymptomatic. A seventh male dancer, Heywood
"Woody" McGriff Jr., left the company in 1987 to teach at the University
of Texas, Austin. He died of AIDS-related causes in 1994.
3. Dance/USA, "AIDS in the Dance/Arts Work Place," 12.
4. Jordan, "Jupiter and Antinous."
5. Hayden White, "Bodies and Their Plots," 234.
6. The notion that contagion lived at the level of the skin was almost

surely the result of the public health training that accompanied a previous epidemic of herpes, which can in fact be transmitted by touch. See Brandt, *No Magic Bullet*.

7. This British film is set in the mid-1990s, but in my view the issues that it explores seem more characteristic of the mid- to late 1980s.

8. Hayden White, "Bodies and Their Plots," 234.

9. Douglas, *Purity and Danger*, 3.

10. Douglas, *Natural Symbols*, 87.

11. That is, sweating—as medical symptomatology—is in an indexical relationship (in the Peircean sense) to the syndrome that causes it. Laura Mulvey, in a 1998 guest lecture at UCLA titled "The Index and the Uncanny," illustrated the special characteristic of medical symptoms as signifiers, a notion for which she draws upon the work of Charles S. Peirce (Peirce, "Logic as Semiotic") and Umberto Eco (*A Theory of Semiotics*). I am grateful to her for providing these references in a subsequent telephone conversation (10 April 1998).

12. Gere, "Thoroughly Modern Misha," p. C7.

13. In his eponymous introduction to *AIDS* (pp. 3–16), Crimp puts forward the view that artists bear a special responsibility to serve as activists in this time of AIDS and that art can actually contribute to finding a cure—for example, by goading drug companies to speed their drug trials. The second and arguably more trenchant of the points made in the 1987 volume was that, just as the HIV virus that causes AIDS is deadly, so too is the irrational assumption that gayness is equivalent to AIDS. Crimp's introduction is reprinted along with other essays in his *Melancholia and Moralism*.

14. Berkowitz and Callen, *How to Have Sex*, 3.

15. Treichler, "AIDS, Homophobia, and Biomedical Discourse," 32, 40. This essay is reprinted in Treichler's *How to Have Theory in an Epidemic*.

16. Ibid., 42.

17. Ibid., 32, 33. These are just three of thirty-eight items listed by Treichler in her catalog of the "epidemic of meanings," each of which is footnoted in her text. Here I am quoting her paraphrases of those sources.

18. Leader, "AIDS: Dancing for Life." This is a common sentiment underlying AIDS reportage emanating from the dance field, including much of my own from the late 1980s and early 1990s. Jody Leader's article is just one example.

19. Hays, "Nureyev's Death a Reminder."

20. Dunning, "Choreographing Deaths of the Heart."

21. Croce, "Discussing the Undiscussable."

22. Shapiro, "Daring Young Man."

23. Jones interview by Charlie Rose.

24. The New York choreographer Senta Driver tells of the special arrangements she made when touring with an HIV-positive dancer who carried a Hickman catheter in his chest. Driver made elaborate plans to deal safely with blood spillage should the dancer be involved in a collision or should his catheter leak, and she reports that she had to put them into action on at least one occasion (Driver interview).

25. For a thorough and eloquent reading of Athey's work, very much related to this discussion of blood and homophobia, see Román's *Acts of Intervention*, pp. 149–53. Athey's piece was performed at the Walker in May 1994 and again at New York's P.S. 122 that October. See also Catherine Gund's documentary film *Hallelujah! Ron Athey: A Story of Deliverance*.

26. Keith Hennessy, personal communication (e-mail), 12 November 2002. The performance took place 17–18 September 1993, at San Francisco's Footwork Studio.

27. *The Test* was performed as part of the Danger Zone performance festival at Theater 200 in UCLA's Dance Building, 9–12 February 1995. Martínéz described the piece and its development on 18 April 1995, as a guest in the UCLA class titled "AIDS and Dance."

28. The reconstruction of *Saliva* is based on two articles by the critic Rachel Kaplan ("Spit Your Way to the Holy Land," and "Body Fluids."), the videotaped document of a 1989 performance at Highways Performance Space in Santa Monica (courtesy Keith Hennessy), and my personal recollections of the live 1988 performance in San Francisco. I am grateful to Hennessy for correcting subtle, though important, details of my description of the piece in an e-mail dated 12 November 2002.

29. Hennessy is a San Francisco–based choreographer, dancer, and performance artist. In his own words, as offered in press materials from 1990,

Keith was born in Sudbury, Ontario, Canada in late 1959, the fifth of six opinionated children. Sudbury (250 miles north of Toronto) is a nickel mining town controlled by a ruthless multi-national based in NYC. Keith is a fifth or sixth generation Canadian— mostly Irish and French blood. His parents still live in the same house he grew up in except in winter when they retire to Texas.

After high school Keith ran fast and hard; first to France and then to Montreal where for three years he was enrolled in McGill University's Faculty of Management. In college he discovered he was angry, bisexual, and good at organizing demonstrations. He became an anarchist, vegetarian, improvising, juggler/ dancer who recycled. He quit school and moved to California

by accident. The public speaking, diving, gymnastics, freestyle
skiing, jitterbugging, juggling, languages and organizing became performance life/art.

Hennessy joined Contraband in the mid-1980s and began creating
his own work in 1988. He is currently on the faculty of the cultural activism program at New College of California.

30. It is worth noting that Hennessy's *Saliva*, like much of the work
discussed in this study, incorporates text. I would suggest that, on its
own, movement offers a more complex semiosis than words, that it is
more porous to interpretation. As such, movement allows the viewer to
wrest a degree of authorial control from the creator, if only because each
viewer takes responsibility for his or her own active reading of the
work. In this sense movement makes each viewer an author. The tendency for choreographers in the AIDS era to incorporate words in their
work could be explained as part of a more general trend toward combining text and movement in postmodern performance. But there may
be something more particular to this text-and-movement formulation
as it pertains to AIDS: If part of the project of making choreography in
the age of AIDS is to find ways to foreclose the audience from unwanted interpretations, to prevent the audience—if that were possible—from homophobic or AIDS-phobic responses, one way to do this
would be to incorporate text as a way of narrowing the frame of meanings. Thus the use of text in movement-based work may constitute an
effort on the part of choreographers to regain control of authorship.

31. In his 1934 discussion of bodily techniques, Marcel Mauss relates
the story of a little girl who did not know how to spit. It seems that her
father's family—in fact, his entire village—did not possess this skill.
Mauss taught her by offering her coins in exchange for expectoration.
She was saving up for a bicycle. Significantly, he does not, however, address the issue of taboos (Mauss, "Techniques of the Body, 472).

32. Nonoxynol 9, long touted as a protection against HIV, was later
discovered to be a suspected causal link to HIV infection in cases of
frequent use and resultant irritation. See "Detergent/Care Briefs:
Nonoxynol-9 (N-9)," *Chemical Market Reporter,* 24 July 2000.

33. Kaplan, "Spit Your Way."

34. In his e-mail to me Hennessy reveals that "Jake is a nickname
from my first two initials J K (for John Keith)."

35. Kaplan moved to the Bay Area in the mid-1980s, having recently
graduated from Wesleyan University. As a writer for the *Bay Times,*
High Performance, and (under the pseudonym Lucy Nees) *San Francisco
Weekly,* she immediately became a respected commentator on fringe
dance and performance work in the Bay Area. She is the author of a

collection of performance texts, *The Probable Site of the Garden of Eden,* and has taught collaborative process in the arts and performance art at San Francisco State University.

36. Kaplan, "Spit Your Way."

37. This reconstruction is based on repeated viewings of the video-tape *Seize Control of the FDA.* ACT UP was formed in March 1987 as "a diverse, nonpartisan group united in anger and committed to direct action to end the AIDS crisis." The acronym ACT UP stands for AIDS Coalition to Unleash Power. The organization was, in part, the brainchild of the playwright and AIDS activist Larry Kramer, who devised the idea after being pushed out of Gay Men's Health Crisis (GMHC), the New York organization he had cofounded in the early days of the AIDS epidemic. ACT UP was born in New York, but by 1990 there were autonomous branches in Chicago, Los Angeles, San Francisco, Atlanta, Boston, Denver, Portland, Seattle, Kansas City, New Orleans, Berlin, London, and Paris. By the mid-1990s ACT UP had lost much of its energy, but other groups branched off from it, for example, New York's Sex Panic (Crimp, *AIDS Demo-Graphics,* 13; Kramer, *Reports from the Holocaust,* 137–39).

38. This statistic was offered 11 June 1988 by the epidemiologist Jim Curran in Stockholm in his yearly speech to the International AIDS conference (Shilts, *And the Band Played On,* 607).

39. Crimp, *AIDS Demo-Graphics,* 81.

40. Moore interview.

41. For all his book's faults Shilts offers important and comprehensive coverage of these blood issues in *And the Band Played On.* See in particular pp. 206–7, 220–26, and 242–43.

42. A passionate debate preceded and followed upon the announcement of the CDC guidelines, with the San Francisco Coordinating Committee of Lesbian and Gay Services issuing a policy statement likening the refusal to accept the blood of gay donors to miscegenation blood laws that divided black blood from white (Shilts, *And the Band Played On,* 220). Shilts portrays this as an irresponsible position, and it does seem in retrospect that, in the interest of saving lives, blood from so-called high-risk groups had to be culled. (The CDC guidelines preceded the highly effective test for HIV antibodies that would have made culling unnecessary.) However, the net effect of the CDC's guidelines was to cast the blood of all gay men as dangerous, regardless of their specific sexual practices, contacts, or HIV status. The legacy of that decision continues to reverberate in the generalized danger associated with gay male body fluids. As of this writing, blood banks in the United States still do not accept donations from men who have sex with men.

43. Crimp, *AIDS Demo-Graphics,* 76.

44. The demands submitted to the FDA included the following: "Shorten the drug approval process. . . . No more double-blind placebo trials. . . . Include people from all affected populations at all stages of HIV infection in clinical trials." These are just three of the ten demands (Crimp, *AIDS Demo-Graphics*, 79–80).

45. The SILENCE = DEATH graphic was the creation of a design collective called the SILENCE = DEATH Project, which lent the logo to ACT UP (Crimp, *AIDS Demo-Graphics*, 7 n.8).

46. That protest on 28 July 1988 at the New York City Department of Health featured two posters with bloody handprints. One read, YOU'VE GOT BLOOD ON YOUR HANDS, STEPHEN JOSEPH. THE CUT IN AIDS NUMBERS IS A LETHAL LIE. Another said, YOU'VE GOT BLOOD ON YOUR HANDS, ED KOCH. NYC AIDS CARE DOESN'T EXIST (Crimp, *AIDS Demo-Graphics*, 73).

47. Ibid.

48. *Seize Control of the FDA*, videocassette.

49. Crimp, *AIDS Demo-Graphics*, 33.

50. For a detailed discussion of ACT UP and its use of media see Juhasz, *AIDS TV*.

51. *Seize Control of the FDA*, videocassette.

52. Crimp, *AIDS Demo-Graphics*, 83.

53. ACT UP was not officially formed until 1987 (see Kramer, *Reports from the Holocaust*, 127–39). But as the choreographer and activist Tim Miller told me by e-mail (28 October 2002), there was already a "proto-activist energy" stirring in 1986, as exemplified by a "zap" organized by the Gay and Lesbian Alliance Against Defamation (GLAAD) in New York, against the *New York Post*. For a more thorough account see Alwood, *Straight News*, 236–37.

54. GMHC was founded in the summer of 1982 by the playwright Larry Kramer, along with a small group of friends and associates who took it upon themselves to raise money following the announcement of an epidemic plaguing gay men in major U.S. cities. By the mid-1990s GMHC had become the largest nongovernmental AIDS service organization in the world. See Simon Watney's introduction to the updated and expanded version of Kramer, *Reports from the Holocaust*, xvii; and Kayal, *Bearing Witness*.

55. Jason Childers, personal communication (e-mail), 28 October 2002.

56. Childers, personal communication (e-mail), 12 November 2002.

57. For a discussion of Shawn's closetedness, see my foreword to Sherman and Mumaw, *Barton Mumaw, Dancer*, xiii–xix; and Foulkes, "Dance Is for American Men," 113–46, and Foster, "Closets Full of Dances," 147–207, in Desmond, *Dancing Desires*.

58. Jowitt, "Perfecting Imperfection," 85.

59. The *Voice*'s Burt Supree reviewed the second program of the same evening, including works by Ishmael Houston-Jones, Ching Gonzalez, and Remy Charlip and Ronald Dabney, Neil Greenberg, and Stephen Petronio (Supree, "Is a Puzzlement," 85, 87).

60. Jowitt, "Perfecting Imperfection," 85.

61. Barber, "'Dancing for Our Lives,'" 50.

62. *Eye on Dance*, videocassette.

63. Connors, "To Dance for Life," 97.

64. Among the group of approximately ten at that first meeting were Robert Yesselman, then executive director of the Paul Taylor company; Cora Cahan of the Feld Ballet; Richard Caples of Lubovitch's company; Art Bukovsky of the Merce Cunningham Dance Company; and Charles Dillingham of American Ballet Theatre. Yesselman says that Lubovitch called the group to his studio and, "in his inimitable, very quiet, but very passionate way, [said] that it was high time the dance world acknowledged there was this thing called AIDS." He proposed a benefit performance, saying emphatically, "'We ought to do this.' And he was absolutely right" (Yesselman interview). Everyone in the room agreed.

65. Connors, "To Dance for Life," 97.

66. Yesselman interview.

67. The three-part event would have taken place at the New York State Theater, City Center Theater, and the Brooklyn Academy of Music. Yesselman estimated production costs at close to $700,000: "The economics were immoral; we would have spent too much to make too little" (Connors, "To Dance for Life," 97).

68. Once the format was settled upon, however, they had yet another major hurdle to surmount: raising the upfront money they needed to plan and publicize the event. According to Yesselman, corporate funders were slow to ante up: "This was 1985. The corporations were still not touching AIDS very much . . . because of the stigma. It was gays, it was drug dealers. It seems almost unthinkable now, but corporations didn't want to deal with the issue of AIDS, and they certainly didn't want to be known for putting up money to underwrite an AIDS benefit" (Yesselman interview).

Charlie Ziff, Yesselman's best friend and a leading arts marketer, volunteered his work and that of his firm, Ziff Marketing, to develop strategy for and market the entire event. His first step was to run a full-page advertisement, designed and placed pro bono by his firm, in the *New York Times*. Zack Manna, who worked in public relations (in 2003 he was president of Broadway Cares/Equity Fights AIDS), convinced AT&T, his employer, to pay for the *Times* ad. Ziff was diagnosed with AIDS about four months into planning for the event and, according to Yesselman, "took this on with a passion." The plan was to raise the upfront money by selling advance tickets. But then, on the basis of AT&T's contribution—which, as it turns out, inspired a hate-mail campaign—Yesselman was able to go to Phillip Morris and say, "'AT&T just did it, why don't you do it?' And they came in with fifty thousand bucks" (Yesselman interview). Another major contribution came from Lincoln Center itself, when Peter Martins, co-ballet-master-in-chief of the New York City Ballet, managed to arrange to use the New York State Theater, "and he got it for free," Yesselman says. Martins also brought in Anne Bass, a new-to–New York society woman who sat on the board of the New York City Ballet. She served as cochair of the event, drawing on an old alliance between Martins's ballet company and the New York elite, and—although this was not articulated explicitly by the participants—between a profession dominated by gay men and largely supported by society women. "Anne Bass was fantastic," Yesselman says, "selling fifty-thousand-dollar box seats, [securing] catering at cost, flowers from the fanciest place in town for cheap. She made it an event. Of course, all the board members of all the dance companies had to be there—that was a lot of presold tickets" (Yesselman interview). American Ballet Theatre kicked in too by bringing in Nan Kempner as social cochair and by lending the company's artistic director, Mikhail Baryshnikov, as host and featured dancer in a new work by Mark Morris, *Drink to Me Only with Thine Eyes*. This would give the benefit star presence and, for the critics, a coveted sneak preview of the Morris dance.

Once the planners had worn down most of the organizational and corporate resistance to the idea of a benefit, the biggest responsibility facing the committee shifted to programming: whom to invite to perform—and in what repertory. According to Connors, "As word of the event spread, it seemed everyone in the dance world wanted to participate" (97), which put the organizers in an enviable but uncomfortable position. (Years later the organizers still worry that certain choreographers have not forgiven them for being left off the list.) The committee members, especially Yesselman and Ziff, working with Robbins, felt that the benefit had to spotlight the bigger uptown companies, which would maximize box office appeal while still including representatives from the downtown scene. "This is an artistic event, but it is an artistic event which must raise $1.4 million," Yesselman explained to Connors. "Once that was mentioned, I think most of the choices became rather obvious" (Connors, "To Dance for Life," 98). In the end the thirteen companies chosen to participate ranged from the big ballet troupes (New York City Ballet, American Ballet Theatre, Joffrey Ballet, Dance Theatre of Harlem) to the major modern dance companies (Alvin Ailey American Dance Theater, Merce Cunningham Dance Company, Martha Graham Dance Company, Paul Taylor Dance Company, and Twyla

Tharp Dance) to a subset of relatively new, relatively small dance organizations (Laura Dean Dancers and Musicians, Feld Ballet, Lar Lubovitch Dance Company, and the Mark Morris Dance Group; Morris was
then just breaking in to the bigger leagues). The truly small upstart
groups were not even considered, because, as I mentioned earlier, they
had in fact bested the big guns by holding their own community benefit the year before. Mark Russell, director of P.S. 122, threw his full support behind *Dancing for Life* in Connors's *Village Voice* article. "It's not
the way of downtown to get involved in this big kind of thing," he said.
"People know it's happening, and we're glad they got it together. I almost had a benefit that same week, then pulled it when I heard about
this. That's where all the money should go that week" (Connors, "To
Dance for Life," 98).

As for which dances would be performed, that was largely left to
Robbins to negotiate. New York City Ballet and American Ballet Theatre
had never danced on the same stage before, which raised the stakes on
their offerings, and Yesselman felt he was in no position to tell Merce
Cunningham which of his dances to put on the stage. "We needed
somebody who could keep people in control . . . somebody well respected and strong," Yesselman recalled. When he approached Robbins,
the renowned choreographer had just lost a close associate to AIDS and
was immediately receptive. "We asked him, as artistic director, to put
the evening together. And he did it," Yesselman says. Moreover, Robbins did it with enormous invention, evoking what Anna Kisselgoff described in the *New York Times* as "an aura of collage, based on its wide
swings in dance aesthetics" (Kisselgoff, "Dance"). Robbins decided that
the dancing would begin with Laura Dean's ritualistic *Magnetic*, then
veer toward ballet with a pas de deux from Gerald Arpino's *Kettentanz*
for two members of the Joffrey, shift to modern dance with an excerpt
from Cunningham's *Fabrications*, and whirl in the direction of a fast
waltz with the final movement of Eliot Feld's *Embraced Waltzes* for four
couples. Then, in a smart stroke of programming, three separate companies in succession would dance to Bach: Mark Morris's dancers in the
first section of his *Marble Halls*, Dance Theatre of Harlem in the second
movement of Balanchine's *Concerto Barocco*, and, in a lucky convergence, the last movement of the same Bach concerto as choreographed
by Paul Taylor in *Esplanade*. Then the program returned to a more eclectic assemblage, with the Graham company dancing *Acts of Light*, based
on the basic Graham technique class; Dudley Williams performing as a
soloist in Ailey's *A Song for You*; and Twyla Tharp reprising her drunken
dance from *Eight Jelly Rolls*. Two works to Mozart would follow: the central duet from Lar Lubovitch's *Concerto Six Twenty-Two*, and the New
York City Ballet in the first movement of Balanchine's *Divertimento No.*

15. Then Baryshnikov would take his star (ensemble) turn in a preview of Morris's *Drink to Me Only with Thine Eyes,* to music by Ralph Vaughan Williams. The finale would be Balanchine's *Symphony in C,* danced by members of American Ballet Theatre, the New York City Ballet, Joffrey Ballet, and Dance Theatre of Harlem. It would be a packed evening of largely famous dances performed by famous dancers.

Yet, for all its aesthetic strengths, the event would ultimately rise or fall—in financial terms—on its ability to capture the attention of the deep-pocketed New York swells who would care more about being seen than about seeing a particular dance company. The only way to do this was to capitalize on the existing infrastructure and time-tested methods of New York's major arts benefactors, and that meant building a sense of occasion. "I think it turned into a society event," Yesselman says in retrospect. "Would as many high-powered people have gone if it wasn't a major social event? Maybe, maybe not. But, finally, they felt they were there for a good cause. But the reality was that it became the major social event of the New York season" (Yesselman interview).

69. Yesselman interview.

70. Gerard, "Creative Arts Being Reshaped by the Epidemic," C15.

71. Anderson, "Dance Companies Set for Tonight's AIDS Benefit."

72. Connors, "To Dance for Life," 98.

73. Dance/USA, "Dance Companies to Stage AIDS Benefit."

74. Yesselman interview.

75. "AIDS and the Arts," videocassette.

76. Dance/USA, "Dance Companies to Stage AIDS Benefit."

77. "AIDS and the Arts," videocassette.

78. Benefit mailer, courtesy Lar Lubovitch and Richard Caples.

79. Created a decade before the official onset of the AIDS epidemic, *Trinity* appears to have no direct connection to the AIDS crisis. The inspiration for that ballet, however, has been ascribed to a live concert of music by Alan Raph and Lee Holdridge that Arpino and Jim Howell attended (Anawalt, *Joffrey Ballet,* 260). Howell, Arpino's choreographic assistant and close friend, was among the first to die of AIDS, in 1982. It is also worth noting that the original cast of the ballet included Ron Reagan, son of then–California governor Ronald Reagan.

80. Just before the benefit Liz Smith wrote in her nationally syndicated daily gossip column: "I believe that this is the first time Mrs. Ronald Reagan has lent her name to an AIDS benefit. It is hoped she may even attend" (Smith, "Beatty Movie of Hughes"). She did not.

81. By the time the invitations were distributed, all $50, $100, and $150 tickets had already sold out, with the remaining tickets ranging in price from $250 to $5,000, the latter including a gala dinner dance on the New York State Theater promenade hosted by Bass and Kempner.

82. Siegel, "A Wide-Angle Look."

2. Melancholia and Fetishes

1. This reconstruction is based on my multiple viewings of the dance in live performance, 1990–92; the accounts in Parish, "San Francisco," and Ricketts, "AIDS Onstage"; and repeated viewings of two videotaped performance documents, an undated (and incomplete) version provided by Rhoades's former manager, Joe Tuohy, and a 1990 version incorporated in a 1996 compilation designed for public viewing by Dancers' Group Footwork, as part of its Dedication Project.

2. Born 17 July 1961, Tracy Rhoades grew up on the Monterey Peninsula in northern California, where he sang in several choirs, played trombone, and served as drum major of his high school band. He received his bachelor of fine arts in dance from the California Institute of the Arts in Valencia in 1986, then spent a year dancing in New York with Mark Dendy, Pooh Kaye, and the Joyce Trisler Dance Company. Rhoades subsequently moved to the San Francisco Bay Area, where he danced with the San Francisco Moving Company (later renamed the Della Davidson Dance Company) and the High Risk Group. He also choreographed his own work, forming a company, Exploding Roses, in 1990. He died of AIDS complications 13 January 1993. See "Tracy Rhoades," and Green, "Tracy A. Rhoades."

3. We have clues that some elements of Requiem were choreographed in 1984, but Rhoades did not transform it into its current state until after Poche's death, when the choreographer revised it for an AIDS benefit. See "Tracy Rhoades."

4. Parish, "San Francisco," 7.

5. The repetitions and use of isolated gestures also serve to identify Requiem as postmodern, and its relationship to the music and its rich signifying properties place it at the center of what Sally Banes has termed "the rebirth of content" characteristic of 1980s and 1990s postmodern dance. See her Terpsichore in Sneakers, xxiv.

6. Parish, "San Francisco," and Ricketts, "AIDS Onstage," offer this same interpretation.

7. See statistics provided by the U.S. Centers for Disease Control and Prevention, National Center for HIV, STD and TB Prevention, Divisions of HIV/AIDS prevention, at http://www.cdc.gov/hiv/stats (28 August 2003).

8. For a quick overview of then-current AIDS drugs and early test results, see the 1989 issues of John James's remarkable self-published AIDS Treatment News, archived at http://www.aids.org/immunet/atn.nsf/page (28 August 2003).

9. The Centers for Disease Control did not consider the opportunistic infections specific to women until 1990. For important work on the politics of HIV/AIDS for women in the United States and other

primarily Western countries, see Patton, *Last Served?* and Roth, *Gendered Epidemic.*

10. Centers for Disease Control website.

11. Ibid.

12. Freud, "Mourning and Melancholia," 134.

13. Dewey, "Dance Spectrum." A closing note to Dewey's article said that others had died of AIDS but that their names were not included "in compliance with their last requests."

14. Schnitt, "AIDS Deaths among Professional Dancers," 129.

15. Dendy choreographed *Back Back* in 1992. Goode created *Their Names Must Be Spoken* for World AIDS Day 1991, as a commission for the San Francisco Fine Arts Museums.

16. Kristeva, *Black Sun.*

17. In *Eros in Mourning* Henry Staten outlines in particularly lucid terms the parameters for the interrelationship of these two states of being in Western thought: "The phenomena I treat under the heading of mourning are those commonly treated today under the heading of desire; yet, for the religious-philosophical tradition in which Western literature is rooted, mourning is the horizon of all desire. In a study of this tradition it is thus not only possible but necessary to transpose the problematic of desire into the key of mourning" (xi).

18. Freud, "Mourning and Melancholia."

19. Ibid., 125, 127.

20. Although Moon's essay appears to have been published for the first time in 1995, a reference to an earlier version—presented at the 1988 convention of the Modern Language Association during a panel titled "AIDS and Our Profession"—appears in Crimp's "Mourning and Militancy," p. 10. The same Moon paper, or perhaps a later variant of it, is cited (undated) as "Memorial Rags, Memorial Rages" in Sedgwick, *Tendencies*, 258 n.4.

21. According to the entry in the *Oxford Companion to English Literature, elegy,* from the Greek, has signified differently in various periods from Old English—when a specific elegy in the Exeter Book concerned the "transience of the world"—to the sixteenth century onward, when it referred to "a reflective poem." Later still, the term applied specifically to poems of mourning. Corelis, in *Roman Erotic Elegy,* explains that the Greeks used the term, ca. 700 B.C. to refer to a specific meter—a hexameter followed by a pentameter—and that it comprised three types of poems: "drinking songs, military subjects, and laments and epitaphs. From these latter two uses of the meter we have inherited our modern use of the term 'elegiac' to mean 'sad'" (5). Corelis goes on to explain that other themes were also considered suitable for the elegy form, including (significantly) erotic ones.

22. Moon, "Memorial Rags," 233.

23. Emerson as quoted in Moon, "Memorial Rags," 233.

24. Ibid., 234.

25. Ibid., 236.

26. Freud, *An Outline of Psycho-Analysis*, 59–60.

27. Moon, "Memorial Rags," 238.

28. Whitman, "The Wound-Dresser," 311.

29. Moon, "Memorial Rags," 239.

30. Butler, "Melancholy Gender/Refused Identification," 23.

31. Butler uses this paradigm to argue for the melancholy incorporation of the lost gender (i.e., the gendered man who holds within him the possibility of the gendered woman, otherwise denied), but her analysis could also be applied to the experience of the gay man whose lover, fuck buddy, or friend has died.

32. Harris, "On Reading the Obituaries," 163–64.

33. Ibid., 164.

34. Ibid., 165.

35. Ibid., 166–67.

36. I draw attention to Lowe's whiteness, and to the whiteness of the choreography of his funeral, in order to reinforce the visibility and tangibility of whiteness for gay white men, especially the unspoken conflation of whiteness and gayness. This move becomes particularly important when, later in this chapter, I make attempts to theorize blackness. See Richard Dyer, *White*.

37. Born 1 August 1953, Joah Lowe was a San Francisco choreographer and body worker who taught what he called "Lessons in the Art of Flying," based in part on his private therapeutic practice, which combined elements of Aston Patterning, Feldenkreis, and Laban techniques. Lowe was raised in Henderson, in provincial east Texas, the son of watermelon farmers. After seeing Alvin Ailey Dance Theater as an undergraduate at the University of Texas, Austin, Lowe decided to dance and sought training at the North Carolina School of the Arts. He received his bachelor's degree in dance (with honors) from Connecticut College in 1976, as a protégé of Martha Meyers. That year he danced with Pauline Konor Dance Consort in New York. In 1978 Lowe traveled to Asia on a Watson Fellowship, and his subsequent choreographic work reflected this influence. In *Savage Gestures for Charm's Sake* (1985), for example, Lowe performed in the style of the Japanese male performer who is trained specifically to play female roles. Upon moving to the Bay Area in the late 1970s, Lowe danced with Lucas Hoving and performed his own choreography, including both solo and group works. He also worked as a movement educator at the San Francisco Orthopaedic and Athletic Rehabilitation Center and with Somacare, a

Bay Area medical practitioners' cooperative. He died 7 January 1988 in a hospital in Texas ("Dancer Joah Lowe Dies"; Gere, "Joah Lowe"; and Gere, "Corpses Dancing, Dancing Ghosts").

Lowe's death took his friends almost completely by surprise. After performing a new solo at Footwork Studio in San Francisco's Mission District in October 1987, he fell ill with pneumonia. This was not the "gay" *Pneumocystis carinii* pneumonia, however, but a garden variety infection of the lungs. When he had partially recovered by Christmastime and expressed the desire to visit his family in Longview, Texas, for the holidays, his doctor encouraged him to go. Almost immediately upon arriving in Texas, however, his pneumonia worsened, and within days he was in intensive care in a ward that had never treated an AIDS patient. The diagnosis was now *Pneumocystis*. As a former lover and as his caregiver, I flew to Texas to be with him. After instructing me that he would like a "party" to be held in his honor after he died, he danced a merengue in his hospital bed on New Year's Eve and breathed his last labored breaths when his ventilator was turned off.

Back in San Francisco, a first gathering—significantly, it was held in Lowe's house, amid the fetishes of his possessions and books—was held to plan a memorial. It began as a debriefing. What were his final thoughts and wishes? Had he been in much pain? Had he been reconciled to dying? When did he know he had AIDS? Each of these questions was attended by much storytelling and thinking aloud, with members of the group openly philosophizing on death and ruminating on the meaning of Lowe's life. Had he really not known that he had AIDS until a month and a half before his death? Why hadn't he said anything about it? Indeed, Lowe had not revealed the results of his HIV test to more than three or four friends and then only because I, as his caregiver, was feeling overwhelmed and needed assistance in nursing him. Lowe was openly gay and was widely loved by legions of friends, both gay and straight. Why hadn't he told them of his illness? Lowe had been concerned that his diagnosis would affect his massage business (who would want to engage a masseur with AIDS?). He was protecting his livelihood. Compounding the economic consequences of revealing his HIV diagnosis was the sheer human difficulty of relinquishing one's independence and asking for help. This response to the stigmatization of AIDS is noteworthy.

38. This reconstruction of Joah Lowe's memorial service is based on my recollections of the event, an interview with a participant (Murphy interview), and photographs provided by Diana Vest Goodman. One of Lowe's friends had just returned from Bali and brought along the umbrella to mark the site of Lowe's death ritual.

39. As I mentioned earlier, Lowe, like so many gay men before and

after him, told few people that he was HIV positive, which is why his death after a short bout with *Pneumocystis* was such a great shock. His reasons included fear of negative reaction, fear for his livelihood, denial. But the pall of AIDS stigma fell heavily on Lowe's memorial for another reason: He had died in a provincial hospital, where his nurses, with the significant exception of the compassionate head nurse, Cindy Medlin, had treated him with hatred and disdain. This was reported to Lowe's San Francisco friends, who mourned not only the loss of Lowe but also his having to die amid the signs of homophobia and AIDS-phobia.

40. Alvin Ailey was born 5 January 1931 in rural (and segregated) southeast Texas. The world of his youth was characterized by participation in black church ceremonials (later reflected in his *Revelations* [1960]) and the bawdy courtship rituals of the Dew-Drop Inns (as incorporated in *Blues Suite* [1958]). When he was a teenager, his single mother moved to Los Angeles to work in the aerospace industry, and Ailey followed. There he met the dancer Carmen de Lavallade in high school and followed her to Lester Horton's dance studio where she took class. Ailey excelled there, though he was erratic as a student, and he eventually joined the Horton company. In the mid-1950s he traveled to New York to appear in Broadway shows, and eventually to start his own company, Alvin Ailey American Dance Theater, in 1958. He choreographed dozens of works for the company, which traveled around the world. He died of complications of AIDS on 1 December 1989 (Dunning, *Alvin Ailey*).

41. Ibid., 405.

42. Ibid.

43. Ailey, *Revelations*, 20–21. Dunning reports additional details provided by Ailey's classmate James Henley, including the spelling of the older boy's name as "Chancey" (Dunning, *Alvin Ailey*, 18–19).

44. DeFrantz, "Simmering Passivity," 113. See also his new book on Ailey, *Dancing Revelations*.

45. Dunning, *Alvin Ailey*, 74–75.

46. Ibid., 144.

47. Ailey, *Revelations*, 17–19.

48. Ibid., 145–46.

49. Harper is one of a small but important group of theorists considering these issues. Two others are Kobena Mercer *(Welcome to the Jungle)* and, before his death, the poet Essex Hemphill *(Brother to Brother* and *Ceremonies)*.

50. Harper, *Are We Not Men?* 5.

51. Harper prefers the word *homosexual* because, in the African American community, *gay* connotes whiteness (205 n.10). I will follow Harper's practice in this discussion.

52. Ibid., 19.

53. Ibid., 11.

54. Ibid., 7.

55. The reconstruction of Alvin Ailey's funeral is based on the account in Dunning's *Alvin Ailey,* along with repeated viewings of *Going Home: Alvin Ailey Remembered,* the hour-long edited video document of the service produced by WNET, the public television station in New York City.

56. Harper, *Are We Not Men?* 9.

57. But as Ailey himself often said, the church in his heart was the church of his childhood, a modest wood-frame structure in Rogers, Texas, where he was baptized (Dunning, *Alvin Ailey,* 116ff).

58. Harper, *Are We Not Men?* xii.

59. *Going Home,* videocassette.

60. I am grateful to Thomas DeFrantz, associate professor in the department of theater at the Massachusetts Institute of Technology and the archivist of Alvin Ailey American Dance Theater, for identifying Gray in the videotape and for offering important critiques of this analysis.

61. Reiter, "Dance: Thirty Years and Still Dancing," 7, 73–74.

62. Born in 1952 to a family of storytellers and sharecroppers, Jones traveled from Florida to central New York, where he attended high school. He attended the State University of New York at Binghamton, where he ran track and studied classical ballet and modern dance. While in college he met Arnie Zane, who became his artistic collaborator and life partner. After spending a year in Amsterdam, Jones returned to Binghamton, where he cofounded the American Dance Asylum in 1973 with Zane and Lois Welk. He and Zane toured widely as a duo in the late 1970s and early 1980s, and in 1982 they formed the Bill T. Jones/Arnie Zane Dance Company. In addition to choreographing for their shared group, Jones has created commissioned works for Alvin Ailey American Dance Theater, the Boston Ballet, and Lyon Opera Ballet, among others. He also works frequently with opera companies and on television. In 1994 he was the recipient of a MacArthur "Genius" Fellowship. See Jones, *Last Night on Earth,* and Zimmer and Quasha, *Body Against Body.*

63. Jowitt, "Bill as Bill."

64. Jones and Zane interview.

65. Ibid.

66. "AIDS and the Arts," videocassette.

67. In his introduction to *AIDS: Cultural Analysis/Cultural Activism,* Crimp decries the conflation of AIDS and the arts, likening it to the linkage of Jews and banking (4–5). Yet to deny dance as queer work is to deny the honor of this predominantly gay profession.

68. "AIDS and the Arts," *MacNeil-Lehrer Newshour,* videocassette.

69. Bill T. Jones, master class and discussion, UCLA Department of World Arts and Cultures, 7 May 1998, handwritten notes by author.

70. In 1982 *Hand Dance* would be reincarnated in solo and group versions titled *Continuous Replay* (Zimmer and Quasha, *Body Against Body,* 139–40).

71. The footage converted into the *Untitled* hologram derives from documentation of the Bill T. Jones/Arnie Zane Dance Company's 1985 season at the Joyce Theater in New York, specifically, of Zane performing his *Continuous Replay.* I am grateful to Bjorn Amelan for providing this information.

72. This reconstruction of the live version of *Untitled* is based on repeated viewings of the 1991 videotaped documentation at American Dance Festival, augmented by the John Sanborn 1989 PBS version of *Untitled.* All text is transcribed from the 1991 videotape.

73. Zane had toyed with fetishizing Jones's body choreographically in Zane's *Black Room,* which was inspired by Robert Mapplethorpe's homoerotic photographs of black men. The 1985 dance was a duet for Jones and Heywood McGriff Jr., who died of AIDS in 1994.

74. In the last year of his life, Zane was told by his acupuncturist and herbalist to record his dreams. He then used these recordings as material for *Untitled.* Jones provided this information at the 7 May 1998 master class and discussion held at UCLA.

75. Jones shares this same story in his memoir, implying that the Reinharts were so offended by his text that ten years went by before they invited him back to the festival. Presumably, this 1991 performance marks his return. The passage from Jones's book reads:

And so it was at ADF in 1981 that I also did a largely improvised solo built on oppositional statements. *I love women,* I would say. Then, *I hate women. I love white people. I hate white people. I'd like to kiss you. I'd like to tear your fucking heart out. Why didn't you leave us in Africa? I'm so thankful for the opportunity to be here.* I said something very personal about Arnie, who was in the audience. I also made reference to an article in that day's paper that quoted the co-director of the festival as saying that careers would be made or broken that weekend.

The solo shocked many. My anger—and my vehemence in expressing it—shaped the way I was perceived for many years to come. I wasn't invited back to the American Dance Festival for ten years. (Jones, *Last Night on Earth,* 165)

76. This richly elegant song, which was written for voice and piano in 1832 and orchestrated in 1843, is one of a larger cycle that depicts the

states of love. One song addresses springtime love, another eternal love, and several comment on the subject of lost love, which is uniformly depicted as a bittersweet state through which life can be experienced with spectacular vividness. (The texts are by Théophile Gautier, the poet who wrote the libretti for such quintessentially romantic nineteenth-century ballets as *Giselle*.) All translations are from the liner notes to the compact disc sound recording of *L'Enfance du Christ* and *Les nuits d'été*, text translated by Arrand Parsons, BMG 09026-61234-2. The recording used as accompaniment by Jones may be Régine Crespin appearing with *l'Orchestre de la Suisse Romande* in performances of Maurice Ravel's *Shéhérazade* and Berlioz's *Les nuits d'été* (London OS 25821), though slight deviations are evident between this recording and the 1991 documentation videotape.

77. At the recapitulation of the refrain, Jones offers a compression of much of the previous material, with the addition of a memorable moment when he falls to the floor as if Rodin's sculpture *The Thinker* had been tumbled to the ground, chiseled legs and arms all askew. In another iconographic moment his legs swim in slow motion as he balances on the floor on one hip, turning to each of the cardinal directions.

78. Jones directly quotes four lines from the refrain of the song: "I think we're alone now. / There doesn't seem to be anyone around. / I think we're alone now. / The beating of our hearts is the only sound." The complete lyrics are on the web at http://www.elyrics.net/go/t/Tommy_James_&_The_Shondells/I_Think_We're_Alone_Now/ (11 September 2003).

79. The specific set of references here includes Dance Theater Workshop (DTW), a key downtown New York performance space; the National Endowment for the Arts (NEA), the government arts agency that was then embroiled in the so-called culture wars; a gay club called The Cock Ring, the name of which is an allusion to a ring-shaped device that, when placed at the base of the penis, helps maintain an erection; the St. Mark's Baths, a gay sex club in New York; amyl nitrate, popularly known as poppers, inhaled to enhance sexual pleasure; various locations to which Jones and Zane toured, including the American Dance Festival (ADF), as well as places where the two lived. "Charlie" and "Melissa" are not identifiable.

3. Monuments and Insurgencies

1. Brecht, *Brecht on Theatre*, 20–22.
2. Ibid., 23.
3. Ibid., 34.
4. The best example of this is Arlene Croce's infamous review of Bill

T. Jones's *Still/Here,* in which she critiques Jones's work, which she has not seen, on the basis of established critical verities, meanwhile failing to acknowledge the politics inherent in those verities. She also accuses Jones of didacticism—the standard critique of openly political art—and of producing art to fulfill "this or that social need" (Croce, "Discussing the Undiscussable"). In a response Homi K. Bhabha, in "Dance This Diss Around," argues that Croce's intellectual practice can only be interpreted as a "frankly ideological maneuver" meant to undermine a specific artistic project. Bhabha writes: "If *Still/Here,* present in her argument only as the spectral subject of controversy, prepublicity, rumor, and report, is by any standard an example of what Croce deplores as the use of art 'to meet this or that social need,' she in turn uses the work to make this or that political argument" (19).

Thus Croce's argument against politics in art serves her own political aims. It is just such ideological maneuvers that I am committed to exposing, and to resisting.

5. Brecht, *Brecht on Theatre,* 35.

6. Crimp, "AIDS: Cultural Analysis/Cultural Activism," 15.

7. Ibid., 5, 7.

8. Crimp, "Mourning and Militancy," 8–9.

9. In what might actually be a conciliatory gesture toward gay men whose activism took the form of memorial activities, Crimp suggests in "Mourning and Militancy" that "there is no such thing as ever fully achieving normalcy, for *anyone*" (7) (the emphasis is Crimp's).

10. Though his essay was published in 1989, Crimp appears to have been writing about an experience that took place before 1986, when the *Times* changed its policy. "Companions" are now listed. I am grateful to Annette Grant, an editor at the *New York Times,* for tracking down the date of the policy change.

11. Crimp, "Mourning and Militancy," 8–9.

12. De Certeau, *The Practice of Everyday Life,* xi–xii.

13. Ibid., xviii, xix.

14. Ibid., xix.

15. Some might consider this silence itself to be strategic, designated to isolate those with HIV. I am grateful to Clyde Smith for this insight.

16. Raised in rural Summerfield, North Carolina, Rickey Lynn Darnell attended high school at the North Carolina School of the Arts as a music student. He majored in theater design and technology at the University of North Carolina, Greensboro, graduating in 1982 (Sparber, "[Rick Darnell] Re-Forms Dance Group"). At Greensboro Darnell met Clyde Smith, who would later become a key member of the High Risk Group, and began his initial involvement with dance creation and performance. After living briefly in Durham, current site of the American

Dance Festival, Darnell enrolled in 1985 in the master of fine arts program at Bennington College in Vermont. In 1986 or 1987, Darnell relocated to San Francisco and formed his first company, Rickey Lynn and the Rangers. He also began his involvement with collectively run live/work spaces as a cofounder of Studio 4, 1800 Sq. Ft., and Work Site, where he rehearsed and produced his performances as well as those of others. Currently Darnell lives in San Francisco and works to provide assistance to homeless artists; he is completing a degree in social work.

I am indebted to Clyde Smith for providing details of Darnell's genealogy, for correcting details in this chapter, and for sharing his own acute insights. Thanks also to Peter Carpenter for research assistance.

17. Wendy Perron and Tony Carruthers, under the auspices of the Bennington College Judson Project, had arranged a show of video materials, interviews, and still photographs from the Judson era, and Darnell saw the exhibition. Years later Darnell would teach his own choreographic workshops "inspired by and . . . reflect[ing] the aesthetics and methods that are generally associated with the ground breaking Judson Church Group." In the literature for these courses, he would write of his interest in the notion of "task," of dances based not on ideas but on disjunct actions. In a press release from the late 1980s Darnell would list his major influences: "The courage, daring, witt [*sic*], and sheer beauty of those who were involved with and know the Judson Church group."

18. "Like garage music, our movement represents a rebellion against standards," Darnell wrote a few years later in marketing and press materials. "We express a dissatisfaction with the 'dry patina' of formalist post modernism and traditional modern dance."

19. Kaplan, "Eat That Idiom."

20. In that first concert Darnell and two colleagues performed a piece titled *27 Ways to Say I Love You* to music by Johnny Cash and Led Zeppelin (Darnell, "Centerspace Presents"). The trio of two men and one woman danced this new work on the street, with speakers pointed outside through the lobby windows. Darnell's coy everydayness, his smooth elisions from simple walking to dynamic athleticism, and his soon-to-be trademark ungainly saunter were already evident in the choreography. Just as evident was his interest in opening up space for new and multiple visions of love.

21. In addition to enjoying the comparison with a then-popular musical style, he twice in the late 1980s rented garage or warehouse spaces and converted them into performance venues.

22. Kaplan, "Risky Business," 55.

23. In some of Darnell's promotional literature the date of the name change is given as 1987, but most company narratives fix the moment of the switch as December 1988.

24. Regarding the gender composition of the High Risk Group, Clyde Smith points out that "there were women in the first concert I did with the company, we then kicked them out, women returned after I left" (Smith, personal communication [e-mail], 21 October 2002).

25. Kaplan, "High Risk Group: A Bitter Pill."

26. Vaucher, *Muses from Chaos and Ash,* 147.

27. Darnell, "Footwork's Sixth Annual Edge Festival."

28. Footwork lost its lease in 1999, during the dotcom-driven real estate boom in San Francisco. As of 2003, it does not exist as a studio space, but its parent organization, Dancers' Group, continues as a service organization.

29. The program for the Edge Festival performances (Darnell, "Footwork's Sixth Annual Edge Festival") acknowledges grants from Dance Bay Area, the local dance service organization; the Zellerbach Family Fund, which offered grants of as much as $5,000 for young artists and new companies; and a large and extremely competitive collaboration grant of $25,000 from the Wallace Alexander Gerbode Foundation that would support the premiere of the company's 1992 *Passions.* The company did not apply for money from the National Endowment for the Arts. Says Darnell, "The NEA won't touch us." He also refused to sign a California Arts Council pledge for a drug-free workplace, declaring it "fascist" (Wright, "High Risk Dancers Live Up to Name").

30. Clyde Smith notes that women had always been involved in the High Risk Group as collaborators, notably the videographer Liz Weinberg, whose documentation "we felt closest to" (Smith, personal communication).

31. Darnell, "Footwork's Sixth Annual Edge Festival."

32. The reconstruction of the prologue to *Falling* is based on my viewing of the live performance and repeated viewings of Liz Weinberg's video documentation of a performance at Footwork's San Francisco studio in October 1991. Also on that High Risk Group program was the company member Clyde Smith's *Homeboys.*

33. The text is not quite audible on the videotape document; I have pieced it together after repeated hearings.

34. For a discussion of the power of effeminacy, see Gere, "*29 Effeminate Gestures.*"

35. Neil and Jon Greenberg grew up in St. Paul. "We were both little gay boys in Minnesota watching *The Wizard of Oz* on TV and listening to Judy Garland," Neil explained to an interviewer, only partly in jest (Kaplan, "My Brother, My Self," 35). As young adults both brothers moved to New York City; although they lived near one another, they were not close. Neil studied dance at Juilliard, eventually landing a gig with Eliot Feld's company and then with Merce Cunningham, with whom he performed for more than six years. Jon "flailed around a bit,"

eventually finding his grounding in ACT UP and as a member of the Mary's, an ACT UP affinity group. On 22 January 1991 Jon was among the group that stormed into the studio of the *MacNeil-Lehrer Newshour* to protest the blackout of AIDS reporting during the Persian Gulf War, and his was a prominent voice in the struggle to find funding for research into non-Western medical treatments. Neil was the artist, Jon the activist. Although they had been gradually drifting apart, their lives converged again when Jon became more seriously ill.

As Neil recounted in an oral history for the New York Public Library Dance Collection, in 1993 he began to spend a great deal of time with Jon, who demonstrated a passion for the music of RuPaul, the drag singer, by programming his computer with an excerpt from "You Better Work," which played when he turned it on. Jon also was becoming more and more interested in eastern religion, especially Zen Buddhism, as he neared death. But even as RuPaul and Zen entered his sphere, Jon remained the passionate AIDS activist, inspiring the mood of his own funeral with his only slightly sardonic request to burn and eat his body—"in the street" (Greenberg interview).

36. Kaplan and Hennessy, *More out Than in*, 35.

37. Larry Kaplan, "My Brother, My Self," 35.

38. *ACT TV: Tim Bailey Funeral and Jon Greenberg Funeral*, videocassette.

39. The reconstruction of Jon Greenberg's funeral is based on the ACT TV video documentation.

40. A more ambiguous point of comparison would be the London funeral of Princess Diana in August 1997, which served both insurgent and monumental functions. In duplicating great state funerals of the past, it established Diana as a figure of enduring power. But in deviating from the script of the state funeral—especially with elements of informality and modernity, such as the musical offering by Elton John, and with the public excoriation of the royal family by Diana's brother— it also demonstrated the extent to which she had been removed from the center of power and now existed at its (relative) margins. Hence, the funeral of Princess Diana hovered between the tactical and the strategic, the insurgent and the monumental.

By contrast, one of the speakers at Jon Greenberg's funeral references a similarly tactical funeral for another activist, just two weeks before, in which the body of the dead man, Tim Bailey, was carried to the gates of the White House in Washington, D.C., in a dramatic gesture of grief and anger. "Something's wrong," a speaker cries out, horrified that even such gestures cannot stop the continual dying.

A 1998 political funeral in front of the White House, for the AIDS activist Steve Michael, evoked similar themes: that, even as new treatments are supposed to be controlling the disease, people continue to die; and that, in frightening ways, AIDS activism itself is in the throes of death. An article in *New York Magazine* noted that Michael's procession included only two hundred marchers: "Six years ago, during the dramatic 'ashes action' on the Capitol, more than 5,000 showed up to dust the White House lawn with the powdery remains of their lovers, parents, children, and friends." Ann Northrop, who had run for vice president (on Michael's presidential ticket) from the AIDS Cure Party, remarked, "It's discouraging to think you can bring a dead body to the White House and not have the whole country stand up and pay attention" (France, "The Body Politic," 21).

41. The final eulogist is an extremely articulate unidentified woman with defiance in her eyes. "He did not want to die," she says. "He wanted to buy a Volvo station wagon and spend the summer visiting friends. He wanted to complete the protocols for clinical testing of alternative treatments. He wanted to write fiction. He wanted to fall in love. In the last week of his life, he told me repeatedly that he was not dying."

I include an extended account of her eulogy here to demonstrate how, in words, she performs work parallel to the work of the funereal choreography. She tells us that he was not resigned to death, that he did not want to go quietly. He still had fight in him. Her rhetoric instructs the viewer that Jon's funeral should be about anger, not resignation and acceptance: "We sat with him, after he slipped into a coma and while he died. After his heart stopped beating, he continued to breathe. He fought dying as much as he accepted it. He was a man full of contradictions and challenges."

She then performs a curious and significant rhetorical maneuver. After offering an alternative definition of family that embraces the gay and lesbian, she comforts that family, acknowledges its ongoing losses, then goads it to action. To use Crimp's phrase, she entreats her listeners to convert mourning to militancy:

Jon loved his lesbian and gay family. His loss to us is in many ways greater than we can bear, being one of many losses we will each accumulate every year of this epidemic. We cannot replace Jon, and so his loss to us is irreconcilable. All that we can do is accept the challenge to become stronger, to become more than we are already, to do what we believe it is impossible to do. Jon would like that.

In its first form, that action should be channeled into caregiving, she suggests, into tending for the ill.

The night Jon died, the nurse who was taking care of him, Keith, told me how wonderful it was to see Jon surrounded by his friends and being so well cared for into his death. Then he mentioned to me that he hadn't seen this kind of support system for a couple of years now. This was in St. Vincent's Hospital. This makes me furious. No one should go through this without a support system.

She vents her fury at the lesbian and gay community, for failing always to protect itself, "for we are alone in many ways," she says. If the nation will not care for us, we must care for ourselves: "Jon was proud to have a lesbian and gay family that could take care of him. We must proudly acknowledge and maintain the incredible response of the gay community to this epidemic. It is terribly painful, but we are alone in many ways and we must not abandon each other now. The only way to survive now is to plunge through whatever barriers we face and to do the work that is needed" (*ACT TV* videocassette)

42. *ACT TV* videocassette.

43. As Neil Greenberg recollects it (personal communication [e-mail] with author, 19 September, 2003), the procession through the streets that follows the funeral on the ACT TV videotape actually preceded it. The sequence may have been edited hastily out of order. In any case, my analysis holds.

44. As to the question of how the public funeral managed to go forward without a permit and without police intervention, Neil Greenberg offers the following recollection (from personal communication [e-mail] with author, 19 September, 2003):

The ACT UP contingent among Jon's friends were concerned that the police might try to stop us. The police were not alerted in any way that the funeral was going to occur. Everyone was told to gather near the subway entrance on First Avenue and First Street—there's a little park there. Jon's coffin was picked up from Reddin's funeral home in the West Village in a van (I think I was part of that, but have no vivid recollection. I know I had to sign papers releasing Reddin's from any responsibility). This was before mobile phones, but I think some of the ACT UP people had walkie-talkies. It all felt quite cloak and dagger. We waited in the van near 3rd Ave and Houston—I remember this more clearly—and drove it to 1st & 1st only after all had assembled. Then we got the coffin out of the van, and proceeded slowly up the east side of 1st Ave, across 7th Street, and into Tompkins Square Park. The coffin was closed as we carried it, but opened once we were in the park. The van driver (no idea who that was) delivered the little p.a. sound system to the designated location in the park while we were marching.

I remember some police were around when we brought the coffin to 1st and 1st. But they never, in any way, tried to stop us. I also remember some police around in the park. But they never got in the way of anything. Neither did we block traffic in any way—we marched on the side of the street, not down the middle. So: there was a police presence, but for some reason they decided to let the whole thing pass. We all were working under the belief that what we were doing was completely illegal, and I think it was, but the police ignored this. Don't know why, but I'm glad that they did. I would go as far as to say the police were appropriately respectful.

45. Neil Greenberg reports that, in order to symbolically satisfy the second part of Jon's request, that on his death they "burn me in the street and eat my flesh," some of his friends met on the year anniversary of his passing and swallowed some of his ashes (personal communication [e-mail] with author, 19 September 2003).

46. This reconstruction is based on direct observation of the quilt ceremony, 11–13 October 1996, on the National Mall. In addition, I have repeatedly viewed a prescriptive videotape prepared by the NAMES Project (Thompson, NAMES Project Volunteer Training, videocassette).

47. Wilson, "High Noon on the Mall," 143.

48. Streatfield, "The Olmsteds and the Landscape," 117.

49. Streatfield (117–18) cites these details based on a set of papers compiled by Glenn Brown for the Senate Committee on the District of Columbia, *Papers Relating to the Improvement of the City of Washington, District of Columbia*, 56th Cong., 2d sess., 1901, S. Doc. 94, 192.

50. See the reproduction of Olmsted's plan in Streatfield, "The Olmsteds and the Landscape," 119.

51. Quoted in Streatfield, "The Olmsteds and the Landscape," 122.

52. According to Thomas Hines, the City Beautiful movement was "the dominant motif and motivating force in American urban design from 1893 to 1917." The central principle of the movement was that quality of life is contingent upon environmental aesthetics. See Hines, "The Imperial Mall," 79.

53. Streatfield, "The Olmsteds and the Landscape," 124–25.

54. Ibid., 125.

55. Wilson, "High Noon on the Mall," 163.

56. For a discussion of Coxey's Army, see Schwantes, *Coxey's Army*.

57. Backscheider, *Spectacular Politics*, 8. (See also Foucault, *Discipline and Punish*, 227.)

58. Backscheider, *Spectacular Politics*, 231.

59. Patterson continues: "I'm from what you might call a middle-class

background, and I don't know anyone [who has died of AIDS]. But this is so big. I wanted to do it [the unfurling] here. I heard this was the last time it would be displayed in its entirety. But I didn't realize how much it would affect me." I ask whether and how the movement changed during the ceremony. "We definitely got better at unfolding it, working more as a unit," she says, noting that Bob gave fewer verbal cues as the ceremony proceeded. "He [Bob] described it as a ritual, a ceremony. It didn't feel so much like that at first. We were laughing and joking when we were bringing the quilt out [from storage]. And then, when the unfurling started, we were just trying to do it right. But we started knowing what to do, and it was a lot more somber."

60. Pinsker and Patterson, "Goucher Students Travel to View AIDS Memorial" (original typescript, including additional paragraph cut from published article).

61. Mike Smith, former executive director of the NAMES Project, reported this information to quilt volunteers, of which I was one, during the summer of 1987.

4. Corpses and Ghosts

1. This reconstruction is based on David Weissman's 1988 film *Song from an Angel* (film converted to video as part of a compilation tape created for Dancers' Group Footwork's Dedication Project) and on my live viewing of the film that same year. I am grateful to David Weissman for reading this chapter and offering factual corrections and citations.

2. The melody is adapted from Weill's "One Life to Live."

3. At the conclusion of the tap-dance sequence, the film cuts abruptly, and Price reappears in his drab hospital garb, although he continues to sing with animation. "Come here and spark up my love life," he beckons. "You need a new kind of scene." He leans forward. "Caress and hug me, and whirlpool tub me." He closes his eyes in ecstasy. "Forgive me when I get mean." He sing-speaks the last line in an angry tone but quickly turns mock sincere:

> I need romance in my life, dear.
> Please try to open your heart.
> Let's face this fear as it happens.
> You'll be richer right from the start.

He makes a gesture from his heart, as if to scatter ashes before him.

> 'Cause when they scatter my ashes,
> The things I've said will ring true.
> We're both the winner, but you'll go to dinner,

'Cause I've got less time than you, yeah,
Less time than you.

4. Born in 1950 in Pittsburgh and raised in Cleveland, Rodney Price was an early member and artistic director of the San Francisco theater collective Angels of Light, which, in the era before AIDS, symbolized "the innocence and exuberance that characterized San Francisco theater in the 1970s," according to the *San Francisco Examiner* critic Robert Hurwitt ("'Angel of Light.'") Before moving west in 1970, Price attended the Columbus School of Art and Design, and he worked briefly as a book illustrator in New York. Angels of Light was formed by Hibiscus, also the originator of the Cockettes, with the central participation of Price, Beaver Bauer, and Brian Mulhern. The Angels were big fans of Broadway extravagance, but to maintain what Bauer called their "purity," they strove to replicate Broadway on a shoestring. From 1970 to 1979 all their performances were free. "They loved all the old Broadway musical production values," the experimental theater artist Laura Farabough told Hurwitt after Price's death, "and they figured out a way to do them with almost no budget." Not surprisingly, when Price died in August 1988, he was virtually penniless. Hurwitt's obituary for Price listed an address where fans and friends could send contributions for his burial plot (Hurwitt, "'Angel of Light'"; for more on the Angels of Light, see Mark Thompson's "Children of Paradise: A Brief History of Queens," in *Gay Spirit*).

5. Phelan, *Mourning Sex*, 154.
6. Guthmann, "Rodney Price Film," C3.
7. Jones, *Last Night on Earth*, 184–85.
8. An example of this is recorded in a program by DIVA TV (Damned Interfering Video Activist Television), a subgroup of ACT UP, that documents the 1993 funeral of Tim Bailey in front of the White House in Washington, D.C. See *ACT TV: Tim Bailey Funeral and Jon Greenberg Funeral*, videocassette.
9. Derrida, *Aporias*, 55.
10. For a discussion of New Age philosophy not specifically related to gay culture, see Hanegraaff, *New Age Religion and Western Culture*.
11. More research at such sites as the Gay and Lesbian Archive of the San Francisco Public Library will be necessary to document these phenomena in the lives of a wide range of gay men. The ethnography presented here, however, draws upon my conversations and interviews, collected over two decades, with and about James Bergeron, Jeff Brandenburg, Richard Brandt, Djola Bernard Branner, Victor Brown, Tom Burke, Peter Carley, Debra Carroll, Doug Conaway, Graham Cowley, Vickie Dodd, Edward Duke, Larry Goldfarb, Daniel Goldstein, Diana

Vest Goodman, Eric Gupton, Eric Hellman, Paul Hill, Bill Huck, Betty Lowe, Joah Lowe, Richard McIntyre, Tim Oates, Tom O'Connor, Steve Rostine, Daniel Sauro, Stephen Steinberg, and Richard Whitesell.

12. According to his oral history, which is housed at the Dance Collection of the New York Public Library, Diaz was born in 1963 and brought up in three Bay Area suburbs: Castro Valley, Union City, and Hayward. He ran away to Los Angeles as a young teenager, because his father, a member of the Assemblies of God, was "too strict" during the period when the son was becoming sexually active. Eventually, the younger Diaz found his way back to the East Bay, where he studied at the Shawl-Anderson studio and with Priscilla Regalado. He has been diagnosed with AIDS and directs an organization called Movement Coalition for AIDS Awareness (Diaz interview by Kraft). See also Román, "Latino Performance and Identity."

13. Diaz interview by Kraft, 35. Presumably his HIV status would be visible in the form of physical symptoms or his face would become associated with AIDS by virtue of his performing this AIDS dance in a public place. In one version of the dance Diaz does emerge from the bag, but beneath it he is covered head to toe in a white body suit, including a full head mask (Diaz, *One AIDS Death. . .*, 1992 videocassette).

14. Diaz cites Michaelangelo's *Crouching Boy, Dying Slave, Rebellious Slave, Youthful Captive,* and "most of Michaelangelo's 'unfinished' statues" as early influences. As for the body bag, "I originally wanted to use a larger than life latex condom, but it would have been too expensive and there would have been no way to breathe" (Diaz, Catalog for *Dance, Dance, Dance Till You Drop,* 6). The stretchy fabric might also evoke Martha Graham's *Lamentation,* but Diaz suggests that, at most, he might have been influenced by a photograph he once saw of Graham's piece. In the oral history interview by Kraft he says, "Someone asked me, Are you influenced by Graham? Or, Did you copy this from Graham? I said, No. I think Martha Graham's piece was about a woman's suffering, a woman's grief. I don't think that Martha Graham had AIDS" (37–38).

15. This reconstruction is based on repeated viewings of video documentation housed in the Dance Collection of the New York Public Library (Diaz, *One AIDS Death. . .*, 1990 videocassette) and Diaz's account of the performance in the accompanying catalog (Diaz, Catalog).

16. Diaz, *One AIDS Death. . .*, 1990 videocassette; Diaz, Catalog.

17. Diaz, Catalog, 11.

18. The eventual outcome was that Diaz and Nolan moved farther up Stockton Street on Union Square. "It was not a very good spot to raise money," Diaz writes in his catalog. "Just another AIDS day for me. I was still trying to collect money for an AIDS Hospice in the Castro" (Diaz, Catalog, 13).

19. This comment was offered in relation to Goode's *Deeply There: Stories of a Neighborhood* (1998). This work, which I discuss in the epilogue, explores the perspective of what Goode calls the "AIDS widow." The DCA meeting was held in New York at Lincoln Center's Rose Building, 11 July 1998.

20. This description is based on my review of Goode's *The Reconditioning Room* and *Remembering the Pool at the Best Western* for the *(East Bay) Express* (Gere, "Dance Beyond the Body"); in style this description piece derives from George Haggerty's entry on gothicism in *Gay and Lesbian Literary Heritage*, 335. Resources for the reconstruction of Goode's work include my viewings of live performances at several stages of the piece's development, February 1990 through June 1991, as well as the company's videotape documentation of *The Reconditioning Room* and *Remembering the Pool*.

21. Goode was born in Presque Isle, Maine, in 1951 and moved to Hampton, Virginia, when he was seven. Escaping his working-class upbringing, he earned a bachelor of fine arts in drama from Virginia Commonwealth University in 1973 and subsequently moved to New York City to become an actor, director, and choreographer. In New York he studied dance with Merce Cunningham and Viola Farber. In 1979 he relocated to the Bay Area and danced with the Margaret Jenkins Dance Company for four years. His first major independent piece for his own Joe Goode Performance Group, *The Ascension of Big Linda into the Skies of Montana* (1986), won two Isadora Duncan Awards for its evocative layered narrative and audacious site-specific staging. Another significant work from the early years of his own company is *29 Effeminate Gestures* (1987), a solo broadcast on PBS's *Alive from Off Center* in 1989. He won a 1999 New York Dance and Performance Award ("Bessie") for *Deeply There*.

22. For a complete description of the era, and of critical theories offered in the attempt to explain its rise, see Haggerty, "The Gothic Novel." Many of these same characteristics appear in the romantic ballets of this and the period immediately following it, ballets such as *La Sylphide* and *Giselle*. See Aschengreen, "The Beautiful Danger"; Banes, *Dancing Women*; and Meglin, "Representations and Realities." From the disciplines of literature and sociology, respectively, see Holland, *Raising the Dead*, and Gordon, *Ghostly Matters*.

23. Sedgwick, *Between Men*, 92.

24. Haggerty, "The Gothic Novel," 240.

25. Gere, "Dance beyond the Body."

26. Merck, "Figuring Out Andy Warhol," 233.

27. Patricia White, "Female Spectator, Lesbian Specter," 157.

28. Fuss, *Inside/Out*, 3.

29. Merck, "Figuring Out Andy Warhol," 233. I must acknowledge José Muñoz, "Ghosts of Public Sex," for leading me to Merck and Castle.

30. This reconstruction is based on my viewings of live performances of *Remembering the Pool* in 1990 and 1991, as well as a video document of the 19 June 1991 performance at Theater Artaud in San Francisco. I have transcribed all text from the video document. I am grateful to Joe Goode for his careful factual corrections of this text.

31. Goode later changed the line about Frankie Valle to: "I woke to the sounds of Johnny Mathis on the clock radio. (sung) Look at me. I'm as helpless as a kitten up a tree'" (Goode, personal communication [e-mail], 19 November 2002).

32. The comic dialogue spoken during the dance of the two cadaver-ghosts comprises a series of questions that implicitly question the boundaries of reality:

APPARITION: Let me pose it to you in the form of five simple questions. One: Have you ever stood outside yourself and really looked at yourself, only it wasn't you?

GOODE: No (voice cracking), never.

APPARITION: Two: Have you ever taken a ride that you never really intended to take?

GOODE: No. No, I haven't, ever, I . . .

APPARITION: Three: Have you ever felt soft and liquid, like you were floating? [The last words are practically sung, suggestively high.]

GOODE: No, I haven't. [Mimicking the floating of her voice. The audience laughs.] No.

APPARITION: Four: Have you ever felt inertia, really experienced the weight and stillness of it? Have you ever thought that that inertia might be a jumping-off place?

GOODE: No.

APPARITION: Five: Have you ever felt the quiet that is so quiet, so quiet that every little sound was punctuated and crisp, even the rustling of paper or the distant flush of a neighbor's toilet?

GOODE: No, never, I, I, I haven't, ever, no, no, no, I honestly . . . no, no, no, no.

33. The complete text of this passage is as follows:

I realize I've been sitting there for twenty minutes, staring off into space, reconstructing the dream and these strange dream entities. It occurs to me that it's getting late, and I should get on with my day. But still, I sit there immobile, virtually locked in this quasi-dream state. I decide to confront the inertia, to look at it squarely, the inertia and me. I wonder where the strange pronunciation of that word comes from. I shake myself. I shake myself back to some semblance of reality. I struggle back to the narrow focus of my life, to the straight-ahead world I've grown accustomed to, with no sideways movement, no vestigial dream people cluttering its path.

But still, I can't move. I am invaded by an overwhelming sadness.

34. Joe Goode reports, "This is a valid reading of the moment, but not what I intended. My intent was more that the dead friend was 'bucking' me off of him" (Goode, personal communication).

35. Wright, "Goode Humor Man."

36. Bredbeck, "Narcissus in the Wilde," 52.

37. Sontag, "Notes on 'Camp,'" 279.

38. Ibid.

39. Ibid., 280.

40. Ibid., 277.

41. Foucault, "A Preface to Transgression," 35.

42. D. A. Miller, "Sontag's Urbanity," 213.

43. Ibid.

44. Meyer, introduction to *The Politics and Poetics of Camp*, 7.

45. Ibid., 1.

46. Ibid.

5. Transcendence and Eroticism

1. James Miller, "Dante on Fire Island," 265–305.

2. Ibid., 266.

3. Among these works are Helgi Tomasson's *When We No Longer Touch* (1995) for San Francisco Ballet and Ulysses Dove's *Dancing on the Front Porch of Heaven* (1993) for the Royal Swedish Ballet. In general, classical ballet has had a particularly tortured relationship with AIDS, owing no doubt to its long history of heterosexual deflection.

4. A postmodern choreographer whose work consistently deals with HIV/AIDS, David Roussève strives, in his own words, "to create a dialogue with as many communities and audiences as possible, both on and off stage, by using African American culture to speak on universal issues of the heart." Roussève, who was born in Houston and is now based in Los Angeles and New York, works in several media to accomplish this goal. He is at once choreographer, writer, director, dancer, and actor. In work for his own Reality company and his commissions for

other ensembles, Roussève attacks racism and sexism while addressing the timeless search for dignity, humanity, and hope in the face of loss and oppression. After graduating from Princeton University magna cum laude in 1981, Roussève danced in the companies of Jean Erdman, Senta Driver, Kathryn Posin, Stephanie Skura, Yoshiko Chuma, and Toronto Dance Theater. He formed Reality in 1989, creating ten full-length works for the company during the ensuing decade, including three commissions from the Brooklyn Academy of Music. Roussève now serves as professor and chair of the Department of World Arts and Cultures at the University of California, Los Angeles. See Kisselgoff, "The Lifelong Pursuit of a Father's Love," and Albright, *Choreographing Difference,* 150–51.

5. This brief reconstruction is based on repeated viewings of video documentation of Roussève, *Whispers of Angels,* as performed at the Brooklyn Academy of Music, 1995.

6. Terry Creach is a postmodern dancer and choreographer whose company is based in New York City. A native of Springfield, Missouri, and a faculty member at Bennington College in Vermont since 1987, Creach has performed with Jamie Cunningham's Acme Company, Vanaver Caravan, Jane Comfort, Annabelle Gamson, and Rachel Lampert, and he has been a guest choreographer and teacher at the Milwaukee campus of the University of Wisconsin, Ohio State University, New York University, and the Juilliard School, among others. He has most frequently worked with Stephen Koester. The duo began dancing together in 1980 and formed their joint Creach/Koester as an all-male dance company in 1986. Since Koester's departure in 1996 the New York–based group has been renamed Creach/Company. See Anderson, "Reverently Naked for Rites in Church"; Dohse, "Consecration"; and Kaufman, "To Creach His Own."

7. This brief reconstruction is based on video documentation of Creach, *Study for a Resurrection,* videocassette.

8. A photographer turned dancer and choreographer, Arnie Zane was cofounder and co-artistic director of Bill T. Jones/Arnie Zane and Company. At first in duets with Jones and subsequently as a choreographer in his own right, Zane developed a theatrical brand of postmodern dance, replete with text and attractive stage designs created by such famous collaborators as the designer Willi Smith and the visual artist Keith Haring. In Zane's obituary in the *New York Times* Jennifer Dunning writes: "[Zane's] interest in formal values and stylish visual design played an important part in the development of his and Mr. Jones's dance, with its distinctive mix of the abstract and the anecdotal" ("Arnie Zane"). Zane was born in the Bronx and received his bachelor's degree from the State University of New York at Binghamton. He began

working with Jones in 1971, and together they formed the American Dance Asylum with Lois Welk in 1973 in Binghamton. Zane briefly created his own dance company in the early 1980s and then cofounded the Jones/Zane company in 1982. Zane and Jones received a New York Dance and Performance Award, a "Bessie," in 1986. He was thirty-nine when he died 30 March 1988, in Valley Cottage, New York. See the 1987 Zane interview by Farlow in which the choreographer discusses his childhood, education, and collaborations with Jones; the discussion of Zane's battle with AIDS in the Goldhuber interview by Kraft; Zimmer, and Quasha, *Body Against Body;* and Zane, *Continuous Replay.*

9. Dunning, "Dance: Jones and Zane."

10. More than a decade later the notion of a "gift" has taken on a new valence. In the current popular lingo of bare-backing—anal sex without the protection of condoms—the gift is the virus itself, given, or received, through an act of anal penetration. For the debate currently raging on the prevalence, or rarity, of this practice, see Freeman, "Bug Chasers"; Sullivan, "Sex- and Death-Crazed Gays Play Viral Russian Roulette!"; Savage, "Savage Love"; and Hogarth, *The Gift,* a documentary film.

11. This brief reconstruction is based on repeated viewings of video documentation of Jones, *The Gift/No God Logic,* videocassette.

12. Zimmer and Quasha, *Body against Body.* Many thanks to Alison Schwartz, operations director of the Bill T. Jones/Arnie Zane Dance Company, for confirming the frequency with which *The Gift/No God Logic* has been performed since Arnie Zane's death.

13. Larkin, *The Divine Androgyne.* I am grateful to Don Shewey for drawing my attention to this text, to Ray Soto of UCLA's Young Research Library for tracking it down, and to the University of Riverside Special Collections Library for lending it. After writing this chapter I found my own used copy for which I paid the bargain price of $150.

14. Ibid., 112.

15. Ibid., 2.

16. Larkin, who assumed the name Purusha in his forties, was born in 1934 in St. Louis, earned his bachelor's degree in philosophy from Notre Dame and his master's in theology from St. Michael's College of the University of Toronto, and then spent three years as a lay theologian and counselor at Thomas More House, Yale's Roman Catholic ministry. By his own report, Larkin appeared to be on his way toward the priesthood, or to a life as a monk, when, in the summer of 1976, he spent time at a beach house on Fire Island and joined a different kind of community of men, "having a lot of sex with myself and others, smoking marijuana daily for the first time, inhaling amyl nitrite [*sic*] regularly during sex, doing an occasional LSD or MDA trip, and re-reading Norman O.

Brown's *Life Against Death.*" (Larkin, *The Divine Androgyne*, 3.) On Fire Island Larkin became especially interested in Brown's notion of an ideal life as one in which Freudian repressions are lifted. "I became increasingly curious," he wrote,

> about how human culture itself is built largely upon the sublimations of repressed erotic instincts in forms of de-eroticized energy which are redirected toward substitute gratifications, and I wondered whether the lifting of repressions would really lead to the beautiful eroticizing of the whole body and all of life which Brown hypothesizes. At any rate, since I had leisure time, energy and resources to spare through the loving generosity of my parents, I decided to undertake personal explorations with a view toward lifting some of my own repressions, and that seems to me now the moment of decision when I finally woke up as if from a long sleep and nightmare. (3)

By the time he published *Divine Androgyne* about five years later, Larkin had devised a complex polysyllabic term for the state of being to which he aspired. He called it "cosmic erotic ecstasy in an Androgyne body-consciousness" (7), hence the title of the book.

17. Ibid., 12.

18. For discussions of New Age spirituality and its rhetoric, see Hanegraaff, *New Age Religion and Western Culture*, and Perry, *Gods Within*.

19. Larkin, *The Divine Androgyne*, 39.

20. Ibid., 32.

21. Ibid., 32–33.

22. Morin, *Anal Pleasure and Health*.

23. Ibid., 89. The specific sexual practices that Larkin references here involve not just simple penetration with a finger or other small object but rather a kind of massive penetration that allows the entire hand or arm to be inserted into the anus. This set of practices he refers to as "fistfucking" or "handballing," to be discussed in greater detail later in the chapter.

24. Shewey, "Joe Kramer Sings."

25. Herrman, *TRUST / The Hand Book*.

26. Ibid., 11.

27. Ibid., 12.

28. By way of example, see retreats for men listed at http://www.bodyelectric.org, accessed 2 November 2003. The "Butt Camp" workshop was held October 2003 at the Easton Mountain Retreat in the Hudson Valley, thirty miles north of Albany.

29. Shewey, "Joe Kramer Sings." Shewey's article includes his own

account of participating in Kramer's workshops. For yet another account see Rist, "Erotic Resurrection."

30. The reconstruction of *Sanctuary* is based on repeated viewings of the documentary videotape of the 10 January 1993 performance, with additional support and corroboration from the three published reviews by Dunning, Jowitt, and Thom (Dunning, "Dance in Review"; Jowitt, "All That Jazz"; and Thom, "Jim Self, Danspace Project."

31. Sally Banes with Noël Carroll, "Dance and Spectacle in the United States in the Eighties and Nineties," in Banes, *Writing Dancing,* 340.

32. Jim Self is an experimental downtown New York choreographer now living in Ithaca and teaching at Cornell University. He has been choreographing professionally since 1972. Born in Greenville, Alabama, he moved to Evanston, a Chicago suburb, with his family when he was fifteen. He began studying modern dance in Chicago with Jackie Radis, Shirley Mordine, and Tom Jaremba and ballet with Edward Parish. Self's first professional dance experience was performing for Mordine's Chicago Dance Troupe, 1972–74. Self was also a cofounder of MoMing in Chicago. He moved to New York City and studied with Merce Cunningham and Maggie Black, and from 1976 to 1979 he danced with the Merce Cunningham Dance Company. From 1980 to 1988 his own company, Jim Self and Dancers, toured throughout the U.S. and Europe. He graduated with a bachelor's degree from Cornell in 1996, majoring in ritual and performance, and now is on faculty at Cornell, teaching movement explorations, postmodern technique, dance history, and video and performance. See Banes, *Writing Dancing,* 268–73, 333–40.

33. Many thanks to Jim Self for providing a copy of the program, dated 7–10 January 1993.

34. As in the earlier discussion of the High Risk Group, the term *effeminate* is in no way meant pejoratively. For a discussion of the word and its significance, see David Gere, "*29 Effeminate Gestures.*"

35. Shewey, personal communication (e-mail), 24 October 2002. My thanks to Shewey for reading and critiquing this chapter.

36. Self, like other postmodern choreographers, has used popular music before but never with such labored sincerity.

37. This scenario is a common one in Native American mythology, though I have not been able to find an example specifically from the Pacific Northwest. In most versions of the myth an outcast or orphan is cared for by animals, and he then is able to bring esoteric knowledge back to the community from which he had been ejected. I am thankful to my colleague Peter Nabokov for this insight.

38. Another choreographer who has experimented strongly in the area of healing and HIV / AIDS is Anna Halprin, whose *Circle the Earth:*

Living with Life on the Line and *Steps Theater Project* were early and not-able attempts to view performance as efficacious, maybe even life sav-ing. Halprin's bold work in the Bay Area deserves full treatment in a text with a different focus as I am treating here works exclusively by gay male artists and activists. See the forthcoming biography of Hal-prin by Janice Ross, *Performance as Experience*, for a detailed considera-tion of these works.

39. Self explains that the red cloths were meant to reference the Red Ribbon Project initiated by his old friend and collaborator Frank Moore, through the New York–based organization Visual AIDS (Self, personal communication [e-mail], 2 May 2002).

40. Self, personal communication (e-mail), 30 October 2000.

41. I should also note that my assessment of the piece as an aesthetic entity is not so different from theirs. However, I do not take it as my role in this chapter to critique the piece as art so much as to describe it closely and to theorize its attempt to create an environment of healing through eroticism.

42. Bataille, *Erotism*, 24.

43. Self doesn't quite fit the pattern. He describes himself as "a lapsed Methodist" who nonetheless boasts many ministers in his fam-ily (Self, personal communication [e-mail], 12 August 2003).

44. Surya, *Georges Bataille*.

45. Surya tells us that the young Bataille lived in Madrid for a year in 1922 and that after his time there he seemed to be of two natures, on the one hand pious and fervently Christian and on the other "beginning to be disturbed by the most fierce and equivocal pleasures." The truth of the man is not to be found between these two poles, Surya argues, but at the two simultaneous extremes (*Georges Bataille*, 44). By 1923 Bataille was adamantly antireligious and had renounced his conversion.

46. Bataille, *Blue of Noon*, 11.

47. Bataille, *Visions of Excess*, x.

48. Bataille, "The Solar Anus," in *Visions of Excess*, 6.

49. Bataille, *Visions of Excess*, xi.

50. André Breton, *Manifestoes of Surrealism*, trans. R. Seaver and H. R. Lane (Ann Arbor: University of Michigan Press, 1969), 184, quoted in Stoekl's introduction to Bataille, *Visions of Excess*, xi.

51. Bataille, *Erotism*, 7.

52. Ibid., 8.

53. Ibid., 8–9.

54. Ibid., 9.

55. As an aside, I should mention that de Sade provides a frequent touchstone in *Erotism*. At times Bataille seems almost to be serving as an apologist for de Sade, from whose name we have inherited *sadism*, in

suggesting that the linkage between death (especially violent death) and desire established by de Sade is something not so cruel or forbidden as one might think. Bataille suggests that the death-desire valence is universal in humans and that it is made visible in our deep yearnings for connectedness.

56. Ibid., 11.

57. Ibid., 17.

58. Ibid.

59. Ibid., 24.

60. Bersani, "Is the Rectum a Grave?" 197–222. Bersani's text is couched as a review of Simon Watney's *Policing Desire: Pornography, AIDS, and the Media* (1987), but its import is larger than any single book review might suggest. The starting point of the essay is sex aversion, in both its "benign and malignant forms" (198) and especially the public's aversion to homosexual sex. "The criminal, fatal, and irresistibly repeated act . . . is of course anal sex" (211). It must be noted that it was Watney who first wrote, "AIDS offers a new sign for the symbolic machinery of repression, making the rectum a grave" (Watney, *Policing Desire*, 126). Bersani takes Watney's formulation and runs with it.

61. Douglas discusses this subject in the chapter of *Purity and Danger* titled "External Boundaries." She suggests that the body is generally viewed by human societies in terms similar to social organization, the margins or boundaries of the body as analogs for the borders of a polity: "The body is a model which can stand for any bounded system. Its boundaries can represent any boundaries which are threatened or precarious" (116). Furthermore, Douglas offers the opinion that "all margins are dangerous. If they are pulled this way or that the shape of fundamental experience is altered. Any structure of ideas is vulnerable at its margins. We should expect the orifices of the body to symbolise its specially vulnerable points" (122). Thus Douglas provides theoretical support for the serving of significant symbolic functions by orifices of the body, particularly the anus.

Epilogue

1. Croce, "Discussing the Undiscussable," 54–60.

2. Roussève interview.

3. Ibid.

4. Goode interview.

Bibliography

Books and Articles

Abelove, Henry, Michele Aina Barale, and David M. Halperin, eds. *The Lesbian and Gay Studies Reader*. New York: Routledge, 1993.

Ailey, Alvin. *Revelations: The Autobiography of Alvin Ailey*, with A. Peter Bailey. New York: Birch Lane Press, 1995.

Albright, Ann Cooper. *Choreographing Difference: The Body and Identity in Contemporary Dance*. Hanover, N.H.: University Press of New England/Wesleyan University Press, 1997.

Alwood, Edward. *Straight News: Gays, Lesbians, and the News Media*. New York: Columbia University Press, 1996.

Anawalt, Sasha. *The Joffrey Ballet: Robert Joffrey and the Making of an American Dance Company*. New York: Scribner, 1996.

Anderson, Jack. 1987. "Dance Companies Set for Tonight's AIDS Benefit." *New York Times*, 5 October 1987.

———. "Reverently Naked for Rites in Church." *New York Times*, 7 October 1997.

Ariès, Philippe. *The Hour of Our Death*. Tran. Helen Weaver. New York: Oxford University Press, 1991.

Aschengreen, Erik A. "The Beautiful Danger: Facets of the Romantic Ballet." Trans. Patricia N. McAndrew. *Dance Perspectives* 58 (1974): 1–52.

Backscheider, Paula. *Spectacular Politics: Theatrical Power and Mass Culture in Early Modern England*. Baltimore, Md.: Johns Hopkins University Press, 1993.

Baker, Houston A. Jr. *Modernism and the Harlem Renaissance*. Chicago: University of Chicago Press, 1987.

Baker, Rob. *The Art of AIDS: From Stigma to Conscience*. New York: Continuum, 1994.

Banes, Sally. *Dancing Women: Female Bodies on Stage.* New York: Routledge, 1998.

————. *Democracy's Body: Judson Dance Theatre, 1962–1964.* Ann Arbor, Mich.: UMI Research Press, 1983.

————. *Terpsichore in Sneakers: Post-Modern Dance.* 2d ed. Middletown, Conn.: Wesleyan University Press, 1987.

————. *Writing Dancing in the Age of Postmodernism.* Hanover, N.H.: Wesleyan University Press, 1994.

Barber, Charles. "'Dancing for Our Lives': New York's Dancers Raise Spirits, Funds for AIDS." *Advocate,* 4 March 1986, pp. 50–51.

Barkun, Michael. "Coxey's Army as a Millennial Movement." In *Popular Culture and Political Change in Modern America.* Ed. Ronald Edsforth and Larry Bennett, 17–40. Albany: State University of New York Press, 1991.

Barthes, Roland. "Rhetoric of the Image." In *Image Music Text.* Trans. Stephen Heath, 32–51. New York: Noonday Press, 1977.

————. *S/Z.* Trans. Richard Miller. New York: Hill and Wang, 1974.

Bataille, Georges. *Blue of Noon* (originally published as *Le Bleu du Ciel*). Trans. Harry Mathews. 1957. Reprint, New York: Marion Boyars, 2002.

————. *Erotism: Death and Sensuality.* Trans. Mary Dalwood. 1957. Reprint, San Francisco: City Lights Books, 1986.

————. *Visions of Excess: Selected Writings, 1927–1939.* Ed. Allan Stoekl. Minneapolis: University of Minnesota Press, 1985.

Berger, John et al. *Ways of Seeing.* London: British Broadcasting Company/Penguin, 1972.

Berkowitz, Richard, and Michael Callen. *How to Have Sex in an Epidemic: One Approach.* Pamphlet. New York: News from the Front Publications, 1983.

Berlandt, Konstantin. "Gay Victim Dances over Death." *Bay Area Reporter,* 11 November 1982, p. 10.

Berman, Janice. "An Evening of Commitment to 'Life.'" *New York Newsday,* 7 October 1987.

Bersani, Leo. "Is the Rectum a Grave?" In Crimp, *AIDS: Cultural Analysis/Cultural Activism,* 197–222.

Berube, Allan. *Coming Out under Fire: The History of Gay Men and Women in World War Two.* New York: Free Press, 1990.

Bhabha, Homi K. "Dance This Diss Around: Homi K. Bhabha on Victim Art." *Artforum* 33, no. 8 (April 1995): 19–20.

Bordowitz, Gregg. 1987. "Picture a Coalition." In *AIDS: Cultural Analysis/Cultural Activism.* Ed. Douglas Crimp, 183–96. Cambridge, Mass.: MIT Press, 1987.

Boyce, Joanna, Ann Daly, Bill T. Jones, and Carol Martin. "Movement and Gender: A Roundtable Discussion." *Drama Review* 32, no. 4 (winter 1988): 82–101.

Brandt, Allan M. *No Magic Bullet: A Social History of Venereal Disease in the United States since 1880*. Expanded ed. New York: Oxford University Press, 1987.

Brecht, Bertolt. *Brecht on Theatre: The Development of an Aesthetic*. Ed. and trans. John Willett. New York: Hill and Wang, 1964.

Bredbeck, Gregory W. "Narcissus in the Wilde: Textual Cathexis and the Historical Origins of Queer Camp." In Meyer, *The Politics and Poetics of Camp*, 51–74.

Bronski, Michael. "AIDS, Art and Obits." In *Personal Dispatches: Writers Confront AIDS*. Ed. John Preston, 161–66. New York: St. Martin's Press, 1989.

————. "Death and the Erotic Imagination." In Carter and Watney, *Taking Liberties*, 219–28.

Browne, Carl. *When Coxey's "Army" Marcht on Washington, 1894*. Pamphlet. San Francisco: 1 May 1944.

Browning, Frank. *The Culture of Desire: Paradox and Perversity in Gay Lives Today*. New York: Crown, 1993.

Burt, Ramsay. *Alien Bodies: Representations of Modernity, "Race" and Nation in Early Modern Dance*. London: Routledge, 1998.

————. *The Male Dancer: Bodies, Spectacle, Sexualities*. London: Routledge, 1995.

Butler, Judith. *Bodies That Matter: On the Discursive Limits of "Sex."* New York: Routledge, 1993.

————. *Gender Trouble: Feminism and the Subversion of Identity*. New York: Routledge, 1990.

————. "Melancholy Gender/Refused Identification." In *Constructing Masculinity*. Ed. Maurice Berger, Brian Wallis, and Simon Watson, 21–36. New York: Routledge, 1995.

Calhoun, Craig. "Introduction: Habermas and the Public Sphere." In *Habermas and the Public Sphere*. Ed. Craig Calhoun, 1–48. Cambridge, Mass.: MIT Press, 1992.

Callen, Michael, ed. "PWA Coalition Portfolio." In Crimp, *AIDS: Cultural Analysis/Cultural Activism*, 147–68.

————. *Surviving AIDS*. New York: HarperCollins, 1990.

Carter, Erica, and Simon Watney, eds. *Taking Liberties: AIDS and Cultural Politics*. London: Serpent's Tail, 1989.

Case, Sue-Ellen. *The Domain-Matrix: Performing Lesbian at the End of Print Culture*. Bloomington: Indiana University Press, 1996.

————. "Theory/History/Revolution." In *Critical Theory and Performance*. Ed. Janelle G. Reinelt, 418–29. Ann Arbor: University of Michigan Press, 1992.

————. "Toward a Butch-Femme Aesthetic." In Abelove, Barale, and Halperin, *The Lesbian and Gay Studies Reader*, 294–306.

————. "Tracking the Vampire." *Differences* 3, no. 2 (summer 1991): 1–20.

Castle, Terry. *The Apparitional Lesbian*. New York: Columbia University Press, 1993.

————. *The Female Thermometer: Eighteenth-Century Culture and the Invention of the Uncanny*. New York: Oxford University Press, 1995.

Certeau, Michel de. *The Practice of Everyday Life*. Berkeley: University of California Press, 1984.

Connors, Thomas. "To Dance for Life." *Village Voice*, 6 October 1987, pp. 97–98.

Corelis, Jon, trans. *Roman Erotic Elegy: Selections from Tibullus, Propertius, Ovid, and Sulpicia*. Salzburg, Austria: University of Salzburg, 1995.

Cott, Nancy F. *The Grounding of Modern Feminism*. New Haven, Conn.: Yale University Press, 1987.

Crimp, Douglas. "AIDS: Cultural Analysis/Cultural Activism" In *AIDS: Cultural Analysis/Cultural Activism*. Ed. Douglas Crimp, 3–16. Cambridge, Mass.: MIT Press, 1987.

————. *AIDS Demo-Graphics*, with Adam Rolston. Seattle: Bay Press, 1990.

————. "The Boys in My Bedroom." In Abelove, Barale, and Halperin, *The Lesbian and Gay Studies Reader*, 344–49.

————. "How to Have Promiscuity in an Epidemic." In Crimp, *AIDS: Cultural Analysis/Cultural Activism*, 237–71.

————. *Melancholia and Moralism: Essays on AIDS and Queer Politics*. Cambridge, Mass.: MIT Press, 2001.

————. "Mourning and Militancy." *October* 51 (winter 1989): 3–18.

————. *On the Museum's Ruins*. Cambridge, Mass.: MIT Press, 1993.

————. "Portraits of People with AIDS." In *Cultural Studies*. Ed. Lawrence Grossberg, Cary Nelson, and Paula Treichler, 117–33. New York: Routledge, 1992.

————, ed. *AIDS: Cultural Analysis/Cultural Activism*. Cambridge, Mass.: MIT Press, 1987.

Croce, Arlene. "Discussing the Undiscussable." *New Yorker*, 26 December 1994–2 January 1995, pp. 54–60.

Daly, Ann. "The Balanchine Woman: Of Hummingbirds and Channel Swimmers." *Drama Review* 31, no. 1 (spring 1987): 8–21.

————. *Done into Dance: Isadora Duncan in America*. Bloomington: Indiana University Press, 1995.

Dance/USA. "AIDS in the Dance/Arts Work Place." *Update* 6 (special issue), October–November 1988.

————. "Dance Companies to Stage AIDS Benefit." *Update* 5, no. 1 (July 1987): 6.

"Dancer Joah Lowe Dies at 34." *San Francisco Sentinel,* 15 January 1988.

Dangerous Bedfellows, ed. *Policing Public Sex: Queer Politics and the Future of AIDS Activism.* Boston: South End Press, 1996.

Darnell, Rick. "Centerspace Presents Openstage, February 20, 1986." Program. 1986. Photocopy.

―――. "Footwork's Sixth Annual Edge Festival 1991." Program. 1991. Photocopy.

Debord, Guy. *Comments on the Society of the Spectacle.* Trans. Malcolm Imrie. London: Verso, 1990.

―――. *The Society of the Spectacle.* Trans. Donald Nicholson-Smith. New York: Zone Books, 1994.

DeFrantz, Thomas. *Dancing Revelations: Alvin Ailey's Embodiment of African American Culture.* New York: Oxford University Press, 2003.

―――. "Simmering Passivity: The Black Male Body in Concert Dance." In *Moving Words: Re-writing Dance.* Ed. Gay Morris, 107–20. New York: Routledge, 1996.

Denby, Edwin. *Dance Writings.* New York: Alfred A. Knopf, 1986.

Derrida, Jacques. *Aporias.* Trans. Thomas Dutoit. Stanford, Calif.: Stanford University Press, 1993.

―――. *Specters of Marx: The State of the Debt, the Work of Mourning, and the New International.* Trans. Peggy Kamuf. New York: Routledge, 1994.

Desmond, Jane. "Dancing Out the Difference: Cultural Imperialism and Ruth St. Denis's 'Radha' of 1906." *Signs: Journal of Women in Culture and Society* 17, no. 1 (1991): 28–49.

―――, ed. *Dancing Desires: Choreographing Sexualities On and Off the Stage.* Madison: University of Wisconsin Press, 2001.

Dewey, Lucia. "Dance Spectrum." *Drama-Logue* (21 December 1989–3 January 1990): 35.

Diaz, Paul Timothy. Catalog for *Dance, Dance, Dance Till You Drop: The AIDS-Specific Dance Collection of Paul Timothy Diaz/Movement Coalition for AIDS Awareness (1988–1996).* Dance Collection, New York Public Library. 1996.

Dohse, Chris. "Consecration." *Village Voice,* 21 October 1997.

Dolan, Jill. *The Feminist Spectator as Critic.* Ann Arbor, Mich.: UMI Research Press, 1998.

―――. "Practicing Cultural Disruptions: Gay and Lesbian Representation and Sexuality." In *Critical Theory and Performance.* Ed. Janelle G. Reinelt, 263–75. Ann Arbor: University of Michigan Press, 1992.

Dollimore, Jonathan. "Different Desires: Subjectivity and Transgression in Wilde and Gide." In Abelove, Barale, and Halperin, *The Lesbian and Gay Studies Reader,* 626–41. New York: Routledge, 1993.

―――. *Sexual Dissidence: Augustine to Wilde, Freud to Foucault.* Oxford: Clarendon, 1991.

Doty, Alexander. *Making Things Perfectly Queer: Interpreting Mass Culture*. Minneapolis: University of Minnesota Press, 1993.

Douglas, Mary. *Natural Symbols: Explorations in Cosmology*. New York: Routledge, 1996.

————. *Purity and Danger: An Analysis of the Concepts of Pollution and Taboo*. New York: Routledge, 1996.

Dunning, Jennifer. *Alvin Ailey: A Life in Dance*. Reading, Mass.: Addison-Wesley, 1996.

————. "Arnie Zane, 39, Choreographer and Dancer, Dies." *New York Times*, 1 April 1988, p. A20.

————. "Choreographing Deaths of the Heart in a Singular Age." *New York Times*, 22 March 1992, p. 26.

————. "Dance in Review: Jim Self, St. Mark's Church." *New York Times*, 11 January 1993, p. C12.

————. "Dance: Jones and Zane." *New York Times*, 21 June 1987.

Dyer, Richard. "Don't Look Now: Richard Dyer Examines the Instabilities of the Male Pin-up." *Screen* 23 (September–October 1982): 61–73.

————. *White*. New York: Routledge, 1997.

Eco, Umberto. *A Theory of Semiotics*. Bloomington: Indiana University Press, 1976.

Edmundson, Mark. "Emerson and the Work of Melancholia." *Raritan* 6 (1987): 120–36.

————. *Nightmare on Main Street: Angels, Sadomasochism, and the Culture of the Gothic*. Cambridge, Mass.: Harvard University Press, 1997.

Elias, Norbert. *The Loneliness of the Dying*. Trans. Edmund Jephcott. New York: Basil Blackwell, 1985.

Farlow, Lesley. "Dancing for Life: How AIDS Has Affected Contemporary Choreography." Master's thesis, New York University, 1993.

Fee, Elizabeth, and Daniel M. Fox, eds. *AIDS: The Burdens of History*. Berkeley: University of California Press, 1988.

Foster, Hal. *The Anti-Aesthetic: Essays on Postmodern Culture*. Port Townshend, Wash.: Bay Press, 1983.

Foster, Susan Leigh. *Choreography and Narrative: Ballet's Staging of Story and Desire*. Bloomington: Indiana University Press, 1996.

————. "Closets Full of Dances: Modern Dance's Performance of Masculinity and Sexuality." In Desmond, *Dancing Desires*, 147–207. Madison: University of Wisconsin Press, 2001.

————. "Dancing Bodies." In *Incorporations*. Ed. Jonathan Crary and Sanford Kwinter, 480–95. New York: Zone, 1992.

————. *Reading Dancing: Bodies and Subjects in Contemporary American Dance*. Berkeley: University of California Press, 1986.

————, ed. *Choreographing History*. Bloomington: Indiana University Press, 1995.

————, ed. *Corporealities: Dancing Knowledge, Culture and Power*. London: Routledge, 1996.

Foucault, Michel. "A Preface to Transgression." In *Language, Counter-Memory, Practice: Selected Essays and Interviews by Michel Foucault*. Ed. Donald F. Bouchard, 29–52. Ithaca: N.Y.: Cornell University Press, 1977.

————. *Discipline and Punish: The Birth of the Prison*. Trans. Alan Sheridan. New York: Vintage, 1979.

————. *The History of Sexuality: An Introduction*. Vol. 1, trans. Robert Hurley. New York: Vintage, 1978.

Foulkes, Julia L. "Dance Is for American Men: Ted Shawn and the Intersection of Gender, Sexuality, and Nationalism in the 1930s." In Desmond, *Dancing Desires*, 113–46.

France, David. "The Body Politic: Cocktail Hangover." *New York Magazine*, 22 June 1998, pp. 20–21.

Franko, Mark. *Dancing Modernism/Performing Politics*. Bloomington: Indiana University Press, 1995.

Freeman, Gregory A. "Bug Chasers: The Men Who Long to be HIV+," *Rolling Stone* (6 February 2003).

Fressola, Michael. "Dimmed Lights, Blank Walls: Potent Symbols." *Staten Island Sunday Advance*, 29 November 1992.

Freud, Sigmund. *An Outline of Psycho-Analysis*. Trans. and ed. James Strachey. 1940. Reprint, New York: W. W. Norton, 1969.

————. "Fetishism." [1927]. In *Freud: Sexuality and the Psychology of Love*. Ed. Philip Rieff, 214–19. New York: Collier, 1963.

————. "Mourning and Melancholia." [1917]. In *A General Selection from the Works of Sigmund Freud*. Ed. John Rickman, 124–40. New York: Doubleday Anchor, 1957.

————. "The 'Uncanny.'" [1919]. In *The Standard Edition of the Complete Psychological Works of Sigmund Freud*. ed. James Strachey, 17:218–52. London: Hogarth, 1959.

Fuss, Diana, ed. *Inside/Out: Lesbian Theories, Gay Theories*. New York: Routledge, 1991.

Gallagher, Catherine, and Thomas Laqueur, eds. *The Making of the Modern Body: Sexuality and Society in the Nineteenth Century*. Berkeley: University of California Press, 1987.

Garafola, Lynn. "Black Dance: Revelations." *Nation*, 17 April 1995, pp. 536–39.

————. *Diaghilev's Ballets Russes*. New York: Oxford University Press, 1989.

Gates, Henry Louis Jr. "The Body Politic." *New Yorker*, 21 November 1994, pp. 112–24.

Gerard, Jeremy. "Creative Arts Being Reshaped by the Epidemic." *New York Times*, 9 June 1987, pp. A1, C15.

Gere, David. "Corpses Dancing, Dancing Ghosts." In *Loss Within Loss: Artists in the Age of AIDS*. Ed. Edmund White, 88–97. Madison: University of Wisconsin Press, 2001.

————. "Dance Beyond the Body: Joe Goode Performance Group." *(East Bay) Express*, 23 February 1990.

————. "Dancing to the End." *(East Bay) Express*, 23 December 1988.

————. Foreword to Jane Sherman and Barton Mumaw, *Barton Mumaw, Dancer: From Denishawn to Jacob's Pillow and Beyond*. Hanover, N.H.: Wesleyan University Press/University Press of New England, 2000.

————. "Joah Lowe" (obituary). *In Dance* 15, no. 3 (March 1988): 1–2.

————. "Mavericks Are Marvelous in Mainstream," review of performance by Rick Darnell and Tracy Rhoades. *Oakland Tribune*, 4 February 1991.

————. "Thoroughly Modern Misha." *Oakland Tribune*, 22 August 1993, p. C7.

————. "*29 Effeminate Gestures:* Choreographer Joe Goode and the Heroism of Effeminacy." In Desmond, *Dancing Desires*, 349–81. Middletown, Conn.: Wesleyan University Press, 2001.

————, ed. "Dance and AIDS." Special issue of *Dance/USA Journal* 9, no. 4 (spring 1992).

Gilman, Sander L. *Disease and Representation: Images of Illness from Madness to AIDS*. Ithaca, N.Y.: Cornell University Press, 1988.

Golden, Thelma. *Black Male: Representations of Masculinity in Contemporary American Art*. New York: Whitney Museum of Art, 1994.

Goldstein, Richard. "Dancer from the Dance." *Village Voice*, 4 January 1994, p. 25.

————. "No Sex, Please, We're Gay." *Village Voice*, 3 March 1998, pp. 50–51.

Gordon, Avery. *Ghostly Matters: Haunting and the Sociological Imagination*. Minneapolis: University of Minnesota Press, 1997.

Green, Judith. "Tracy A. Rhoades, 31, Dancer, Choreographer." *San Jose Mercury News*, 22 January 1993.

————. "Unbearable and Inescapable." *Movement Research Performance Journal* 10 (winter–spring 1995).

Greskovic, Robert. "13 Troupes Join 'Dancing for Life' War on AIDS." *Los Angeles Times*, 7 October 1987.

Grover, Jan Zita. "AIDS: Keywords." In Crimp, *AIDS: Cultural Analysis/Cultural Activism*, 17–30. Cambridge, Mass.: MIT Press, 1987.

Guthmann, Edward. "Rodney Price Film—'Angel' Exits Dancing." *San Francisco Chronicle*, 20 August 1988, pp. C3, C8.

Habermas, Jürgen. *The Structural Transformation of the Public Sphere: An Inquiry into a Category of Bourgeois Society*. Trans. Thomas Burger. Cambridge, Mass.: MIT Press, 1991.

Haggerty, George E. "Gothicism." In *The Gay and Lesbian Literary Heritage*. Ed. Claude J. Summers, 335–37. New York: Holt, 1995.

————. "The Gothic Novel, 1764–1824." In *The Columbia History of the British Novel*. Ed. John Richetti, 220–46. New York: Columbia University Press, 1994.

————. "*O Lachrymarum fons:* Tears, Poetry, and Desire in Gray." *Eighteenth-Century Studies* 30 (1996): 81–95.

Hanegraaff, Wouter J. *New Age Religion and Western Culture: Esotericism in the Mirror of Secular Thought*. New York: E. J. Brill, 1996.

Hanson, Ellis. "The Telephone and Its Queerness." In *Cruising the Performative: Interventions into the Representation of Ethnicity, Nationality, and Sexuality*. Ed. Sue-Ellen Case, Philip Brett, and Susan Leigh Foster, 34–58. Bloomington: Indiana University Press, 1995.

Harper, Phillip Brian. *Are We Not Men? Masculine Anxiety and the Problem of African-American Identity*. New York: Oxford University Press, 1996.

Harris, Daniel. "On Reading the Obituaries in the *Bay Area Reporter*." In *Fluid Exchanges: Artists and Critics in the AIDS Crisis*. Ed. James Miller, 163–68. Toronto: University of Toronto Press, 1992.

————. *The Rise and Fall of Gay Culture*. New York: Hyperion, 1997.

Hawkins, Peter S. "Naming Names: The Art of Memory and the NAMES Project AIDS Quilt." *Critical Inquiry* 19, no. 4 (summer 1993): 752–79.

Hays, Tom. "Nureyev's Death a Reminder of AIDS' Toll on Dance World." Associated Press, 1 November 1993.

Held, David. *Introduction to Critical Theory: Horkheimer to Habermas*. London: Hutchinson, 1980.

Hemphill, Essex, ed. *Brother to Brother: New Writings by Black Gay Men*. Boston: Alyson, 1991.

————. *Ceremonies: Prose and Poetry*. New York: Plume, 1992.

Herrman, Bert. *TRUST/The Hand Book: A Guide to the Sensual and Spiritual Art of Handballing*. San Francisco: Alamo Square Press, 1991.

Hines, Thomas S. "The Imperial Mall: The City Beautiful Movement and the Washington Plan of 1901–1902." In Longstreth, *The Mall in Washington,* 79–99. Hanover, N.H.: University Press of New England, 1991.

Holland, Sharon Patricia. *Raising the Dead: Readings of Death and (Black) Subjectivity*. Durham, N.C.: Duke University Press, 2000.

Houston-Jones, Ishmael. "Lost and Found: Memories of John Bernd at St. Mark's Church." *Movement Research Performance Journal* 17 (fall–winter 1998): 11.

Hurley, Kelly. *The Gothic Body: Sexuality, Materialism, and Degeneration at the Fin de Siècle*. Cambridge: Cambridge University Press, 1996.

Hurwitt, Robert. "'Angel of Light' Rodney Price Dies." *San Francisco Examiner,* 18 August 1988, pp. D1, D7.

Jackson, Kenneth T. *Crabgrass Frontier: The Suburbanization of the United States.* New York: Oxford University Press, 1989.

Jacobs, Ellen. "In the Mail: Who's the Victim?" *New Yorker,* 30 January 1995, p. 11.

Jakobson, Roman. "Closing Statement: Linguistics and Poetics." *Semiotics: An Introductory Anthology.* Ed. Robert E. Innis, 145–75. Bloomington: Indiana University Press, 1985.

James, John. *AIDS Treatment News.* http://www.aids.org/immunet/atn.nsf/page (28 August 2003).

Johnson, Fenton. "Death into Life." *New York Times,* 24 December 1994.

Johnston, Jill. *Marmalade Me.* New York: E. P. Dutton, 1971.

Jones, Bill T. *Last Night on Earth.* New York: Pantheon, 1995.

Jordan, John. "Jupiter and Antinous: Geometry, Effeminacy, and Same-Sex Desire in William Hogarth's *Dancing Masters.*" Paper presented at the annual meeting of the Congress on Research in Dance, Pomona, Calif., 3 December 1999.

Jowitt, Deborah. "All That Jazz," review of Jim Self's *Sanctuary. Village Voice,* 2 February 1993.

———. "Alvin Ailey, 1931–89." *Village Voice,* 12 December 1989, p. 114.

———. "Bill as Bill." *Village Voice,* 20 October 1992.

———. "Diminished, Yet Enriched." *Village Voice,* 5 May 1987, p. 85.

———. "Forests, Trees," review of works by Edward Stierle performed by Joffrey Ballet. *Village Voice,* 19 March 1991, p. 75.

———. "In Memoriam: Marvin Gordon and Tim Wengerd." *Village Voice,* 24 October 1989, p. 93.

———. "In Memoriam: William Carter." *Village Voice,* 27 September 1988, p. 76.

———. "Jeff Duncan, 1930–89." *Village Voice,* 13 June 1989, p. 87.

———. "Obituaries: Juan Antonio, Vic Stornant, Demian Acquavella." *Village Voice,* 26 June 1990, p. 88.

———. "Perfecting Imperfection," review of *Dancing for Our Lives! Village Voice,* 28 January 1986, p. 85.

———. "Robert Joffrey, 1930–88." *Village Voice,* 12 April 1988, p. 91.

Juhasz, Alexandra. *AIDS TV: Identity, Community, and Alternative Video.* Durham, N.C.: Duke University Press, 1995.

Kaplan, Larry. "My Brother, My Self: Choreographer Neil Greenberg Touches Nerve with AIDS Work." *POZ,* April–May 1995, pp. 34–35.

Kaplan, Rachel. "A Bitter Pill to Swallow: AZT Why Can't I Love You? The High Risk Group, 1800 Square Feet." *San Francisco Bay Times,* June 1990.

————. "Body Fluids." *Dance/USA Journal* 9, no. 4 (spring 1992): 28, 30, 32.

————. "Eat That Idiom Spit It Back: The High Risk Group, Julian Theatre at New College, Apr. 23." *San Francisco Bay Times*, May 1989.

————. "High Risk Group: A Bitter Pill to Swallow: or AZT Why Can't I Love You?" *High Performance* (winter 1990).

————. "High Risk Group: *Falling.*" *High Performance* (spring 1992): 47.

————. *The Probable Site of the Garden of Eden.* San Francisco: Abundant Fuck Publications, 1992.

————. "Risky Business: An Anarchist of Dance Unleashes Violent 'Passions.'" *San Jose Mercury News*, 8 May 1992, pp. 43, 55.

————. "Spit Your Way to the Holy Land," review of Keith Hennessy's *Saliva. Coming Up!* January 1989, p. 29.

Kaplan, Rachel, and Keith Hennessy, eds. *More out Than in: Notes on Sex, Art, and Community.* San Francisco: Abundant Fuck Publications, 1995.

Kaufman, Sarah. "To Creach His Own: A Choreographer's Man-Made Success." *Washington Post*, 24 February 1997.

Kayal, Philip M. *Bearing Witness: Gay Men's Health Crisis and the Politics of AIDS.* Boulder, Colo.: Westview Press, 1993.

Kaye, Elizabeth. "Bill T. Jones." *New York Times Magazine*, 6 March 1994.

Kinney, Katherine. "Making Capital: War, Labor, and Whitman in Washington, D.C." In *Breaking Bounds: Whitman and American Cultural Studies.* Ed. Betsy Erkkila and Jay Grossman, 174–89. New York: Oxford University Press, 1996.

Kirstein, Lincoln. *Movement and Metaphor: Four Centuries of Ballet.* New York: Praeger, 1970.

Kisselgoff, Anna. "Dance: Lubovitch Troupe," *New York Times*, 9 April 1986.

————."Dance: 13 Companies in 'Dancing for Life,' an AIDS Benefit." *New York Times*, 7 October 1987.

————. "The Lifelong Pursuit of a Father's Love." *New York Times*, 30 November 1995.

Kramer, Larry. *Reports from the Holocaust: The Story of an AIDS Activist.* New York: St. Martin's Press, 1994.

Kristeva, Julia. *Black Sun: Depression and Melancholia.* New York: Columbia University Press, 1989.

————. *Powers of Horror: An Essay on Abjection.* New York: Columbia University Press, 1992.

Krouse, Mary Beth. "The AIDS Memorial Quilt as Cultural Resistance for Gay Communities." *Critical Sociology* 20, no. 3 (1994): 65–80.

Laine, Barry. "N.Y. Performance Art: Art Without Boundaries, in Tempo with the Times." *Advocate*, 7 July 1983, pp. 51–59.

Laqueur, Thomas. *Making Sex: Body and Gender from the Greeks to Freud.* Cambridge, Mass.: Harvard University Press, 1990.

Larkin, Peter (Purusha). *The Divine Androgyne According to Purusha: Adventures in Cosmic Erotic Ecstasy and Androgyne Bodyconsciousness.* San Diego: Sanctuary Publications, 1981.

Leader, Jody. "AIDS: Dancing for Life." *(Los Angeles) Daily News,* 8 July 1991, pp. 9, 11.

Lechte, John. "Art, Love, and Melancholy in the Work of Julia Kristeva." In *Abjection, Melancholia, and Love: The Work of Julia Kristeva.* Ed. John Fletcher and Andrew Benjamin, 24–41. London: Routledge, 1990.

Lewis, Matthew. *The Monk.* Ed. James Kinsley and Howard Anderson. Oxford: Oxford University Press, 1980.

Library of Congress. *The Grand Design: An Exhibition Tracing the Evolution of the L'Enfant Plan . . .* Washington, D.C.: Library of Congress, 1967.

Longstreth, Richard, ed. *The Mall in Washington, 1791–1991.* Hanover, N.H.: University Press of New England, 1991.

Lyons, Bridget Gellert. *Voices of Melancholy: Studies in Literary Treatments of Melancholy in Renaissance England.* London: Routledge, 1971.

McMurry, Donald L. *Coxey's Army: A Study of the Industrial Army Movement of 1894.* Seattle: University of Washington Press, 1968.

Manning, Susan. *Ecstasy and the Demon: Feminism and Nationalism in the Dances of Mary Wigman.* Berkeley: University of California Press, 1993.

Marcus, Greil. *Lipstick Traces.* Cambridge, Mass.: Harvard University Press, 1989.

Martin, Emily. *Flexible Bodies: Tracking Immunity in American Culture—From the Days of Polio to the Age of AIDS.* Boston: Beacon, 1994.

Martin, John. "The Nature of Movement." In *Introduction to the Dance,* 31–55. Brooklyn: Dance Horizons, 1965.

Mauss, Marcel. "Techniques of the Body." (1934). In *Incorporations.* Ed. Jonathan Crary and Sanford Kwinter, 455–77. New York: Zone, 1992.

Mazo, Joseph H. "In Memoriam: Alvin Ailey (1931–1989)." *Dance Magazine,* February 1990, p. 111.

Meglin, Joellen. "Representations and Realities: Analyzing Gender Symbolism in the Romantic Ballet." Ed.D. diss., Temple University, Philadelphia, 1995.

Mercer, Kobena. *Welcome to the Jungle: New Positions in Black Cultural Studies.* New York: Routledge, 1994.

Merck, Mandy. "Figuring Out Andy Warhol." In *Pop Out: Queer Warhol.* Ed. Jennifer Doyle, Jonathan Flatley, and José Esteban Muñoz, 224–37. Durham, N.C.: Duke University Press, 1996.

Meyer, Moe. "The Signifying Invert: Camp and the Performance of Nineteenth-Century Sexology." *Text and Performance Quarterly* 15, no. 4 (October 1995): 265–81.

———, ed. *The Politics and Poetics of Camp*. New York: Routledge, 1994.

Miller, D. A. "Sontag's Urbanity." In Abelove, Barale, and Halperin, *The Lesbian and Gay Studies Reader*, 212–20.

Miller, James. "Dante on Fire Island: Reinventing Heaven in the AIDS Elegy." In *Writing AIDS: Gay Literature, Language, and Analysis*, Ed. Timothy F. Murphy and Suzanne Poirier, 265–305. New York: Columbia University Press, 1993.

Miller, Tim. *Shirts and Skin*. Los Angeles: Alyson Books, 1997.

Modleski, Tanya, ed. *Studies in Entertainment: Critical Approaches to Mass Culture*. Bloomington: Indiana University Press, 1986.

Moon, Michael. "'The Blood of the World': Gender, Bloodshed, and the Uncanny in the Fourth (1867) Edition of *Leaves of Grass*." In *Disseminating Whitman: Revision and Corporeality in Leaves of Grass*, 171–222. Cambridge, Mass.: Harvard University Press, 1991.

———. "Flaming Closets." In *Bodies of the Text: Dance as Theory, Literature as Dance*. Ed. Ellen W. Goellner and Jacqueline Shea Murphy, 57–78. New Brunswick, N.J.: Rutgers University Press, 1995.

———. "Memorial Rags." In *Professions of Desire: Lesbian and Gay Studies in Literature*. Ed. George E. Haggerty and Bonnie Zimmerman, 233–40. New York: Modern Language Association of America, 1995.

Morin, Jack. *Anal Pleasure and Health*, rev. 3d ed. San Francisco: Down There Press, 1998.

Mulvey, Laura. "The Index and the Uncanny." Paper presented at Department of Art, University of California, Los Angeles, 8 April 1998.

———. "Visual Pleasure and Narrative Cinema." In *Art After Modernism: Rethinking Representation*. Ed. Brian Wallis, 361–74. New York: New Museum of Contemporary Art, 1984.

Muñoz, José Esteban. *Disidentifications: Queers of Color and the Performance of Politics*. Minneapolis: University of Minnesota Press, 1999.

———. "Ghosts of Public Sex: Utopian Longings, Queer Memories." In Dangerous Bedfellows, *Policing Public Sex*, 355–72.

Murphy, Jacqueline Shea. "Unrest and Uncle Tom: Bill T. Jones / Arnie Zane Dance Company's *Last Supper at Uncle Tom's Cabin/ The Promised Land*." In *Bodies of the Text: Dance as Theory, Literature as Dance*. Ed. Ellen W. Goellner and Jacqueline Shea Murphy, 81–105. New Brunswick, N.J.: Rutgers University Press, 1995.

Ness, Sally Ann. *Body, Movement, and Culture: Kinesthetic and Visual Symbolism in a Philippine Community*. Philadelphia: University of Pennsylvania Press, 1992.

Novack, Cynthia J. *Sharing the Dance: Contact Improvisation and American Culture*. Madison: University of Wisconsin Press, 1990.

Odets, Walt. *In the Shadow of the Epidemic: Being HIV-Negative in the Age of AIDS*. Durham, N.C.: Duke University Press, 1995.

Parish, Paul. "San Francisco," review of Tracy Rhoades's *Requiem*. *Ballet Review* (fall 1990): 7–10.

Parks, Gary. "Passion's Progress: New Lease on Lar." *Dance Magazine*, November 1986, pp. 54–57.

Patton, Cindy. *Inventing AIDS*. New York: Routledge, 1990.

_____. *Last Served? Gendering the HIV Pandemic*. London: Taylor and Francis, 1994.

Peirce, Charles S. "Logic as Semiotic: The Theory of Signs." In *Semiotics: An Introductory Anthology*. Ed. Robert E. Innis, 4–23. Bloomington: Indiana University Press, 1985.

Phelan, Peggy. *Mourning Sex: Performing Public Memories*. New York: Routledge, 1997.

Pinsker, Sarah, and Erin Patterson. "Goucher Students Travel to View AIDS Memorial." *Quindecim*, 23 October 1996.

Reiter, Susan. "Dance: Thirty Years and Still Dancing with the Alvin Ailey Company—Dudley Williams . . ." *Los Angeles Times Calendar*, 12 February 1995, pp. 7, 73–74.

Renan, Ernest. "What Is a Nation?" (1882). In *Nation and Narration*. Ed. Homi Bhabha, 9–22. New York: Routledge, 1990.

Ricketts, Wendell. "AIDS Onstage." *Dance Ink* 4, no. 3 (fall 1993).

_____. "Talking Dance/Talking AIDS." *Dance/USA Journal* 9, no. 4 (spring 1992): 6–14.

Rist, Darrell Yates. "Erotic Resurrection." *New York Native*, 20 April 1992, p. 23.

Roach, Joseph. *Cities of the Dead: Circum-Atlantic Performance*. New York: Columbia University Press, 1996.

Román, David. *Acts of Intervention: Performance, Gay Culture, and AIDS*. Bloomington: Indiana University Press, 1998.

_____. "'It's My Party and I'll Die If I Want to!': Gay Men, AIDS, and the Circulation of Camp in U.S. Theatre." *Theatre Journal* 44, no. 3 (October 1992): 305–27.

_____. "Latino Performance and Identity." *Aztlan* 22 (1997): 151–68.

_____. "Not-about-AIDS." *GLQ: A Journal of Lesbian and Gay Studies* 6, no. 1 (2000): 1–28.

_____. "Performing All Our Lives: AIDS, Performance, Community." In *Critical Theory and Performance*. Ed. Janelle Reinelt and Joseph Roach, 208–221. Ann Arbor: University of Michigan Press, 1992.

Román, David, and Alberto Sandoval. "Caught in the Web: Latinidad,

AIDS, and Allegory in *Kiss of the Spider Woman*, the Musical." *American Literature* 67, no. 3 (1995): 553–85.

Román, David, and Tim Miller. "Preaching to the Converted." *Theatre Journal* 47, no. 2 (May 1995): 169–88.

Ross, Janice. *Performance as Experience: Dance, American Culture and Anna Halprin*. Berkeley and Los Angeles: University of California Press, forthcoming.

Roth, Nancy L., and Katie Hogan, eds. *Gendered Epidemic: Representations of Women in the Age of AIDS*. New York: Routledge, 1998.

Sadownick, Doug. "ACT UP Makes a Spectacle of AIDS." *High Performance* (spring 1990): 26–31.

Saussure, Ferdinand de. "The Linguistic Sign." In *Semiotics: An Introductory Anthology*. Ed. Robert E. Innis, 24–46. Bloomington: Indiana University Press, 1985.

Savage, Dan. "Savage Love: Bug Chasers," thestranger.com. 30 January–5 February 2003. http://www.thestranger.com/2003-01-30/savage.html (28 August 2003).

Savigliano, Marta E. *Tango and the Political Economy of Passion*. Boulder, Colo.: Westview, 1995.

Schnitt, Diana. "AIDS Deaths Among Professional Dancers." *Medical Problems of Performing Artists* 5, no. 4 (December 1990): 128–30.

Schwantes, Carlos A. *Coxey's Army: An American Odyssey*. Lincoln: University of Nebraska Press, 1985.

Scott, Pamela. "'This Vast Empire': The Iconography of the Mall, 1791–1848." In Longstreth, *The Mall in Washington*, 37–58.

Sedgwick, Eve Kosofsky. *Between Men: English Literature and Homosocial Desire*. New York: Columbia University Press, 1985.

————. *Epistemology of the Closet*. Berkeley: University of California Press, 1990.

————. "Queer Performativity: Henry James's *The Art of the Novel*." *GLQ* 1 (1993): 1–16.

————. *Tendencies*. Durham, N.C.: Duke University Press, 1993.

Sember, Robert. "Seeing Death: The Photography of David Wojnarowicz." In *The Ends of Performance*. Ed. Peggy Phelan and Jill Lane, 31–51. New York: New York University Press, 1998.

Shapiro, Laura. "The Daring Young Man: Rudolf Nureyev . . ." *Newsweek*, 18 January 1993, p. 21.

Shelton, Suzanne. *Divine Dancer: A Biography of Ruth St. Denis*. New York: Doubleday, 1981.

Sherman, Jane and Barton Mumaw. *Barton Mumaw, Dancer: From Denishawn to Jacob's Pillow and Beyond*. Hanover, N.H.: Wesleyan University Press/University Press of New England, 2000.

Shewey, Don. "Joe Kramer Sings the Body Electric." *Village Voice*, 21 April 1992.

Shilts, Randy. *And the Band Played On: Politics, People, and the AIDS Epidemic*. New York: St. Martin's Press, 1987.

Siegel, Marcia B. "A Wide-Angle Look at America's Dance Scene—All at Once," review of *Dancing for Life. Christian Science Monitor*, 13 October 1987.

_____. *The Shapes of Change: Images of American Dance*. Boston: Houghton Mifflin, 1979.

_____. "Survival by Drowning." *New York Press*, 7 April 1989, p. 13.

Silverman, Kaja. "Fassbinder and Lacan: A Reconsideration of Gaze, Look, and Image." *Camera Obscura* 19 (1989): 54–85.

Singer, Linda. *Erotic Welfare: Sexual Theory and Politics in the Age of Epidemic*. New York: Routledge, 1993.

Smith, Liz. "Beatty Movie of Hughes Is on Runway," item regarding *Dancing for Life. New York Daily News*, 1 October 1987.

Sontag, Susan. *Illness and Metaphor; and AIDS and Its Metaphors* (New York: Picador, 2001).

_____. "Notes on 'Camp.'" In *Against Interpretation and Other Essays*, 275–92. New York: Dell, 1966.

Sparber, Gordon. "(Rick Darnell) Re-Forms Dance Group Near His Roots." Photocopy of clipping ca. 1993 from unidentified North Carolina newspaper, provided to author by Rick Darnell.

Staten, Henry. *Eros in Mourning: Homer to Lacan*. Baltimore, Md.: Johns Hopkins University Press, 1995.

Streatfield, David C. "The Olmsteds and the Landscape of the Mall." In Longstreth, *The Mall in Washington*, 117–43.

Stuart, Otis. "Dancing for Life at the New York State Theater: Resplendent Relief." *Dance Magazine*, January 1988.

Sturken, Marita. "Conversations with the Dead: Bearing Witness in the AIDS Memorial Quilt." *Socialist Review* 22, no. 2 (April–June 1992): 65–95.

_____. *Tangled Memories: The Vietnam War, The AIDS Epidemic, and the Politics of Remembering*. Berkeley: University of California Press, 1997.

Sullivan, Andrew. "Sex- and Death-Crazed Gays Play Viral Russian Roulette!" Salon.com. 24 January 2003. http://www.salon.com/opinion/sullivan/2003/01/24/rolling/(28 August 2003)

Supree, Burt. "Bright Spirits." *Village Voice*, 9 December 1986.

_____. "Is a Puzzlement," review of *Dancing for Our Lives!*, *Village Voice*, 28 January 1986, pp. 85, 87.

_____. "John Bernd: 1953–88." *Village Voice*, 13 September 1988.

Surya, Michel. *Georges Bataille: An Intellectual Biography*. Trans. Krzysztof Fijalkowski and Michael Richardson. New York: Verso, 2002.

Thom, Rose Anne. "Jim Self, Danspace Project at St. Mark's Church-in the-Bowery, January 7–10, 1993." *Dance Magazine*, April 1993.

Thompson, Mark, ed. *Gay Spirit: Myth and Meaning*. New York: St. Martin's Press, 1987.

Tomko, Linda J. "*Fete Accompli:* Gender, 'Folk-Dance,' and Progressive-era Political Ideals in New York City." In *Corporealities: Dancing Knowledge, Culture, and Power*. Ed. Susan Leigh Foster, 155–76. London: Routledge, 1996.

"Tracy Rhoades." *San Francisco Bay Guardian*, 9 May 1990, pp. 25, 27.

Treichler, Paula A. "AIDS, Homophobia, and Biomedical Discourse: An Epidemic of Signification." In Crimp, *AIDS: Cultural Analysis/Cultural Activism*, 31–70.

———. *How to Have Theory in an Epidemic: Cultural Chronicles of AIDS*. Durham, N.C.: Duke University Press, 1999.

U.S. Centers for Disease Control and Prevention, National Center for HIV, STD and TB Prevention, Divisions of HIV/AIDS Prevention. http://www.cdc.gov/hiv/stats (28 August 2003).

Vaucher, Andréa R. *Muses from Chaos and Ash: AIDS, Artists, and Art*. New York: Grove Press, 1993.

Wallace, Michele. *Black Popular Culture*. Ed. Gina Dent. Seattle: Bay Press, 1992.

Watney, Simon. "'Lifelike': Imagining the Bodies of People with AIDS." In *The Masculine Masquerade: Masculinity and Representation*. Ed. Andrew Perchuk and Helaine Posner, 63–68]. Cambridge, Mass.: MIT Press, 1995.

———. *Policing Desire: Pornography, AIDS and the Media*. 2d ed. Minneapolis: University of Minnesota Press, 1989.

———. *Practices of Freedom: Selected Writings on HIV/AIDS*. Durham, N.C.: Duke University Press, 1994.

———. "Representing AIDS." In *Ecstatic Antibodies: Resisting the AIDS Mythology*. Ed. Tessa Boffin and Sunil Gupta, 165–92. London: Rivers Oram Press, 1990.

Weinstein, Jeff. "Acts: Live Boys." *Village Voice*, 11–17 March 1981.

Whitman, Walt. "The Wound-Dresser." In *Leaves of Grass*. Ed. Sculley Bradley and Harold W. Blodgett, 308–11. New York: W. W. Norton, 1973.

White, Edmund. "Esthetics and Loss." *Personal Dispatches: Writers Confront AIDS*. Ed. John Preston, 145–52. New York: St. Martin's Press, 1989.

White, Hayden. "Bodies and Their Plots." In Foster, *Choreographing History*, 229–34.

———. *The Content of the Form: Narrative Discourse and Historical Representation*. Baltimore, Md.: Johns Hopkins University Press, 1987.

White, Keith. "Passionate Communions." *Bay Area Reporter*, 13 October 1988.

White, Patricia. "Female Spectator, Lesbian Specter: *The Haunting.*" In Fuss, *Inside/Out*, 142–72.

Wiegman, Robyn. *American Anatomies: Theorizing Race and Gender*. Durham, N.C.: Duke University Press, 1995.

Wilson, Richard Guy. "High Noon on the Mall: Modernism Versus Traditionalism, 1910–1970." In Longstreth, *The Mall in Washington*, 143–67.

Woods, Gregory. "Rage and Remembrance: The Uses of Elegy." In *AIDS: The Literary Response*. Ed. Emmanuel S. Nelson, 155–66. New York: Twayne, 1992.

Wright, Frankie. "Goode Humor Man." *Los Angeles Times*, 7 March 1991.

––––––. "The High Risk Dancers Live Up to Name." *Los Angeles Times*, 25 September 1991.

Yingling, Thomas. "AIDS in America: Postmodern Governance, Identity, and Experience." In Fuss, *Inside/Out*, 291–310.

Zane, Arnie. *Continuous Replay: the Photographs of Arnie Zane*. Ed. Jonathan Green. Introduction by Bill T. Jones, with essays by Susan Leigh Foster et al. Cambridge, Mass.: MIT Press, 1999.

Zimmer, Elizabeth. "Dance of Death: AIDS Takes Its Toll on the Dance World." *Advocate*, 6 November 1990, pp. 36–40.

Zimmer, Elizabeth, and Susan Quasha, eds. *Body Against Body: The Dance and Other Collaborations of Bill T. Jones and Arnie Zane*. New York: Station Hill Press, 1989.

Videography, Filmography, and Discography

ACT TV: Tim Bailey Funeral and Jon Greenberg Funeral. Public access series directed by James Wentzy. Produced by DIVA TV (Damned Interfering Video Activist Television), ACT UP/New York, 1993. Videocassette. Courtesy Neil Greenberg.

"AIDS and the Arts." *MacNeil-Lehrer Newshour*. Reported by Joanna Simon. Produced by PBS. July 1987. Videocassette.

Bernd, John. *Surviving Love and Death*. Documentation of a performance at P.S. 122, New York, 25–28 December 1981 and 22–25 January 1982. Videocassette. Harvard Theatre Collection, Cambridge, Mass.

Creach, Terry. *Study for a Resurrection*, Documentation of a performance at St. Mark's Church, New York, 5 October 1997. Presented by Danspace Project.

Darnell, Rick. *Falling*. Documentation of performance at Footwork Studio, San Francisco, 17–19 October 1991. Videography by Liz Weinberg. Videocassette. Courtesy Rick Darnell.

Diaz, Paul Timothy. *One AIDS Death. . . .* Documentation of performance outside Macy's, San Francisco, December 1990. *Dance, Dance,*

Dance Till You Drop: The AIDS-Specific Dance Collection of Paul Timothy Diaz/Movement Coalition for AIDS Awareness (1988–1996). Catalog code: C).1). Dance Collection, New York Public Library, 1990. Videocassette. Courtesy Paul Timothy Diaz.

———. *One AIDS Death. . . .* Documentation of performance at Union Square, San Francisco, 5 April 1992. *Dance, Dance, Dance Till You Drop: The AIDS-Specific Dance Collection of Paul Timothy Diaz/Movement Coalition for AIDS Awareness (1988–1996)*. Catalog code: L).4).a. Dance Collection, New York Public Library, 1992. Videocassette. Courtesy Paul Timothy Diaz.

Eye on Dance: Positive Perspectives on AIDS. Ernie Horvath, Charlie Ziff, and Irene Dowd, interview by Celia Ipiotis. Produced by ARC Videodance. Recorded 13 June and telecast 29 September 1988. Produced by Celia Ipiotis and Jeff Bush. Dance Collection, New York Public Library, 1988. Videocassette.

Going Home: Alvin Ailey Remembered. Recorded at the Cathedral of St. John the Divine, New York, 8 December 1989. Produced by WNET, 1990. Videocassette.

Goode, Joe. *The Reconditioning Room*. Documentation of performance installation, Capp Street Project, San Francisco, February–March 1990. Directed by Ted Helminski. Videocassette. Courtesy Joe Goode Performance Group.

———. *Remembering the Pool at the Best Western*. Documentation of performance, Theater Artaud, San Francisco, 19 June 1991. Videocassette. Courtesy Joe Goode Performance Group.

Gund, Catherine, dir. and prod. *Hallelujah! Ron Athey: A Story of Deliverance*. 1999. Videocasette. Aubin Pictures.

Hennessy, Keith. *Saliva*. Documentation of performance, Highways Performance Space, Santa Monica, 1989. Videocassette. Courtesy Keith Hennessy.

Hogarth, Louise. *The Gift*. Documentary film, Dream Out Loud Productions, Los Angeles, 2003.

Howell, James R. *Ritual: The Journey of the Soul*. Documentation of performance, James R. Howell Studio, San Francisco, May 1982. Direction and camera operation by James R. Howell. Edited by Bruce John Short. Courtesy David Román.

Jones, Bill T. Documentation of performance, American Dance Festival, Durham, N.C., 14 June 1991. Also included are *The Gift/No God Logic* and *Continuous Replay*. Videocassette.

———. *Still/Here*. Documentation of performance, Brooklyn Academy of Music, 2 December 1994. Videocassette. Courtesy UCLA Center for the Performing Arts.

———. *Untitled*. Created and performed by Bill T. Jones. Dream text

by Arnie Zane. Directed by John Sanborn and Mary Perillo. Produced by PBS/Alive from Off Center, 1989. Videocassette. Courtesy
Neil Sieling.

Lucas, Craig. *Longtime Companion*. Directed by Norman René. Avant-
Garde Cinema. Metro Goldwyn Mayer, 1990.

Miller, Tim. *Live Boys*. Documentation of performance. Hallwalls Performance Space, Buffalo, N.Y., April 1981. Videocassette. Courtesy
Tim Miller.

Rankin, Liz. *Alive and Kicking*. Directed by Nancy Meckler. Written by
Martin Sherman. Produced by Martin Pope. First Look Pictures,
1997.

Rhoades, Tracy. *Requiem*. Documentation of performance, unknown location, 1990. Included in compilation tape created for Dancers'
Group Footwork's Dedication Project, 10–26 October 1996. Videocassette. Courtesy Footwork/Wayne Hazzard.

————. *Requiem*. Incomplete documentation of performance, unknown location and date (1991?). Videocassette. Courtesy Joe Tuohy.

Roussève, David. *Whispers of Angels*. Documentation of performance at
the 1995 Next Wave Festival, Majestic Theater, Brooklyn Academy of
Music, 2 December. Videocassette, recorded by Character Genera-
tors Inc. Courtesy David Roussève.

Seize Control of the FDA. Directed by Gregg Bordowitz and Jean Carlomusto. Produced by Gay Men's Health Crisis, 1988. Videocassette.
Courtesy Robert Sember.

Self, Jim. *Sanctuary: Ramona and the Wolfgang Work for a Cure*. Videotape
of 10 January 1993 performance, Danspace Project at St. Mark's
Church, New York. Courtesy Jim Self.

Song from an Angel. Featuring Rodney Price. Directed by David Weissman. 1988. Videocassette. Frameline.

Thompson, David, dir. and prod. *NAMES Project Volunteer Training*.
1996. Videocassette. Courtesy NAMES Project Foundation.

Zane, Arnie. *The Gift/No God Logic*. Documentation of performance at
the American Dance Festival, 11 June 1991. Videocassette. Courtesy
Bill T. Jones/Arnie Zane Dance Company.

Interviews

Acquavella, Demian. Interview by Maya Wallach. September 1989.
Oral History Project. Dance Collection, New York Public Library.

Bromberg, Ellen. Interview by author, telephone, 29 March 1998.

Diaz, Paul Timothy. Interview by Susan Kraft. 31 May 1996. Oral History Project. Dance Collection, New York Public Library.

Driver, Senta. Interview by author, New York City, 6 November 1997.

Goldhuber, Lawrence. Interview by Susan Kraft. 19 February 1997. Oral History Project. Dance Collection, transcript call number MGZMT 3–2041, New York Public Library.

Goode, Joe. Interview by author, telephone, 7 November 1998.

Greenberg, Neil. Interview by Susan Kraft. Oral History Project. 27 February 1995. Dance Collection, New York Public Library.

Jacobs, Ellen. Interview by author, telephone, 24 April 1998.

Jones, Bill T. Interview by Charlie Rose. PBS. World AIDS Day broadcast. Transcript #1260, 1 December 1994.

―――――. Interview by Lesley Farlow. 14 July 1993. Oral History Project. Dance Collection, New York Public Library.

Jones, Bill T., and Arnie Zane. Interview by author. Tape recording and partial transcript. Dia Foundation Studio, New York, 1 June 1987.

LeBlond, Richard. Interview by author, telephone, 16 August 1998.

Moore, Patrick. Interview by author, telephone, 16 April 1998.

Murphy, Edie. 1998. Interview by author, telephone, 31 May 1998.

Roussève, David. Interview by author, telephone, 12 November 1998.

Russell, Mark. Interview by Lesley Farlow. P.S. 122, New York, 8 January 1993.

Sexton, Lucy. Interview by author, telephone, 30 March 1998.

Yesselman, Robert. Interview by author, telephone, 12 November 1997.

Zane, Arnie. Interview by Lesley Farlow, Valley Cottage, New York, 23 December 1987. Oral History Project of the New York Public Library Dance Collection.

Index

abjection, 12, 35, 62, 167–69, 178–79; and African American culture, 117, 119–22, 132; and mourning, 102, 134

Acquavella, Demian, 236

ACT UP. *See* AIDS Coalition to Unleash Power

activism, 7, 65, 75, 137, 143, 265; and artists, 50, 80–83; and ethnography, 197

Agee, James, 267

AIDS, 4, 28, 47, 96–97, 109, 150; anxiety surrounding, 41, 43, 60, 208; as associated with gay men, 41, 86, 170; and bodily transformation, 199; continued presence of in choreography, 264–68; cultural analysis, 28; czar, 147; funerals, 109–14, 119–22, 160–68, 195; gothic, 206–13; heterosexual transmission of, 14; as murder, 159; as new public sphere, 180–81; popular views of, 7, 47; and semiotics, 45–48; societal effects of, 5; statistics concerning in 1989, 96; and stigma, 24; theater, 29–30; transmission of as gift, 307n.10; and underreported groups, 96; and U.S. presidents, 146–47; volunteerism, 5. *See also* dance

AIDS Coalition to Network, Organize and Win, 6. *See also* AIDS Coalition to Unleash Power

AIDS Coalition to Unleash Power (ACT UP), 8, 34, 63–76, 77, 78, 154; and corpses, 195; founding of, 66; and media, 67, 69, 72–75; *Seize Control of the FDA*, 64, 68–76, 69, 71, 73

AIDS Community Television, 161

Ailey, Alvin, 34, 84, 114–17, 289n.40; funeral of, 119–22

Alive and Kicking (Martin Sherman), 42–43

Alive from Off Center, 124

American Ballet Theatre, 40

American Dance Festival, 125, 131, 135

American flag, 69, 179

American Foundation for AIDS Research (AMFAR), 87

American Institute of Architects, 175

anal eroticism, 237, 241–43, 259–61

anastasis, 230, 234

Angelou, Maya, 120–21

Angels of Light, 25. *See also* Price, Rodney

Antoinette, Marie, 222

Arce, Elia, 50

Ariès, Phillippe, 10

333